Jewish Sanctuary in the Atlantic World

The Carolina Lowcountry and the Atlantic World
Sponsored by the Program in the Carolina Lowcountry and the Atlantic World of the College of Charleston

Money, Trade, and Power
Edited by Jack P. Greene, Rosemary Brana-Shute, and Randy J. Sparks

The Impact of the Haitian Revolution in the Atlantic World
Edited by David P. Geggus

London Booksellers and American Customers
James Raven

Memory and Identity
Edited by Bertrand Van Ruymbeke and Randy J. Sparks

This Remote Part of the World
Bradford J. Wood

The Final Victims
James A. McMillin

The Atlantic Economy during the Seventeenth and Eighteenth Centuries
Edited by Peter A. Coclanis

From New Babylon to Eden
Bertrand Van Ruymbeke

Saints and Their Cults in the Atlantic World
Edited by Margaret Cormack

Who Shall Rule at Home?
Jonathan Mercantini

To Make This Land Our Own
Arlin C. Migliazzo

Votaries of Apollo
Nicholas Michael Butler

Fighting for Honor
T. J. Desch Obi

Paths to Freedom
Edited by Rosemary Brana-Shute and Randy J. Sparks

Material Culture in Anglo-America
Edited by David S. Shields

The Fruits of Exile
Edited by Richard Bodek and Simon Lewis

The Irish in the Atlantic World
Edited by David T. Gleeson

Ambiguous Anniversary
Edited by David T. Gleeson and Simon Lewis

Creating and Contesting Carolina
Edited by Michelle LeMaster and Bradford J. Wood

Jewish Sanctuary in the Atlantic World

A Social and Architectural History

Barry L. Stiefel

With the Assistance of David Rittenberg   Foreword by Samuel D. Gruber

THE UNIVERSITY OF SOUTH CAROLINA PRESS

Published by the University of South Carolina Press
Columbia, South Carolina 29208

www.sc.edu/uscpress

Manufactured in the United States of America

23 22 21 20 19 18 17 16 15 14   10 9 8 7 6 5 4 3 2 1

Stiefel, Barry, author.
  Jewish sanctuary in the Atlantic world : a social and architectural history /
Barry L. Stiefel.
     pages cm. — (The Carolina Lowcountry and the Atlantic World)
  Includes bibliographical references and index.
  ISBN 978-1-61117-320-8 (hardbound : alk. paper) — ISBN 978-1-61117-321-5 (ebook)
1. Sephardim—America—History. 2. Jews—America—History. 3. America—
Ethnic relations. I. Title.
  E29.J5S75 2013
  973'.04924—dc23
  2013027981

To all my teachers

Who is wise?
One who learns from every person, as it is said:
From all my teachers I grew understanding.

Ben Zoma, *Sayings of the Fathers,* 4:1

Contents

Illustrations

Figures

Tables

Foreword

In April 2007 I joined scores of people to attend a special service at the Snoa—the venerable synagogue of Curaço, built in 1732, home to Congregation Mikvé Israel-Emanuel, the oldest surviving synagogue in the Americas, where no Sabbath or major holiday has gone uncelebrated in 278 years. Inside, through the arched entrance portal with the inscription from Psalm 26, B'makhelim abarekh ha-shem ("In the congregations I will bless the Lord"), all 144 candles were burning in the three large chandeliers and the sconces attached to the four big columns.

In the past twenty years I have visited many of the "Jewish sanctuaries in the Atlantic World" described by Barry Stiefel in this book, including the well-known synagogues of Amsterdam, London, Newport, and Charleston. But when I was at the service in Curaçao held to commemorate the 275th anniversary of the dedication of the building, I felt the strength of the historical continuum of Judaism in the New World, and the richness of the traditions of the Atlantic Jewish communities. Through their language, liturgy, and architecture, these communities—originally exclusively Sephardic—reach back to a distant past. In their establishment in circumstances of freedom and tolerance, however, they are the foundation on which modern American Judaism is built.

The survival of the Snoa represents centuries of a culture of tolerance and cooperation of the sort Jews have rarely enjoyed elsewhere in the world. The great columns and the wooden ceiling vaults recall those in the Portuguese Synagogue in Amsterdam (known as the Esnoga), the "mother" congregation of Curaçao's Jews, who first settled "on the island" in 1651, making Willemstad the oldest surviving Jewish community in the Western Hemisphere. It was the erection of the monumental Amsterdam Esnoga in 1675, celebrated with a week's festivities that recalled the rededication of the Temple at the time of the Maccabees, that signaled a new age of opportunity for Diaspora Jews, and it was in the successful colonies established by Jews from Amsterdam, and later London, that this freedom was most fully realized over the next 350 years.

The foundation of Jewish liberty and opportunity in the United States—a country where George Washington emphatically pronounced to the Sephardic Jewish congregation of Jeshuat Israel (better known as the Touro Synagogue) in Newport, Rhode Island, that government "to bigotry gives no sanction, to persecution no assistance"—this foundation has its strong roots in the tolerance and support provided to Jews by Dutch Protestant reformers in seventeenth-century Amsterdam, capital of Europe's first modern republic, and then in the Dutch colonies.

And yet this is a history that today remains distant and continues to dim for most American Jews, who are mostly Ashkenazic, not Sephardic, and who trace their roots to central and eastern Europe, not to the world of Atlantic Judaism. *Jewish Sanctuary in the Atlantic World* should help bridge that distance. Stiefel brings these oft-forgotten communities back into the historical narrative, so that their history is a vital link in the Atlantic and American historical continuum. But he also makes the case that they constitute through their circumstances, customs, and architecture a distinct and successful phase of Jewish history from which we still benefit, and from which we should still learn. Even in an age before modern communications, in a big watery world, distant Jewish communities stayed in close contact. This is symbolically represented in the Snoa in the three great wooden barrel vaults of the synagogue's ceiling, which also contribute to the Snoa's excellent acoustics. They are shaped like the inverted hulls of ships, reminiscent of those that carried Jews to this safe haven. Their appearance suggests ships that were somehow beached but were raised on walls to make a sanctuary. (In truth, the vaults were cut and fitted in the Netherlands, then shipped to Curaçao for on-site assembly—an early instance of prefab construction.)

The long benches of the Snoa on which I and the entire community sat are narrow and hard, and only a few had cushions (they predate our modern-day era of extra-wide Jewish posteriors). The old benches are arranged in the common Sephardic fashion, as in Amsterdam, London, and Venice, and throughout the Caribbean. They face the open central space between Hechal (Ark) and Tebah (Bimah), which functions as a (rectangular) arena where the drama of the service, including processions with the Torah scrolls, takes place. Behind one range of benches, against the north wall, is a raised dais, or banca, where the leaders of the congregation sit. To emphasize the still-strong Dutch roots of Caribbean Jewry, a Dutch rabbi from the Liberal Synagogue of The Hague, located in the former Sephardic Synagogue (the Snoge), built in 1726 and therefore an architectural "sibling" of the Snoa, joined in the celebrations.

As we sat on that bench, the scene seemed exotic and out of time, though I knew that until the 1820s almost all Jews who prayed in the New World would have experienced something very similar. Today, however, most American Jews find little direct connection to Amsterdam, London, or Curaçao. Rather, most American Jews seek their past, real and imagined, beyond these once-vital centers—in Poland often, or other places east. Other times, they seek their past in their own backyards, in their own stories of sanctuary. The Atlantic World, which was once a central network that helped knit Diaspora

Judaism together, is now at best peripheral both geographically and historically to contemporary American Jewish concerns. Only Jewish New York—once a relatively insignificant stop on Jewish Atlantic trade routes—is a place of consequence. But while the importance of New York is due in the nineteenth century, to its role as an Atlantic port, it is important now because of the immigration of hundreds of thousands of Ashkenazi immigrants by way of central Europe and the Baltic and North Seas, rather than through the success of or a continuity with the Sephardic culture of the Atlantic communities from which the city developed.

In Curaçao the Snoa is the most-visited historic site of the entire island, but though it is the best-known of all Jewish sites in the Caribbean, it is only one of many. There has been a Jewish presence in the Caribbean and throughout much of the Americas for more than five hundred years, since the first voyages of discovery by European explorers. For much of that time, American Judaism played a small but vital role in a world network of maritime commerce. Despite long oppression by the Spanish government and Catholic Church, there have been Jewish communities established in territories colonized by the Dutch and English since Dutch Jews settled in Brazil in the 1620s and following, until their expulsion by the Portuguese in 1654. Jewish colonization on Dutch and then English islands took place in the 1640s through the 1670s, and these communities have continued for the most part until today. Subsequently, formal Jewish communities were established in many former Spanish dominions once they obtained independence beginning in the nineteenth century.

Just about the time that Willemstad's Jews were planning their impressive new house of worship, the much smaller Jewish community of Shearith Israel (Remnant of Israel), far to the north in the Dutch-founded but now British New York, was preparing for its small synagogue, the very first erected in North America. In 1728 a plot of land was purchased in the same neighborhood where the first synagogue was located, and the congregation appealed for funds to sister communities in London, Jamaica, Barbados, Surinam, and Curaçao. These congregations formed a community of interest, but also one of family and business ties. On September 8, 1729, four cornerstones were laid according to the tradition of the Great Synagogue of the Portuguese Jews in Amsterdam and the new Mill Street Synagogue (as the new Shearith Israel was popularly called), was dedicated the following April.

The Mill Street building was a masonry building, thirty-five feet square, and twenty-one feet high, with a gallery on three sides for women. It had tall windows running through the two levels, and like the Snoa of Curaçao (and like the Sephardic synagogues of Amsterdam and London), the men sat on wooden benches running lengthwise along the north and south sides of the space. And like the men of those congregations, New York Jews were a diverse lot, but most were engaged in trade, and many made their living through the transatlantic import and export business facilitated by their friendly relations with other Jews. Records of the synagogue include mention of the ark, the reader's desk, the banca for the parnas presidente, the wooden tablets of the Law, and a glass lamp for the eternal light, and they also reveal much about the familiar connections, public behavior, and personal wealth of the congregants. Scenes of Jewish religious and community life familiar in Curaçao and New York through the early nineteenth century were replicated in synagogues throughout the Atlantic World, many of which shared the same formal, architectural, and decorative features.

Jewish communities mostly founded by Spanish and Portuguese Sephardic Jews by way of the Netherlands and England were spread up and down the Atlantic littoral. These outposts of Judaism were often far distant from one another but were connected by a common history, tradition, and language and stayed close through ties of trade, kinship, and marriage. Some of these communities, such as Dutch Curaçao and British Gibraltar, continue today. Many historic synagogues are well known, often well maintained and frequently visited. Some are active synagogues, while the sites of former synagogues are now being reidentified and researched through documentary and archaeological investigation. Throughout the Atlantic, there have been or are now scores of known Jewish heritage sites, including communal and religious properties, urban areas of settlements, and private plantations. Sites include cemeteries, mikva'ot, schools, and commercial and domestic structures; foremost among these are the synagogues, with their rich history.

Other Jewish centers, such as the tiny island of St. Eustatius, have all but disappeared, leaving only the visible remains of a synagogue and cemetery, and a dim memory of the important role that community played in helping to arm the Continental Army during the American Revolution. Excavations in Spanish Town, Jamaica, and Bridgetown, Barbados, are bringing to light valuable information about the first synagogues of these islands. Recent investigations have also revealed a possible synagogue on the island of Nevis, and there may have been one on St. Martin was well.

Jewish Sanctuary in the Atlantic World collects in one place for the first time the known information about these buildings, their congregations, and the historic circumstances of their inception, and sometimes their demise. It brings together research of scholars, architects, preservationists, and local historians from four continents and many islands, written in many languages, over many years. Brought together, these myriad local historians become a single flowing history of a successful, confident, and proud Jewish world, shaped and linked by the constancy of Atlantic Ocean winds and currents, and commitment to a Jewish community, even at the edges of the world.

Samuel D. Gruber
SYRACUSE, NEW YORK

Acknowledgments

Jewish Sanctuary in the Atlantic World was a labor of love that took me on adventures to its geographic four corners. Nonetheless, I could not have done it without some very special people and institutions. To begin with is David Rittenberg. His editorial assistance and fact checking was solid in an area where I had little experience at this level. For any remaining inaccuracies that may exist in this publication I accept full responsibility.

The Special Collections at the College of Charleston Library, especially Dale Rosengarten, allowed me unfettered access to the William A. Rosenthall Judaica Collection. For assistance that allowed the research for this study to really take off, thanks to the Carolina Lowcountry and Atlantic World Program at the College of Charleston, for the Hines Prize; to the American Jewish Historic Society, for the Sid and Ruth Lapidus Fellowship; and to the Jewish Endowment Foundation of New Orleans, for the Wolff Memorial Scholarship. I am very grateful for the immense patience and understanding of Linda Fogle and Alexander Moore, at the University of South Carolina Press. I am also indebted to Jonathan Sarna of Brandeis University; Samuel Gruber of the International Survey of Jewish Monuments; Aviva Ben-Ur of the University of Massachusetts, Amherst; Howard Adelman of Queens University; and Robert Russell of Salve Regina University for their guidance and valuable review of earlier drafts and excerpts for material content. My graduate student assistant, E. Megan Funk, was also of exceptional help in preparing the final images for this project.

I also wish to thank Eugene Cizek and Colin MacLachlan at Tulane University for their support and guidance over the years. Special thanks to the Department of History at the University of Michigan, who took me in while Tulane University was closed in the aftermath of Hurricane Katrina in the fall of 2005. My colleagues Sherri Andrews and Catherine Wright, at ASM Affiliates in Carlsbad and Pasadena, California, gave valuable editing and formatting assistance.

The research phase of this study took me to the corners of the Atlantic world. From all these lands that were part of my research I encountered a plethora of fantastic people to whom I am grateful: In North America—George

Goodwin in Rhode Island; Arlene Hicks at Touro Synagogue in Newport, Rhode Island; Alan Singer at Shearith Israel in New York; Randy Belinfante at the Library of the American Sephardi Federation in New York. In the Caribbean—Grant Gilmore, director of the St. Eustatius Center for Archaeological Research in St. Eustatius; Nicole and Anthony Henriquez and Simon Wolfson for their research assistance in Curaçao; Ainsley Cohen Henriques and the United Congregation of Israelites, Kingston, Jamaica; Miri and Jason Bowen in Barbados; Derek Miller and Michael Stoner for sharing their doctoral research on Barbados; Karl Watson of the University of the West Indies. In South America—Lily Duym at Nederlandsch-Israelietische Gemeente in Paramaribo, Suriname; Rachel Frankel in Suriname; Tania Neumann Kaufman in Brazil. In Europe—Sharman Kadish, director of Jewish Heritage UK in the United Kingdom and Gibraltar; Abraham Benady of Holy Land Travel in Gibraltar; Brenda Soiza in Gibraltar. And in Israel—Tania Coen Uzzielli at the Israel Museum in Jerusalem; and Seth Fersko.

Archival research was conducted at (North America) the Center for Jewish History in New York; the American Jewish Archives at Hebrew Union College–Jewish Institute of Religion in Cincinnati; Special Collections at the College of Charleston in South Carolina; South Carolina Department of Archives and History; the Jewish Theological Seminary in New York; National Museum of American Jewish History in Philadelphia; the Jewish Museum of New York; the Jewish Public Library in Montreal; Jewish Women's Archive in Brookline, Massachusetts; Beth Ahabah Museum and Archives and the Valentine Richmond History Center in Richmond, Virginia; William Clements Library at the University of Michigan in Ann Arbor; the John Carter Brown Library in Providence, Rhode Island; the Huntington Library in San Marino, California; the Getty Research Institute in Los Angeles; the Library of Congress in Washington D.C.; (Caribbean) the Mongui Maduro Library in Curaçao; the Jewish Cultural Historical Museum in Curaçao; the Nidhe Israel Museum in Barbados; (South America) Nationaal Archief Suriname in Paramaribo; Arquivo Historico Judaico de Pernambuco in Recife, Brazil; (Europe) the Jewish Museum in London; the Joods Historisch Museum in Amsterdam; the Museo Sefardi, Toledo, Spain; (Israel) the Israel Museum in Jerusalem; and the Jewish National and University Library in Jerusalem.

Finally I would like to thank my family, especially my father, Gilbert, and stepmother, Kathy Stiefel, and my in-laws, Aliza and Morty Hoch. Last, but certainly not least, is my wife, Lori. I first met Lori just as I was beginning my doctoral studies, and she was with me through thick and thin—from hurricanes in New Orleans, to blizzards in Montreal and wildfires in southern California, swimming with the piranhas in the Suriname River of South America, and playing with the monkeys in Gibraltar. We even acquired two little additions to our family along the way, with the births of Izzy and Corinne. As my best friend and partner, Lori was my travel companion on every research trip and provided assistance with the graphics and illustrations for this book. I could not have accomplished what has been done without her love and support.

Introduction

Sanctuary from expulsion, torture, extortion, and riot: this was the haven offered by the New World for the crypto-Jews and New Christians fleeing repression as Iberian Catholic monarchs endorsed persecution.[1] Beginning in the seventeenth century, however, more tolerant Protestant societies of the Netherlands, England, and Denmark opened their doors. Jewish refugees who settled in the Netherlands and England, then followed Dutch and British imperial expansion to the Americas. As Iberia itself was abandoned—though crucially not the powerful imprint of Sephardic culture—the art and architecture of synagogues built in the Atlantic world, whether in northern Europe or the Americas, came to express a new prosperity and social acceptance that Jews had not known for centuries.[2] As conditions for Jews improved under Protestant rule, synagogues that had started off as modest structures became grander in scale and more impressive architecturally.

Before the Inquisition gathered full force, Spain and Portugal were themselves seedbeds of Jewish talent and energy. At the dawn of the Age of Discovery (c. 1420), Jewish minorities were already involved in the great endeavor of exploration. They figured as scientists or inventors in the development of navigation and, what is more important, as translators of relevant Arabic and Hebrew scientific treatises into Latin, Spanish, and Portuguese. This contribution ended at a stroke between 1492 and 1498 when the Spanish, Portuguese, and Navarrese edicts of expulsion struck: at a minimum, Jews faced exile from Spain and Navarre and forced conversion in Portugal. Some, concealed as crypto-Jews during the sixteenth century, continued to serve Iberian rulers in the exploration and the conquest of foreign lands as New Christians. Others, beginning in the seventeenth century, contributed to the imperial expansion of the Dutch and British, and, to a lesser extent, of the Danes and French. These Jews often prospered as port merchants who shipped goods between the colonies and mother countries; as planters who owned and raised cash crops; and as shopkeepers, and artisans.[3]

Wherever a numerically substantial Jewish community established itself under a tolerant regime, a synagogue was built to meet religious, social, and cultural needs. Jonathan Sarna in his indispensable survey, *American Judaism*,

A History (2004), observed that, during the colonial epoch (1654–1776), each community of Jews constituted one congregation.[4] As it happens the Hebrew word associated with a house of worship is semantically inclusive: *kahal* means both "spiritual congregation" and "community of people," while a synagogue named Kahal was most often modified by the adjective "kodesh," which means "holy," thus becoming the "Holy Congregation/Community."[5] Typically a single building housed a synagogue. But there were instances when, because of population growth, site considerations, or religious politics, a satellite building was erected, as was in (Dutch) Brazil, Surinam, Curaçao, and (English) Barbados. But, for all practical purposes, the synagogue-community relationship established c. 1636 by the Sephardic Jews of Amsterdam disseminated across the Sephardic communities of the Netherlands, Great Britain, and their respective empires, lasting for two centuries (until c. 1825).

Conceived and built mostly in the New World between 1636 and 1822, these religious structures followed two models—Amsterdam's Portuguese Synagogue (called the Esnoga) and London's Bevis Marks Synagogue. This London synagogue, whose official Hebrew name is Kahal Kodesh Sha'ar Hashamayim (Holy Congregation / Community Gates of Heaven), was built off of a street, Bevis Marks, in the Aldgate ward. Both demonstrate a characteristically Sephardic open central aisle floor plan integrated with Dutch Baroque or Georgian architectural elements.[6] This conjunction is hardly peculiar: after many Iberian Jews fled the Inquisition to settle first in the Lowlands, soon after in England. As happened wherever they were admitted, the Jews responded to their immediate architectural environment. Both the Dutch Baroque and Georgian styles embody the prestigious Roman classicism of Andrea Palladio; aesthetically and theologically this architecture articulates both Dutch Reform and Puritan aversion to iconography, a sensibility consonant with the age-old iconoclasm of Jewish doctrine, art, and architecture. There were regional variants of Palladian classical design as climate and the availability of building materials required, such as synagogues with sand-covered floors in the Caribbean and South America.

Clandestine Jews in the far-flung Spanish, Portuguese, and French Empires also left an identifiable mark on religious practice and synagogue design. When we survey the Dutch, British, Danish, and French colonial empires, as well as the nascent United States forty-six synagogue structures were built between 1636 and 1822. These synagogues triangulate or striate the Atlantic World, from Montreal, Canada, to Recife, Brazil, and, across the ocean, to Gibraltar. The forty-six structures were built by some thirty-one congregations, which is to say, certain congregations constructed more than one building, either sequentially, as a larger structure replaced an older one, or additionally, as satellite buildings accommodated population growth.[7] There were other congregations in the Atlantic World, however, that never managed to build a synagogue and were forced to accept makeshift quarters.

A "synagogue" here means a Jewish community's purpose-built house of worship, while the Atlantic World Jewish community (c.1625–1825) refers to European states that bordered the Atlantic and their colonies or former colonies. Inevitably colonization implies "familial" bonding—home countries figure as parents, colonies as dependents. To a degree, this kind of relationship defined New World Jewry in regard to the Esnoga or Bevis Marks. Sometimes colonies would help each other too: larger, more established Jewish communities on Curaçao, Surinam,[8] and Jamaica would aid newer, less prosperous congregations.

Where the Atlantic touches the Mediterranean, there is a special case. Gibraltar had been inaccessible to Jews from the onset of the Spanish Inquisition (1492) until 1714, when Spain ceded the territory to Britain at the end of the War of Spanish Succession. So the Jews who moved to the fortress-city under British rule resembled in some respects colonists in the larger Jewish diaspora. To an uncanny degree, British Gibraltar's economy and society were similar to those of a fortified Caribbean island, akin to Dutch St. Eustatius, dependent on a valuable port rather than a developed commercial center in a continental European state.

Even Gibraltar's synagogues were shaped by this Atlantic colonial perspective. The Great Synagogue (Shaar Hashamayim, built 1781–83) and the magnificent Flemish Synagogue (Nefutsot Yehuda/Dispersed of Judah, built 1799), similar to synagogues found in the Caribbean, testify to the strong cultural bonds that once existed. These houses of worship are elegant expressions of Sephardic design, built with fine materials. But Gibraltar's modest Etz Chaim (Tree of Life, built 1783) and Abudarham (built 1821) Synagogues are different: these represent vernacular style appropriate for a dense population. No such examples survive in the Americas or elsewhere in the Atlantic World.

Several groups of Jews populated the Atlantic World in our period. Beyond question, the most influential were the Iberian Sephardim. Jews who had lived productively under Muslim-ruled Iberia between 711 and 1492. The Sephardim were the cultural progenitors of Jews in the colonial Atlantic—those who later built the synagogues of the seventeenth, eighteenth, and early nineteenth centuries while establishing a Jewish presence in the New World. Before 1492 the Sephardim had developed strong mercantile and banking skills, as well as experience in experimental sugarcane cultivation in southern Iberia and the outlying Atlantic islands of the Azores, Canaries, Cape Verde, Madeira, and São Tomé.

When the Spanish monarchs Ferdinand and Isabella declared summary expulsion in 1492, many Sephardim fled to North Africa, the Italian states, and the Ottoman Empire.[9] But from the early sixteenth century Jews who remained on the Peninsula or sought out Iberian colonies became *conversos*. These covered a spectrum, ranging from changed religious belief to social accommodation as a disguise for ancestral faith: there were Jews who became sincere Christians; partial converts who shifted between Christianity and Judaism; converts who remained faithful to Judaism in conviction although adopting a Christian façade; and atheists, deists, or agnostics—those who personally rejected religion, while privately preserving some Jewish identity out of deference to family or friends. Until the tolerance formally granted by Protestant rulers in the seventeenth century, Jews in the Netherlands, England, and their overseas dependencies also practiced religious subterfuge, very much in line with the "converted" of the Catholic empires Spain, Portugal, and France.

At the end of the sixteenth century, as Protestant European states prevailed in bitter conflicts with Catholic forces, oppression of the Jews began to dissipate. This was conspicuous in the newly independent Netherlands (c. 1580) and Cromwellian England (c. 1655), two ardently Protestant polities. To them came the crypto-Jewish émigrés who wanted to shed any Christian façade and re-embrace normative Sephardic Judaism. For many putting aside converso camouflage—especially for later generations of converts with no direct knowledge of Judaism—the course back to Judaism called for effort.

Adopting Jewish belief and practice could be problematic. Because a recent returnee to Judaism neither read Hebrew nor understood Jewish ritual, he or she often felt lost. Traditional worship probably challenged an uneducated person, who could find no corollaries to Christian formulas like praying with hands clasped together, counting beads as memory aids, or kneeling before an altar. Some wealthier, more educated returnees to Judaism—they had received extensive instruction in Catholic doctrine at universities and were multilingual (in Spanish, Portuguese, French, and Latin)—faced different tests of an intellectual order. They had to learn a different interpretation (indeed an alternative historiography) of the Torah or Hebrew Bible—no longer regarded as "the Old Testament" anticipatory of Christian revelation; the canon of the Oral Law (the Talmud); and the Hebrew language itself, with strange characters contained in an utterly unfamiliar prayer book. The children of such upper-class repatriates to Judaism mastered this knowledge and acquisition of ritual.

On balance conversos responded quickly to newly tolerant environments: adaptation, flexibility, selective memory, and resilience were their main psychological tools in putting aside the repression launched by the Inquisition. Still, although returnees to Judaism soon came to regard Amsterdam and London as rightful and natural homes, the memory and religious attitudes of the converso past sometimes lingered.[10] Nor was this adaptive experience confined to the Netherlands or England in the seventeenth century, the most active arenas and period of return for Sephardim migrating from Iberia. The memory, indeed the reality, of liberation was alive as late as the early nineteenth century. David Henriques Valentine served as sexton of Shearith Israel in New York from 1821–35. He supposedly bore scars on his wrists from chains used when he was a prisoner during the Portuguese Inquisition (extant until 1821). Clearly immediate exposure to crypto-Jewish or persecuted experience, and its permutations, was alive for the Sephardim centuries after the first crisis of expulsion in the 1490s.[11]

The Inquisition forced Jews to accept an entirely new socioeconomic, cultural, and geographic condition. Sephardim in Protestant states not only sustained contacts with Iberian Jews migrating to the Mediterranean but also encountered or corresponded with the native Jews of North Africa, the Ottoman Empire, and several Italian states. At the same time, both the Atlantic and Mediterranean Jews were in contact with New Christians in the far-flung Spanish and Portuguese Empires. Whether overtly or covertly connected, the Jewish social, mercantile, and cultural network thus created was impressive. It paralleled the vast, international scope of the Iberian rulers, whose imperial ventures stretched from the Americas through Europe, the Mediterranean, and the Middle East to India and East Asian coasts or islands.

Beginning with the arrival of Jews in the Netherlands and England (c. 1580–1655), religious culture was sustained by an inter-Sephardic conversation. The Jews of Amsterdam and London, including at first many who had been conversos, frequently sought historical insight, knowledge of rabbinic traditions, and community "best practices" from their coreligionists in the Sephardic Mediterranean diaspora. Everywhere this interaction—at once pragmatic, absorptive, and cohesive—was embodied in the synagogue-community. By providing, in the words of Daviken Studnicki-Gizbert, "the physical locus for the recognition of a common 'national' symbol, synagogues opened spaces in which links could be established between individuals who did not have a more primary connection—such as kinship, common provenance, or class affiliation—to tie them together."[12] Bonded in this way, as well as by a peninsular background, Iberian Jews and their descendents developed a distinct cultural and historical identity that they called La Nación, meaning "Hebrews of the Spanish and Portuguese Nation."[13] With this name the Sephardim of the Atlantic World at once referred to and differentiated themselves from Ashkenazic or Mediterranean Jews. In a sense, membership in La Nación provided an intangible, transportable "sanctuary" for postexilic Sephardim—a preserve of memory and likeness within the wider, more variegated Jewish diaspora.

The Mizrachim are another Jewish population encountered in the Atlantic World. *Mizrach* means "east" in Hebrew and refers to Jews indigenous to North Africa and the Middle East.[14] Those from Morocco and Algeria are sometimes known as Maghribim, after the Arabic word "Maghrib," or "west," since North Africa, seen from the Arabian peninsula, was at the western edge of the Islamic world. After 1492 some Sephardim fled to North Africa and the Middle East, so their relationships with the Mizrachim compounded and deepened. Iberian Jews shared the experience of having lived under Islamic rule.

But interactions with Moslems was definitely not the case with the third Jewish population of the Atlantic World, the Ashkenazim. They were indigenously European—though neither Iberian nor Mediterranean—and lived in a wide geographic zone from the Rhine and Alsace in the west, through Germany, Austria, and Poland, to Lithuania, Russia, and Ukraine in the east. *Ashkenaz* in Hebrew refers to the Rhineland and later connoted all Jews in western, central, and eastern Europe. In the seventeenth century, burgeoning economic and mercantile development in the Netherlands and Great Britain attracted Ashkenazic immigration. Then in 1648 the notorious Chmielnitzki Pogroms erupted in Poland, only to be followed by further anti-Semitic outbursts across central and eastern Europe. This time Ashkenazic Jews sought the sanctuary offered by the Dutch and British, whether in Europe or the growing overseas empires.[15]

From 1600 to 1825, the composition of a given Jewish community varied; the Atlantic World included Sephardim, Ashkenazim, and Mizrachim. Members of each were often multilingual, an important asset for conducting trade among Jews and non-Jews alike. The polyglot diversity was striking: Even though a given speaker's experience varied, Sephardim from the Netherlands and Britain often spoke, besides Dutch and English, Portuguese, Spanish, and Hebrew; Mediterranean Sephardim were conversant in Arabic, Ladino, Italian, Turkish, and Hebrew; the Mizrachim were familiar with Judeo-Arabic, Turkish, and Hebrew; and the Ashkenazi spoke Yiddish, Dutch, English, German, and Hebrew. Assimilated Iberian New Christians and crypto-Jews, if formally educated, would have known Spanish, Portuguese, and Latin too. Other languages included French, Danish, Polish, and Russian. Jewish merchants on the colonial frontiers picked up indigenous languages and even contributed to new creole languages, such as Papiamento and Djoe-tongo.[16]

There were minor variations in religious custom (Hebrew *minhag*) among the main populations constituting the Jewish Atlantic World. For non-Iberian Jews, however, acquisition of Sephardic minhagim often provided a functional passport to the robust social and commercial network growing rapidly during the seventeenth century. So Ashkenazis frequently deferred to Sephardic practice set by the congregations of Amsterdam and London. That is why both rituals and synagogue architecture across so broad an Atlantic expanse bear a Sephardic stamp.

Amsterdam's Portuguese Synagogue (1636–39) was followed soon after by the construction of Zur Israel (Rock of Israel) synagogue in the Dutch colony of Recife, Brazil (1640).[17] Although a few Jews had begun their clandestine sojourn in the New World by sailing with Columbus in 1492, Dutch-occupied Brazil provided the first opportunity for Jews in the Americas to practice their religion openly, free from persecution. An important era had begun. It would last until the 1820s, its passing in effect marked architecturally by the last synagogue designed on Sephardic lines, Beth Shalome (House of Peace) in Richmond, Virginia (completed 1822). In that very year the position of chief Sephardic rabbi of Amsterdam, the spiritual head of all Dutch Sephardic Jewry, was left vacant, not to be filled again until 1900.[18] By the mid-1820s the social cohesion and posture of the Atlantic Sephardim had frayed emphatically. Differences in minhagim, not to mention a vigorous interest in religious reform, created tensions that split many synagogue-communities into enclaves of provenance—such as German and Polish Ashkenazim worshipping apart from Sephardim. The result was a diverse community of synagogues.[19] This is the social context—other large forces were at work too—that led to the notable expansion of synagogue design during the 1830s and 1840s.

Before 1825 Jews of non-Iberian origin had, for the most part, conformed to Sephardic minhagim, even in communities where non-Sephardim made up a majority. But demographic changes would alter this religious landscape. During the eighteenth century, as religious tolerance fostered by the Enlightenment affected the Americas, non-Sephardic Jews came to the New World in ever larger numbers. These were Ashkenazim from central and eastern Europe, and, to a lesser extent, North African Mizrachim. By 1825 the recent Ashkenazic immigrants were separating themselves from their Sephardic predecessors. They founded their own congregations, favoring synagogue designs that did not copy Sephardic architectural models. Thus in the United States members of Sephardic synagogues created breakaway Ashkenazic institutions, like B'nai Jeshurun (Children of Righteousness, 1825) in New York. Moving westward as settlers seeking new opportunities, Ashkenazim also founded new congregations where Jewish life had not existed before, such as Bene Israel (Children of Israel, 1824) in Cincinnati. The pioneering momentum, of Jewish immigrants was not confined to the United States. Brazil, newly independent from Portugal in 1825, adopted a policy of religious tolerance toward non-Catholics. Soon, a wave of Moroccan Mizrachim arrived to take advantage of the growing rubber trade, settling in Belém at the mouth of the Amazon River. By 1828 the congregation in Belém, called Shaar Hashamaim, erected a synagogue architecturally distinct from any other in the Americas.[20] Moreover, unlike the Sephardim who had settled in the Dutch and British Empires, in the Americas the Ashkenazic and Mizrachic immigrants were uninterruptedly Jewish, never having undergone the trauma of conversion and the loss of religious memory.

The year 1824 also witnessed the rise of American Reform Judaism in Charleston, South Carolina, where a group from Beth Elohim (House of God) established the Reform Society of Israelites. This movement spread across North America; Britain and particularly Europe were influenced by a contemporary reform development in Germany. By the mid-nineteenth century, Reform Judaism had decisively affected American and British Jewish culture, both in ritual and synagogue design. The new religious practices included mixed-gender seating (not men divided from women, as was the age-old Orthodox custom), services conducted in English (not Hebrew), and the introduction of pipe organs. Reform Jews also began to call their houses of worship "temples."[21]

The Sephardic hegemony of Amsterdam and London had waned. Their Atlantic communities were influenced by political events and, most importantly, by large-scale Ashkenazic migration with different cultural preferences. Such socio-political changes were evident in novel synagogue architecture as early as 1825, when Philadelphia's Sephardic congregation built Mikveh Israel (Hope of Israel), in the Egyptian Revival style. Soon after Classical Revival and Greek Revival synagogues appeared in New York, Montreal, Charleston, and in England, at Brighton and Ramsgate; Gothic Revival in Barbados; and a hybrid Gothic-Greek Revival synagogue in St. Thomas. Strikingly nowhere in the Americas were Palladian synagogues built after 1822. The cultural discourse had changed.

By the 1830s La Nación would have realized that a whole way of life was in decline. The axis of economic and cultural power had shifted. In 1838, for example, after fire destroyed Charleston's first Beth Elohim synagogue (completed in 1794), the congregation contacted the traditional Atlantic Sephardic network in the United States, Britain, the Netherlands, and the Caribbean for help in building a new structure. The appeal fell on deaf ears. In fact the one congregation to offer (admittedly token!) aid was the Ashkenazic Jewish community in Cincinnati, which sent a check for $119.50.[22] No princely sum, but good intentions, based on common religious and social perceptions, registered: soon after, the Jewish communities of Cincinnati and Charleston became allies and propagators of Reform Judaism in the United States.

This passing of Sephardic dominance did not take place in a vacuum. The Iberian Jews of the Diaspora, like everyone in the Atlantic World, were directly or indirectly subject to the great twin revolutions that forever changed western European societies (and eventually those in contact with that West) during the last three decades of the eighteenth century. Political revolution in America and France, and industrial revolution, emerging first in England but soon crossing the Atlantic, marked the birth of a world we recognize as our own. The European Enlightenment had launched a paradigm shift in Western society that shaped the most fundamental areas of experience: the redefinition of civil and political rights under the rubric of egalitarian universality; the role of reason in secular and scientific thought and how this affected religious belief; the accepted relationship between religion and government; and the emerging sovereignty of science as a scourge of superstition. Add to these categories the seminally revolutionary material changes brought on by the onset of industrialization with its new division of labor. Modernity was in embryo.

So the way of life among the Sephardim changed radically between 1775 and 1825. By the end of this period, the Inquisition, which had brought oppression and exile to so many Jews for so long, finally ceased. In geopolitics the American and French Revolutions, followed by the Napoleonic Wars, had redrawn national and imperial borders. There were the palpable effects of Enlightenment liberty affecting economy, society, and ideology: the legal end of the international slave trade; the rise and spread of the abolitionist movement, particularly in the Americas; and the initial emancipation of the Jews throughout most of continental Europe and its colonial dependencies.

Within this fifty-year span—the period of one lifetime—the situation for Atlantic and for much of European Jewry had been turned on its head. The Inquisitor's flames were extinguished, ghetto walls came down, and newly emancipated Jews could join civil society in the post-Napoleonic era. During the nineteenth century, Jews were free to describe these great changes in the art and architecture of the synagogue on both sides of the Atlantic. After 1825 western European and North American Jews began to venture into the professions of architecture and building construction: No longer were surrogates hired to design or craft synagogues. For Jews the house of worship had become not only a sanctuary but, quite literally, a home of their own.

CHAPTER 1

The Origin of the Atlantic World Synagogue

Buildings, like people, contain multitudes: so too the Atlantic World synagogues built between the early seventeenth and early nineteenth centuries. Like people these houses of worship can also be understood as telling distinct, though at times synchronous, narratives: of Jews as they left Europe and settled in the Americas during the early modern period; of architecture as a formal artistic endeavor with aesthetic roots in Roman culture; of the synagogue in its evolution following the destruction of the Second Temple (c. 75 C.E.). Weaving through these narratives is the relationship among the three Abrahamic monotheisms. During the first Christian centuries, Judaism crucially influenced the infant "Jesus movement"; by the fifth century, a robust Christianity had reciprocated with identifiable impact on synagogue architecture and Jewish art. Then, as Islam arose in the seventh century and spread with remarkable vigor, a third great religion inflected the historical narrative. If we take the broadest perspective, the synagogues of the Atlantic World, however distinctive they may seem, belong to this dense, multiform genealogy.

Because the history of the synagogue has ancient origins, few actual records have survived.[1] Etymology, however, is suggestive: "synagogue," based on Middle English *synagoge*, derives from the Greek *synagein*, meaning "to bring together," while the corollary in Hebrew are two words, *beth kenesset*, translatable as "house (beth) of gathering." In any case it seems likely that early synagogues arose as informal community centers well after the destruction of the First (or Solomon's) Temple in 586 B.C.E. This date, besides marking the manifest crisis of Babylonian captivity and exile, is an extremely important cultural and ritual demarcator: whereas animal sacrifice conducted by priests was at the center of Jerusalem's cultic Temple worship, no sacrifice was ever practiced in the precincts of synagogues. The synagogue familiar to us today developed slowly over a millennium and emerged mostly in a postcultic environment, as rabbis gradually supplanted the role of priests.[2]

After the destruction of the Second (Herod's) Temple in 70 C.E., rabbis began to codify the prayer-oriented practice of Judaism that became the form of worship recognizable today. Again we must emphasize how this transition was seminal—away from cult, sacrifice, and hierarchy toward ethics, texts, and community. Another Hebrew phrase marks a new (and lasting) meaning of synagogue—*beth tefilah,* or "house of prayer." The Greek word *proseuche* ("place of prayer") was sometimes used as a vernacular reference to a house of worship during this early period among many peoples of the eastern Mediterranean who gathered to pray, and sometimes applies to Jews during the first centuries C.E. Moreover the synagogue was also established as a center of Jewish learning; accordingly the building, or an area within it—later to be housed separately—was usually called *beth midrash,* or "house of study" in Hebrew. Again there are etymological signposts: the Yiddish (Ashkenazic) term *shul* and Ladino (Sephardic) *esnoga* are derived from the Latin word *scola,* meaning "school."[3] Eventually, after migrations across the Atlantic between 1500 and 1800, similar semantics define *snoa,* a word in the Papiamento creole language spoken in the Caribbean islands of Aruba, Bonaire, and Curaçao.[4]

As three key functions of the synagogue (community center, prayer house, and school) became institutionalized during the first and second centuries C.E., the architectural design components became more fixed. Unlike either the First or Second Temples, in which the most sacred ritual aspect was a *place*—an interior sanctuary known as the Holy of Holies—the most sacred element of a synagogue is *a text*—the Torah, a handwritten scroll recording the Five Books of Moses, or Pentateuch. The Torah remains at the core of Jewish thought, practice, and identity—both a theological and a historical document, determining that prayer and education must be central activities in the synagogue. Although in the mature, fully evolved synagogue, these three functions would converge, they may have had different gestations. Looking at the Hebrew names of communal institutions, in a given community, one or more of the key roles might have predominated at first (c. 200 B.C.E.–600 C.E.), later to merge as a tripartite formation under a single roof.[5] In any case there is a consensus that the development of the synagogue was multifaceted, complex, and hardly linear.[6]

Since the early centuries of the common era, Torah scrolls have been stored in transportable containers. These suggest the Ark of the Covenant, which had enclosed the tablets of the Ten Commandments in the First Temple's Holy of Holies.[7] Eventually the containers became permanent fixtures of a synagogue and were placed along the wall closest to Jerusalem. For synagogues located in Europe, North Africa, and the Americas, this wall is on the east; in Mesopotamia, Asia, and Australia it is on the west. The English word—hearkening back to the Tabernacle—for the place containing the tablets is *ark,* but in the Atlantic World, Jews used the term *hechal.*

Within Atlantic World synagogues, above the hechal was often an iconic motif, or *lukhot,* showing the dual tablets inscribed with the Ten

The hechal at the Portuguese Synagogue of 1675 in Amsterdam during the holiday
of Simchat Torah. Engraving by Bernard Picart, *Cérémonies et coutumes religieuses
de tous les peuples du monde*, Amsterdam, 1723. William A. Rosenthall Judaica
Collection, Special Collections, College of Charleston Library.

Commandments.[8] Near the hechal we find a lamp, called a "ner tamid," always kept lit as a reminder of the menorah that stood in the First and Second
Temples. Given the placement of the hechal on the wall nearest Jerusalem,
the primary entrance to the synagogue was usually on the west side, or occasionally the north or south side, of the building. In order not to distract the
congregation, the entrance was placed on the side opposite the hechal.

Along with the hechal, we find a reader's table on which the open Torah
scroll was placed. This table was positioned variously: in the middle of the
sanctuary or, depending on local tradition, either in the center of the room
or near the western wall opposite the hechal. The Sephardic Jews called the
platform a *tebah*; it would later be named a *bimah* by Ashkenazim.[9] While the
reader's platform often served as a pulpit, it sometimes became a separate element, designated the *amud*, and usually placed near the tebah or the hechal.
At this speaker's lectern stood either the *chazzan* (prayer leader) or the rabbi,
who would give a *drasha*, the Jewish equivalent of a sermon.

Another ubiquitous architectural fixture was the *mechitzah*, a partition between men and women. For larger basilica-like synagogues, this division might
create a separate (sometimes elevated) area for women, the *ezrat nashim*,

The tebah at the Portuguese Synagogue of 1675 during the holiday of Rosh Ha-Shanna, the Jewish New Year. In the above background can also be seen the ezrat nashim, or mechitzah. Engraving by Bernard Picart, *Cérémonies et coutumes religieuses de tous les peuples du monde*, Amsterdam, 1723. William A. Rosenthall Judaica Collection, Special Collections, College of Charleston Library.

which echoed an area within the Second Temple precincts by the same name, more commonly called the Women's Courtyard. The gender-separated areas of two-story structures would seat men on the main floor and women in an upstairs balcony or gallery. In one-story synagogues a partition was often used. Although the tradition of separate seating is ancient, its exact origins within the synagogue are controversial.[10] Not until 1851—starting with Anshe Emeth (People of Truth) in Albany, New York—did Reform congregations gradually eliminate gender separation by replicating the practice of Protestant denominations.[11]

Another synagogue feature evoked Temple antiquity—a curtain in front of the hechal known as the *parokhet*. It seperated the inner sanctum from the Holy of Holies. In the Atlantic World, Sephardim hang the parokhet inside the hechal. This is in contrast to the Ashkenazic custom, where the parokhet is often placed outside the ark. The Sephardim also used a "banca," which was a special elevated seating area on the north wall of the sanctuary, for the congregation's leaders and elders.[12] Many synagogues have courtyards or squares for outdoor courtyards, as did the Temples in Jerusalem. These spaces were sometimes used for religious purposes, such as blessing the New Moon, wedding ceremonies, and sukkah structures for the holiday of Sukkoth.[13]

Besides the architectural elements just described, certain rabbis also prescribed a proper method for building a synagogue. During the 1560s the Sephardic rabbi Yosef Karo of Safed, Israel, compiled a significant amount of Jewish law into a single work called the Shulchan Aruch. Ten years later Rabbi Moshe Isserles of Krakow, Poland, supplemented Karo's work with an Ashkenazic commentary in a work named the Mappah. The combined works, uniting the texts of Karo and Isserles, became authoritative for Jews all over the world.

Regulations within the Shulchan Aruch are quite precise on certain aspects of synagogue design and site planning. For example: A synagogue was to be built at the highest point of a town or of a neighborhood in a city; a synagogue was to be taller than any nearby residence; a synagogue ought not to be torn down until a new one has been built or purchased; and any ruined synagogue (or its contents) remained holy and therefore was to be respected. The entrance of a synagogue was never to be opposite congregants who face the hechal in prayer, while the tebah was to be located in the center of the sanctuary. Moreover a *yeshiva* (house of study) was not to be made into a synagogue, although a synagogue could be converted into a yeshiva since it serves a holier purpose.[14] Behavioral requisites existed too: the attic above a synagogue was not to be used for immodest purposes.[15] Even though these prescriptions were meant as mandatory, they were often treated as idealized goals given the subjugated status of Jews in medieval Christian and Muslim kingdoms. As the institution of the synagogue developed into the Jewish house of worship, somewhat different traditions emerged among Ashkenazim in central Europe, Italkim in Italy, Sephardim in Iberia, and Mizrachim in North Africa and the Middle East. These local customs, called "minhag," included liturgical and ritual variations, or "nusach."

From the first century B.C.E., Jewish communities built synagogues with various floor plans. Today we find floor plans in the Americas and Europe that follow four chief patterns: open central aisle, theater-style, central bimah (tebah), and open double aisle.[16] Sometimes called the "Sephardic Plan," the open central aisle model predominated in the Atlantic World prior to 1825. Here the hechal was placed along the sanctuary's eastern wall, and opposite the tebah was located toward the room's western half (often as far as the western wall). Starting at the northern and southern walls, rows of seats are arranged horizontally on an east-west axis, leaving a large open central space, or "aisle," with an unobstructed view of the room between hechal and tebah. The banca is raised within the row seating adjacent to the north wall.

By contrast the theater-style plan situates the tebah-bimah in front of the hechal: both project from the eastern wall and are opposite row seating that projects from the western wall. The rows of seats in a theater or auditorium

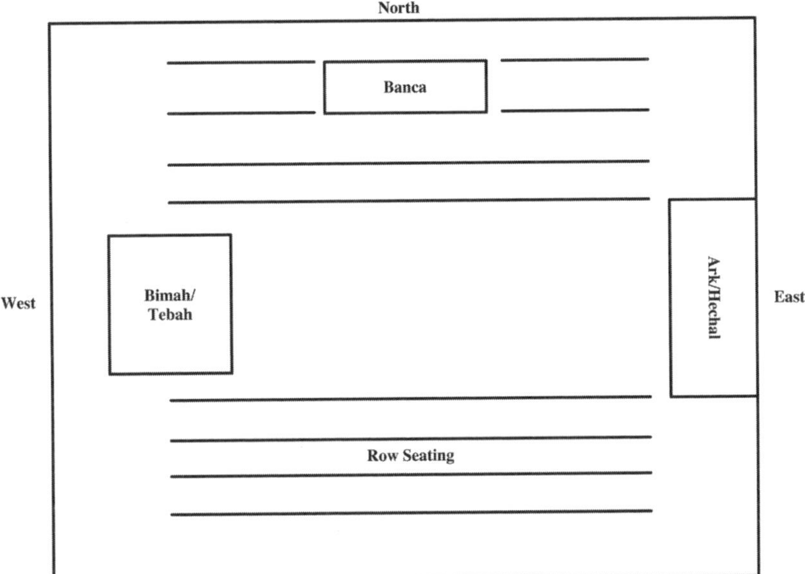

A schematic of the open central aisle plan. Drawn by E. Megan Funk. Personal collection of the author.

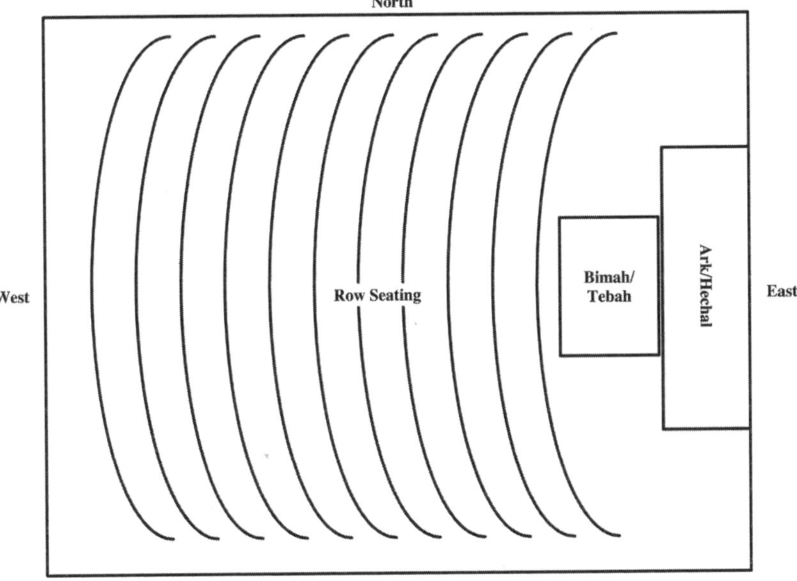

A schematic of the theater-style plan. Drawn by E. Megan Funk. Personal collection of the author.

     Jewish Sanctuary in the Atlantic World

are sometimes arranged in semicircular arcs following the curvature of the sanctuary room. This floor plan became popular in the nineteenth century as the Reform movement gave greater emphasis to the rabbi's or cantor's sermon in contrast to other elements of the service.

In the central bimah-tebah plan, the hechal stands at the eastern wall of the sanctuary and the tebah in the middle of the room, while the row seating faces east and is opposite the central tebah. This style is common in Ashkenazic design but is seen in some non-Ashkenazic synagogues.

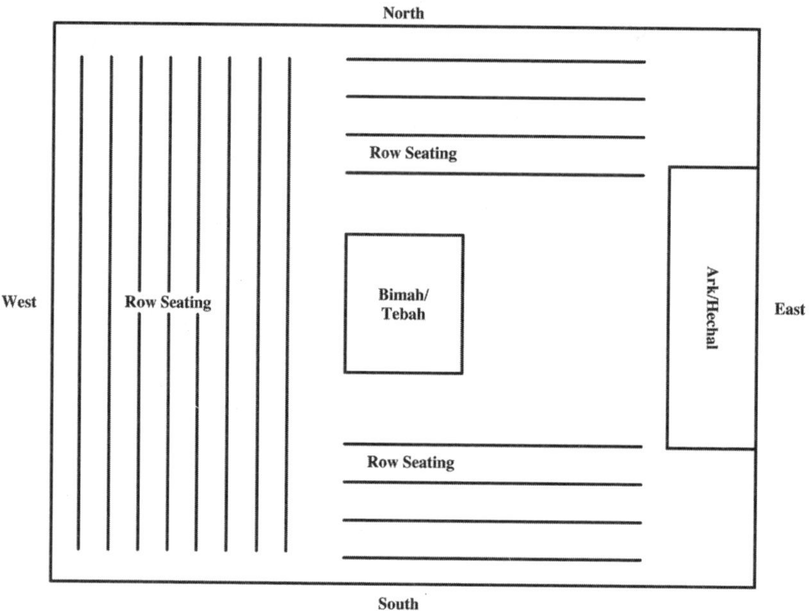

A schematic of the central bimah-tebah plan. Drawn by E. Megan Funk. Personal collection of the author.

The last model, the open double aisle plan, is close to the open central aisle plan: the hechal parallels the eastern wall, with the tebah extending from the center toward the western wall. Yet this plan differs in that central rows of seats create two open aisles within the sanctuary; at the same time, seats are oriented north-south. Mizrachim and other western Asian Jewish groups favored this double aisle plan.

Architectural nomenclature suggests an anomaly. Even though the open central aisle synagogue prevalent in the Atlantic World is designated "Sephardic," structures of that type—the Anglicized case of Gibraltar excepted—do not actually appear on the Iberian peninsula. So Iberia refers to culture, not geography. Once in the Americas, Jewish immigrants of Iberian origin regarded Amsterdam's Esnoga and London's Bevis Marks as norms. They embraced a synagogue design unlike what had existed in Spain or Portugal before

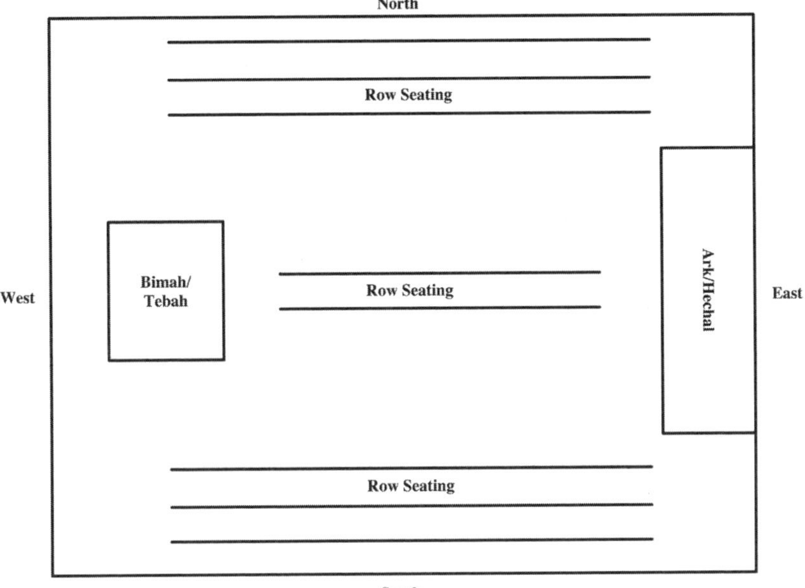

A schematic of the open double aisle plan. Drawn by E. Megan Funk.
Personal collection of the author.

1498. Hence, cultural identity, not to mention practice, defies literal-minded provenance: Sephardic Atlantic Jewry was, and was not, Iberian.

Only a handful of pre-expulsion (1492–98) synagogues remain on the Iberian Peninsula. Most typically, the remnant survived in Christian avatar, with synagogues converted into churches or some other use. These rare surviving examples include the Samuel ha-Levi Abulafia Synagogue, later named the Nuestra Senora del Transito Church, or El Transito, and the Joseph ben Meir ibn Shoshan Synagogue, later known as Santa Maria La Blanca Church, both in Toledo. Based on the scant available evidence, the style of synagogues before 1492 differed markedly from the Atlantic World Sephardic synagogues that appeared later.

In Italy—whose native Jews were known as the Italki—rather than in Iberia, evidence from the fifteenth and early sixteenth centuries exists of the open central aisle synagogue plan prognosticating later Atlantic World structures. Because of circumstances quite like those in Iberia itself, the study of pre-sixteenth-century Italian synagogues is problematic. In the early decades of the sixteenth century, parts of Italy were ruled by Spain, whose anti-Jewish king, Ferdinand, ousted Italian Jews just as he had done slightly earlier in Spain.[17] Venice had decided to restrict its Jews to a ghetto —Venetians themselves having coined the word, a reference to an island with a foundry (called *ghetta*) of the same name in the proximate lagoon—in 1516; other Italian

The engraving of the Joseph ben Meir ibn Shoshan Synagogue is by D. Ramée, Nicolas-Marie-Joseph Chapuy, and Hastings, from *Le moyen-âge monumental et archéologique; vues, détails et plans des monumens les plus remarquables de l'Europe, depuis le 6e jusqu'au 16e siècle*, 1843, Paris. William A. Rosenthall Judaica Collection, Special Collections, College of Charleston Library.

states followed suit throughout the sixteenth century—often in reaction to the surge of Jewish refugees from Iberia. In 1555 Pope Paul IV decreed that all Jews in the Papal States had to live in a ghetto and that each town or city's ghetto could only have one synagogue. His successor, Pope Pius V (1566–72), closed over a hundred synagogues within the Papal realms, reducing the number of ghettos to three locations (Rome, Ancona, and Avignon) for a period of time.[18] Whether through abandonment, seizure, demolition, or renovation into churches or something else, the ancient synagogues of Italy disappeared even as new houses of worship arose in the Italian ghetto. It was not a comfortable world for Jews: in the extremely crowded ghettos of Rome, Ancona, Ferrara, and Pesaro, for example, the authorities allowed only one synagogue building for the entire community. Perforce, Jews from different lands, with different minhagim, had to pray under one roof. In this kind of

Samuel ha-Levi Abulafia Synagogue, renovated as a church, artist unknown.
William A. Rosenthall Judaica Collection, Special Collections, College of Charleston Library.

synagogue-community, camaraderie jostled with conflict. On the Italian peninsula, Jewish communities comprised Italki, who had lived in Italy since the Roman Empire; Sephardic and Provençal refugees from Iberia and southern France; Ashkenazim, themselves often refugees or merchants from central and eastern Europe; and Mizrachi (sometimes called Levantine), Jews from the Middle East involved in trade.

From the cultural exchange of Italy's ghettos during the fifteenth and sixteenth centuries, Jewish customs were transferred to other regions on the highways of commerce. A synagogue-community following Italkic minhag was built in Salonika, Greece, as early as 1423; it no longer survives. Yet the Jewish community in Salonika grew robustly in the sixteenth century, maintained strong ties with the Sephardic community in Venice, and also had an open central aisle floor plan synagogue.[19] Remarkably, this Venetian-Salonikan relationship would bear fruit later, in the training and selection of Sephardic religious leaders for seventeenth-century Amsterdam.

Furthermore the Sephardic communities in Italy, Greece, and Asia Minor became so dominant that they not only outnumbered Italkic and Romaniot Jewry (Jews native to Greece and Ionia) but also literally absorbed many of their communities. In late fifteenth-century Istanbul, on the eve of the Spanish edict of expulsion, the city had an estimated Jewish population of twenty-five hundred to three thousand families. By the mid-sixteenth century, swelled by Iberian refugees, Istanbul's Jewish population had grown to eight thousand families.[20] Furthermore, like Italy and Iberia, because of the different suppressive regimes, Greece and Asia Minor lack intact ancient synagogues. In the eastern Mediterranean, during the long centuries of Byzantine rule, Jewish culture—most conspicuously, houses of worship—seems invisible until Ottoman hegemony arrived in the mid-fifteenth century.

Italy's oldest intact synagogue is Venetian, the Scuola Grande Tedesca (Great German Synagogue), dating from 1528–29.[21] This building is an architectural hybrid: constructed by Ashkenazim, not as we might suppose by Italkim or Sephardim, its original interior followed the characteristic Ashkenazic design (with the bimah in the middle of the sanctuary). But early in the congregation's history—sometime in the late sixteenth century—the structure was renovated to include an Italkic open central aisle floor plan. Thus, the Scuola Grande Tedesca provides one of the earliest examples of the cross-cultural interplay between Jewish groups in Italy at the beginning of the sixteenth century. It seems that the Venetian Ashkenazim, while carefully maintaining their minhag and nusach (both liturgical texts and musical elements of worship), considered themselves sufficiently "Venetian" to recognize certain cultural norms of their ghetto neighbors, the Italki. Constructed slightly later than the Grande Tedesca was Venice's Scuola Spagnola (Spanish Synagogue, built between 1555 and c. 1590). Like the other eight Venetian synagogues, as well as Sephardic synagogues throughout the Italian peninsula, the Scuola Spagnola uses the characteristic open central aisle plan.[22] Clearly Sephardic refugees, however pressured by regional laws, adapted well enough to establish themselves in much of Italy. Venice became special: For Jews, the seventeenth-century Republic would come to represent achievement: they were vital to all maritime trade and their own religious scholarship flourished.

Sephardic architectural influence, at least in its effect on Atlantic World synagogues, goes beyond the floor plan, although this was the single most conspicuous element in design. Another ubiquitous feature is the banca. It was a special booth, prominently placed on the sanctuary's northern wall, where the congregation's executive board sat. Sephardic practice also approved widespread reference to biblical numerology in Atlantic synagogues. For example, in Amsterdam and Curaçao, there are four structural supporting columns in the center of the sanctuaries, representing the four matriarchs from the book of Genesis (Sarah, Rebecca, Rachel, and Leah). Other design motifs are based on significant numerical correspondences: seven (for days in the week or the seven-day period of the Creation plus the Sabbath), ten (for the Commandments), twelve (the tribes of Israel), and forty (for the years the Israelites wandered in the wilderness). Occasionally an element of *gematria* —the system of assigning numbers to letters of the Hebrew alphabet— decorates a synagogue.[23] For instance above the synagogue main entrances in Amsterdam and Curaçao names of notables in construction, or the completion date, encrypted within a quote from scripture can be found.

Besides the physical design of the Atlantic World synagogue, the congregations also had a social structure of their own. The ordained religious leader was called a *haham*, not rabbi.[24] In fact, ordination itself was rare. While the paradigmatic Bevis Marks (London) and Esnoga (Amsterdam) were led by formally ordained, educated, scholarly figures, as were a few of the larger New World congregations, this was hardly true, despite popular perception, of most Jewish communities. The fact remains that North America did not have a permanent resident ordained rabbi (or haham) until c. 1840. It was the chazzan, less formally trained than a haham, who guided worship and, as cantor, led the mode of the service. During the eighteenth and nineteenth centuries, non-Jews, and even some Jews, referred to the chazzan as "reverend," which mistakenly caused these two words to conflate then expand, so that the titles reverend, minister, rabbi, and chazzan became synonymous. Other Jewish communal positions included the *shochet*, who butchered livestock according to kosher ritual, the *shamash*, who served as the sexton, and the schoolteacher *(melamed)*. Given the size, wealth, and sophistication of a given Jewish community, a single individual might fill all or several of these roles.[25]

The first congregations of what would become the Jewish Atlantic World took root in Amsterdam during the early years of the seventeenth century. Congregation Beth Jacob (House of Jacob) was organized in 1604 as a secret "chevra" (religious society) by Rabbi Uri ben Joseph Halevi. Two other congregations, Neve Shalom (Abode of Peace 1608) and Beth Israel (House of Israel, 1618) followed as the population increased. But these groups had to wait before worshipping in purposely built synagogues, as opposed to renovated buildings. Moreover, until they could educate their own religious leaders in the seventeenth century, Amsterdam's Sephardim welcomed Italian or Ottoman religious authorities who taught normative Judaism and ancestral Sephardic customs.[26] Hahamim Joseph Pardo (d. 1619) and Isaac Uziel (d. 1622) were among the prestigious rabbis who came to Amsterdam from the Sephardic diaspora in the Mediterranean.

Between 1636 and 1639, Amsterdam's three Sephardic congregations—Beth Jacob, Beth Israel, and Neve Shalom—merged to form Talmud Torah (Study of the Torah), representing the entire Sephardic community. As part of this merger, Beth Israel's building, Amsterdam's first purposely built synagogue was chosen as the home for the united community.[27] Unfortunately neither the premerger buildings for these congregations nor precise visual images of these structures survive. But, based on extant contemporary buildings used by various non-Jewish clandestine religious groups, the earliest Jewish houses of worship in Amsterdam were similar in design and function to the Dutch *schuilkerk* found through most of the Lowlands. A schuilkerk is a disguised house of worship used by Roman Catholics and nonconforming Protestant groups (as well as Jews) between the late fifteenth and the early nineteenth centuries. This need for secretive venues was hardly novel: Jews, Protestants, and Catholics all over Europe resorted, when necessary, to clandestine meeting houses during this epoch scarred by bloody wars of religion and subsequent suppression of minorities. Most urban schuilkerken were located in houses, although warehouses were sometimes used in cities, as were barns in rural villages. By the middle seventeenth century, some schuilkerken were purposely built as houses of worship, although exteriors offered no such indication. Nevertheless however plain the exterior was, many schuilkerken contained richly decorated interiors. Outside the Lowlands, such as in Alsace, surviving schuilkerk-like synagogues can be found dating from the eighteenth century, such as in Traenheim. But the designs of those in Alsace are Ashkenazic rather than Sephardic.[28] During the long, complex turmoil of Reformation and Counter-Reformation, clandestine houses of worship followed the trajectory of European settlement and appear in parts of the Americas.

Looking more closely at Amsterdam's Jewish population, we see the Sephardim had made an attempt to build a synagogue prior to Beth Israel's success, beginning in 1636. In 1612 congregation Neve Shalom had actually hired Hans Gerritszoon, a Dutch contractor, to build a synagogue meant for public worship but encountered hostile outcry from the dominant community. A compromise was thus made with the Dutch authorities. An edifice was permitted to be completed as a schuilkerk under the condition it was owned by a Christian (who turned out to be a Catholic), who would lease it to the Jews.[29] Two decades later congregation Beth Israel purchased a plot of land for what became the city's first recognizable (nonclandestine) house of worship, in 1636–39, which became the home of the merged Talmud Torah Sephardic community, and was called the Portuguese Synagogue. This building was a larger edifice than the one originally planned by Beth Israel.[30] After the merger of the three Sephardic congregations was completed in 1639, both the Beth Jacob and Neve Shalom buildings were sold. Surviving seventeenth-century illustrations of the Portuguese Synagogue reveal an interior with an open central aisle floor plan.[31] In any case the intellectual and human capital among the Sephardim was definite. There were four gifted hahamim guiding this Jewish community during the 1630s: Saul Levi Morteira, David Pardo, Isaac Aboab da Fonseca, and Menasseh ben Israel. Even though Amsterdam's Sephardim, successfully immersed as they were in foreign trade, would probably have been familiar with synagogues elsewhere in Europe and North Africa, these four hahamim remained the ultimate authorities on synagogue design and Sephardic minhag.

Certainly the background and education of this same religious leadership allows us to identify the increasingly Sephardic tendency of Jewish life in Amsterdam. For instance both Isaac Aboab da Fonseca (1605–93) and Menasseh ben Israel (1604–57)—he was from Madeira—were Portuguese conversos who had arrived at a young age in Amsterdam. Since in Portugal itself no intact synagogues survive from before the expulsion (1497), it seems unlikely da Fonseca or ben Israel had much to say about Amsterdam's first Sephardic synagogue. The only Jewish houses of worship they would have had intimate familiarity with were the makeshift ones of Beth Jacob, Neve Shalom, and Beth Israel, that they had come of age in.[32]

Haham Saul Levi Morteira is one likely possibility as the one who conceived the final design of Amsterdam's Talmud Torah, Portuguese Synagogue, with the merger in 1639. Although Morteira came from the Ashkenazic community of Venice, it was the great Adriatic city's large population of Iberian and Jewish émigrés who, starting in the mid-sixteenth century, had instituted Sephardic customs.[33] Morteira may have attended the Scuola Grande Tedesca—despite its Ashkenazic name, the Scuola featured an open central aisle—and adopted Sephardic customs on taking his appointment as haham in Amsterdam. He was named chief haham of Amsterdam's Sephardic Jewish community when the Sephardim there merged. Significantly, the chief Sephardic communal organization in Venice, like the one in Amsterdam, was called Talmud Torah.[34]

There is another possible progenitor of the signature open aisle style outside of the Mediterranean—first in Amsterdam, then, following that template, in the entire Atlantic World—Haham David Pardo (d. 1657). Prior to the formation of the Talmud Torah congregation from the merger, David Pardo had served as haham for the Beth Israel congregation, which had initiated construction of Amsterdam's first synagogue in 1636. He was born into Salonika's Sephardic community but as a youth moved to Amsterdam, where his father, Joseph Pardo, became haham of the Beth Jacob congregation during the early 1600s. Again there is suggestive nomenclatural convergence: Amsterdam's Sephardic embraced the congregational name Talmud Torah, from their coreligious in Salonika, who had borrowed the same name and traditions from their common brethren in Venice.[35] The Pardo family projected a certain dynastic (or in any case widespread) rabbinical authority: from Greece, Italy, and the Netherlands, they would go on to secure rabbinates in London, Curaçao, and Jamaica.

Salonika's Talmud Torah Synagogue was built in the 1540s. Its communal organization and bylaws, or *hascamoth*, were very similar to those adopted by Amsterdam's Talmud Torah: the congregants of both were governed by virtually the same forty-two regulations. While the open central aisle plan, specified by Joseph Pardo, might have been evident in the three discrete pre-1636 Sephardic houses of worship (Beth Jacob, Beth Israel, Neve Shalom), there is no definite historical data to support this conjecture. Unfortunately the sixteenth-century Talmud Torah Synagogue in Salonika was destroyed by fire; hence, direct comparisons cannot be made. To summarize: available facts, heuristic not definitive, indicate that either David Pardo or Morteira prescribed the Sephardic open central aisle plan for Amsterdam's prestigious Portuguese Synagogue (1636–39), the structure that in turn would be replicated across the Atlantic World for most of the next two centuries years.

The relationship formed in the sixteenth century between the Salonikian and Venetian Talmud Torah congregations was substantive.[36] We know that the two were founded contemporaneously—precise dating is not possible—as Sephardim fled, then recuperated from, Iberian expulsion in the 1490s. Once again evidence has been lost: the original records of the Venetian by-laws do not survive intact, so we can't say whether the Salonikan hascamoth (the forty-two regulations) were also identical.[37] But the Sephardic diaspora bears the imprint of several congregations and synagogues named Talmud Torah, all spanning the sixteenth and seventeenth centuries: those in Fez, Morocco (1603); Rome (1617); and Hamburg, Germany (1627). In any case Talmud Torah, with its broad meaning of the "study of the Torah," had a commensurately wide usage, not only among Sephardim but also for Ashkenazim and other Jewish groups. Venice's Ashkenazic community also had its own institution, also called Talmud Torah.[38]

Jews from the Netherlands built the first Atlantic World synagogues in Dutch Brazil. While there are no extant records of what the Dutch Brazilian synagogues looked like, we may posit a design model similar to Amsterdam's Portuguese Synagogue. It was, after all, the most familiar—"natural"—house of worship for the Dutch Jews who arrived in Recife, the capital of the northeastern Brazilian state of Pernambuco, where Zur Israel (Rock of Israel) was built in 1640–41. Inferences here about the Sephardic nature of Zur Israel are surely factually based: the hascamoth of Zur Israel mirrored those of Amsterdam's Talmud Torah, and the chief haham of Pernambuco was none other than Haham Isaac Aboab da Fonseca.[39]

Leaving Recife on its capitulation to Portugal, da Fonseca returned to Amsterdam and, as successor to Haham Morteira, was appointed the city's chief Sephardic haham (c. 1660). In 1670 he urged the Talmud Torah congregation, which had outgrown its 1639 structure, to construct a new, larger synagogue. This "new" building has already figured in our account: commonly called by the Ladino word for synagogue, the Esnoga was completed in 1675 and became the template for subsequent Atlantic World Jewish communities. Why? We must never forget that—insofar as our analysis belongs to history, not philosophy—the material (architecture) is a vehicle for the immaterial (thought, belief, custom, religion, beauty). In any case, the emergence of Dutch Jewry into particular prominence at this time cannot be seen apart from the transformations and achievements of Dutch society itself.[40]

By 1600 only 150 years after Guttenberg's invention, the publishing industry in Amsterdam and Leiden was robustly developed. It had already played a vital role in the preservation and dissemination of Protestant religious literature. So too, if with a far smaller readership in mind, did this contemporary publishing industry—unthinkable without a general post-Renaissance environment emphasizing literacy, scholarly inquiry, and economic expansion in the Netherlands—affect and motivate Dutch Jewry. Surely one critical element advancing the religious authority—it would become preeminent for Atlantic World Jews during the seventeenth century—of Amsterdam's Talmud Torah must have been the availability of Jewish Hebrew printing presses.[41] This was not just a matter of technology. These presses represented an industry controlled by Sephardic religious leaders; important is that the publications, both books and pamphlets, were written or sanctioned by the rabbinic leadership. The first, most influential press was founded by Haham Menasseh ben Israel in 1626. For more than a century, a multitude of the prayer books, rabbinic texts, and other forms of Jewish literature disseminated into the Atlantic World—and elsewhere—were printed in Amsterdam. Printed materials were reviewed and censored by the religious leaders there. The most important documents of Judaism are not printed but handwritten—the Torah scrolls. But these were often of Dutch provenance, obtained through Amsterdam's Talmud Torah.

Across the English Channel, one and only one rival to Amsterdam's Jewish religious stature arose during the eighteenth century. London's Sha'ar Hashamayim (Gates of Heaven), the Sephardic congregation that would complete Bevis Marks Synagogue in the first years of the eighteenth century, adopted in 1664 the same forty-two bylaws that governed Talmud Torah in Amsterdam. All future congregations in the British Empire would follow the precept and example of Bevis Marks in the eighteenth century. But the Sephardim of London and Amsterdam—those two prime conduits of Judaism to the Dutch and English-speaking Atlantic colonies—agreed substantially on religious, theological, and congregational issues during the eighteenth century.[42] Only the realignment of political forces brought on by the Napoleonic Wars would lead to divergence between Bevis Marks and the Esnoga.[43] In fact, we can now see that the four Sephardic rabbis of Amsterdam who were active during the Talmud Torah consolidation period—after Beth Jacob, Beth Israel, and Neve Shalom reorganized as one congregation in 1639—were responsible for a remarkable fusion and transference. As so often happened in Jewish history, these Dutch Sephardic rabbis became the chief interpreters of exile. In the middle seventeenth century, they erected vital cultural, historiographic, and religious bridges between two extraordinary epochs of Jewish achievement: the all-but-dead medieval Spanish-Portuguese golden age that had flourished in Iberia and the early modern Dutch golden age that arose in the Netherlands and permeated into the New World.

Between the Iberian and Dutch golden ages, we find that Sephardic Jewish culture found respite in lands undergoing their own respective golden ages during the sixteenth and early seventeenth centuries, which were in some of the Italian states and the Ottoman Empire. Within these Mediterranean realms, developments were formative for Sephardic hahamim who traveled to these places for study. Tellingly, Hahamim such as Joseph Pardo, Saul Levi Morteira—those luminaries of Amsterdam—and David Nieto—this master scholar from Livorno became the leader of London's Spanish-Portuguese Jewish community—received their formal religious education in these Mediterranean academies. They then passed the rabbinic torch to the next generation of hahamim, who went on to lead congregations in the Dutch and British Americas. This pedagogy was decisive: Sephardic identity and community, a diachronic construct of Iberian, Italian, Ottoman, Dutch, and English elements, matured into the cultural formation that would cross the Atlantic and prove so robust for so long.

When we return to the architectural record, there is a last, unique feature that vividly marks certain New World synagogues—sand used to cover floors made from wood or some other material. These sand-covered floors are not in North America and no longer in Europe. While Sephardic Jews migrating to Central America and other parts of the Caribbean considerably after 1825 (our boundary date) would later use sand as a floor cover, this practice was learned from the eighteenth-century Jews who first populated these islands. Built in 1732, Mikve Israel (Hope of Israel, founded c. 1651) in Willemstad, Curaçao, is the oldest surviving synagogue with a sand-covered floor. Another that is similar in age was Zedek ve Shalom (Righteousness and Peace) in Paramaribo, Surinam (built 1735).[44] Elsewhere in the Caribbean, archaeological studies—at Honen Dalim (Charitable to the Poor, built 1739) on St. Eustatius and at Berakha ve Shalom (Blessings and Peace, built 1685) in Jodensavanne, Surinam—as well as historical records for synagogues on Barbados, Jamaica, and St. Thomas, indicate the same use of sand. Thus, from an early date, sand covering was rather ubiquitous—not confined to the Dutch Caribbean, but also found in British and Danish colonies. In fact sand-covered floors may well have been seen somewhat earlier in the Dutch Brazilian synagogues of Zur Israel and Magen Abraham (Shield of Abraham), both c. 1640s. Unfortunately, no accounts survive describing the interiors of these synagogues. Evidence for a sand-covered floor would have been obliterated following Pernambuco's reconquest by Portugal in the 1650s, when Magen Abraham was destroyed (1653) and Zur Israel became the private property of João Fernandes Vieira (1654), before he gave it to the Catholic Church several years later.[45]

Yet the question arises: why sand? As long as migration, displacement, or new settlement shape human experience, there is an anomaly of sorts: those who have long forgotten (or who have long been separated from) one-time homelands often preserve, if unconsciously, ancestral customs. How that process affected early Atlantic World Jewry and the use of sand is a case in point. Oral traditions and popular lore describe several plausible origins for this practice, none per se exclusionary. The first is an "Iberian" hypothesis, in which émigrés, once crypto-Jews, now safe in a new environment, remembered their former clandestine synagogues, where floors were muffled with sand to silence the footsteps of worshippers. Another explanation is a health measure: sand was a prophylactic to discourage pests and insects. A third, metaphorical association comes from Genesis 22:17, where God promises the patriarch Abraham that he "shall surely bless you and greatly increase your offspring like . . . the sand on the seashore." But a fourth theory is the most evocative. Many Jews believed that as long as they were not back in Israel, they were symbolically exiles, wandering in search of the Promised Land: the sand-covered floors of the Caribbean become an immemorial signifier, Exodus translated into Diaspora.[46]

However that may be, the archaeological examination of Berakha ve Shalom Synagogue does not definitively establish that Surinamese congregation as the oldest with sand floors, though documentation establishes it as the earliest confirmed with this feature. Such customs, as we have seen, generally follow an indirect, circuitous trajectory of settlement. The founders of Berakha ve Shalom in 1685 came from various places, not only the Netherlands and Italy, but also—they were émigrés who relocated—from Barbados, Cayenne, and Dutch Brazil. In fact, the Jewish communities of Barbados and Cayenne, whose first synagogues have not survived, were some ten to twenty years older than Berakha va Shalom. But we do know that Jews from Barbados, Cayenne, and Surinam arrived as refugees from northeastern Brazil after Portugal, with its Inquisition, reconquered its territories from the Dutch (c. 1654). So it is a most plausible inference that the pioneer Brazilian synagogues, Zur Israel (Recife) and Magen Abraham (Mauricia), built in the 1640s, had sand-covered flooring. Our question of architectural or ritual practice has now migrated south from the Caribbean to Brazil itself: how did this customary use of sand emerge in seventeenth-century Dutch Brazilian congregations?

The Jewish community that established itself in Dutch Brazil came from two principal sources: the first was immigrants from the Netherlands; the second was Brazilian crypto-Jews, who openly affirmed Judaism when the Dutch conquered much of northern Brazil in the 1630s. There is no surviving record of interiors in the earliest Amsterdam synagogues, those makeshift buildings of Beth Jacob, Beth Israel, and Neve Shalom. An examination of detailed historical images reveals that the 1639 Portuguese Synagogue and the 1675 Esnoga had wooden flooring. Having visited the beautiful Esnoga, I saw exposed wood deal flooring with no sand. But a brochure published by the congregation, entitled "The Portuguese Synagogue," states: "The deal floor is covered with fine sand, in the old Dutch fashion, to absorb dust, moisture and dirt from shoes and to muffle the noise."[47] No author, sources, or dates are specified for this document. When I consulted staff experts at the Jewish Historical Museum in Amsterdam on this matter, I learned that sand was historically used in Dutch buildings to keep mud out of buildings.[48] Although using one kind of dirt to combat another may strike us as counterintuitive, dry sand attaches to wet mud on a shoe or boot and has an absorptive effect. In fact when the Esnoga was built, it was located near the city limits, where streets and walkways were unpaved and often very muddy. Eventually the surrounding streets were paved, thus eliminating the need for sand-covered floors.

Years later the travel account of Harry Simonhoff was brought to my attention. Simonhoff had visited the Esnoga during the early 1950s. Of the synagogue he observed: "Yom Kippur, I worshipped in the famous Portuguese shule, built in 1675. In this spacious, grim sanctuary, electricity is taboo. Hundreds of candles flickered in somber, half mysterious light. The chief rabbi S. Rodriques Perreira could give no reason *why sand is strewn upon the wide-beamed, old floor*" (author's emphasis).[49] Therefore documented testimony of sand-covered floors within the Esnoga exists for the middle twentieth century. This confirmed evidence, as well as the information from Amsterdam's Jewish Historical Museum, lead to further research on this "old Dutch fashion" for non-Jewish buildings, which brought to light William Elliot Griffis's 1899 publication *The American in Holland,* an account of his travels there. On visiting the town of Zaandijk, Griffis wrote: "Both Waterland and the Zaanland have been famous in the history of the Mennonites, my hostess being one of them. Wishing to see a modern Mennonite meetinghouse, we took carriage and rode down toward Zaandam. We called on the Domine, who lived next door to the edifice, and so had a good guide. The structure was reared in 1680, and restored in 1873. The floor, scrubbed as clean as a butter firkin, *was covered with fine sand*" (author's emphasis).[50]

So neither Caribbean Jews nor their coreligious in the Netherlands invented sand-covered floors. The 1680 Mennonite meetinghouse in Zaanland was built only five years after the Esnoga was completed. Today a thirty-minute train ride from Amsterdam takes us to Alkmaar, Netherlands, where a well-preserved Remonstrant church built in 1658 has sand-covered wood flooring.[51] Both the Mennonite and Remonstrant houses of worship were clandestine schuilkerken. Sand does not appear limited to sacred purposes either: Amsterdam's second oldest tavern, De Karpershoek Bar, opened continuously since 1629, features sand-covered floors.[52] Looking at the Dutch Empire through this lens leads us to Laura Fischer's *Life in New Amsterdam:* "floors were sometimes *covered in fine white sand or straw* to keep them dry" (author's emphasis) during the seventeenth century.[53] This information raises the plausibility if the Jewish house of worship in late seventeenth century New Amsterdam (and early eighteenth century New York) could have had sand on its floor. Unfortunately such a conclusion is speculative with the available historical record. Indeed there is the possibility that New Amsterdam's Jews used straw instead, in which case this Jewish house of worship would be unto itself in the New World. Nevertheless, straw suggests that further research into this subject matter should not be confined solely to the use of sand. One such example is the eighteenth-century church of San Juan Bautista in Chamula, Mexico, where pine needles mat the floor, although this custom probably relates to a Mayan tradition.[54]

To date the weight of evidence supporting a Netherlands-based source for sand-covered floors in Caribbean synagogues cannot exclude an alternative of a Brazilian-Portuguese origin. Either or both seem chronologically feasible; the use of the sand to muffle noise or control mud supplies a rational causation, in the event that sand covering was more common throughout the Atlantic World than we had supposed, whether in Europe or the Americas. What we do know is that Caribbean Jewish congregations sustained the custom of sand-covered floors long after it had disappeared among non-Jewish populations (the Dutch) in Europe. Put another way, the Jews who crossed the Atlantic adhered strictly to tradition even though the likeliest first causes for using sand (to achieve stealth, quiet, or cleanliness) no longer applied. This suggests that the preservation of custom—that is, minhag—however consciously informed or not, was central to Jewish Atlantic World identity—and arguably to a greater degree than was evident among non-Jews who also put sand on floors of buildings.

There are also tales surrounding the Caribbean's synagogues with sand-covered floors claiming that the material came from Israel. In a revealing letter from 1756, David Lopez Penha of Curaçao cited correspondence between Amsterdam and Smyrna, Greece (then Ottoman Izmir), about an order of sand from the Holy Land, stating, "we have received two bags of holy earth sent from Safed through Messrs Da Costa and Lameira of Izmir, one for our synagogue and the other for Curaçao, which we are forwarding."[55] Earth from Israel is known to have been used commonly in burial rites across the Jewish Diaspora, symbolizing a mystical connection to the Holy Land, and relates to prophecies treating death and the Messianic Age. Tellingly, with the kind of shipment just mentioned, Dutch and Caribbean Sephardic Jews could have sprinkled small quantities of sand from Israel with local sand for the floors of sanctuaries.

The moving of large quantities of sand across half the globe would have been a significant undertaking, but not impossible. Besides brick and stone, sand is also recorded as having been used as ballast in transatlantic shipping.[56] The brick, stone, and sand ballast were left in the New World, where it was often used as raw building materials. The ship either returned to the mother country or to another colonial port laden with newly acquired goods for trade. Theoretically a large shipment of sand could have hitched a transatlantic voyage from Israel as ballast. Further research is warranted if seventeenth- or eighteenth-century merchants frequented ports in Ottoman Palestine and brought back sand as ballast from the Holy Land on their return trips in order to fulfill orders made for Dutch and Caribbean Sephardic synagogues.

If the tradition of sand-covered synagogue floors does derive from the Iberian crypto-Jewish experience (secret prayer rooms) as opposed to the Dutch schuilkerk (concealed churches), we can see the lasting imprint of the Spanish and Portuguese Inquisitions. Even though conversos would return to Judaism openly, the interior design of many Atlantic World synagogues conveys the memory of oppression. The use of sand may also have been a common European practice from the sixteenth century, when Spanish Habsburgs dominated the Lowlands. However, synagogues with sand-covered floors today are rare—found only in the Caribbean and Surinam, as well as Central America, where Sephardic Caribbean Jews migrated to during the nineteenth century.

In sum, from a transatlantic perspective, a particular historical inquiry—why sand was used in religious sanctuaries (such as Alkmaar, Amsterdam, and Zaandam)—takes us to a more fundamental dialectic, that between the Reformation and Counter-Reformation. Granted the Jewish exile was launched by the Spanish and Portuguese expulsions in the closing decade of the fifteenth century. But the subsequent Jewish story becomes entwined amid rival dominations and alliances: whether Catholics or Protestants—Habsburgs and Bourbons or the House of Orange and the German, Swiss, and English reformers—prevailed in a given time or place, the religious conflicts of the sixteenth and seventeenth centuries affected all forms of worship, all houses of prayer, all populations—not least those forced to be clandestine.

The building of the Esnoga in Amsterdam instituted a kind of template for synagogue construction in the Atlantic World. Conventions included the auctioning of cornerstones with proceeds used to defray construction costs. For the winning bid, a donor or donors not only received the distinction of laying the cornerstone at the synagogue's ground-breaking ceremony, but also the honor of a dedicated special prayer on the official inauguration or anniversary of the synagogue's completion for as long as the building stood. This was no small recognition: in Amsterdam, the seventeenth-century sponsors have been remembered in prayer for centuries. Following the completion of a synagogue, there was a special dedication ceremony celebrated in conjunction with the closest major holiday.[57] It was after all those leaders and patrons who turned community and memory into material reality who stand as the perdurable architects of Atlantic World sanctuaries.

Atlantic World Synagogues as a Historical Type

At this point, given the complex permutations of Jewish exile, settlement, and cultural transfer, we should briefly scrutinize the status of the Atlantic World synagogue as a clearly differentiated historical and aesthetic category. Thus far perforce we have examined the most influential or illustrative synagogue-communities in Europe and the Americas during the period c. 1635–1825.

But we could have looked at other European instances too: To begin with, some synagogues should be considered geographically part of the Atlantic World. There were Jewish communities in various cities or towns, such as The Hague and Exeter. While smaller than Amsterdam and London, these urban populations were by no means insignificant economically, culturally, or politically. We have already seen the special nature of British Gibraltar—with its peculiar parallels, despite its strategic peninsular and Mediterranean location, to the island colonies of the Caribbean. Yet in each case the Sephardic congregations in these places were guided doctrinally, ritually, and often economically by two determinative religious centers—the Esnoga of Amsterdam and Bevis Marks of London. Again and again in this era, we have seen how Amsterdam and London were the Jewish culture bearers; all others were receivers. In any case selection is necessary in any historical analysis, and my chief concern in this study must be on first things: on the relationship between the Euro-Atlantic cultural core and Jewry in the American-Atlantic sphere.[58]

Nor do the Sephardic synagogue-communities of either the Italian states or the Ottoman Empire, both of which belong to our narrative, fit within the Atlantic World paradigm. We must never forget that it is the compromise and suppression of identity necessitated by the Iberian Inquisition that marked peninsular Jews in exile or hiding. But for the most part the Sephardim of Italy and the Ottoman Empire never had to undergo the trauma of living as crypto-Jews, at least not for any lengthy, multigenerational period. This stability was certainly not the case in the Dutch or English Atlantic World, where the experience of living as crypto-Jews for more than one generation had a powerful effect on the communal and individual religious psyche. Crucially, Italy and the Ottoman lands had older, existing, native Jewish communities that provided some assistance to Sephardic refugees. Not so in the Netherlands and England. While, at some level, the crypto-Jewish experience may have manifested empirically through such practices as sand-covered floors in Caribbean synagogues, forced self-containment and dilution of cultural norms very likely forged in Atlantic World Jews a consciousness quite unlike what we see in most other Jewish communities.

Nonetheless the most conspicuous aesthetic reason for recognizing a distinctive Atlantic World synagogue style, one different from Mediterranean models, can be identified in artistic and architectural values per se. This is by no means to propose that art has some autonomous status apart from its practitioners or cultural determinants. The Atlantic World synagogue grows out of a specific cultural environment, hence the reliance on Dutch Baroque and English Georgian styles. In contrast Mediterranean synagogues were built in a plethora of styles, most often Italian Baroque, Rococo, Moorish, and classical Ottoman. While the aesthetic differentiation between the Italian and Dutch Baroque—generically linked at the hip as they are—may seem marginal from a discrete European art historical perspective, synagogue design, as an expression of Jewish historical adaptation, has invariably been a synthetic, absorptive process. Ever since the biblical period, Jews have borrowed from their host country's religious architecture, then modified it to suit Jewish doctrine, identity, and cultural predilections. For example, the Second Temple following King Herod's renovation (c. 20 B.C.E.) most certainly used classical architectural ornamentation, which had been made fashionable through Roman influences. That is why, considered macroscopically throughout history, synagogues have resembled at any given time a Hellenistic temple, a Christian church, an Islamic mosque, or a Confucian pagoda. What in my view marks the Atlantic World synagogue as normative and heuristically coherent is geographic distribution: Jewish sanctuaries emerged from northwestern Europe to follow the trade routes and colonial settlements of the Dutch, British, and Danish Empires. This vast territory effectively triangulated Gibraltar, British Montreal, and Dutch Recife. As the Dutch and British Empires expanded during the seventeenth and eighteenth centuries, it is exclusively Dutch Baroque and English Georgian architectural forms that Jews accepted. So we can most profitably read these Atlantic synagogues as a distinctive intersection of European and colonial architectural styles in a demarcated period. Inevitably, as we move toward our own century, away from the political, social, and economic conditions that forced Iberian Jews to flee and to resettle, other styles—Greek, Egyptian, and Gothic Revival—would find favor after 1825. The forms of Dutch and English Atlantic Jewry, except for occasional detours into nostalgia, did not outlive the age that produced them.

The Emergence of Synagogue Architecture
in the Protestant Atlantic World

One evident difference between Atlantic World synagogues and those found in other areas of Western or Central Europe is the relative freedom of expression evident in exterior design. Here, we see the benevolent (or at least less intrusive) effect of Dutch and British colonial administrations when compared to their counterparts in the Holy Roman Empire. The Dutch Baroque- and Georgian-style synagogues of the Atlantic World are notable for their simplicity, even austerity, which replicates the Baroque manner of the Netherlands and Great Britain, though the various colonial adaptations of these architectural styles was everywhere less ornate than the European models.

Dutch and British Protestants, as well as the Jews, deliberately eschewed the elaborate ornamentation we associate with other regional Baroque style types of Central Europe, Italy, France, or Spain, which were predominantly Catholic.

The Reformation in the Netherlands witnessed a strict architectural embrace of minimalism—a reduction to essentials, spiritual purity embodied in purity of form—beginning in the sixteenth century and lasting until the advent of the Enlightenment in the eighteenth century. Famously, when the Iconoclastic Revolt erupted across the Netherlands in 1566, the Dutch launched a movement of ideological force, in which Protestant fervor, linked to nationalism, promulgated aesthetics.[59] And literally so: reformers gathered into mobs that "de-ornamented" churches and public buildings, removing the deplorable religious-political iconography articulating Catholic doctrine and Habsburg hegemony. While the Dutch struggle for independence from Spain lasted eight decades, until 1648 and the more general peace enacted by concluding the Thirty Year's War, architecture in the Netherlands focused on nonecclesiastic structures. This, for a perfectly practical reason in a famously practical land: neither Protestants nor Catholics were willing to invest capital in churches during the violent years of the Dutch Reformation, when buildings were "redesigned" or eliminated by one party or the other. Minimalist Baroque architecture—in common with the plain English Puritan or Quaker meeting houses—posited asceticism meant to oppose, even rebuke, the flamboyant sensibility of the Catholic Church. In the event we know that Catholicism with its exuberant Baroque ecclesiastic style did not prevail in the Netherlands.

Dutch government buildings likewise reflected this minimalist orientation. In their tutorial journeys to Italy and France, those epicenters (and classrooms) of Renaissance and Baroque accomplishment, Dutch artists and architects studied their Raphael, Bernini, Palladio, Mansart, and Le Vau but steadfastly rejected what domestic Dutch taste would condemn as foreign ornamental extravagance. It was rather an adapted, essentialist interpretation of Italian and French models that Dutch artists achieved in their Baroque designs.[60] Moreover, during the war for independence against Spain, the influence and wealth of the hereditary aristocracy waned, depriving Dutch society of its traditional patrons of art and architecture. In their place emerged an altered upper class—it absorbed to a degree members of the older nobility— substantively made up of wealthy merchants, government officials, and professionals. It was this new commercial patriciate, allowing successful mercantile and professional Jews to gain burgher status, that would sponsor the arts and architecture during the Dutch golden age recorded by the likes of Rembrandt and Hals.

The network of relationships binding the Dutch to the English, codified by Elizabeth's definitive break with Catholicism, then her confrontation with

Habsburg Spain, would only grow more vigorously in the seventeenth century. The affinities—political, religious, cultural, economic—between these emerging Protestant maritime powers would compound until William of Orange married Mary Stuart (1678) and went on to rule England (1689). Correlations in art and architecture were inevitable as well: the Protestant (whether Dutch Reform or Puritan) theological insistence on direct, untrammeled communication between believers and the divine valorized precisely those minimalist ideals (simplicity, purity, austerity) that shaped Dutch and English Baroque.

With remarkable synchrony given the earlier fifteen-hundred-odd years' divergence between Judaism and Christian practice, Jews and Protestants could now theologically and aesthetically converge by expressing profound iconoclasm, as stipulated in the Second Commandment (Exodus 20:4), which rejected iconographic representations in religious sanctuaries. The Hebrew Bible's prohibition against engraved images, interpreted by Jews as an attack on idolatry, determined an identical Calvinist view endorsed by Dutch and English reformers.[61] Atlantic synagogues based on Dutch Baroque and English Georgian modes sustain iconoclastic identity in a doctrinally consistent fashion, unlike synagogues built in the more elaborate Baroque of Italy or the Holy Roman Empire. Curtailing ornament, these Italian, French or central European synagogues were, in one sense, forced to contravene the dynamic, opulent impulses often associated with Baroque invention in order to create an appropriate environment for Jewish worship. Dutch Baroque architecture consciously attains clarity and sobriety in an aesthetic commensurate with the less-stratified, mercantile character of Protestant Reformed society. This same Dutch preference for structural simplicity—we must not forget the cultural and religious conversation between the Netherlands and England—comported with seventeenth-century English taste and, to a degree, with the gestation of Georgian architecture.

Hendrick de Keyser (1565–1621) and Jacob van Campen (1596–1657) were the two leading architects responsible for establishing what we might call the qualified Baroque of Dutch sensibility. De Keyser was instrumental in bringing Renaissance architecture and design to the Netherlands in the late sixteenth century. Inigo Jones (1573–1652), who knew and worked with van Campen, played a similar role in England. Their long relationship, based on the tenets of Palladio and their enthusiasm for contemporary Italianate neoclassicism, was a kind of harbinger. Over the next century and a half (c. 1600–1750), Anglo-Dutch artistic affinities would follow the colonial expansion of these twin Atlantic trading powers. Nicholas Stone, who trained with Inigo Jones, became de Keyser's assistant and accompanied the Dutch architect when he returned to the Netherlands. In Amsterdam de Keyser's architectural contribution was prodigious, as he designed the East India House (built 1606), the Exchange Building (built 1608–11), Haarlem Gate (built 1615–18), and Bartolotti House (built 1621). But at least equal influence must be assigned to de Keyser's theoretical compilation *Architectura Moderna* (1631).[62]

Younger than de Keyser, and like him an acolyte who traveled to Italy, where the Palladian example proved decisive, was the most influential Dutch architect of the next generation (c. 1630–50), Jacob van Campen. His most famous designs, the Mauritshuis in The Hague (1633–44, with the assistance of Pieter Post) and the Town Hall in Amsterdam (1648–55), resonated in both the Netherlands and England. Representatively for the age and our concerns here, the Mauritshuis (1633) was built by the general and statesman Johan Maurits van Nassau-Siegen (1604–79), who went on to become the governor of Dutch Brazil and prince of Nassau-Siegen. As governor, he desired that his Brazilian estate, Vrijburg Palace in Mauricia, resemble his Mauritshuis in The Hague, and he brought with him Pieter Post (1608–69) to design this edifice.[63] Post was a painter and architect from Haarlem, who designed several buildings in the Netherlands but gained notoriety as the prince of Nassau-Siegen's architect in Dutch Brazil, where he designed public buildings and fortifications.[64]

The architect of Amsterdam's Beth Israel-Portuguese Synagogue (built 1636–39) remains unknown. Yet extant exterior illustrations of that building place it firmly in the early seventeenth-century Dutch Baroque, one that owes something to van Campen's Mauritshuis. Furthermore, the Jews of the Netherlands and its overseas empire revered Prince Johan Maurits van Nassau-Siegen for his steady policy of tolerance toward religious minorities. On his recall from Brazil to the Netherlands in 1644, Dutch Brazilian Jews, who wanted to convert the building into a synagogue, offered Prince van Nassau-Siegen six hundred thousand guilders for his Recife residence.[65] Though this generous offer to Prince van Nassau-Siegen was declined, the Jews most likely wanted the building not just for purposes of flattery, but out of need or desire. Due to their prosperity and success in Dutch Brazil, and the belief that it would continue, the colony's Jews sincerely believed they needed to expand their infrastructure. Though no images of Dutch Brazil's synagogues survive, there may have been consanguinity between the evolution of Amsterdam's synagogues and their satellites built in northeastern Brazil with Prince van Nassau-Siegen's respective residences.

While Amsterdam's Portuguese Synagogue was a noteworthy edifice with respectable exterior architectural design, its preeminence lasted only a handful of decades before greater synagogues rose to cast it in shadow. Towering high above its neighbors, and standing prominently on a city square connected by a major thoroughfare of streets and a canal, was the Grote Sjoel (Great Shul in Dutch) for Amsterdam's burgeoning Ashkenazic community. Built in the Dutch Baroque style by Daniel Stalpaert (1615–76), assisted by Elias Bouman (1636–86), in 1670–71, the prominent brick edifice measured approximately fifty-three to sixty feet at its base. The Grote Sjoel bears many exterior architectural similarities with another prominent Amsterdam building designed at the same time by Stalpaert with Adriaan Dortsman: the Oosterkerk Church, built in 1669–71.[66] These buildings were characteristic of Stalpaert's style—large monumental brick edifices with pilasters, mansard roofs, and tall, round-headed windows.[67] The Grote Sjoel interior was also the first to introduce the galleried basilica that was both popular and expected within the great synagogues of Europe and North America during the nineteenth and early twentieth centuries.[68] Due to the Ashkenazic community's size, three additional synagogues were built next to the Grote Sjoel following its completion: the Obbene Sjoel (built 1686), the Dritt Sjoel (built 1700), and the Nieuwe Sjoel (New Shul, built 1752). The Obbene and Dritt Sjoels were small, vernacular buildings that fell in the Grote Sjoel's shadow. However, the Nieuwe Sjoel, designed by Gerard Frederik Maybaum, was a significant edifice that not only stood shoulder-to-shoulder with the Grote Sjoel but also took architectural inspiration from it.[69]

The work involving Daniel Stalpaert and Amsterdam Jewry also extended beyond the architecture of the synagogue and into city planning. The Grote Sjoel, located within Amsterdam's Vlooienburg neighborhood, was a quarter annexed by the city and under development during this period. This urban expansion and redevelopment of the city's historic core was orchestrated through the *Plan of the Three Canals*, approved in 1607. Authored by Hendrick J. Staets (1575–1649), this plan was brought to fruition by Stalpaert, serving as Amsterdam's city architect. The plan not only regulated land use, but also assigned different districts of the city according to socioeconomic status. Guidelines for streets, canals, and buildings where also regulated by the plan, according to Dutch Baroque paradigms of urban design. The roots for this came from theories developed by Simon Stevin (1548–1620), father of Dutch town planning, which were circulating among architects and engineers at the time, and eventually published (posthumously) in the *Ideal City* in 1649.[70]

Manifestation of Stalpaert's scholarship and practice are seen in the way Jews and other tolerated minority groups, such as Huguenots, were assigned their own neighborhoods, each having their own city square where a market or house of worship could be placed. Only certain types of brick could be used on exterior walls for purposes of architectural uniformity. Primary, secondary, and tertiary streets and canals were established within a hierarchy for regulating the movement of people, water, commerce, and waste within the city. In other words Stalpaert was more than just the Grote Sjoel's architect, but also the urban designer, civil engineer, and planner for the *tout ensemble*.[71] No other synagogue within the Christian world had been so thoroughly incorporated within a city master plan as the Grote Sjoel, in addition to its own grand architectural scheme. Seventeenth-century Dutch Baroque planning philosophy was also the only type developed in Europe to consider minority groups in a respectful manner.[72]

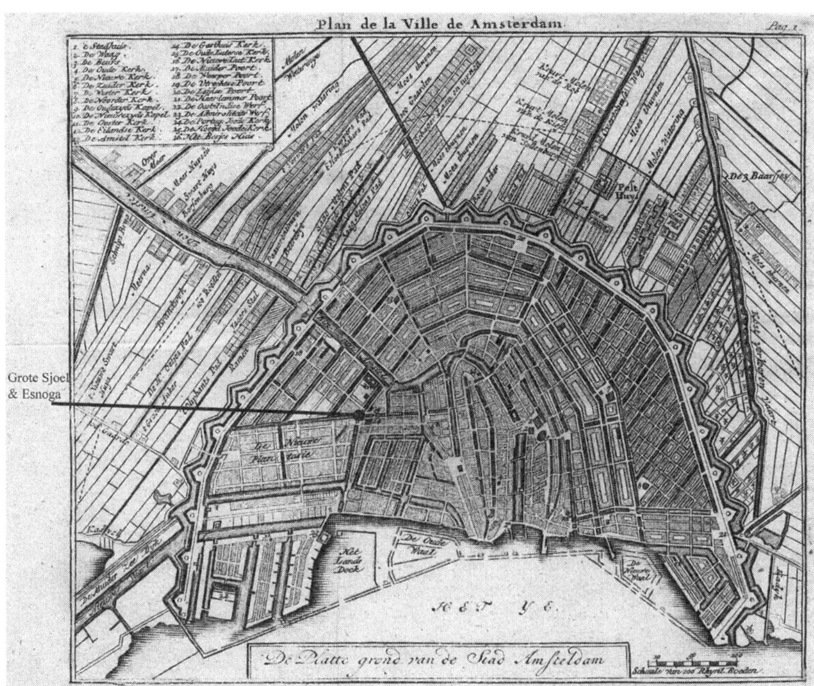

Reprint from 1802 of Daniel Stalpaert's c. 1662 plan for Amsterdam with the locations of the Grote Sjoel and Esnoga. *De platte grond van de stad Amsteldam = Plan de la ville de Amsterdam.* William A. Rosenthall Judaica Collection, Special Collections, College of Charleston Library.

In 1670 Haham Isaac Aboab de Fonesca, then chief haham of Amsterdam's Sephardic community, approached his congregation about the need to build a larger building. He had two concerns. Not only was his Sephardic congregation becoming too large for its building (1636–39), but there was also an issue of prestige, or at least of appropriate dignity, to ponder: the larger, more impressive Grote Sjoel of Amsterdam's Ashkenazim just described. Shortly after, the Sephardic Talmud Torah organized a building committee, and a new piece of land was purchased in the Vlooienburg neighborhood, as it happens across the street from the Grote Sjoel. The building committee invited architects and builders to submit proposals for the new synagogue, and Elias Bouman was selected. Construction of the Esnoga was supposed to take just over a year, with completion set for the spring of 1672. The Third Anglo-Dutch War intervened, however, and all available resources were diverted to the military. So it was that the Esnoga would not be finished until 1675.

Even in the comparatively tolerant Reformed Netherlands, the pursuits of architecture and building remained firmly closed to Jews until the nineteenth

An eighteenth-century view of Mr. Visserplein Street in Amsterdam, with the
Esnoga on the right, the Nieuwe Sjoel in the left foreground (the building with
the domed cupola), and the Grote Sjoel in the left background (the building
with the flat hipped roof). This scene is during the holiday of Sukkoth, as can
be ascertained by the presence of Sukkah structures on the street. Engraving
by P. Wagenaar, *Gezicht Der Portugeesche En Hoogduitsche Jooden Synagogen,*
c. 1781. William A. Rosenthall Judaica Collection, Special Collections, College
of Charleston Library.

century. In these restrictive conditions, the gifted master mason and builder
Elias Bouman—he followed the trade of his father, Claes, who held the same
credentials—was an inspired choice, arguably the best the Netherlands could
offer, as architect-builder of Amsterdam's new Sephardic synagogue. His
professional associations with Stalpaert and van Campen, his own learned
knowledge of architecture, his almost contemporaneous achievement with
the Grote Sjoel—all made his participation seem inevitable. Unsurprisingly
Bouman also designed and built homes for various prominent Amsterdam
Jewish families. For the Esnoga, Bouman, like any Christian architect with
a synagogue commission, would have had a close working and consultative
relationship with his client, the Sephardic leaders of Amsterdam. How otherwise could the religious traditions shaping synagogue design, whether in matters of scope or precise detail, be integrated with the popular Dutch Baroque
vocabulary of the day?

Given the disabling of the direct Jewish practice of architecture, much
less building construction, in most of Europe for some four hundred years

(c. 1400–1800), it seems unremarkable that Jews did not immerse themselves in the historical study or appreciation of architecture.[73] Synagogues, as an aspect of material culture, were, at best, collaborations between informed Jewish scholars and enabled expert Christian professionals. In this narrative of intellectual atrophy and social diminution, one clarion exception was Haham Jacob Juda Leon (1602–75), known familiarly as "Templo." Haham Leon, a scholar and translator of vast, varied learning, was a distinguished rabbi, who ministered to congregations in Hamburg (1628), Middleburg (Netherlands, c. 1640), and Amsterdam (after 1643). Add to these accomplishments Leon's prodigious awareness of architecture. In the 1640s he was fascinated by King Solomon's Temple, of which he produced a series of architectural plans; he published a description called *Retrato del Templo de Selomo* (1642); and he constructed a conceptual model. Since Leon's model and drawings of a storied (even mythopoeic) structure unseen for millennia were rendered in a neoclassical idiom, which was imagined and embodied by Haham Leon from his exposure to Renaissance architecture and studies by others on King Solomon's Temple, such as *Ezechielem Explanationes* (c. 1596) by Spanish Jesuits Juan Bautista Villalpando (1552–1608) and Heronimo del Prado, not to mention his rich knowledge of the Bible.[74] In the event, and Leon's enthusiasms

Haham Jacob Juda Leon (1602–75), with a thumbnail of one of his architectural studies of King Solomon's Temple below his portrait. Engraving by Salom Italia, c. 1641. William A. Rosenthall Judaica Collection, Special Collections, College of Charleston Library.

here are metaphorically though not quantifiably indicative, the Esnoga as a cultural referent for many Jews and philo-Semitic Christians suggested King Solomon's Temple in Jerusalem. This association with the ancient Temple became more pronounced in 1773–74, when—art imitating art—the Esnoga was partially altered to conform with Haham Leon's plans. Slanting buttresses were affixed to the synagogue's rear exterior wall as mimicry of Leon's famous model.

It was also from these studies of King Solomon's Temple that "messianic-inspired" architectural features were incorporated into houses of worship, commensurate with the fervor of the period. These features included site layout and floor plan; number and placement of architectural details, such as columns and seating; and art and ornamentation. This was done so that early modern houses of worship could have an aspect of "divinely inspired" design. By utilizing these features, Jewish as well as Protestant and Catholic religious leaders hoped not only to bring their flocks closer to God but to also facilitate the long anticipated messianic era. Rhetoric pertaining to architecture and urban design in Villalpando and del Prado's *Ezechielem Explanationes* were exemplary of this movement within the Catholic tradition, affecting church design not only across Iberia and its American and Asian colonies but also central and eastern Europe.[75] Johann Valentin Andrease's (1586–1654) *Christianopolis* (1619) is a Protestant example, which had its effects across northern Europe and parts of North America.[76] Haham Leon and his *Retrato del Templo de Selomo* was a mode of transfusion of this paradigm from Christianity to Judaism, and specifically within the Sephardic Atlantic World.[77] Each book, among others, was widely disseminated and translated into multiple languages. Indeed there was much intellectual crossover between theologians and architects from various religious backgrounds about design aesthetics. For instance both Haham Leon and Christopher Wren (1632–1723), an Anglican and England's most distinguished architect during the late seventeenth and early eighteen centuries, were not only familiar with *Ezechielem Explanationes* but may have met when Leon visited London in 1674–75.[78] It was also on this trip that Haham Leon composed one of the first (postreadmission) "Royal Prayers" for London's nascent Jewish community—which would come to be recited by Jews in synagogues across the empire—as a blessing for the reigning British monarch.[79]

Before moving on with the discussion of synagogue architects and builders in the Dutch American colonies, there is one last designer who had significant influence in both the Netherlands and England. This architect was Daniel Marot (1661–1752), who built The Hague's Honen Dal synagogue (called the Snoge) in 1726.[80] Daniel Marot was not Dutch, but a French Huguenot born in Paris, who sought refuge in the Netherlands following the Revocation of the Edict of Nantes in 1685. Therefore Marot represents a unique French Protestant contribution to the Dutch and English experiment in Atlantic World synagogue architecture. Besides the Snoge in The Hague, Marot served as architect at Het Loo Palace to William III of Orange (who later became king of England). After the Glorious Revolution, Marot followed William to England, first working at Kensington Palace and later with Christopher Wren at Hampton Court Palace. Marot also excelled at garden and furniture design. In 1712 Marot published a pattern book entitled *Recueil d'Architecture et d'Ornemens*.[81]

Within the Dutch Atlantic World colonies, the first known architect-builder of a synagogue was Abraham van Edam. Although he built the first Neve Shalom synagogue in Paramaribo, Surinam, in 1718–19, little is known of van Edam, other than his having been recorded as a master carpenter.[82] Considering the emphatically undeveloped, pre-urban environment of early colonial Surinam, van Edam was no doubt a "jack-of-all-trades," as were so many of his peers scattered across the frontiers of the Atlantic World.

Besides van Edam the only other known architect-builder of synagogues in the Dutch colonies was Henderik Schielach. He is credited with building the Mikve Israel (Hope of Israel) synagogue on Curaçao (completed in 1732), often called the Snoa. Unfortunately little is known about Schielach before his arrival in Curaçao, except that he was commissioned to build the synagogue there. Schielach, a Dutch builder, was charged with modeling the Curaçao structure on Bouman's Esnoga. Unfortunately Schielach proved to be an unreliable builder, and the synagogue's construction did not go smoothly.[83] Possibly Schielach, with little repute, was perceived as an affordable contractor. While the exterior of Mikve Israel in no way resembles the Esnoga, the interior bears striking similarities that have been noticed and recorded through the centuries. The differences with the Amsterdam structure may not have been a matter of the architect's ineptitude. After all the Snoa is a much smaller building than the Esnoga; Curaçao's construction resources (skills and manpower) were far less robust than those in the Netherlands; the tropical climate posed challenges; and insular aesthetic tastes might have been in play. In these early days of Atlantic settlement, such conditions frequently affected construction outside of major metropolitan centers.

The conventions of art, especially architectural history, present a certain nomenclatural, or chronological, confusion when we address "Georgian" style. North Americans, with eyes fixed on aesthetics, identify Georgian art as beginning c. 1700.[84] But British academics, with their eyes on reigns, refer to the year of Hanoverian succession, 1714, as the correct start date for the Georgian epoch. Before then, according to the British, buildings in the period between 1689 and 1714 should be named William and Mary or Queen Anne. Here I would argue that academic terminology should aspire toward precision without being needlessly rigid. The coronation of European monarchs are not architectural charrettes; reigns do not issue licenses for aesthetic movements. Rulers and aristocrats have influenced architectural style and interior design, most conspicuously by funding and hiring those who build and decorate. Ruling class tastes were subject to larger ideational, socioeconomic, political, and educational dynamics—domestic and foreign—that determine culture at any given time. We have already seen for example where the Dutch Baroque was in dialogue with English architecture throughout the seventeenth century.

For my purposes I am less concerned with art-historical taxonomy—pace rival academic-political rhetorics—than with finding a pragmatic, coherent language to describe synagogue architecture in the Americas during the eighteenth and early nineteenth centuries. So I will call "Georgian architecture"— no doubt loosely, neither the dates nor the features are impermeable—designs and structures that express the Palladian neoclassical idiom, c. 1700–1830. Moreover, in a ground so well trodden by gifted commentators, my narrative supplies only a précis of the evolving Georgian style—meant heuristically as a preamble to specific instances in the Atlantic World.[85]

Georgian architecture adopted Greco-Roman classical orders, interpreted through forms derived from the Italian Renaissance and French classicism, in order to achieve exact proportion, balance, and symmetry—and quite literally, as precise mathematical ratios, for example, were used to determine the height of a window in relation to its width or to the shape of a room. If the English Baroque was the dialect reserved for palaces and churches, the developed Georgian style had its widest currency beyond royal or ecclesiastic clients, generally in the upper and upper-middle classes, who would consolidate as the governing stratum after 1688. Then too eighteenth-century builders— in a reflection of the Enlightenment's ever-greater concentration on education and empirical knowledge—turned to a new, increasingly available medium, inexpensive architectural design books. As a result the Georgian style became the prevalent vernacular in the training of effectively every ambitious builder, carpenter, mason, and plasterer—those who worked on buildings for the gentry and aristocracy.

But we cannot really do justice to the emerging Georgian aesthetic without mentioning the extraordinary figure who in many ways was its immediate and greatest precursor. Christopher Wren, polymath scientist-philosopher, was a rigorous student of Aristotle, an Oxford professor of astronomy, an anatomist, a mathematician, and a seminal founder of the Royal Society. He most likely came to architecture by way of his undergraduate pursuits in mathematics and astronomy. These disciplines required modeling, drawing scale diagrams, and charting. While the ancient Vitruvius and Wren's great French contemporary Claude Perrault (1613–88) became part of his intellectual formation, he was also drawn to his older countryman Inigo Jones, the progenitor of English Baroque (popular c. 1665–1720).[86]

Jones, whom we have just encountered as van Campen's able assistant, studied architecture in Italy and became nothing less than the ambassador of Palladianism in England.[87] It is an eclectic merger of Jones and Wren that leads to the Georgian vocabulary. Again, however much "Georgian" is considered an authentically "English" idiom, we should underline this force of Palladianism—a common, if varied, seventeenth-century inheritance from the Cinquecento—and the Dutch Baroque example when assessing the mature Georgian style.

Shortly after the restoration of Charles II (1660), Wren became an advisor for the repair of (old) St. Paul's Cathedral. Then in 1666 came the catastrophe of the Great Fire of London: two-thirds of the western Europe's largest city was destroyed. Although Wren promptly submitted plans for rebuilding, none were officially implemented. But from 1669 until 1718, he held the royal appointment as surveyor-general. So Wren was much invested in the heroic, often Augean effort of reconstruction, notably the design of some fifty-one new churches. In the midst of such labors, there can be no doubt about his signature masterpiece: between 1675 and 1710, Wren was the designer and architect of one of Europe's supreme structures, (new) St. Paul's Cathedral.[88]

Wren's ecclesiastical architecture varied. St. Paul's itself, with so much novel effect, is generally regarded as a magnificent late Renaissance-Baroque composition. We know that Wren left Gothic conceptions behind when he introduced—as he often did—large clear windows and clerestories into his churches so that the interiors seem sculpted in light, as well as scaling sanctuaries according to classical proportions.[89] There is even in Wren's designs the occasional Gothic revivalist tendency—the Tom Tower (Christ Church, Oxford, built 1681–82), where we see an elaboration of the late Gothic spire. This was an element that architects subsequently redacted, during the eighteenth century, on decidedly more neoclassical lines, achieving the familiar Georgian church tower.

Another general effect of Protestantism on ecclesiastic design follows from the centrality of reading the Bible in Protestant worship. After the great vernacular biblical translations of the sixteenth and seventeenth centuries; after the emergence of relatively affordable publications printed in moveable type; after, too, the not unassociated rise in literacy, Christians were no longer bound to a largely incomprehensible Latin Vulgate cited and interpreted by the clergy. It was no small part of Lutheran and Calvinist worship to inculcate "the priesthood of all believers" by frequent reference to biblical texts in a language known to all congregants. So preaching assumed a new, authoritative status in Reformation culture. Sermons given in church had to be read and heard—which is precisely where architects responded with certain complementary innovations. During the seventeenth and eighteenth centuries, the interior designs of sanctuaries began to emphasize the pulpit, both as an empirical matter of acoustic audibility and as a symbolic focus on the power of language in the discourse between the human and the divine. Nor was this development confined to churches and the Protestant faithful. Atlantic

World synagogues reveal a comparable emphasis on the tebah: its size and ornamentation became more prominent within the sacred space of worship.[90]

However religiously tolerant early modern Protestant societies may have been in relation to medieval dispensations, the bald historical statement still seems astonishing: the first synagogues built in English-ruled lands after the expulsion of the Jews in 1290 appeared almost four centuries later, not in England but in the Caribbean. Bridgetown (c. 1660s) and Speightstown (c. 1670s) in the Barbados, Port Royal in Jamaica (c. 1680s), and Charlestown in Nevis (c. 1680s) were the sites of these earliest colonial Jewish sanctuaries. There are few surviving records of what these buildings looked like, but they were most likely built in a vernacular style with simple, if any, exterior architectural ornamentation. Indeed, considering the time period that these buildings were erected, vernacular architectural elements of the late English medieval or Jacobean styles could have been what was present. As a comparison, two surviving Barbadian buildings from the 1650s, St. Nicholas Abbey and Drax Hall, exhibit precisely this. A possible surviving image of Bridgetown's Nidhe Israel synagogue appears in the background of a painting from c. 1742, called *Governor Robinson Going to Church*. The synagogue is small within the illustrated landscape but gives an idea of what the building looked like.[91]

Back in England itself, congregation Sha'ar Hashamayim was constituted in the seventeenth century, but not openly at least until Oliver Cromwell (1599–1658) permitted the return of Jews in 1655. Before then, crypto-Jews could well have organized this London congregation. Making do with temporary rental spaces before a synagogue could be built, Sha'ar Hashamayim was completed in 1701 and has represented Judaism in Britain ever since. It occupied a parcel of land near the city's edge at Bevis Marks—the eponymous name that has figured so often in our account. At the time Jews were still legally prohibited from land ownership in England, so the construction had to be launched on a rental basis.[92] The congregation chose master builder Joseph Avis as the designer in charge of the entire project.

Avis was a Quaker. He had worked for the gifted Robert Hooke (1635–1703), a scientist, sometime architect, and collaborator with Wren in the surveying and rebuilding effort after the Great Fire. The Royal Observatory (built 1675) at Greenwich and St. Paul's were Wren designs that engaged Hooke too. As we might suppose, the association with Wren shaped Hooke's own architectural practice.[93] Avis likewise worked on Wren's designs, notably St. Bride's Church on Fleet Street. Neither an eminent establishment-favored Anglican, nor a designer as famous as Wren or even Hooke, Avis might have seemed more accessible to London's Jewish community leaders. His Quaker background, with its nonconformist (non-Anglican) insistence on simplicity in places of worship, comports with a certain rigor evident in Bevis Marks. We should mention, too, the possible design contribution of an expert carpenter, one Henry Ramsay. In the event, Avis imported many important elements from Bouman's Esnoga (built 1675): a rectangular brick structure; tall round-arched windows on the exterior; a women's balcony with a latticed parapet supported by twelve columns; brass chandeliers; and a tripartite hechal, with an upper level over a central bay containing a lukhot.[94]

Thus a kind of formula emerges here: as with Bevis Marks, so with the other synagogues in the growing British Empire of the eighteenth century. Formula has a more exact connotation too. English architectural books, manuals, and design compilations were a main vehicle for synagogue plans and construction in the Americas. These texts must have helped in constructing the first Shearith Israel (Remnant of Israel, built 1730) synagogue in New York, built by Stanley Holmes.[95] This synagogue, formerly located in lower Manhattan, is the only recorded building attributed to him. Little is known about Holmes other than that he obtained his freemanship in New York on 20 February 1728, just two years prior to the project.[96] The first well-known colonial architect to build a synagogue was Peter Harrison, who designed Jeshuat Israel (now called Touro Synagogue, the name used hereafter) in Newport, Rhode Island. Like his contemporary Avis, Harrison (1716–75) was born a Quaker in Yorkshire, England, but he immigrated to Rhode Island, where he became an Anglican and a successful businessman and merchant.

Harrison's travels as a merchant took him back to England from 1743 to 1745, where he studied architecture under Richard Boyle, third Earl of Burlington (1694–1753). Lord Burlington was a gentleman scholar who became enamored with architecture following a series of Grand Tours he took during the 1710s. He subsequently became a collector of architectural drawings and publications, such as those by Inigo Jones (1573–1652) and Andrea Palladio (1508–80), and used them as inspirational resources for practicing Palladian architecture.[97] Peter Harrison did the same, incorporating aspects of architectural books by Inigo Jones, John Webb, and James Gibbs.[98] Lord Burlington's practice was always conducted in conjunction with a building contractor, as he was an artist of architecture, unskilled with the engineering component. Evidently, Harrison practiced architecture in the same way, for the synagogue's construction was completed by Joseph Hammond as contractor and Naphtali Hart and Company as developer.[99]

With architectural pattern books available to part-time architects like Peter Harrison, Georgian-Palladian architecture spread across the British Empire. During this period full-time professional architects did not yet exist in the British Americas, and those who practiced architecture did so while pursuing other economic endeavors. Harrison's known architectural accomplishments also include the Redwood Library (built 1747–49) and Brick Market Building (built 1762–72) in Newport, Rhode Island; King's Chapel (built 1749) in Boston and Christ Church (built 1759–60) in Cambridge, Massachusetts; and Antigua's courthouse (built 1747–50).[100] While conducting business related to other matters of trade, Harrison used his time in that location—such as elsewhere in New England or the Caribbean—to squeeze in an opportunity to work on an architectural project. This is how he worked on projects in Newport, Boston, and Antigua at approximately the same time and made each profession a viable pursuit. Unfortunately the breadth of Harrison's architectural career is difficult to ascertain, especially his works outside of New England. At the onset of the American Revolution, Harrison sided as a Loyalist, and his papers were destroyed by a mob of Patriots shortly after his death.[101] For his design of Touro, Harrison's only American precedent would have been New York's Shearith Israel. He very likely knew the designs of both Bevis Marks and the Esnoga: there can be scant coincidence in Touro's architectural debts: to the exterior of Avis's London synagogue and the interior of Bouman's Amsterdam one.

As the American Revolution drew to its end, it was appropriately the Philadelphia congregation Mikveh Israel (built 1782)—proleptic of the new republic—that constructed the newest synagogue to appear in the United States. Designed and built by John Donohue, a carpenter, and Edward McKegan, a bricklayer, this synagogue had a simple design similar to Shearith Israel. It would seem that Donohue and McKegan, like Holmes in New York, were little known and relied on the architectural literature of the era.[102]

Two pairs of brothers built the synagogue in Charleston, South Carolina: the Steedmans (James and Charles) and the Horlbecks (Peter and John), who, confusingly if naturally, called their architecture and construction firm "Steedman & Horlbeck." Apparently one fraternal group—it is frustrating, but we do not know which individuals—designed and constructed the building. In fact work attributed to the Steedmans is difficult to determine. But the Horlbecks certainly were associated with Charleston's Exchange Building, built in 1771. This was the last public building in the thirteen colonies commissioned by the British before the American Revolution. Congregation Beth Elohim used Steedman and Horlbeck to build their first synagogue in 1794: its exterior traces a handsome Georgian ecclesiastic plan (complete with tall steeple), while the interior resembles Bevis Marks, with the addition of certain Ashkenazic elements. Here, we see eclectic cultural preference: Beth Elohim was largely made up of Ashkenazim. The tall steeple and façade of the synagogue are reminiscent of St. Michael's (then Anglican, now Episcopalian) Church in Charleston, a congregation that flourished during the second half of the eighteenth century.[103]

Not to be forgotten, yet has almost been, is John C. Evans, who built Mickve Israel's synagogue in Savannah, Georgia, c. 1820. Evans was a ship carpenter by training. Little else is known about him or the projects he worked on.[104]

The synagogues of the Atlantic World, derived from Anglo-Dutch architecture in both its formal and vernacular syntax, should be considered links within a continuous, if varied, Jewish cultural history. These seventeenth-century sanctuaries connect a storied Sephardic past to eighteenth-century mercantile experience—captured in a neoclassical architectural vocabulary—and by so doing point the way to later, postimperial developments. Nor do we have to wonder why these synagogues arose where they did. Transplanted by the trade routes and migration patterns of European maritime powers entering the Atlantic World, these houses of worship may be categorized as the first Jewish building type to span hemispheres (east and west, as well as north and south).

On aesthetic grounds, we should not exaggerate the aesthetic achievement represented by the earliest (c. 1640–1730) synagogues in the Americas.[105] They were, for the most part, small and architecturally plain. As for the nascent congregations in both North America and parts of the Caribbean in the mid-eighteenth century, we should recall that, despite Ashkenazic majorities, minhagim generally tended to be Sephardic. This must have been done purposefully, at least on a socioeconomic basis: Atlantic Jews, whatever their origin, recognized the importance of remaining connected to the common, larger Sephardic trading network and its familiar religious practices. So it was for Montreal's Shearith Israel, whose Ashkenazic members carefully preserved Spanish-Portuguese nusach in 1768.

During the seventeenth and eighteenth centuries, when compared to European urban centers, colonial cities and towns in the Americas were economically and demographically underdeveloped. Some telling figures: in 1776 Philadelphia, the largest North American city, had twenty-five thousand residents; London, the largest metropolis of western Europe, had 650,000. To a degree, for all the penalties and suffering of anti-Semitism, Jews in early modern Europe dealt with surplus: land could be leased (though not legally owned until later in the eighteenth century), synagogue designers readily identified, skilled builders commissioned, and materials purchased. This situation was nearly reversed in the colonies: materials and land were cheap and available, but human labor and skills (whether for design or construction) in limited supply and costly. Whether in North America or the Caribbean, settlement away from the ocean could quickly bring encounter with difficult frontier conditions.

Many of the white Europeans who peopled the British Americas were financially indentured. In North America, the proportion may have been as great as fifty percent. African slaves made up about forty percent of the population in the southern United States in 1787.[106] In an economic environment with such levels of compulsory or forced labor, civil society in the Americas presented new and revolutionary challenges. But paradoxically, in the midst of such contradictions, there was embryonic liberty too: the American frontiers, continental and Caribbean, could offer some measure of religious freedom to minorities—not least to Jews. The oppressed and compromised of the

Netherlands and England could leave behind the schuilkerks and clandestine synagogues that had consigned them to the margins of European experience. But as time passed in the eighteenth century Atlantic World, Jewish communities grew in numbers. As an expression of this newly acquired success, Jews would build synagogues whose designs and materials enter architectural history as beautiful, substantial, and memorable.[107]

Map and index of the Atlantic World synagogues that have been identified as having been built between 1636 and 1822. Specific information on each synagogue can be found in the appendix.

TABLE 1. The known synagogues of the Atlantic World
between 1636 and 1822

Name of congregation / synagogue	Translation	Years extant	Location
Talmud Torah / Portuguese Synagogue (I)	Study of the Torah	1636–1931	Amsterdam, Netherlands
Zur Israel	Rock of Israel	1640–1900s	Recife, Pernambuco, Brazil
Magen Abraham	Shield of Abraham	1648–1653	Mauricia, Pernambuco, Brazil
Unknown	n/a	1661–1667	Cayenne, French Guyana
Nidhe Israel	Scattered of Israel	1660s–1831	Bridgetown, Barbados
Semah David	Branch of David	1660s and 1670s–1739	Speightstown, Barbados
Unknown	n/a	1671–after 1685	Thorarica, Suriname
Mikve Israel (I)	Hope of Israel	1674–1692	Willemstad, Curaçao
Talmud Torah (II) / Esnoga	Study of the Torah	1675–present	Amsterdam, Netherlands
Neve Zedek (I)	Abode of Justice	c. 1684–1692	Port Royal, Jamaica
Unknown	n/a	c. 1684–1772	Charlestown, Nevis
Berakha ve Shalom	Blessing and Peace	1685–after 1832	Jodensavanne, Suriname
Mikve Israel (II)	Hope of Israel	1692–1703	Willemstad, Curaçao
Sha'ar Hashamayim / Bevis Marks	Gates of Heaven	1701–present	London, United Kingdom
Mikve Israel (III)	Hope of Israel	1703–1730	Willemstad, Curaçao
Neve Shalom	Abode of Peace	1704–1907	Spanish Town, Jamaica
Shaar Ha Shamaim (I)	Gates of Heaven	after 1704–1744	Kingston, Jamaica
Santa Irmandad	Holy Brotherhood	1710s–1720	Tucacas, Venezuela
Neve Zedek (II)	Abode of Justice	c. 1719–at least 1815	Port Royal, Jamaica
Neve Shalom	Abode of Peace	1719–1835	Paramaribo, Suriname
Shearith Israel (I)	Remnant of Israel	1730–1818	New York, New York, United States
Mikve Israel / Snoa (IV)	Hope of Israel	1732–present	Willemstad, Curaçao
Zedek ve Shalom	Justice and Peace	1735–present	Paramaribo, Suriname
Honen Dalim	Charitable to the Poor	1739–after 1800	Oranjestad, St. Eustatius
Shaar Ha Shamaim (II)	Gates of Heaven	c. 1744–1882	Kingston, Jamaica
Neve Shalom	Abode of Peace	1746–after 1864	Willemstad, Curaçao

Name of congregation / synagogue	Translation	Years extant	Location
Shaar Hashamayim (I)	Gates of Heaven	1749–1766	Gibraltar, United Kingdom
Jeshuat Israel / Touro Synagogue	Salvation of Israel	1763–present	Newport, Rhode Island, United States
Unknown	n/a	1764–1765	St. Croix, Virgin Islands, United States
Shaar Hashamayim (II)	Gates of Heaven	1768–1781	Gibraltar, United Kingdom
Shearith Israel	Remnant of Israel	1777–1824	Montreal, Quebec, Canada
Darkhe Yesharim	Path of the Righteous	1779–1800	Paramaribo, Suriname
Shaar Hashamayim (III) / Great Synagogue	Gates of Heaven	1781–present	Gibraltar, United Kingdom
Mikveh Israel	Hope of Israel	1782–1825	Philadelphia, Pennsylvania, United States
Unknown	n/a	1783–before 1828	Philipsburg, St. Maarten
Etz Chaim	Tree of Life	1783–present	Gibraltar, United Kingdom
Shaare Yosher	Gates of the Upright	1789–1837	Kingston, Jamaica
Beth Elohim	House of God	1794–1838	Charleston, South Carolina, United States
Beraka ve Shalom ve Gemilut Hasadim (I)	Blessing and Peace and Acts of Piety	1796–1804	St. Thomas, Virgin Islands, United States
Mikveh Israel	Hope of Israel	1796–1895	Spanish Town, Jamaica
Nefusot Yehudah / Flemish Synagogue	Dispersed of Judah	1799–present	Gibraltar, United Kingdom
Beraka ve Shalom ve Gemilut Hasadim (II)	Blessing and Peace and Acts of Piety	1813–1831	St. Thomas, Virgin Islands, United States
Shearith Israel (II)	Remnant of Israel	1818–1833	New York, New York, United States
Mickve Israel	Hope of Israel	1820–1829	Savannah, Georgia, United States
Abudarham	n/a	1821–present	Gibraltar, United Kingdom
Beth Shalome	House of Peace	1822–1934	Richmond, Virginia, United States

CHAPTER 2

Jews and Conversos during the Age of Discovery

A geographer would look at the *terra firma* of the Atlantic World—whether continental, coastal, peninsular, or island—and observe that the land, always bounded by the ocean, strides the hemispheres between Canada (Montreal) in the north and Brazil (Recife) in the south. Yet in this vastness, I have placed my focus firmly on the American Atlantic and the Jewish settlements to be found there. As we have seen, the historiographic perspective that takes this same zone as its subject of inquiry begins in the early fifteenth century in Portugal and Spain. Here we encounter familiar themes—most often told from a Europeanized cultural vantage—of Europeans exploring, then colonizing, territories in, or islands en route to, Africa, North America, Central America, South America, and the Caribbean.[1]

We should never become blasé about the scale of this endeavor undertaken by discoverers living on the cusp of the early modern epoch. Voyages were launched across the earth's second largest body of water, on a metric covering nearly one-fifth of the planet's surface, with maritime technology that, however inventive and adaptive, still should make us marvel at those adventurers, sailors, and merchants traveling, for them, great unknown distances in, for us, relatively small wooden ships. In ancient Greek history, the eponymous name "Atlantic"—it refers to the Titan Atlas—was first mentioned by Herodotus (c. 450 B.C.E.).[2] The Hebrew Bible contains its first reference to what might be the Atlantic World when the prophet Obadiah (c. early 600s B.C.E.) places Jews in the land of "Sepharad," a name later (c. 200 C.E.) associated with the Iberian Peninsula.[3] This is the etymological source of the name Sephardim, denoting the Spanish-Portuguese Jews whose migrations and traditions we have traced so attentively. If we go farther back in time (c. 1500–300 B.C.E.), there was Israel's neighbor Phoenicia, whose homeland—northern Canaan in the biblical Hebrew geography—stretched along the coastal Levant. The Phoenician sphere of settlement or maritime trade moved westward, impressively, from Tyre (in the east) through the entire Mediterranean, probably beyond the Straits of Gibraltar, and, at least as a commercial network, expanding into the Atlantic to touch southern Britain and northwestern Africa. Whatever associations might plausibly have existed between the Hebrews and the Phoenicians, we have no archaeological record of Jewish settlement to corroborate Obadiah's reference—that hypothetical presence of Jews near Gibraltar or in Iberia—until fully seven centuries later.[4]

From the first century C.E., there is the first actual physical evidence of Jews in contact with the Atlantic, specifically in the Roman provinces of Hispania (Spain), Gallia (French Gaul), and Mauretania (Morocco).[5] Of course, for historical priority, dauntless exploratory zeal, and navigational brilliance, neither Columbus nor any other European people took precedence over the Vikings. Beginning in the ninth century, their small ships were rowed and sailed across the North Atlantic, reaching both Greenland and Newfoundland. But by the fifteenth century, the Norse settlements of North America were abandoned.[6]

During the high Middle Ages (c. 1000–1300), European demand for luxury items from both Arab lands and Asia—spices, silks, sugar, and precious stones and metals—grew steadily as news of Acre and Jerusalem was augmented by a new awareness of China. First returning Crusaders—they would periodically militate toward the Holy Land for almost two centuries after the first expedition in 1095—reported on the fabulous wealth of Muslim rulers. Then Marco Polo (1254–1324) described the Silk Road and the riches to be found not only among the Mongols but also along the central Asian trade arteries. European imaginations were sparked; their coffers were opened for trade. In this expanding market, Jewish merchants, bringing an expert knowledge of Arabic as well as familiarity with various Muslim societies, would play a part. Certainly their Mediterranean contacts, financial skills, and mobility proved useful in the import of valuable goods into the West. For Jews, whether in the Levant, North Africa, or Iberia, this economic role often led to wealth coterminus with exceptional cultural accomplishment. This was the world that produced Moses ben-Maimon (1138–1204), also called the Rambam as well as Maimonides. Let him serve as an icon of philosophical, intellectual, and scholarly achievement that was broadly based and influential.

For medieval Jews, however, there was a dichotomy, or perhaps more correctly, opposed realities: they could, and did, thrive under Islam, while they frequently suffered from Christian biases or hostility. In the Christian West, we find expulsion, persecution, and massacre in Germany, England, and France. Yet especially in Muslim Iberia, to a large extent in the Levant, in Mamluk-Turkic lands, in Persia between the mid-seventh and mid-twelfth centuries, and in the Arab Middle East, Jews for the most part experienced a rich epoch, gaining considerable acceptance, cultural authority, and the right to a large measure of financial integration in Moorish North Africa and Iberian, as well as Muslim Levantine society.

Although Marco Polo's name has become synonymous with the medieval European "discovery" of China, that accolade should also be given to an extraordinary twelfth-century Jewish traveler. Benjamin of Tudela came from Navarre, in northern Iberia, and ventured to Asia a century before the more famous Venetian. Both crossed the Mediterranean, Mesopotamia, and central Asia, tracing the fabled Great Silk Road and leave compelling accounts of their journeys. Jewish dynamism appeared unusually—in this instance, almost atypically—in the region of the North Caucasus and the Pontic steppe along the Caspian Sea, ruled (c. 600–1000) by the Khazars. Their nobility and aristocracy converted to Judaism, although how much of the general population did so is not clear.[7] The Radhanites—both etymology and usage here remain disputed—was the name given to Jews in commerce across the vast Eurasian landmass in the early Middle Ages (before the eleventh century). These Jews were the neutral, or de facto, the permitted traders who made possible economic relations between otherwise hostile civilizations—the Christian West and Islamic East. While quite literally spreading the wealth, these same Jewish merchants, whose profits provided revenue to Christian kings, opened a conduit between what had been the Roman Empire and Asia.[8]

Yet for medieval western Europeans, the Oriental cornucopia, with its luxuries from China, India, Persia, and the Middle East, was far too distant, too mediated. Had it not been for the "proximate" mediators—the Moorish Iberian, North African, northern Italian (Venetian, Pisan, Genoese), Byzantine, Mamluk, and Arab mercantile systems (often reliant on Jews) that exerted seemingly cartel-like pressures at times on the price structure of goods brought into Europe—trade with the Far East would have been impossible for the Christian West. Sustainable commerce with the Orient was at least one pressing material motivation for Europeans to undertake what we call the Age of Discovery and, in its wake, the Atlantic World: to dispense with Eurasian-Mediterranean routes, thus radically reducing costs by sea transportation around Africa—or some other route—would yield great wealth. And in Portugal by the 1420s, given advances in cartography, maritime science, and navigational technology, that idea achieved critical mass.

Early Explorations in the Age of Discovery

In 1415 Prince Henry the Navigator (1394–1460)—properly the Infante Dom Henrique of Portugal—conquered a strategic port lodged on the northwestern tip of Africa. The fall of Ceuta, opposite Gibraltar, marked an epoch, one given impetus by commercial initiative, Christian confrontation with Islam, and an urge to explore. Portugal not only would launch military campaigns across Moorish North Africa, but, far more important, would send expeditions that discovered—at least according to the European narrative—Atlantic islands west and south of Ceuta, and would continue to trace the entire west coast of Africa, circumnavigating the continent at the Cape of Good Hope and the Horn of Africa, and onward to India. Although there is much exaggeration that attaches to the "scientists"—anachronism is inevitable when discussing an episteme during which empirical experiment was still grafted to natural philosophy—assembled in the court of Prince Henry, he certainly employed skilled cartographers to help chart navigational expeditions. Not least among these mapmakers was the Majorcan Jew Judah Cresque (c. 1350–1427), whose gifts as a brilliant drawer of maps and designer of nautical instruments would command the attention of Prince Henry.[9]

The Portuguese explored and colonized the West African Atlantic rapidly during the first half of the fourteenth century. They first found outlying island groups—Azores (c. 1427–32), Madeira, Cape Verde, São Tomé—then further south Cape Bojador (1434), a northwestern promontory off the Saharan coast. By the 1470s Portuguese mariners had ventured so far down the West African coast that, on passing the equator, they lost sight of the North Star (Pole Star)—which had up to that time had been their defining point of orientation when navigating the North Atlantic and Mediterranean. Yet the Spaniards were not lax. It was Castile, not Portugal, who colonized the Canary Islands.[10]

There were great contributions by various Jewish scientists, like Yehuda ibn Verga (c. fifteenth century), Joseph Vecinho (late fifteenth century), and Abraham Zacuto (1452–1515).[11] Their applied studies and technical knowledge made possible the improved maps, metal astrolabes, and astronomical tables that allowed sailors from Iberia—Columbus, de Gama, and Magellan most famously—to venture into uncharted waters with more reliable awareness of nautical location. Abraham Zacuto's Hebrew text *Ha-Hibbur ha-Gadol* (The Great Compilation) of 1472 accurately predicted the sun's seasonal position relative to the earth. This seminal work was much translated, first into Latin by Joseph Vecinho as *Almanach perpetuum coelestium motuum,* and later into Spanish and Portuguese. Some Jews traveled on West African expeditions to record geographical data, as did Vecinho in 1485; others, notably Zacuto, helped translate the corpus of Arabic, Greek, and Hebrew scientific and mathematical literature, especially on astronomy and navigation, into Latin, Portuguese, and Spanish.[12] Not for the first time in the chronology or orbit of Jewish diaspora, language skills would prove invaluable. Soon enough Jews and New Christians would thrive in the Atlantic World as translators, settlers, merchants, and advisors, whose linguistic abilities provided indispensable communication.

In the fifteenth century, labor-intensive cash-crop plantations were established in the Portuguese island colonies of the Azores, Madeira, Cape Verde, and São Tomé, as well as in the Castilian Canary Islands.[13] New products began to enter the European repertoire—like the famous Madeira wine, named after the archipelago where it was made. But excellence notwithstanding,

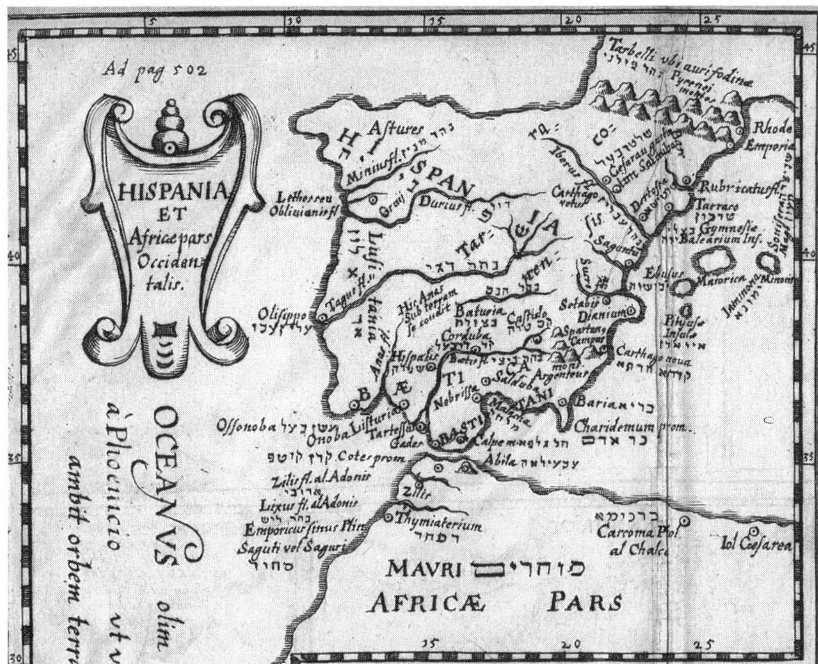

The bilingual Latin-Hebrew map *Hispania et Africa pars Occidentalis,* c. 1700, illustrating Iberia and northwest Africa, is an example of how multilingualism was a valuable skill within the field of cartography in the Atlantic World. Artist unknown. William A. Rosenthall Judaica Collection, Special Collections, College of Charleston Library.

wine was an economic sideshow, as were all other agricultural commodities, compared to one great innovation: sugarcane. It would—when transformed into its crystalline form, as well as into molasses and rum—yield white gold: profits that decisively affected the Atlantic European economy and, once triangulated into the mature European slave commerce during the seventeenth and eighteenth centuries, determined the very history of the modern world.[14] Before the fifteenth century in Europe, sugar was restricted to the rich, a luxury that came to the West through the Eurasian–Mediterranean–North African trade networks. The tropical plant originated in New Guinea and southern Asia.[15] Europe's climate (except in Cyprus, Sicily, Crete, and small areas of southern Iberia) precluded wide cultivation: sugarcane needs constant, abundant water and warm temperatures. With entrepreneurial zeal many Genoese, Iberian Jews, and New Christians—those Jews driven to convert by the Inquisition—became early colonists on the Portuguese-Spanish islands off of Africa. They organized the first sugarcane plantations in the Euro-Atlantic world, an enterprise that prospered with quicksilver speed.[16] By the

1460s Madeira had become the largest single producer of sugarcane in the Western world. The mostly non-Portuguese sugarcane producers had made cultivation so profitable that native Portuguese commercial agents and aspirant cultivators, resentful at exclusion, complained to João II about a foreign-run monopoly. In 1481 a royal license requirement was introduced to contain foreign dominance in sugarcane production and sale. But this nativist attempt was quickly doomed. In 1489 the king decreed that all sugarcane plantation owners and traders could become Portuguese subjects—recognition that their wealth and expertise had become indispensable bulwarks of the general economy.[17]

In the capitalist plantation system developed during the early modern epoch, sugarcane required both abundant land and a large-scale work force.[18] It was the labor requisite that launched economic, then humanitarian and political consequences of the most profound, disturbing order. To work their plantations the Portuguese brought increasingly large numbers of enslaved Africans who lived and toiled under notoriously brutal, dangerous, and arduous conditions. The Roman Catholic Church sanctioned this slavery to a considerable degree, at least during the last half of the fifteenth century.[19] Pope Nicholas V, in his bull Dum Diversas (1452), authorized Alfonso V of Portugal "to invade, search out, capture, and subjugate the Saracens and pagans and any other unbelievers and enemies of Christ wherever they may be." Here was ideology linked to profit at the dawn of the Atlantic colonial project: if papal doctrine sustained the Church's hostility toward Islam and pagan cults, there was at the same time the crafting of a policy that encouraged the material and imperial ambitions of Iberian Catholic monarchs. A series of similar papal endorsements of African slavery followed rapidly.[20] Clearly the Church's position helped bind the destiny of Africans, Europeans, and slave traders to the emerging wealth of the Atlantic World. Here we encounter a dark destiny indeed: From our historical vantage today, when we scrutinize the economic initiative of the European merchants who colluded with willing African slave-trafficking partners, it is impossible not to regard the colonized Atlantic World, despite its wealth and political potential, as contaminated by, and inseparable from, tragedy, violence, greed, and opportunism. Thus beginning in the mid-fifteenth century, the west central African kingdom of Kongo—or rather that portion of Kongo located now in northern Angola—began to supply a preponderance of slaves to Portugal's island colonies.[21] Fortunes were made: as the sale and transportation of human beings became institutionalized, the growing profits shaped the character of New World societies populated by dominant Europeans. But Jews—and this point needs emphasis to counteract anti-Semitic distortions—played only a minor role in the overall slave economy.[22]

However significant its development would become, slavery figures as only one element that led Europeans to probe the Atlantic in the fifteenth century.

There were various forces at play—most conspicuously the vision of distant lands, the drama of exploration, and as so often, the seduction of wealth attainable through new maritime routes. In sailing westward from Europe, rather than south along the African coast, as did the Portuguese, it was one of history's heroic discoverers, the Genoese mariner Christopher Columbus, who mounted the archetypal effort.[23] During the 1480s, he sought royal patronage for his idea of sailing across the Atlantic to reach the "Indies"—then a catch-all geographic conflation of South and East Asia. As a mariner, Columbus was familiar with the Mediterranean and a swathe of the eastern Atlantic, from Ireland (possibly Iceland) and the English Channel to the northwest African coast.[24] Columbus believed the world was a sphere, itself far from a novel idea. Aside from being common knowledge of European geographers and navigators in the fifteenth century, the conception of the earth as a globe bespoke an ancient, famous lineage: Pythagoras (570–495 B.C.E.), Plato (428–348 B.C.E.), and Aristotle (348–322 B.C.E.) all postulated that the earth was a sphere. Approximately 240 B.C.E., the Greek mathematician Eratosthenes (276–195 B.C.E.) used trigonometry to calculate a reasonably accurate estimate of the earth's circumference. Ptolemy (Claudius Ptolemaeus, 90–168 C.E.), who lived in Roman-ruled Egypt, produced a *Geographia* and *Almagest* (an astronomical study) that became the main conduits of Hellenistic astronomy to Roman–western Christian culture and to the Byzantine and Islamic traditions. But starting in the twelfth century, ancient authorities, especially Aristotle, Ptolemy, and Euclid (c. 300 B.C.E.), were introduced to the West by Arabic translators of Greek, whose works in turn were translated into Latin. While much of this great effort in translation was based in northern Italy and Sicily, equally vital in cultural dissemination was Iberia, with Toledo as a center. In any case Jewish scholars under Arab rule distinguished themselves as multilingual translators of various scientific texts (c. 900–1300), for instance Isaac ibn Sid (c. 1250), whose astronomical compilations, revised three centuries later by Abraham Zacuto, were invaluable to Columbus.

This was the conspectus of Greco-Roman-Islamic thought that the West had acquired—or had sustained if, at some level, we regard the Roman provinces of Hispania, Gallia, and Britannia as embryonic "western European"—by the late fifteenth century. And this was, accordingly, the rich intellectual ferment that made possible the great voyages of discovery. When Columbus, seeking support for his venture, approached João II of Portugal, the king rejected any such expedition because his experts rightly understood the circumference of the earth to be much greater than Columbus supposed.[25] One of the key royal advisors in this instance was the mathematician Joseph Vecinho, who had studied with Abraham Zacuto in Spain. Unlike his famous teacher, Vecinho opposed the proposal of Columbus.[26] Since the Portuguese—and, for that matter, most informed—geographers of the age believed that no land interposed between Europe and Asia, they sensibly argued that ships and crews could not be supplied to survive so long a voyage. Over such uncharted distances with presumably no landfalls en route, there was no port to offer food, water, and repairs—so argued learned and professional opinion. It was this "impossibility," not the fear of a flat earth, that negated attempts to traverse the "Ocean Sea."[27]

But there was something besides mathematics that would be determinative. Columbus was the first to appreciate the Atlantic's easterly and westerly trade-wind currents—an understanding that proved to be sine qua non, allowing the most rapid transit for a sailing vessel to leave port, cross the Atlantic, and return. He did suppose his voyage plausible in the first place because he had incorrectly downsized the earth's circumference by some 15,888 miles. Yet this error, not to mention the survival of all mariners of his first expedition of 1492, was made good—or at least offset—by the land encounter that would immortalize Columbus—San Salvador in the Bahamas (sighted 12 October 1492). On later voyages, the admiral would go on to visit various Caribbean islands, Central America, and South America.

Ultimately, as most of us have learned to recite from childhood, Ferdinand II and Isabella (Los Reyes Católicos), Spain's king and queen, decided to sponsor Columbus on his way west. Less recited, perhaps, are those European rulers (from Venice, Genoa, England, Portugal) who squelched the discoverer's appeals for funding. And even Spanish royal patronage had been denied earlier (1486), when a panel of experts rejected the expedition of Columbus. But that first rejection was somewhat softened by the timely opinion of the eminent astronomical authority Abraham Zacuto. He considered the plan of Columbus acceptable, a judgment that had great weight five years later when Columbus at last won royal approval.[28]

This decision to authorize exploration emerged from a particular, triumphalist context: Ferdinand and his wife had just successfully conquered Granada (1492), the last Muslim emirate on the Iberian Peninsula.[29] By combining their respective royal houses of Aragon (Ferdinand) and Castile (Isabella), the Spanish rulers went far toward the creation of a Catholic national entity. The victory in Granada closed the last page on the Reconquista, the nearly eight-century-long Christian campaign (722–1492) to end Muslim rule in Iberia. Reconquest likewise turned a page for Spain's Jews too. The Alhambra Decree (31 March 1492) was the royal edict expelling all Jews who refused to accept Catholicism. This interplay between national unification, Atlantic discovery, Muslim decline, and Jewish exile effectively marks 1492 as an *annus mirabilis et terribilis.* Terror followed, as execution, forced conversion, expropriation, and exile would soon afflict the non-Christian victims of oppression—those Muslims and, especially, Jews who had lived so long and productively in Iberia, and then wonder, as Spain would become the wealthiest European empire of the age, claiming vast resources from continents unknown to Columbus when his three ships left the Andalusian port of Palos de la Frontera (3 August 1492).

Still another Spanish incentive for helping the doggedly determined Columbus was the financial ambition to rival the prospective wealth of Portugal. Its explorer Bartolommeo Diaz had sailed around the tip of Africa in 1488; clearing the Cape of Good Hope, he had thus pointed the way toward direct maritime commerce with India and China. For the Spanish monarchy, whose cash reserves were depleted by the Reconquista, ready access to the riches of the Indies must have been tempting. However tentative (or credible) Columbus's proposition, if successful, there beckoned a cornucopia of wealth, prestige, territory, naval dominion, and, not least, the missionary opportunity to bring "pagan" souls from afar into the one true Catholic faith. Their royal gambit linked to the luck, skills, and vision of Columbus, proved providential. A new world of power, profit, and exploration would be Spanish.

In the new environment created by discovery and expulsion, various Jewish associations with the achievement of Columbus are not hard to detect. King Ferdinand's powerful financial advisor, Luis de Santangel (d. 1498), was the main broker of the funding arrangements between the monarchs and the admiral. Santangel was born Christian, but his grandfather had converted and belonged to a large once-Jewish family that included bankers, speculative tax investors ("tax farmers"), and financiers active throughout Aragon, Castile, and Valencia.[30] We know that Ferdinand and Isabella, indebted from their struggle against Islam, could only partially support Columbus. Most of the financing was supervised by Santangel, who drew on the resources of three other experienced court figures of converso origin: Gabriel Sanchez (d. 1505), Ferdinand's treasurer; Juan Cabrero, royal chamberlain; and Alfonso de la Caballeria, vice-chancellor of Aragon. There may well have been further funding through an undisclosed lender, possibly the Portuguese-born Jewish philosopher, statesman, and financier Isaac Abrabanel (1437–1508).[31] In any case when Columbus promptly mounted his second expedition in 1493, Ferdinand and Isabella were less hard pressed to find funding: it came from the considerable amassed wealth of confiscated Jewish property.[32]

Anti-Semitism in Iberia was age-old. Visigoths (418–720 C.E.) stigmatized and harmed Jews, practices largely unaffected by the gradual Christianization of the peninsula beginning in the first Christian century. Under Muslim rule (711–1492) too, Iberian Jewry was occasionally persecuted, even more so when the Almohad Dynasty (c. 1130–1269) was in power there and in northern Africa.[33] As the Reconquista gathered force, but long before the crisis of 1492, Jews emigrated to escape harassment and violence. The greatest Jewish philosopher with ties to Iberia, Moses Maimonides (1137–1204), was born in Cordova, only to leave after the Almohad invasion in 1148. Most of his life was spent in Egypt, where he moved in 1168.[34] But, at some level, the memory of Iberia seems to have lingered: Maimonides is known to have signed

Representatives of Spain's Jewish community before King Ferdinand and Queen Isabella. Among them was Isaac Abrabanel, requesting that the monarchs reconsider the expulsion of the Jews set forth in the Alhambra Decree. Engraving by Alonzo Chappel, from *History of the World: Ancient and Modern* (New York: Johnson, Fry, and Co., 1866–71). William A. Rosenthall Judaica Collection, Special Collections, College of Charleston Library.

his name "Moses the son of Maimon the Spaniard."[35] This self-description connotes a Hispanic memory of Sephardic-Moorish-Christian provenance, centuries before the unified Catholic kingdom formed.

By 1300 conditions for Hispanic Jewry had worsened. Notoriously bloody anti-Semitic massacres broke out across Spain in 1391. Hundreds, probably thousands, of Jews were murdered, among them prominent leaders and scholars. These deaths terrified the Jewish community, launching an exodus of scholars, scientists, and physicians.[36] At the same time, the violence of 1391 caused large numbers of Jews to adopt Christianity, effectively creating a social stratum, the converso (or New Christians), whose activities have appeared throughout our account.[37]

In the actual human circumstances, the nature, or spectrum, of conversion for the Sephardim was malleable and calibrated. Many conversos sincerely became Catholic; others adopted a Christian façade but lived and worshipped as Jews in secret. There were converts who made a public return to Judaism after initial anti-Semitic violence abated. Still others gradually returned to Judaism with the encouragement of family, friends, or neighbors. In any case the shadows cast by coercion and apostasy are hard to delineate. Amidst all this religious ambiguity, psychological pain, and social dysphoria, relations between Jews and conversos were often sustained on a civil basis during the fifteenth century. But this same ambiguity—as to the authenticity of the faith of a New Christian—proved anathema to the Catholic Church, which regarded the relapse of conversos to Judaism as an abomination, and social pathogen. The Spanish Inquisition, established by Ferdinand and Isabella in 1478 if less than enthusiastically endorsed by Pope Sixtus VI, targeted *relapsos* (relapsed Jews among New Christians) as heretics. They were an evil who could pollute souls. That archetype of execution, the auto-da-fé, in which the condemned were burned publicly, first appeared in Seville in 1482.[38] The entire regime of intimidation, interrogation (with torture as needed), and formal trial would extend for more than 350 years—declining after the Enlightenment —throughout Spain and its empire. Whatever the motive forces—nationalism, doctrinal zealotry, greed for expropriated property—forging so perdurable an instrument, there can be little doubt that Ferdinand and Isabella grafted state power and religious orthodoxy to achieve unity, obedience, and cultural cohesion. According to the policies brought on by the final Moorish capitulation at Granada, Jews and conversos immediately, then Muslims slightly later, would face stark choices: accept Catholicism unqualifiedly, leave Spain, or die.

The Alhambra Decree forbade Jews to remain in Spain after 31 July 1492. There was a slight delay; however, by the evening of 1 August 1492, the final contingent of Spain's Jewish community—those who continued to affirm their Judaism—sailed away from El Puerto de Santa Maria, on the Bay of Cadiz.[39] Ironies abound, indeed almost biblically: 1 August 1492, according to the Julian calendar (since the Gregorian was not adopted by Spain until 1582) corresponds to 9 Av 5252 on the Hebrew calendar—a date that, by Jewish tradition, marks the 2,077th and 1,421st anniversaries, respectively, of the destruction of the First and Second Temples.[40] These twin ancient catastrophes are commemorated in Judaism by an annual day of fasting and mourning, known as Tisha B'Av, when the book of Lamentations is often recited. On 3 August 1492, Columbus set sail from Palos de la Frontera for the Canary Islands (where he reprovisioned), his last landfall before crossing the Atlantic. Later, in his only reference to Jews in all his writings, the admiral—technically, the first royal appointment was styled "Captain General," but "Admiral" is more familiar—recalled the Jewish expulsion, that manifest socioeconomic dislocation, as a mnemonic, a point of reference for his personal drama. In the introduction to his account of his first voyage, as submitted to the king and queen, Columbus wrote: "In the same month in which Their Majesties issued the edict that all Jews should be driven out of the kingdom and its territories—in that same month they gave me the order to undertake with sufficient men my expedition of discovery to the Indies."[41] But, as it happens, this calendrical device misleads. The actual Columbian expedition was hardly free of Jewish association, or in the case of the first voyage, converso participation. Among his crew members were a few recently baptized converso sailors, including the admiral's designated interpreter, Luis de Torres. He had worked as a translator during the Reconquista and chose baptism shortly before the August 1492 deadline.[42] Torres was very likely the first Jew to set foot in the Americas.

Almost at the same time, Jews in Portugal—many had just exited Spain—continued the work of maritime discovery for several more years. All Iberia would soon become Jew-free. In this environment, the great Zacuto abandoned the University of Saragossa for Lisbon (1492), where he was soon appointed royal astronomer. In Portugal, Zacuto advised Vasco da Gama, as he had Columbus earlier, and certainly provided the Portuguese mariner with his authoritative astronomical tables (the *Almanach Perpetuum*) as well as a notably accurate copper astrolabe (supplanting the much less exact wooden astrolabe then in common use) before leaving for North Africa following the forced conversion edict of King Manuel I in 1497. These same indispensable navigational tools were available to Pedro Álvares Cabral, the Portuguese mariner who achieved the European discovery of Brazil in 1500. In fact, during the sixteenth and seventeenth centuries, later editions of Zacuto's almanac became the standard astronomical guides for all European mariners and navigators.[43]

Gaspar da Gama (c. 1444–1515)—much involved with, but not an actual relative of, the legendary Vasco da Gama, who was the first to sail from Europe around Africa and arrive in India—may have been the first Ashkenazic Jew involved in Atlantic World exploration. The translator Torres was Sephardic. There are several biographical variants for the remarkable, almost picaresque, Gaspar (*sic,* to avoid confusion with the more famous explorer) and any number of factual discrepancies. We do not even know Gaspar's true family name. That he was a polyglot traveler who had made his way to India is certain. En route he might have been taken prisoner and temporarily enslaved. But Gaspar's 1498 rendezvous with da Gama, returning from Calicut (the port in Kerala) on that famous first voyage, literally made Gaspar's name and career. The explorer forced the wandering Jew to convert to Catholicism, christened with his own surname, then enlisted Gaspar as a translator and pilot through Indian coastal waters. Back in Lisbon, King Manuel I would designate Gaspar translator for other major maritime expeditions.[44]

The encounter with the New World, certainly no less fabulous for European sailors at the time than learning about Africa, India, Asia, or Oceania, would come as Gaspar accompanied Cabral on the Portuguese voyage of discovery to Brazil.[45] Cabral's destination was India, following da Gama's route; he sailed southwest, crossed the Atlantic, and came upon Brazil. But then Cabral and Gaspar continued on, emulating Vasco da Gama, to the Cape of Good Hope and India. During their return to Portugal, c. 1501–2, Gaspar da Gama met the Florentine Amerigo Vespucci—himself appointed to yet another Portuguese Brazil-bound expedition—at Beseguiche, near the Cape Verde islands. With Vespucci, Gaspar shared his navigational knowledge, not to mention Cabral's, of both India and Brazil. And it was this information that very likely helped the much-traveled Florentine, who never visited India, to his axial geographic finding: the Americas were neither Asia nor the Indies, but in fact two connected continents (with outlying islands) previously unknown. Indeed, in a letter to Lorenzo di Pierfrancesco de' Medici (1463–1503), Vespucci acknowledged that "the said Gaspar, who knows many languages and the names of many provinces and cities: as I say, he is a very trustworthy man, because he has twice made the voyage from Portugal to the Indian Sea."[46] Here crystallized the perspective, one still not held by Columbus on his death in 1506, that allowed Europeans to conceive a New World. Put differently, by introducing a new, more accurate global geography to the European mind, Vespucci, intrepid and insightful, earned his eponymous tribute—"America" derives from Amerigo—and, as so often in great advances, did so collaboratively—in the company of the Portuguese discoverers, Columbus, and not least Gaspar da Gama.[47] After them, but only just barely (1503), the deluge of colonization: early on, Fernão de Noronha—he gave his name to the archipelago some two hundred miles off the Brazilian coast—was one of the many New Christians who helped create Brazil's first export economy based on pernambuco (valuable as a source of fine dense hardwood and a dye) as well as other exotic commodities.[48]

What of the Spaniards who would soon dominate so much of this New World? Having perpetrated Jewish expulsion, persecution, or conversion, the Catholic monarchs Ferdinand and Isabella still could not cull their ranks of former Jews, crypto-Jews, or subjects with Jewish ancestry. This persistence of affiliation can be seen even among bona fide conquistadors—those soldiers whose arms so belligerently and notoriously delivered large swathes of the Americas to Spain in rapid order. In 1519, when Hernando Cortez (1485–1547) landed at Veracruz, the decisive commander who would fell the Aztec Empire was accompanied by a much less known though capable namesake, one whose fate would soon introduce an Inquisition-inflected script to North America—Hernando Alonso.[49] He had been trained as a blacksmith but on the first Cortez expedition worked as a highly skilled carpenter, helping to build crucial equipment used so effectively by Cortez in the capture of Tenochtitlan, Montezuma's great capital.[50] By 1521 Alonso, with many in his fellow ranks, had been rewarded with an encomienda (a land grant whose profits depended on the peonage of indigenous Native Americans).[51] He prospered as a rancher and later as a meat supplier to Mexico City. But in 1528 Alonso was burned in the first public auto-da-fé to be held in Mexico City, the Spanish colonial capital built on the site of razed Aztec Tenochtitlan. Not only was this execution the Inquisition's ritual entrée to the new continent, meant to chastise the Judaizing behavior of the retired conquistador, but the flames also served warning that the punctilio of Iberian religious severity would govern New Spain. How errant was Hernando? If we examine the trial records, charges against him mention his having celebrated Passover while visiting Cuba and having baptized his child twice, the second time by replacing the Christian ceremony with a Jewish one.[52] Because torture elicited these findings, we cannot say how Jewish Hernando was in public or private practice. But we do know that a successful figure like Hernando would have had business rivals. Nor can we ignore the rapid socioeconomic changes in early New Spanish–Mexican society, as the first wave of conquistadors, men like Hernando, were pressured by the successor cadre of civil and Church administrators, careerists who left Iberia to thrive in the New World. Whether motivated by anti-Semitism, greed, envy, class ambition, or insecurity—after all, the Iberian Inquisition was not the peculiar whim of royalty but bespoke common attitudes rooted in a whole society—Christians in imperial Mexico early on came to regard the financial, mercantile, or agrarian achievements of conversos as obstacles to be overcome. Nevertheless Cortez, given the grand title of Marqués del Valle de Oaxaca by Charles V (1500–1558) in 1528, managed to protect most of his own soldiers from encroachment during his first tenure (1518–28) in Mexico.[53]

Yet soon enough the writ of Cortez, Mexico's first Spanish governor and captain general, would be challenged by other ambitious commanders and, whether in Spain or the New World, by various ecclesiastics. In fact, when he made his first return to Spain (1528–30), Cortez sought support from Emperor Charles V to outflank rivals. During his absence Hernando Alonso was doomed, while fellow veteran conquistadors were subject to the hectoring of Inquisition-inspired clerics. Blasphemy uttered by Christian tongues was punishable too, although not necessarily by death. So we find that two erring Christians, Diego de Morales and Diego de Ocana, were spared from the same auto-da-fé in which Hernando Alonso died. Or to use the language of the inquisitors, the errant were "reconciled" to the path of the true Church.[54]

Clearly the environment for New World conversos was becoming harsh and perilous. To protect the religious purity of the faithful from concealed heresy or potential "racial" and doctrinal corruption, the Spanish Crown banned anyone of Jewish origin from crossing the Atlantic for the Americas in 1552. Then, as a state institution, the Holy Office of the Inquisition arrived in Mexico City in 1571, directed by Pedro Moya de Contreras. He was a formidable figure indeed, simultaneously Archbishop of Mexico City, Inquisitor General, and Viceroy. In the quasi-theocratic drive to nullify Judaism, New Spain would emulate the fervor—we would probably choose a different term today—of the Spanish homeland and its Church.[55]

For all the anti-Semitic displacement, violence, and suppression, during the Age of Discovery there are elements of continuity linking the posture of

Jews, conversos, and crypto-Jews to their standing in the Iberian world before 1492. If the Jews of Portugal and Spain had long been tax collectors, doctors, and merchants, some filled such roles in the New World too. Less often, though critically, Jews, then conversos, served as financiers and courtiers, in the orbit of Christian monarchs. But Jews also made brilliant contributions as scientists, mariners, and soldiers—those on the cutting edge of exploration and, it must be said, therefore of exploitation. Too many modern accounts overlook them. It is hard to suppose how Columbus, Vasco da Gama, and Vespucci, for all their boldness, would have succeeded as readily as they did without the aid of men like Abraham Zacuto, Luis de Santangel, Gaspar da Gama, and Luis de Torres.

The Sephardic and Converso Diaspora in the Spanish and Portuguese Empires

While some Jews were caught up in the voyages of discovery, encountering the Americas, Africa, and Asia along with legendary navigators and conquistadors, most of the Sephardic population would respond to the crisis of 1492, as we saw earlier, by seeking refuges nearer to hand. So they left Spain to make their lives somewhere else—briefly in Portugal and elsewhere in Europe, the Mediterranean, North Africa, and the Levant. Conditions of acceptance in these safe havens varied. At least in much of Italy, as well as in the Ottoman Empire, Jews could practice their religion openly. To other sanctuaries, such as the Lowlands or Bordeaux, the Sephardim could emigrate, but only under the façade of Catholicism. A very small number went to inhospitable England, where the exclusion of Jews was still in place after two centuries, but it at least lacked an Inquisition. A substantial minority of Spanish Jews did not flee, instead accepting Christianity sincerely or wearing the crypto-Jewish mantle with all its risks. However, in contrast, the majority of Jews in Portugal were forced to convert in 1497.[56]

Yet Spain's rule of portions of Italy allowed the expulsion program of Ferdinand and Isabella to rapidly penetrate Sicily (1493), Sardinia (1493), and eventually Naples (1541) and Milan (1597). Thus, under variable institutional arrangements and rigor, the Inquisition accompanied the Spanish and Portuguese wherever they ventured.[57] Iberian anti-Semitism was increasingly governed by racism: just having a trace of Jewish ancestry was dangerous and onerous in the first decades of the sixteenth century. Certain safe zones did emerge. Jews in the North African coastal cities of Ceuta, Melilla, Oran, and Tangier, at the doorstep of Spain and Portugal and controlled by them, did not experience expulsion or Inquisition too strictly. Anomalously, despite the proximity of these ports to Iberian power, it was the close contact with the greater Islamic world, not to mention the functional acceptance of Jews among Muslims, that placed a limit on too zealous inquisitorial policy by the Catholic forces.[58]

By the early sixteenth century, the Sephardic diaspora (both practicing as Jews and New Christians) extended from the West Indies through Europe, North Africa, and the Middle East to India. This included a kith-kin-coethnic network that eventually became realized and appreciated as the perfect means of establishing the first interhemisphere mercantile system in the early modern world. Displaced families, friends, and fellow travelers wandered far, often to distant lands.[59] But over so vast an area of settlement, there existed among once-Iberian Jews a common experience rooted in religious identification, expulsion (hence, intolerance), and a shared set of both intellectual and mercantile skills. It would be this contiguity, simultaneously cultural, genealogical, linguistic, and professional, that helped integrate one of the earliest commercial networks in the Age of Discovery and the early modern world. Both native and colonial populations of the Americas, Europe, the Mediterranean, the Levant, Anatolia, the Middle East, and Asia would come to recognize the adaptability, resourcefulness, and scope of the Sephardim. They became, quite literally, citizens of the world and pioneering agents of global economic expansion.

By far most of the Spanish exiles, perhaps some forty thousand, fled to three contiguous polities—Portugal, Navarre, and Provence.[60] But normalcy in a Portuguese refuge was very quickly disrupted. On 4 December 1496, King Manuel I (1469–1521) ordered the expulsion of his country's Jews, allowing them eleven months to leave or become Christian. There were some thirty thousand Portuguese Jews, plus an equal number of Spanish refugees who had arrived after 1492. Portugal's population at the time was about one million.[61] The mass eviction-conversion scheme was caused by Manuel's marriage to Princess Isabel, daughter of King Ferdinand and Queen Isabella. Their Hispanic Catholicizing zeal merged marital consolidation with a purification program meant to cover all Iberia. Yet Manuel had distinct reservations. No enthusiast for the loss of a Jewish population that had long proven so economically critical for his nation, the king proceeded to make expulsion as untenable as possible—often in the cruelest ways, like separating parents from children, who were then forcibly baptized. Far harsher compulsion—including condemnation to death by burning or to enslavement—was then launched against recalcitrant Jewish parents and adults. In fact Manuel wanted to retain these valuable subjects once they had been formally de-Judaized. So Jews were not allowed to leave Portugal without a special royal license and, in general, emigration was only notional. The hard, prevalent fate for Portuguese Sephardim was forced conversion. By 1497, tens of thousands of Jews, under such dangerous pressure, were made into New Christians.

During the fifteenth century, the kingdom of Navarre, straddling the Pyrenees, tried to resist absorption by its larger neighbors. (Spanish annexation came in 1513; in 1589, capitulation to the French.) Even though Navarre allowed entry to some thirty-five hundred Spanish Jews—3.5 percent of the entire Navaresse population—after the Alhambra Decree, relentless pressure by Ferdinand and Isabella, including threat of invasion, forced King John III to expel the Jews of Navarre in 1498. While given sanctuary at first, the refugees and Navarrese Jews were soon given the same bitter choice—expulsion or conversion. This brief interval under John III represented the final respite for a Jewish community living openly and legally in Iberia.[62] In fact, the Inquisition would formally come to Navarre in the wake of Ferdinand's invasion of the small kingdom in 1512, and its subsequent annexation the following year. It was in Navarre, after more than a millennium of vital, sometimes brilliant achievement, that the indigenous chapter of Sephardic history came to an end, not to be reopened, and then mutedly, until the mid-nineteenth century.

To the north of Navarre lay France, to the east Provence. Only a small number of Jewish refugees crossed the Pyrenees, not least because France had expelled its Jews in 1394. For a very brief interval, Provence—it would formally come under French rule in 1486—took in some exiles from Iberia but in 1500 adopted the Iberian and French policies of banishment or conversion toward Jews. This expulsion was the culmination of various local bans that, town by town, often as a sequitur to gang violence against Jews, starting in 1483, when the young Charles VIII of France became the de facto ruler of the storied land bordering the Mediterranean.[63] After 1500, the Pontifical State of Avignon (with its surrounding enclave, le Comtat Venaissin) stood as the only Renaissance polity in southwestern Europe where Jews could live openly as Jews. There was some irony here: the papacy—historical author of inquisitorial scrutiny of heresy, now in disrepute under the ethically dubious tenure of Alexander VI (pope 1492–1503), born Rodrigo Lanzol (1431–1503) in Xàtiva, Spain. He offered this small Provençal bulwark as well as the Italian Papal States (adjacent to Spanish Naples) as a haven against encroaching virulent anti-Semitism perpetuated, at least regionally, by the doctrinal zeal of Ferdinand and Isabella.

During the twelfth century, the medieval Catholic Church began to combat both the great Catharist (Albigensian) religious movement—beginning c. 1140, in Languedoc and Waldensianism, and then c. 1170, in southern France, northern Italy, and Germany—through various ecclesiastic bodies called "inquisitions." These identified and punished heresy; for the most part, they operated either under the authority of local bishops or, as authorized by Pope Gregory IX in 1233 to target the Cathars (using the Dominicans as inquisitors). In the protracted, bloody struggle (c. 1150–1250) to eradicate the Cathars, we see the maturation of the Inquisition (c. 1229) as an instrument of coercion and punishment against a mass community of believers.[64] Especially after 1233 the penalties of torture, hanging, or burning became common tools of suppression, as would happen later in the effort to terrify recalcitrant or crypto-Jews and Muslims in Iberia. When Ferdinand and Isabella inaugurated the Spanish Inquisition in 1478, they supplemented, though gradually, the medieval inquisitorial regimes with specifically Spanish socio-political objectives. For this enterprise the dual Catholic monarchs received the reluctant imprimatur of Pope Sixtus IV (1414–84). As far as the Church was concerned, the purpose of the Inquisition was to root out heretics, defined as *baptized* Christians who disavow orthodox revealed truth. In Iberia this heretical population comprised mostly those who had been Jewish and Muslim. Their conversion to Christianity—which involved baptism—was deemed "false": there was conformity to external religious practice, but privately rejection of Catholic faith. Whether based in deception or error, this behavior was categorically punishable; nor did it matter whether conversion had been voluntary or coerced. Guilty, too, were converts lapsing to their original faith, and those who secretly perverted believers by advocating false doctrine. So Christian heretic ranks, outside Iberia and Catholic Europe, were numerous, including all Protestant, Eastern Orthodox, Nestorian, and Coptic believers. *Unbaptized* Jews, Muslims, and all non-Christians—collectively the majority of the world's population—were, according to Renaissance Catholic teaching, *infidel* (without true faith), thus beyond the Inquisition's remit. Institutionally the Spanish Inquisition was the creature of the monarchy, which administered the apparatus and punishments, although guided in doctrinal matters by the clergy. Rome never unqualifiedly accepted this hybrid structure that encroached on papal authority. For its part the Church recognized the inquisitor generals as the chief officials responsible for directing tribunals under the Spanish crown.[65]

Between 1478 and 1480, Seville's Sephardic community was the first to be confronted by the Inquisition. Tomás de Torquemada (1420–98)—his name would serve as a synonym for unrelenting dogmatic severity—became the first Inquisitor General in 1483. From then until 1530, some two thousand people, mostly Jews, were burned to death.[66] We know how rabidly this spirit of religious intolerance proceeded in the last decade of the fifteenth century—first claiming Spain, then after 1500 extending to Spanish-ruled Italy (Naples, Sicily, and Sardinia) and the Hispanic Atlantic. Though King Manuel I also outlawed Judaism in 1497, papal permission to institute the Inquisition was not obtained until 1536. In this first Iberian phase, Jews were forced to choose between conversion or expulsion (Spain) or forced baptism or death (Portugal) and faced interrogation (which often included torture) and the auto-da-fé if suspected of Judaizing. If one was found guilty of heresy, punishments included humiliation (as part of reconciliation), confiscation of property, enslavement, or even execution. As Ferdinand and Isabella had done, Manuel I confiscated all Jewish communal property, such as synagogues and religious schools.[67]

It would seem plausible, insofar as motives in dangerous existential circumstances can be reconstructed, that the Sephardim who fled Spain, many to settle in Portugal, were governed by a more rooted piety, or sense of Jewish identity, than those who remained and converted. Still, we must respect complexity: under threatened Inquisitorial violence, the reasons for staying in one's native land and deciding to follow the paths of religious renunciation, adoption of a new religion, or crypto-Jewish submission traced a labyrinth of impulses and ambiguities. Given Portugal's brutally coercive mass baptisms in 1497—with stories of countless Jews being dragged to the baptismal font—crypto-Judaism seemed to develop more cohesively in Portugal than in Spain during the first half of the sixteenth century. This inference has to do with numbers, admittedly still a subject of debate. After 1492 Spain was proclaimed a Jew-free kingdom. As for Portugal after 1497 a very high percentage of its Jewish population—some sixty thousand, comprised equally of Portuguese Sephardim and of displaced Castilian refugees—became nominally Catholic, most often under harsh coercion.[68]

In any case, after visiting trauma on the Sephardim, Manuel I declared a twenty-year period (1498–1518) during which the beliefs of converted Jews could be neither scrutinized nor tested. The state demanded that Portuguese conversos maintain the public façade of Catholic practice—in effect, a measure of compensatory leniency, which allowed the psychology and stratagems of crypto-Jewish behavior to incubate. For many, to the world they were Catholic but in heart and mind, Jewish: this was the way of an internal religious exile struggling to sustain Jewish identity. Forced into the shadows of observance, Iberian crypto-Jews preserved, especially during Manuel I's reign, some elements of their former religion and heritage.[69] Yet under such secrecy and suppression, crypto-Jewish religion gradually segregated from normative Judaism during the first decades of the sixteenth century. Religious ritual was confined either to secret meetings or the sanctum of the home. As time passed and the burning or banning of the Hebrew Bible, the Talmud, and prayer books took their toll, Iberian crypto-Jews were forced to rely on the Vulgate as the only source for understanding their scriptures and historicity—a censorship that let Christian hermeneutics shape what Jews had always venerated as their supreme holy-historical narrative, the Tanakh. In fact it would be oral transmission of traditional belief, practice, and prayer that most often oriented crypto-Jews: in an ironic, wounding deprivation, the typological People of the Book were denied their own book. With the passing of the first generation (1492–c. 1540) of *anusim* ("forced ones" in English transliteration)—these were the pre-Inquisition Jews who had once attended synagogues and affirmed their religion without restriction—oral tradition became ever more important, in effect, a substitute vehicle for rabbi, formal observance, and informed study.[70]

Again we must emphasize that the Catholic monarchs who consolidated the Iberian Inquisition were, to some degree, expressing, not fomenting popular will. This is by no means the same thing as labeling all peninsular Christians of the era rabid zealots.[71] Although not common, widespread violence could erupt unpredictably. On Easter Sunday 1506, after an inflammatory sermon by a Dominican friar, some three thousand New Christians were massacred by Lisbon mobs over several days. In reaction King Manuel I ordered the execution of several Dominican clergy who had presided over the massacre. Whatever ambivalences marked Manuel I's policies toward his persecuted, if commercially valuable, New Christian subjects, it was his son João III (1502–57), nicknamed "the Pious," who promoted anti-Jewish policy to the level of a sanctioned national Inquisition. Pope Paul III named Cardinal Henry, João's brother and successor, the first General Inquisitor of Portugal in 1536. Yet by that date, the Portuguese conversos were sufficiently organized to mount some rearguard opposition to anti-Jewish policy. For instance Gracia Mendes Nasi, whose once-Spanish family, resettled in Lisbon, were the owners of an influential international banking and trading syndicate. She used her wealth to mitigate papal support for Joao's Inquisition, causing a delay in its establishment.[72]

The Inquisition institutionally advanced with Iberian navigators and conquistadors as they crossed oceans, explored islands, and staked imperial claims in the Americas, Africa, and Asia. In 1536 Portugal inaugurated Inquisitorial tribunals in Lisbon, Porto, Coimbra, and Évora; to these cities, only twenty-five years later (1560), would be added the Portuguese Indian colony of Goa. For some four decades, when a crypto-Jew was convicted of heresy in Portugal, the sentence—as distinct from sometimes cruel interrogation—was exile to Brazil, thus, relocating undesirables beyond a distant cordon sanitaire. But in 1581, Philip II of Spain (1527–91) united Spain and Portugal under hegemonic Habsburg sovereignty; this new Iberian ruler of a truly global empire at once made Portugal follow the Spanish policy of denying Jews entry to overseas territories.[73] From the earliest years of post-Columbian exploration, both church and state in Spain recognized that the New World could become a sanctuary for conversos escaping peninsular Inquisitions, thereby providing an opportunity for a return to Judaism. According to the letter of Spanish law, any haven in the Americas—exceptions would emerge through the bribing of Spanish bureaucrats—had to be closed off. Indeed the Alhambra Decree, which predates Columbus's first Caribbean landfall by only six months, forbade Jews entry to all Spanish territories. As Spanish possessions swelled, the Alhambra stricture remained in effect. But royal writ could go only so far: official sanctions meant to protect the Spanish empire from converts or refugees did not stop crypto-Jews from settling in the Americas during the sixteenth century.[74] Once again we must be cautious when assessing crypto-Jewish intentions. Although Inquisitorial persecution, dating from the initial ethnic purge launched by Ferdinand and Isabella (1478), seems the evident, paramount reason for flight, the once-Jews who managed to cross the Atlantic after 1492 must certainly have been economically motivated too. In

Spain New Christians, suspected of heresy and deprecated for their ancestry, were often denied jobs and property, much less social acceptance. In such conditions the financial and existential merged.

Meanwhile the Spanish passion for Inquisition, leaping provinces, coasts, and continents, expanded with magnetic force, as simple chronology reveals. The "Holy Office of the Inquisition" (its unabbreviated title) instituted twelve permanent tribunals in Castile and four in Aragon, which included the Balearic Islands (1488) and Canary Islands (1505).[75] Abroad the Spanish momentum was striking too, beginning with tribunal offices opening in Sicily and Sardinia in 1513. Then in 1569–71 Spain brought to its American viceroyalties tribunals—these supplanted various brutal anti-Semitic policies already in place—with offices appearing in Mexico City and Lima. By 1610 Cartageña de las Indias (Colombia) had welcomed the Holy Office. No territory escaped Inquisitorial surveillance, although colonial status and proximity determined jurisdiction. So the distant Spanish Philippines, opened to Europeans by Ferdinand Magellan (1480–1521) in 1521, with Manila designated capital fifty years later, would send its crypto-Jews to Mexico, not Spain, for examination. Similarly the authorities sent those suspected of Judaizing in Brazil and Portugal's African colonies to Lisbon for trial.[76]

An auto-da-fé—here we see the burning of a converso at the stake—was a common Inquisitorial public execution for anyone found guilty of Judaizing. Artist unknown. William A. Rosenthall Judaica Collection, Special Collections, College of Charleston Library.

Auto-da-fé ("act of faith"), the most notorious and storied Inquisition punishment, was not common practice. In the Inquisitorial lexicon, to Judaize was to maintain, adopt, or promote Jewish religious beliefs under the pretext of being Catholic—a grave sin, destructive spiritually and socially, punishable by death. Yet in the event, burning a heretic to death before a community of believers ("auto publico")—as distinct from more private execution before specified witnesses ("auto particular")—was restricted to the most dangerous, unrepentant conversos—Judaizers anathematized as *repeat* offenders. While figures have long been debated, those burned likely amounted to 3 percent of the 49,092 accused Judaizers between 1540 and 1700.[77] As for the two decades after 1478, often regarded as the Jacobin phase of Torquemada's excess, figures remain less certain, but recent scholarship tends to place victims of auto-da-fé in the hundreds, with total victims reaching perhaps several thousand— not at all the much higher numbers once accepted.[78] Most charged Judaizers were eventually "reconciled" after interrogation, submission, and discipline, and they reaffirmed Church doctrine. Only the incorrigible—these included deliberate martyrs to Judaism—and a minority made to be an example of were executed, generally at the hand of state rather than clerical functionaries. But statistically—recall Lisbon in 1506—conversos were likelier to die from anti–New Christian mob violence, provoked by the Inquisition's hate rhetoric, than from purgative flames. First-time offenders were punished in various ways: confiscation of property or possessions, compulsory wearing of the *sambenito* (a penitential garment), banishment, imprisonment, or forced labor (such as rowing in royal galleys). Often enough cases were judged in absentia; if an accused person escaped before investigation or trial, he or she was condemned and burned in effigy. In the event of death of the accused before trial—even if a span of many years separated the two events—the guilty corpse was exhumed and burned as a punishment to the deceased's soul. The Inquisition would also confiscate the property of the deceased from the heirs. In this turgid environment, with evidence compromised and perverted by zeal or malice, prosecutorial confusion and false judgments were rife. Especially in the early decades of the Inquisition, tribunals failed to identify insincere converts to Catholicism, mistook crypto-Muslims (Moriscos) for Jews, and even labeled long-time Catholics as heretics. At the same time, many crypto-Jews managed to confound the authorities and flee Iberia and their overseas territories.[79]

When Philip II gained the Portuguese throne in 1580, thus combining the two crowns, the great expanse of the Spanish empire was opened to all Portuguese subjects, not least conversos. These, as we have seen, had been forced not only to relinquish Judaism but also, by the 1497 diktat of Manuel I, to remain legally bound to Portugal in peninsular confinement. This restriction was sustained under Joao III, who on 14 June 1532, issued a law, often broken, forbidding conversos to leave his kingdom. But suddenly, given Philip II's new

Habsburg dispensation, after eight decades of harassment, conversos could legally cross Portuguese borders—a freedom of movement they embraced vigorously. Wherever opportunity or escape from repression beckoned, the moment was seized. After 1580 large were the numbers of conversos who left Portugal —first, for Spain and the Habsburg Netherlands, then for the Americas— that, between the late sixteenth and eighteenth centuries, the Atlantic World attached a new connotation to the name "Portuguese": it would serve as a near-synonym for New Christians of Jewish ancestry.[80] Yet this increased mobility should not be confused with a lessening of Inquisitorial rigor. That manifestly worsened during the sixteenth century. But the anti–New Christian animus of the Portuguese Inquisition, at pains to root out conversos from an authentic Old Christian population, only kept crypto-Judaism alive.[81]

One hundred years into the Iberian Inquisition declared first by Ferdinand and Isabella in 1478, dialectic had been set in motion. Mounting oppression fomented steady opposition and evasion, which were variegated and, of course, sub rosa. Whether Spain, Portugal, or their widespread imperial possessions, many New Christians replied to the thesis of the Inquisition with the antithesis of crypto-Judaism. For those who wanted to retain Jewish awareness, this counterstatement—however challenged without or diluted and internalized within—sustained Jewish customs, social connection, and antiassimilationist consciousness. During the sixteenth and seventeenth centuries, crypto-Judaism matured in response to an Inquisition policy that regarded converts with fanatic suspicion. A theologically perverse suspicion at that: after all, converts should represent, in the logic of Inquisition, a triumph of Catholic faith—souls saved from error and heresy by the vigilant Church in full partnership with a pious state. But converts of Jewish origin, whether in Madrid, Naples, Mexico City, Lima, Lisbon, Salvador da Bahia, Goa, or Manila, were for the most part seen by the Iberian Inquisitions as false or failed Christians likely to suborn true believers. It was as if the relatively small, suppressed convert minority were poised to corrupt the overwhelmingly majoritarian, immemorial body of the Church. Paradoxically enough it was this mistrustful, anti–New Christian intolerance that ensured the survival of crypto-Jewish culture. As long as New Christians were doubted and hunted, crypto-Jews, their identity under assault, persisted.

An institution as pervasive and lasting as the Iberian Inquisition relied on certain ideological premises. Perhaps the most radical—or the most proleptically destructive, given the racist decimation that would soon befall many New World native peoples and, centuries later, European Jewry—concerned *limpieza de sangre,* "purity of blood" in Spanish (or *limpeza de sangre* in Portuguese). The Castilian experience is particularly significant here. Before the expulsion of 1492, this nomenclature referred to actual religious, sectarian conditions.[82] But as anti-Semitic fervor increased, a Jew who converted to Catholicism was understood to pass along residual "Jewishness" to his or her descendants as an inherited characteristic. This idea of biological/inheritable transmission was critical and came to assume priority over religious belief as such: however sincerely Catholic doctrine was accepted, a Jewish convert was flawed genealogically (for us, genetically), and as a consequence, religiously and socially corrupt. Moreover stigma attached ubiquitously, extending to even the most devout converts, those who entered the priesthood. They too would soon enough be doubted, then ostracized or punished as secret Judaizers. So ideological categories cognate with the Inquisition combined over time: biologism (bloodlines determine social value), religious puritanism (Catholic orthodoxy must defeat heresy), and national exceptionalism (Spain and Portugal epitomize virtue, honor, and valor) became the dominant formulas of an Iberian culture fixated on genealogical prestige.[83] Within the peninsula, the "impure" comprised Semites, converts from Judaism and Islam, then all their progeny and descendants. Outside Europe, as the Iberian empires grew during the sixteenth and seventeenth centuries, all non-Caucasian peoples—Native Americans, Africans, subcontinental Indians—were seen as carriers of more or less dangerous impurity.

Although elements of such racialism can be traced to the Reconquista of medieval Castile, one of the earliest formal legislative acts specifying blood purity emerged during Toledo's anti-converso riots in 1449, when New Christians and their children were denied any official position. The papacy deplored such policies, but the Toledo law itself, soon to be revoked with the restoration of royal authority, still marked the irreducible otherness and social threat posed by Jewish (later Muslim) converts to Catholicism. By 1492 genealogy and religious identity were the key descriptors of otherness: Jews who converted were innately suspect, negating the possibility of embracing Catholicism sincerely—though some did. So the Alhambra Decree, instrument of royal policy as it was, also represents Spain's mature communal rejection of a biological group.

After the Alhambra Decree came the deluge. The Laws of the Indies, which make up the corpus of Spanish decrees laws dating from c. 1513 and governing the entire Spanish Empire, repeatedly banned conversos and their descendants from settling in the Americas.[84] But let us not forget the camouflage religious intolerance gave to socioeconomic competition: a driving motive of limpieza de sangre statutes was to contain the aspirations of New Christian merchants or government servants. If professional work and even intermarriage with aristocrats had been increasingly closed to Jews before 1478, sincere converts to Christianity were free to (and did) pursue upward mobility. This was deplored, while the animus against crypto-Jews usurping positions from longtime Christians soon became harsh and widespread. Whether through law or custom, limpieza de sangre, by securely attesting to Old Christian lineage, conveniently expunged rivalry from graspingly impure heretics. After 1492 many Spanish social groups, whether religious, military, or mercantile (such as guilds), adopted limpieza de sangre regulations. In response conversos bribed relevant authorities to overlook purity stipulations or, more elaborately, produced forged documents demonstrating an Old Christian family history.[85] Although conceived to label peninsular conversos, limpieza de sangre protocols had a broader application in the Americas. The blood purity doctrine imposed an elaborate racial system of multiple, apartheid-like articulations purporting to classify the "non-Hispanics" of the Spanish Empire. Three such coinages are still familiar in English: *mestizo* refers to a person of equally Spanish and Native American parentage; *mulatto* to someone whose parents are Spanish and African; and *zambo,* who is one that has European, African, and Native American ancestry. Inspiring this nomenclature was a profoundly racist, imperialist bias assigning social value according to a person's percentage of European, preferably Spanish, blood.

Conversos Outside the Peninsula

How did conversos fare when they left Iberia? Let us look at a prominent convert family whose patriarch, Luis Carvajal y de la Cueva (c. 1540–95), was born in Portugal, moved to Spain, worked as a royal accountant in the Cape Verde slave trade, then, in 1568, sailed to Mexico (New Spain) as admiral of the Spanish Indies fleet.[86] There he became a scourge of Native Americans, a road builder, sometime slave trader, and developer of mines. Back in Spain (1579), Carvajal received Philip II's joint appointment as governor and captain-general of the new Spanish American province of *Nuevo Reyno de León,* now the state of Nuevo Leon in northeastern Mexico. His writ directed him not only to colonize extensively but also to pacify and catholicize the recalcitrant indigenous population. In this instance, pragmatically enough, the Spanish royal council chose to emend blood purity laws, thus authorizing Carvajal's recruitment of conversos for his difficult mission to an unknown portion of New Spain.

Returning to Mexico in 1580, Carvajal named his first settlement San Luis Rey de Francia. It would in time become Monterrey, modern Mexico's third largest city. But in the late sixteenth century, Nuevo Leon figured as a distant destination for converso immigrants, many of whom were Carvajal's relatives, friends, or contacts. They included sincere Christians as well as crypto-Jews. Whatever the religious affiliation, the quasi-conquistadorial, quasi-familial contingent led by Carvajal was presumably united in seeking wealth and security normally denied conversos. By 1589, embroiled in a territorial dispute with the Viceroy of New Spain, Álvaro Manrique de Zúñiga, first Marqués de Villamanrique (r. 1585–90); Carvajal was seized and imprisoned in Mexico City. There he also faced dubious Inquisition charges of Judaizing. Although cleared of personal heresy, Carvajal died in prison for having concealed his Judaizing relatives. But for all his Machiavellian virtù and his lack of sympathy for crypto-Jews preserving their ancestral faith, he implicated his sister's family only after torture. Eventually that sister, Francisca Nunez de Carvajal, then her four children, were burned at the stake in Mexico City (1596). Given Carvajal's acquisitive tendencies—well suited to any conquistador—his propensity for illegal slave trading in Mexico, yet his consistently Catholic practice, it is hard not to see this adventurer as an opportunist of Jewish descent who long prevailed, but ultimately succumbed, in a dangerously anti-converso environment.[87]

His well-known nephew, heir, and namesake, Luis Carvajal the Younger (1567–96)—whom we shall call Luis here—presents a striking comparison with his uncle. Born in Benavente, Portugal, educated by Jesuits in Latin and rhetoric, Luis was the author of a vivid memoir and letters. He was also the subject of various Inquisition documents recording his interrogation, trial, and death.[88] In fact Luis's memoir, which relates his spiritual, intellectual, and social journey to become an observant secret Jew, stands as one of the most detailed, cogent descriptions of crypto-Jewish experience written in the sixteenth-century Atlantic World. The fate of the Carvajal clan at the hands of the Inquisition sounded a tocsin in San Luis Rey de Francia. If such prominent conversos could be exposed, survival, leave aside socioeconomic opportunity, for other crypto-Jews seemed unlikely.[89] Whether elsewhere in Mexico or the Americas, converts would seek out settlement where the Inquisition apparatus was less avid.

One revealing fact documented about Luis is the important role played by his sister Francisca, and, more generally, by the Carvajal women. Similarly recourse to women for practical support or religious instruction can be seen in the experience of other crypto-Jewish leaders whose lives were marred or ended by the Inquisition (hence noted in tribunal documents of the era). So Tomás Treviño de Sobremonte (1592–1649), who by the time of his execution was regarded as the leader within Mexican crypto-Jewry, was burned in Mexico City during the largest single auto-da-fé held in the Americas. He had learned Jewish ritual from his mother, Leonor Martínez de Villagómez, and, later, from his wife, María Gómez. In fact there was a gender role reversal in the Spanish-Portuguese converso orbit: here women, not men, were central to sustaining observance and precept. Prior to Iberian expulsions and forced conversion, it was men, forgers and beneficiaries of Judaism, who had been foremost in normative religious practice, rabbinic councils, and organized study. Not so for many crypto-Jewish communities in the Atlantic World, when institutional religious structures were dismantled and formal cultural transmission disrupted. In this time of shadow observance, it was women who added to their "natural" familial focus a piety, commitment, and sense of tradition that became a bulwark in difficult exilic circumstances.[90]

From 1500 until 1800, thousands of conversos managed to escape Spanish and Portuguese rule for tolerance elsewhere. Depending on the haven, there were often enough wealthy Sephardic facilitators poised to help individuals, families, or groups of conversos seeking new homes. This kind of assistance, however, predicated a declaration of religious liberation upon resettlement— the discarding of secrecy by conversos and their public assertion of Jewish identity and practice. And just who were the facilitators? We have already mentioned the wealthy Mendes-Nasi banking syndicate with operations covering, at one time or another, Portugal, England, France, the Lowlands, Venice, and the Ottoman Empire. Unsurprisingly, as the Inquisition took hold in Portugal after 1536, members of this powerful, largely crypto-Jewish clan fled Lisbon for Antwerp, Venice, and ultimately Istanbul.

Born *conversa,* inheritor of the commanding Mendes commercial fortune, Dona Gracia Mendes Nasi (1510–69) was a Renaissance grandee, a gifted financier who developed into a notable defender of oppressed Jews. She worked tirelessly. By 1558 Dona Gracia had persuaded Sultan Suleiman I (1494–1566) to let her establish a colony of Iberian Jews near the Sea of Galilee at Tiberias. While this community did not prosper as hoped, it would eventually become (c. 1780) a haven for Polish-Lithuanian Ashkenazim, who then created a center of Jewish learning. The Tiberias project was largely managed by one of the diplomatic and commercial magnates of his time, Spanish-born converso Don Joseph Nasi (1524–79).[91] He was the paternal nephew of Dona Gracia and husband of her daughter, Reyna. Fleeing the Inquisition, Nasi achieved influence in temporary havens (Antwerp, France, Venice), before arriving in Istanbul to join his aunt (c. 1554). There Nasi, with his wide, often personal knowledge of European royalty and financial affairs, became the powerful ministerial advisor of two Sultans, Suleiman I and his son Selim II (1524–74). Among many foreign policy ventures, Nasi's war policy against the Venetian Republic gained Cyprus for the Ottomans (1570), while Nasi, quite openly Jewish in the Sultan's court, also won commercial trading rights with Poland. Striking back at the Iberian Inquisition that had hounded his family and so many Jews across the Mediterranean, Nasi successfully urged William of Orange to lead the Dutch in revolt against Spain, a constant Ottoman enemy. Unsurprisingly the Sultans favored this accomplished strategist with rewards and titles: Nasi was named Lord of Tiberias, Count Andros, and Duke of Naxos and the Seven Islands.[92]

"Out of the crooked timber of humanity," Kant observed, "no straight thing was ever made." He could well have been remarking the enmeshed relationship between Iberian Jews and the oppressors who expelled them. One might suppose that only hostility or disdain could mark such antagonists. Not so. Some Sephardim, whether converts or openly practicing Jewish émigrés, had associations with Christians from the peninsula; nor did Spanish and Portuguese Catholics boycott all Jews who left Iberia. Kant's maxim must cover a multitude of motives.

There is the extraordinary instance of two brothers, Jacob Curiel (born Lopo Ramirez, 1594–1666), and David Curiel (born Duarte Nunes da Costa,

1585–1664), who at different moments in their exilic careers served both Spanish and Portuguese interests.[93] For instance David Curiel, influential within
Amsterdam's wealthy Jewish mercantile community, helping the Portuguese
ambassador negotiate a contract for Dutch weaponry, siege equipment, and
naval supplies that would arm Portuguese king João IV (1603–56) in his war
for independence (1640–68) from the Spain of Philip IV. Yet this allegiance
did not stop David Curiel from later becoming the chief agent of the Spanish Crown in the late 1640s.[94] In turn, Jacob Curiel served as "Agent" of
the Portuguese Crown in Hamburg (1641), while both he and his son Moses advanced Portugal's commercial interests in the Netherlands as well as
in Hamburg. They were rewarded by João IV with the title Cavaleiro fidalgo
da casa real, Knight of the Royal Household. Although outwardly Jewish and
for the most part based in the Netherlands, the Curiel family clung to a Portuguese identity. For instance Moses Curiel claimed to be "a good Portuguese
and faithful servant of His Majesty," João IV.[95] Ambiguities abounded. These
were the very Curiels who fled Portugal after their Judaizing was detected
in 1609 by the Lisbon and Coimbra Inquisitorial tribunals. Efforts on behalf
of Portuguese independence, whether mounted by Sephardic emigrants like
the Curiels or crypto-Jews in Portugal, were evident to the Roman Catholic
Church, not least to Portuguese clergy. If resentment of religiously inspired
Luso-Hispanic persecution seemed the "natural" response of oppressed Jewry,
the actual record is more complex. In fact the intrapeninsular war pitting Portugal against Spain (as well as Catalonia and their failed revolt, 1640–52) also
affected their colonies, dividing New Christian and crypto-Jewish communities along *Luso-Hispanic* nationalistic lines. Such loyalties one might have
supposed atavistic, nostalgic, or passé—the very stuff of crooked timber.[96]

More focused was Antonio Vieira (1608–97), a Jesuit priest, eminent orator
and writer, as well as a capable diplomat. At the age of seven, he left Lisbon to
settle in Brazil with his parents. By 1640 Vieira, who ardently supported both
João IV's war against Spain and against Portuguese (as opposed to imperial
rival Dutch) sovereignty for Brazil, was named a royal preacher. After 1647,
on diplomatic missions to England, France and the Netherlands, he adopted
an Atlanticist perspective on Portuguese New Christians: many formerly or
crypto-Jewish merchants not only sided with João IV but also brought financial expertise to Portuguese trade everywhere. So Vieira became one of the
first ecclesiastic figures of his day—never a majority—who called for reformation of cruel Inquisition procedure and an end to the distinction between Old
and New Christians, and who guaranteed security for non-Portuguese Jewish
traders. They were to be particularly protected from any seizure of shares in
the young Brazil Company at the Inquisition's command. Yet Vieira was not
philo-Semitic as such.[97] He believed, as did many clergy, in millenarian apocalyptic prophecy: the conversion of the Jews was a requisite sign of the Second Coming. Because the Inquisitor's tribunals had failed in persuading Jews

to surrender their faith willingly, Vieira argued, less brutal measures seemed pragmatic commercially and fitting for a people who would bring Revelations to pass. Such reasoning deeply offended the Inquisition, which imprisoned him. But within a year, the eloquent Jesuit was released on condition that he cease writing and preaching. Eventually Vieira was chosen as a favorite papal preacher in Rome. Later still he became the author of a Vatican investigative report that led to the suspension of the Portuguese Inquisition, his longtime adversary, for five years (1676–81).[98]

The end of Portugal's Inquisition was protracted. On the level of ideas, it was the European Enlightenment that brought on the final decline, dissolving Lisbon's embrace of religious passion, institutional racism, and political opportunism. Ultimately reason and reform would overcome bias, and not simply as a matter of abstract ideological preference. In 1768 King José I (1714–77) ordered the elimination of lists naming Portuguese New Christians. Here we see the hand of the Sebastião José de Carvalho e Melo, first Marquess of Pombal (1669–1782), de facto prime minister and one of the great reforming figures in Portuguese history, who effectively set government policy for over two decades after the Lisbon earthquake in 1755.[99] However enthusiastically he accepted Enlightenment ideas—and Pombal's friendship with contemporary reformers would suggest a marked intellectual proclivity—his argument for persuading the king to suppress anti–New Christian blood purity laws in Portugal, not to mention autos-da-fé, was fully in accord with Antonio Vieira's earlier conclusion: the conversos who had fled to the Ottoman Empire, the Netherlands, England, or their American colonies had enriched their economies. These exiles were much needed in a Portuguese economy grown dependent on Brazilian colonial imports, lacking mercantile exchange skills, and in danger of stagnation. So Pombal arranged for a second royal decree in 1773 that made the distinction between New and Old Christians illegal. In the following year, he stopped the Inquisition's longstanding practice of seizing property based on the confession of a convicted party—tantamount to disallowing confiscation through torture, so frequently used in Inquisitorial process.

But at the end, for both Spain and Portugal, the Inquisitors' powers could not survive a cultural imperative guided by Rousseau and Hume, or Diderot and Locke. Nor could the peninsula's Catholic empires escape the maelstrom unleashed in 1789, when France's bourgeoisie, peasantry, and urban population casted off the seignurial triumvirate of monarchy, nobility, and Church. Across the Atlantic, similar Enlightenment arguments, but under different material and social conditions, had just created the new American republic. It is this age of revolution, aflame in both Europe and the Americas, that would bury, figuratively and literally, the Inquisitions that had oppressed Jews for some three hundred years.

Already by the late eighteenth century, Spanish and Portuguese port officials had begun looking the other way when Jewish merchants arrived to trade in New World venues far removed from Lisbon and Madrid.[100] When France invaded Portugal (1807) and Spain (1808), Napoleon, a very different kind of emperor, espousing the religion of reason rather than the dogmas of the Iberian clergy, quickly abolished the Inquisition in both countries. But Bonaparte's diktat, while prescient, did not quite survive Waterloo. It would be 1821 when Portugal's King João VI declared the end of the Inquisition in his lands. The situation in Spain was entwined with the larger struggle between modernizing and conservative forces after the fall of Napoleon. Ferdinand VII (1784–1833) reclaimed the throne in 1814 and reinstated the Holy Office, only to suspend it during an interlude of Liberal administration (1820–23). The last documented victim of Inquisitorial tribunals was accused of neither Judaizing nor Islamasizing but was a Valencian schoolteacher hanged in 1826 for heretical deism. After Ferdinand died, his far more liberal widow and regent, Maria Christina, formally abolished the Inquisition by decree in 1834. As for the Spanish Americas, abolition of the Holy Office followed the flags of the new states that waged their victorious revolutionary wars of independence against the colonial ancien regime during the first quarter of the nineteenth century. The Inquisitors' dispensation gave way to liberators like the great Simon Bolivar, Miguel Hidalgo, and José María Morelos. The structure of intolerance that evolved from religious fervor and royalist realpolitik in Renaissance Castile gained power as a menacing clerical-state apparatus with tentacles throughout the peninsula and vast ranges of the Americas, then finally sputtered to death—far away from the Iberian sun.

The Sephardic and Converso Diaspora in Prerevolutiony France and the French Empire

And what of the European country whose *philosophes* and revolutionaries had done so much, directly and indirectly, to defeat the peninsular Holy Office? How, we may ask, did Jews fare in France itself? Evidently Iberia's special interaction of national unification, supremacist religious policy, and institutional racism did not replicate north of the Pyrenees. This in no way means that the medieval French encouraged tolerance of Jews. In many respects the kingdom and duchies of what became modern France were profoundly, bloodily anti-Semitic: since 1182 there been serial deportations of Jews ordered by French monarchs. It was however the comprehensive expulsion declared by Charles VI (1368–1422) in 1394 that would set the terms for those Jews who entered France in flight from the peninsular Inquisition. Sincerely or not, Sephardic émigrés had to present themselves as practicing Catholics, and in the early decades of the sixteenth century, many of these New Christian or "Portuguese merchants" resettled in southern France.[101] In 1550 Henry II (1519–59) let Iberian New Christians settle in Bordeaux. He wanted to stimulate an Aquitaine economy still relatively depressed a century after the end of the Hundred Years' War. Similarly and gradually, during the second half of the sixteenth century, Jews were allowed into the southwestern region extending from Bayonne, at the intersection of Gascony, Guyenne, and the Basque country.[102]

Rarely could Jews in France of this period manage to abandon their New Christian façade. But so it was with the distinguished doctor Eliau Montalto (d. 1616), who in 1612 accepted the invitation of Queen-Regent Marie de Medici (1575–1642) to serve as court physician. Born in Portugal, a graduate of the University of Salamanca, Montalto had lectured at the University of Pisa before moving to Venice, then Livorno (Leghorn). Granted a papal dispensation at the French queen's urging, Montalto and his Jewish assistants were able to practice their religion openly—although synagogue worship was beyond the pale. Among this favored Montalto circle was Saul Levi Morteira, whom we have already encountered, the future chief rabbi of the Sephardic community in Amsterdam.[103]

At end of the Thirty Years' War (1618–48), France gained the provinces of Alsace and Lorraine and with them a considerable Rhineland-based Ashkenazic population. In an increasingly familiar process, the Crown, on assessing Jewish businesses as economic assets, chose to let the Ashkenazim remain, a legitimization that only spread during the age of Louis XIV (1638–1715). By 1720 Sephardim from Bordeaux and Avignon, already socially and culturally preferred to Ashkenazim, qualified for the next stage of assimilative approval—permission to settle in Paris, that lodestar from which Jews had been banished since 1394.[104]

As a matter of documentary evidence, the first references to Iberian exiles in France as Jews—with no New Christian veneer—date from 1723 in letters patent from Louis XV (1710–74) that renewed their privileges to reside in Guyenne.[105] But Enlightenment thought, however powerfully it catalyzed Parisian salons or other liberal European cadres, did not instantly win tolerance for French Jewry. For example between 1675 and the end of the eighteenth century Jews in Bordeaux, while sometimes allowed by authorities to reveal their religious affiliation, French Jews still worshipped in small, inconspicuous buildings. These were very much like the concealed Jewish-schuilkerken used in the Netherlands. So French Jews would become subjects, later citizens, of a sort: not until 1812, two decades after the Declaration of the Rights of Man and the ideological gales of revolution, did the Sephardim of Bordeaux confidently build themselves a nonclandestine synagogue.[106]

Let the architectural record chronicle the slow evolution of acceptance. In 1741 the first new synagogue on the French mainland was constructed, after a lapse of almost 350 years, in Carpentras. Conceived in Rococo by its talented architect Antoine d'Allemand (1679–1760), this building was erected on the very site of a synagogue dating from 1367. Because Carpentras belonged to the pontifical state of Avignon and was ruled by the papacy rather than the monarchy, the ancient synagogue had been preserved throughout the long epoch of Jewish exile. If we are precise, the Bourbon kingdom would wait until 1782 before Louis XVI (1754–93) approved a synagogue: it was designed by Charles Augustin Piroux (1749–1805) for the Jews of Luneville, Lorraine. There were various clandestine Alsatian synagogues, much of a kind with the schuilkerken of the Lowlands.[107]

There can be no doubt that the condition of French Jewry became entwined with the great Revolution, its effects reverberating far beyond the generation of Danton, the Convention, Thermidor, Napoleon, and Restoration —and, it must be said, affecting European polities irrespective of religious identity. Here we can only summarize. Although first legally emancipated by the National Assembly on 27 September 1791—a first in western European history—French Jews would respond to cycles of liberation and reimposed restrictions during the four decades of Republic, Empire, and Restoration. By 1840, although anti-Semitism would hardly disappear, neither would national acceptance ever return to the harsh mores of the ancien regime. France moved into a world of Jewish political emancipation, social upward mobility, financial security, and remarkable cultural achievement.

As the French began to carve their own Atlantic World empire, Jews figured only slightly. The discoverer Jacques Cartier, sailing from St. Malo in 1534, was the first European to chart Newfoundland and the Gulf of St. Lawrence. The vastness of Canada, which the Bourbons named New France, was declared forbidden ground to non-Catholics through a 1627 proclamation by Cardinal Richelieu (1585–1642), Louis XIII's (1601–43) chief minister. This exclusion targeted Huguenots, not Jews, whose contacts with French North America during the seventeenth and early eighteenth centuries remained limited.[108]

In 1643 the French made their first attempt to colonize Cayenne, the coastal capital of what today is French Guyana, but after only a few years abandoned the project. The territory in 1656 was taken by the Dutch, who opened colonization to Sephardim arriving from the Netherlands and Leghorn in the adjacent settlement of Remire. A Torah scroll was also given by Amsterdam's Jews in 1659 for use in the colony. By 1660 Cayenne's Dutch Jews had built a synagogue in nearby Remire. In 1664 the colony passed once again to France, but on this occasion, as stipulated in the capitulation agreement (signed by Alexandre Prouville de Tracy [c. 1600–70], representative for Louis XIV), that all remaining Jews could freely practice their religion.[109] Thus these Jews in French South America were officially recognized and civically enabled, with no need to pose as Catholics, fifty-nine years (1723) before their coreligious in Bordeaux and Bayonne. Arguably coexistence with Jews came to the French more readily abroad than at home—perhaps due to socioeconomic necessity. In 1667 Remire's synagogue was destroyed when the English, fighting a Dutch-French alliance, sacked the colony in the Second Anglo-Dutch War. Elsewhere among the small Jewish communities in the colonies of the French Caribbean—in Martinique, Guadeloupe, and St. Domingue—as there were no official synagogues, religious worship was most likely conducted secretly.[110]

By introducing sugarcane and cacao production to the French West Indies, Jewish planters and merchants made their economic presence felt. This was in large part due to the financially gifted Jean-Baptiste Colbert (1619–83), who in 1671 encouraged the legalization of specific, capable Jewish merchants. But soon after, and applicable to all French colonies, Louis XIV's Code Noir (1685) not only set comprehensive guidelines for African slavery but also expelled Huguenots and Jews from all overseas possessions. Later that year the Edict of Fontainebleau (which revoked the Edict of Nantes, 1598) created a diaspora of Huguenots in the Protestant Atlantic World due to their expulsion. Catholicism became the one sanctioned religion for both France and her empire. Wherever Jews were tolerated in the Dutch and English empires, Huguenots were also found, creating their own parallel socio-economic familial network. However, in the eighteenth century, a few Jews did trickle back to the French West Indies, doing so under an officialdom that chose to ignore the code's Jew-free strictures, such as in St. Domingue (Haiti) and Louisiana.[111]

In French Louisiana we find the Monsantos, a crypto-Jewish family. But only six years after France ceded Louisiana to Spain at the end of the French and Indian War (1763), the colony's Spanish governor Alejandro O'Reilly ordered the small number of Jews in New Orleans to leave. The merchant Isaac Monsanto, on protesting such treatment, received this reply from O'Reilly: the "departure which I require of you and your entire family is specifically a consequence of an order of the King which expressly forbids all Jews from residing in this state."[112] So Ferdinand and Isabella's 1492 expulsion decree, reiterated in Spain's comprehensive Law of the Indies, seemed alive and well in the last decades of eighteenth-century Spanish Louisiana. As for the Monsantos, they went to British West Florida, a territory only recently won from Spain and under a relatively benign Protestant sovereignty and willing to accept Jews. Yet, when Louisiana became American after its purchase in 1803, the Monsanto family shortly after chose to return to New Orleans.[113]

Any large chronicle of immigration provides remarkable instances, and that of Jews arriving in North America before the French Revolution was no exception. Take Abraham Gradis (1695–1780), who was the scion of a great shipping and mercantile firm from Bordeaux with extensive trade in the England, the Netherlands, Canada, and the Caribbean. He focused much of his energy, not to mention great wealth, on promoting with mercantilist vigor France's North American empire. In 1748 the Gradis house formed La Societe du Canada (Canadian Company), a commercial venture sponsored by the Crown. A similar project, La Societe du Louisiana, never succeeded. But this was not simply a matter of colonial profits. In 1752 Gradis personally accompanied a relief fleet carrying food and supplies to Quebec City as the colony starved during one of its frequent crop failures. Hailed as a savior from the port's wharf on the St. Lawrence, Gradis could not leave his ship, not even during unloading, because two laws, decreed in 1627 and 1685, barred Jews from setting foot in Canada. In fact Quebec City would receive seventeen shiploads of Gradis provisions during famine. With the outbreak of the Seven Years' War in Europe (1756), France's strained resources alone could not sufficiently supply Canada. Into this breach stepped *le maison* Gradis. It effectively became the major—at times the only—conduit of food, munitions, and supplies to all of New France during the war. In 1779, recognizing such loyalty, generosity, and service to the state, King Louis XVI granted Abraham Gradis and his family full equality with the rights of Catholic citizens. The rest of France's Jews would have to wait until the Republic made its declaration of liberation.[114]

The Jewish and Converso Diaspora in England and the English Empire before 1660

In 1290 Kind Edward I (1239–1307) expelled the Jews from England and Wales, giving them until 1 November to leave. Since 1066, when Jews first came to England with William the Conqueror (1028–87), they had been the king's property and were exploited as a source of revenue generation through tax farming and money lending. It is commonly known that after having financially bled his Jews into poverty through taxation, Edward I had them expelled and confiscated what little they owned. Indeed the number of Jews in the British Isles had been on the decline for years due to persecution, with there being only two thousand on the eve of the edict, in contrast to the tens of thousands affected in Iberia two centuries later.[115] However, the 1290 expulsion must also be understood as part of a broader policy for Edward I since it was not the first for one of his realms. In 1287 the king expelled the Jews from his ducal territory of Gascony as an experiment.[116] Anti-Semitic popular opinion, in Gascony as well as England and Wales, approved of the expulsion edicts, which were fueled by the medieval stereotypes that Jews were unfair usurers and the blood libel. Debts owed to Jews were canceled because of the edicts; however, more importantly, the expulsions gave Edward I political capital to negotiate a new tax on all laymen in the 1290 Parliament— since he had disposed of his Jews for the wishes of the people—which generated a substantially larger income for the king.[117]

As in Spain in 1492, English Jews who converted to Catholicism were permitted to remain. Located in London was a *domus conversorum*, a house and institution for Jews who converted to Christianity, which had been founded by Henry III (1207–72) in 1232. On the eve of the 1290 expulsion there were approximately eighty residents. However, what is more surprising is that following 1356—when the last of the pre-1290 converts died—and c. 1600, is that forty-eight additional converts came to reside there. These former Jews came from continental Europe, including Iberia.[118] Mentions of Jews in English historical records also appear elsewhere. For instance, in 1410, the Italian Jewish physician Elias Sabot was brought to attend to the desperate Henry IV (1367–1413), who had been suffering from chronic illness since 1406.[119] In 1494 Ferdinand and Isabella wrote to Henry VII (1457–1509) asserting that their expulsion decree from two years earlier nullified debts of Spanish subjects owed to Jewish exiles living in England. Somewhat later, during the 1520s, the very musical Henry VIII (1491–1547) invited talented Italians to his court as royal musicians. Among them were conversos originally from the peninsula.[120] Presumably Catherine of Aragon (1485–1536), Henry VIII's first wife, would have enjoyed royal concerts performed by conversos who had fled her homeland.

As for Queen Catherine herself, 1525 marks the start of the crisis brought on by Henry VIII's rejection of his Spanish wife. The dilatory pope Clement VII (1478–1534), utterly controlled by Holy Roman Emperor Charles V (of Spain), would not annul Henry VIII's marriage to Charles's aunt; divorce wrangling extended for the next eight years. As theology and law commingled in this marital quarrel, both the Tudor and Spanish parties sought biblical precedent. Here, oddly, given the otherwise heretical status of Judaism in the eyes of Christianity, rabbinic scholarly authority on Levirate marriage came into play. Oddly indeed: prestigious churchmen from two Jew-free Christian states, Spain and England, sought out Jewish religious opinion in Rome, Bologna, and Venice. Hermeneutically at least, insofar as Christian practice evolved from marital stipulations in Leviticus, Jewish knowledge could be mined for cogent evidence. So the views of senior scholars were consulted, with mixed results. Rabbi Elijah Menachem Halfan favored Henry VIII; Jacob Raphael ben Yehiel Haim Peglione ruled for Catherine.[121] Although only a footnote, subsumed by the *forces majeurs* of Henry VIII's ambitions, desires, and nascent Reformation doctrine, this minor recourse to Jewish scholarship foretells a changed role that Jews would later assume in English Protestant society. Henry VIII's divorce, his marriage to Anne Boleyn, and establishment of an Anglican national church (1533) alienated the great Catholic power of Spain for over fifty years. As we would expect, the struggle between these unequal colonial, naval, and religious rivals would extend beyond European waters to the wider Atlantic World.

During the reign of Mary I (1516–58), when the queen's fervent Catholicism and marriage to Spain's Philip II supported a notorious anti-Protestant campaign at home, peninsular conversos, no strangers to the burning of martyrs, avoided England. But because Elizabeth I (1533–1603), whatever her personal preferences, enforced a pragmatic Anglican compromise, England again attracted Jews posing as Christians. But these New Christians were careful to adopt the posture of Protestants, demonstrating how the Reformation —Luther had posted his theses in 1517—had realigned both England and

Europe in only a few decades. But for their part, the Elizabethans would always live under the pressure of Spanish subversion and a Habsburg effort to reinstate Catholicism (it would gradually become the "Old Faith").

Those Jews or converts who did settle in England were often enough allowed to enter because of specific skills. There is the case of Joachim Gaunse, an Ashkenazi miner from Prague, who came to Cumbria in the early 1580s along with other émigrés invited to improve mining technology. He introduced a more efficient method for smelting copper, an essential metal in making cannon and firearms and thus of significant strategic value—not only as Phillip II assembled his invasion fleets but later when English ships probed and fought for New World territory. In 1584, gamely joining Sir Walter Raleigh's expedition to Roanoke Island (North Carolina)—this was to be England's initiation into North American colonization—Gaunse became the first Jew to be recorded among Englishmen on the new continent. When Sir Francis Drake's fleet passed the colony on its way back England in 1585, following successful raiding in the Caribbean, Gaunse sprang at the opportunity to return back to England. This was fortunate for him since the colony would ultimately fail (c. 1590) and its colonists would be "lost." In 1589 Gaunse moved to Bristol, where, a sometime teacher of Hebrew, he was tried for heresy. Yet he was found innocent, his Judaism regarded as infidel, not heterodox. At this point Gaunse was sent to London for further examination by the Privy Council, but all records disappear: this gifted metallurgist, adventurer, member of the Raleigh cadre, and Bohemian transplant to Elizabethan society becomes a cipher.[122]

Besides Gaunse, Portuguese names are listed as participants in the exploration and colonization of Roanoke. The most notable is Simon Ferdinando, who served as a mariner and ship's pilot for the venture, exploring the inlets along the North Carolina coast. He, like Gaunse, was also fortunate in choosing to return to England, where he took up a career of piracy, preying on Spanish ships.[123] While it cannot be substantiated whether these Portuguese figures at Roanoke had Jewish ancestry or practiced crypto-Judaism, their presence is a testament to how dispersed Iberian expatriate settlement was within the English-speaking world. As time passed, colonies were founded in Barbados (1627) and Surinam (1652) by the English, whose number did include a few crypto-Jews.[124] In 1649 one Solomon Franco, a Dutch Sephardic Jew, tried to settle as a merchant in Boston. The city's leaders, vigorously inhospitable to non-Puritans, sent Franco back to the Netherlands at the Bay Colony's expense.[125] We also find early examples in other colonies, such as Virginia from the 1620s and 1630s, where individuals like Elias Legardo, Joseph Moise, and Rebecca Isaacke had Jewish-sounding names, but information is lacking on their cultural and religious identities.[126]

In England itself the Commonwealth (1649–59) was rebuffed by the Dutch in a briefly floated proposal to merge the two Protestant republics. They were soon to become determined naval, commercial, and imperial opponents, fighting three wars between 1652 and 1678. At Cromwell's bidding, Parliament moved decisively to protect overseas commerce by fortifying the first of its Navigation Acts (1651) with the requirement that all imports from the Americas, Asia, and Africa be carried only by English ships. Here was mercantilism tout court and the instigation of the First Dutch War (1652–54), since the Netherlands, in what has justly been called an embarrassment of riches, dominated Atlantic World—not to mention East Indian—shipping and trade.[127] We have already noted that many Sephardic Jews flourished in the Netherlands, established in Amsterdam, Rotterdam, and The Hague, at the heart of the Dutch international trading system. Their success was forged by bonds—an amalgam of familial, professional, historical, cultural, and linguistic affinities—that brought together members of a much-dispersed postexilic, once-Iberian community. These Jews used financial skills to create a reliable network among coreligionists, relatives, and confidants: they provided credit or capital, made loans, shared business contacts or insider information, often in a sophisticated way. So when England's 1651 Navigation Act threatened the interests of Dutch Jewish merchant houses, not least colonial commerce, their response was promptly to move family members or business associates directly into England itself, in effect domesticating among the English what had been foreign enterprise. While New Christian and crypto-Jewish refugees based in Spanish, Portuguese, and French dominions had to contend with the official hostility of their Catholic rulers, Jews in the Netherlands had been shown considerable tolerance, at least since 1603, when Dutch authorities permitted them to practice their religion in secret like the other allowed dissenting protestant sects. At a deeper level, Dutch Sephardic economic activity in England was made possible by the Commonwealth's increasingly open attitude toward Jews. In 1655 Menasseh ben Israel, a Madeira-born rabbi, teacher of Spinoza, and gifted author who became the first printer and publisher of Jewish texts in Amsterdam, actually met with Oliver Cromwell to promote the full legal readmission of Jews to England and her burgeoning empire.

The Lord Protector was sympathetic, although almost certainly not because of ecumenism or commitment to religious pluralism. His millenarian prophetic inclinations—the conversion of the Jews would precede the Second Coming—were duly reinforced by recognition of how important a role Jewish merchants and planters played in the new Atlantic economy. Thriving Dutch plantations owned or administered by Jews in Brazil and the West Indies offered conspicuous evidence of profit. Already small crypto-Jewish settlers were accepted in English Barbados and Surinam because their mercantile expertise benefited colonial enterprise. On a larger scale, readmission would also allow Cromwell to repay London's converso community for its financial, partisan support of his wars against Catholic enemies.

In seventeenth-century England, Protestantism and millenarianism have long been identified as ideological fellow travelers.[128] Undeniably a zeitgeist manifested itself among Europeans and some who ventured across the Atlantic: not just Protestants, but small groups of Catholics and Jews revealed millennialist tendencies too. So we see seemingly strange companions, both Dominican and Jewish apocalyptic thinkers in this era Judaizing Native Americans as one of Israel's Ten Lost Tribes of neobiblical legend, a status certain Protestant evangelical communities would likewise adopt.[129] At the same time, whether we consider functioning monarchies, Calvinist dictatorships, Habsburg empires, or the cruel wars of religion waged by these entities in England, the Lowlands, or Bohemia, the apocalyptic evangelical imagination generated powerful ideological force. The doctrinal roots of millenarianism, not to mention any subsequent admixture of beliefs, reaches back to antiquity. The widespread acceptance of a mystical chronology announced the end of historical time, and the beginning of divine reign over souls redeemed by a messianic figure. This was Christ for the manifold Protestant denominations located in the British Isles, France, the Netherlands, Switzerland, various German territories of the Holy Roman Empire, and Scandinavia. To many of the pious, following some visionary narrative or another, the Kingdom of God on earth would arrive more or less imminently. But by no means was such a vision marginal or confined to fanatic sects.

Here we have a religious environment that, quite uncharacteristically given earlier repression, began to normalize Jews in the diverse landscape of mid-seventeenth century English Protestantism. Most Christian evangelical narratives described the conversion of the Jews to Christian belief as a necessary condition for the final metahistorical chapters: apocalypse and the end of time. It is in this spirit that, all economic considerations aside, English Protestants began to create a new, more acceptable social space for Jews who so recently had been excluded from the kingdom en masse. Moreover harsh conversion of Jews into New Christians in imitation of Iberian methods did not fit into the larger discourse about religious liberty made possible, though in no way actualized, by the Civil War and the Protectorate. English apocryphal vision foresaw Jews willingly acknowledging Christ as the true Messiah. It would be Christian charity that won allegiance, whether in England or among the native peoples of the Americas—in telling contrast with the Catholic Inquisition's resort to compulsion and cruelty.

At the broadest level, the Reformation launched Protestantism into a new, or at least newly imagined, estimation of the Hebrew Bible. There was a remarkable appropriation of and identification with, the archetype of the Israelites as they fled Egypt and sought Canaan.[130] In the book of Exodus, there was the example of an oppressed but elect people defying alien power, led by Moses after great struggle to achieve spiritual and national liberation, finally reaching the Promised Land. This was exactly the kind of mythopoeisis, theologically elaborated, that inspired radical Protestant groups.[131] They included the Puritans and their coreligious allies in colonial America, all actively identifying with Exodus Israel. Certainly there was no lack of militantly redemptive ideology available to John Winthrop when, en route to the Massachusetts Bay Colony, he spoke in his famous 1630 sermon of a city on hill.[132]

It is worth noting that for Jews themselves, as opposed to their prognostic role in Christian evangelical hermeneutics, messianism and millenarianism have an ancient history.[133] In general traditional Jewish messianism posits that the Messiah will descend from King David and restore both his dynasty as well as the Kingdom of Israel. He—almost never she, female messianic figures were exceptional—will also rebuild the Temple in Jerusalem, gather in the Jewish Diaspora, and reestablish the ancient laws and sacrifices under the guidance of Aaron's descendants, once again designated priests of the Temple. Such beliefs had been advanced by various prophets and played no small part in collective Jewish expectation over three thousand years. What distinguishes rational (Jewish) messianism, as outlined by Maimonides, from so much seventeenth-century Christian apocalyptic thought is the idea of continuance: human civilization and the natural world will remain intact, though infinitely improved, under the Messiah.[134] Given the complex gestation of eschatological ideas over time, millenarianism would take different forms in different places—not least among the Jews and crypto-Jews.

Why should we wonder that many European Jews turned to millenarian thinking during the sixteenth and seventeenth centuries? This visionary consciousness was engendered by an irreducible catastrophe, the Iberian exile with its all too concrete consequences. Unsurprisingly, after the battle for survival itself (Where can I be safe?), it was the existential or spiritual crisis (Am I still a Jew?) that would preoccupy Sephardim. For peninsular Jews salvation from suffering and the hope of a better future permeated their wanderings, whether to the relative safety of European Protestant sanctuaries or across the Atlantic to new Promised lands. It is this peculiar intersection of two different Exodus narratives—for Jews, their flight from Spanish-Portuguese oppression; for Protestants, their assault on Rome's institutional corruption of the faith—that accounts for this unexpected millenarian embrace. Two religious cultures previously alienated from each other found, by way of refracted biblical interpretation, common ground in England and the Netherlands.

In December 1655 it fell to Cromwell, aware of the arguments cogently prepared by the extraordinary Amsterdam rabbi, scholar, and diplomatist Manasseh ben Israel, to call a conference at Whitehall in which the merits of readmitting Jews to England were fractiously debated among clergy, merchants, and politicoreligious factions alike. Cromwell and ben Israel's mutual interest in reopening England and her empire to Jewish settlement stemmed from both economic and religious interests. It was no secret that Jews in the Netherlands had proven themselves economically valuable in the Atlantic World as merchants and sugarcane planters, especially through Dutch ventures in Brazil and the West Indies.[135] Some experimentation abroad was already taking place. In 1654 Jewish settlement swelled on Barbados with refuges from the Portuguese reconquest of Dutch Brazil. Taking advantage of an opportunity to booster its embryonic sugarcane economy, and without London's consent, permission was given by the Barbados Assembly for Jews to settle, stating: "On the petition of several Jews, it is ordered that, behaving themselves civilly and doing nothing to disturb the peace, they shall enjoy the privileges and laws of the Island relating to foreigners and strangers."[136]

With a declaration such as this one may ask how could a colony ignore an edict from the mother country that had been enforced for centuries? What we find is that during the Civil War, colonial Barbados navigated a fine line of neutrality between the Parliamentarians and the Royalists. Refugees from the conflict also sought asylum on the island. Neutrality allowed the colony to maintain a degree of political and economic autonomy, enabling it to admit Jews without consent from London. Trade with Dutch ships and merchants, which included Sephardic Jews, strengthened Barbados's independence.[137] So what was Cromwell's response to the admission of Jews to Barbados? Instead of fighting what was taking place on this wayward colony, the Lord Protector conducted his own experiment of singularly permitting two Jews, Abraham and Raphael de Mercado, to settle on Barbados in April 1655, eight months prior to his decision for the rest of the English Empire.[138]

In the following month of May 1655, English forces dispatched by Cromwell and led by Robert Venables (1613–87) and Admiral Sir William Penn (1621–70), invaded Spanish Jamaica. A number of conversos were already residing on the island. Here we find Captain Campoe Sabbatha and Simon de Caceres, who were Iberian New Christians, and possible even crypto-Jews, assisting the English in their conquest. This paved the way for additional Jewish settlement on the island. Caceres also proposed a plan to Cromwell for an invasion of Chile, though it never materialized.[139] Readmission thus became an opportunity for Cromwell to repay the assistance conversos and Jews provided him in England's conflict with Catholic Spain.[140]

Not long after the Whitehall conference, in early 1656 the Lord Protector decided to let London's heretofore crypto-Jewish community remain, unobtrusively, in England. However qualified, this de facto recognition, by unmasking London's increasingly active Jewish mercantile and financial houses, combined fait accompli with harbinger. No edict or act of Parliament was involved, nor would normalization, over the next forty years, be achieved without serious opposition from rival merchant or anti-Semitic clerical interests. But a threshold had been reached. In 1660 Charles II was restored to the English throne. Opponents of the Jews made several petitions to the king to countermand Cromwell's decision and to enforce Edward I's expulsion edict.

The restored king decided against it as the Jews in Amsterdam had also provided him financial assistance during his exile. Four years later the king granted a formal statement of toleration for England's Jews, thus reaffirming Cromwell's decision.[141] In 1674 Charles II reiterated this permission in another declaration that granted Jewish residents the privilege to assemble for worship. Nonetheless the precarious position of Jews in English society was not resolved until the ascent of King William III (1650–1702) and Queen Mary II (1662–94), when Parliament passed the Toleration Act in 1689, which included Jews as one of several tolerated nonconforming religious groups.[142]

Taking a step back for a moment, we see that the "English question" of to be or not to be with Jews was first experimented by the head of state in an Atlantic possession, beyond the shores of the Isles, for both expulsion (Edward I's edict from 1287 in Gascony) and readmission (Cromwell's test in Barbados, early 1655). While religion played an important role in their expulsion and readmission, it was by no means the only factor. Economic incentive, as well as Renaissance-influenced thinking for readmission also played important roles. As the Enlightenment took hold, Jews would gradually make a home in England and its colonies. Their long banishment had come to an end. There were Jews, including some involved in Atlantic enterprises, who chose conversion to Christianity over preservation of a faith that could still impede a career or elicit disdain. For instance the convert Joseph de la Penha, one of the earliest explorers of the Labrador coast (1697), was granted this territory by William III.[143]

The pain exacted by incremental survival as early modern Europeans dealt with their "Jewish problem" cannot not be understated. Whether in England, the European continent, or new found territories across the Atlantic, seventeenth-century Jews lived precariously. If the first epoch of post-Columbian discovery had unleashed fierce Spanish-Portuguese anti-Semitism and cruelty toward Jews and New Christians, early-Reformation Europe was hardly an incubator of tolerance. Whether under French Bourbon, English Tudor, or Habsburg Holy Roman rule, the antagonism directed at Jews did not go away. In the widespread violence and passion consuming Protestants and Catholics during the epoch of religious wars beginning in the sixteenth century, periodic pogroms or property seizures aimed at Jews—those depressingly familiar events—were of a piece with a bloody, ideologically driven age. If Christians divided by absolutist confessional claims often harmed and tormented each other, what respite awaited a problematic minority of non-Christians? It is no wonder that Jews, who had learned to evade Inquisitors through secrecy, would rely on a lowered public presence in their New World forays.

In any case, given the pressures on crypto-Jews—in Iberian lands, an omnipresent Inquisition actively encouraged spies—meeting together for prayer was fraught with risk. Indeed only a single instance of a crypto-synagogue with some resemblance to the normative Jewish house of worship is recorded. In 1415, as part of a nationwide campaign to win over Jews to Catholicism, the synagogue and its community in the far remote town of Barbastro, Aragon, were converted. Though the synagogue was reconsecrated as the Church of San Salvador, it continued to be used by Barbastro's crypto-Jews until the Inquisition discovered it seventy years later (1485). Near the church altar, Hebrew inscriptions from when the building was an official synagogue were left unmolested on the wall. Behind the altar niche was stashed a Torah scroll. Only conversos were permitted to join the congregation.[144] This crypto-synagogue survived for seven decades with a congregation capable of practicing normative religious ritual because its use predates the 1492 expulsion edict. Jews and conversos knowledgeable in Hebrew were close at hand. On the peninsula after the 1490s, with no trained rabbis, no religiously informed laity, no access to the Hebrew Bible or rabbinic literature, Judaism was reduced to a shadow of what it had been before the Inquisition. Paradoxically Hebrew writing on the walls of former Iberian synagogues was not unheard of, even after the 1490s. For instance the Samuel ha-Levi Abulafia Synagogue in Toledo, reconsecrated the Nuestra Senora del Transito Church, has inscriptions on the walls that survive to today. Most frequently and by perforce, crypto-Jews chose inconspicuous, small, sometimes transient sites for worship, ones that by definition could not supply the religious, ritual, social, or intellectual functions of a synagogue cognate with a secure civil order. Though there are recorded instances of conversos visiting the ruins of former synagogues, as well as those buildings converted into churches and other uses after 1492–98, nevertheless, under the watchful eye of the Inquisition, all that could have taken place (Jewishly) would have been private contemplation or meditation.

We know that as the first generation of converts, the *anusim*, passed away, their learning and awareness of traditional practices waned. This same erosion shaped conversos on their various paths to exile, at first to marginal sanctuaries in the Netherlands, France, and England, then far away to the Spanish and Portuguese Americas. Only rarely did an Iberian crypto-Jew arrive in the Americas with enough formal religious training in Judaism to act as "rabbi" for a community. This was true, however, of Juan Pacheco de Leon (b. 1619), who moved from Spain to Livorno as a boy, received a Jewish education, and then left for New Spain in 1639. There he served the crypto-Jewish community of Mexico City until 1642, when he was caught by the Inquisition and condemned to the royal galleys, after which he disappears from the record. Even though the Inquisition accused de Leon of being a *rabino* (rabbi), no documents confirm earlier ordination in Italy.[145] In fact the harassed, deprived circumstances of Iberian crypto-Jewry did not allow for requisites like fully credentialed rabbis (as had previously been the case) or even for insistence on men as religious leaders. That is why women sometimes figured as heads of secret congregations in this world of duress.[146]

The dearth of archeological evidence itself describes negation. Architecturally the beauty and subtle ritual vocabulary of a mature Sephardic synagogue in relatively tolerant Livorno—first built in 1591—was minimized throughout the Americas to spaces chosen for concealment. Inconspicuousness was all: a modest room in a residence or some other structure served for worship, while ritual objects or symbols would have been well hidden from spies. Almost no physical traces of these furtive religious practitioners remain today. Ironically enough it is only Holy Office records that let us identify former congregations, like those that met in the homes of Simon Vaez de Sevilla and Tomás Treviño de Sobremonte, two crypto-Jews who lived in mid-seventeenth-century Mexico City.[147]

One telling reference to these Iberian crypto-Jewish gathering places comes from the documented reminiscences of Mordecai M. Noah (1785–1851). He refers to the Portuguese youth of his great-grandmother Zipporah Nunes Machado Jacobs (1710–99) before her arrival in Savannah, Georgia: "They had no synagogues or places of public worship, but assembled for devotional purposes in each other's houses, and their prayer books were concealed in the seats of chairs, and opened by springs. It had long been observed that the families never ventured abroad Friday evenings . . . [Notwithstanding] suspicions were awakened as to their real faith, although for form's-sake they all attended mass."[148]

For over three centuries (c. 1500–1800), neither structures nor images of secret meeting places survive.[149] This void resounds. Between the voyages of discovery and the Enlightenment, Sephardic Jewry, with the occasional exception, had declined into pale existential half-life. Especially under Inquisitional surveillance, crypto-Judaism in one or two generations (1492– c. 1550) became essentially a religion of oral tradition, spoken memories, and intangible sociological traits. By reciting biblical narratives and by commenting on customs or practices, crypto-Jews tried to sustain identity through word of mouth. Here we observe methods deployed against cultural suppression: to write or use texts, to create any physical object—such as a synagogue, Torah scroll, or prayer book—was to invite the Inquisition and punishment.

In the Mediterranean basin, we know that certain polities, and notably the Ottoman Empire, allowed Jews to settle. For western Europe during the early seventeenth century, as we are well aware, Jewish peninsular refugees would be admitted by the Dutch and the English only as long as their presence was discreet. Yet during the 1600s, whether in the Netherlands or England—markedly less so in France—Jews were granted freedom of religion demarcated by a narrow, almost domestically restricted space. They could be Jewish within their own homes, or gather to worship in inconspicuous sites, but public display or ritual was unthinkable. These conditions were of a different order than Iberian oppression, but obviously still far from normalization. Remember that these schuilkerk restrictions applied to Catholic and dissident Protestant congregations too. Not only homes, but barns and warehouses served the religious needs of nonconformists. Moreover, unlike the conversos of Spain and Portugal, Jews in the Netherlands and England could use sacred and rabbinic texts, such as the Torah and Talmud, as well as ritual objects like wine cups, prayer shawls, and Sabbath lights. Meaningful improvement then, certainly, but only partially so: the schuilkerk reminds us that Jews still wished to remain invisible to a dominant population that had erupted anti-Semitically elsewhere. The process of self-revelation was gradual. Amsterdam's first publically sanctioned synagogue was not completed until 1639.

Looking at realpolitik, the Protestant societies of the Netherlands and England exerted precisely the naval mastery, bureaucratic organization, and adept capitalist commercial adaptation that challenged, then in large measure supplanted, Spanish-Portuguese supremacy in the New World. At this time, alone among the major Catholic powers to achieve successful Atlantic expansion was France, whose North American colonies east of the Mississippi would gradually be conquered by the British until Canada was ceded in 1763. For Jews this geopolitical shift helped lift the boot of Inquisitorial Catholicism. The mercantile and financial skills that first earned Jews a place among the business communities of Amsterdam and London became only more important as the economy of empire expanded during the seventeenth century. In the event, at the far more general level of the history of ideas, the seventeenth century was Janus-like: religious authority, feudal tradition, and superstition, although still entrenched, were subject to the constant propulsive assault of science, capitalism, and emerging modern philosophy. We do not need to rehearse here how the world of Descartes, Galileo, and Newton prepared the ground for the victory of rationalism. What we know is that the intellectual firmament first constructed by Locke and Spinoza gained full momentum only during the eighteenth century, when the contributions of Hume and Smith, of Kant and Lessing, of Diderot and Rousseau would make the prejudice and maltreatment of Jews appear increasingly inhumane, ossified, and irrational. In the Atlantic World as well as Europe, Enlightenment and the great revolutions would create a better world, one where, for Jews at least, opportunities finally beckoned.

CHAPTER 3

Jews under Protestant Dominion before 1675 Brave New World

During the sixteenth century, as rapid-fire exploration and imperial conquest followed in the wake of Columbus and Cabral, we have seen conversos seek out New Spain, Brazil, and Peru. Hoping to escape the Inquisition's tentacles, these New Christians deliberately pursued lives of obscurity far away from Europe. But we know, too, that, Iberia's ideologically charged antiheretic apparatus quickly appeared in the New World. There a crypto-Jewish existence formed for some and remained a compound of deception and fear, one that replicated in the larger arena of the Americas the menace and danger born in Spain and Portugal.

By contrast Jews fared better in Protestant lands poised on the Atlantic—especially in England, the Netherlands, and their colonial projections into the Americas. It would be Curaçao, Surinam, Jamaica, and Barbados where seventeenth-century Jewry would distinctively enter and participate in the new Atlantic sphere. To this end, Amsterdam's Sephardic leadership organized a labor pool of prospective colonial settlers. They insisted that jobless unmarried men between the ages of twenty and fifty find work in Dutch or English territories rather than rely on the Jewish community's poor relief in Amsterdam.[1] Obviously such a policy added to, and in some instances created, a loose network of Sephardic workers—merchants, traders, planters, journeymen—who often thrived abroad. Relationships among colonial Jews, wherever dispersed across the sphere of Anglo-Dutch enterprise, could only help forge a common Sephardic identity: religious sanctuary and economic advantage joined hands in the Atlantic World.

Before looking more closely at Jews in the Dutch Americas, we should consider the preface—how Sephardim, exiled in the 1490s, found a place in the Lowlands, those countries largely coterminous today with the Netherlands, Belgium, and Luxembourg. Most of the territory that was enclosed by the deltas of the Meuse, Scheldt, and Rhine Rivers had been under Habsburg control since 1482. The entire low-lying land mass constituted the Seventeen

Provinces, which had been Burgundian in the Middle Ages but by 1543 contained a single Habsburg administrative polity. This amalgam was then granted in 1549 to Spain's Charles V, the Holy Roman Emperor. He thus became even more of a world-magnate, ruling not only Spain and the Lowlands, but the central European possessions of the Holy Roman Empire, Naples, Sardinia, and Sicily, not to mention vast areas of two American continents and the Philippines.

Even though Iberian policy promptly required any new Habsburg territory outside of the Holy Roman Empire to become as Jew-free as Iberia, few Jews actually lived in the United Netherlands, as the seven northernmost provinces of the seventeen were designated after 1581. De jure the Holy Roman Emperor's anti-Semitic diktat had technically expanded to cover the Dutch, Flemish, and French-speaking territories; in fact Sephardim were able to move freely from Iberia to the Lowlands, their route often beginning in Portugal as Jews readily crossed the porous interior border between Portugal and Spain, then arrived in Antwerp. This great port city of European economic dynamism in the sixteenth century was the chosen destination of many conversos leaving Iberia.[2] Although living in the midst of the ongoing suppression of Flemish Protestantism through its own Inquisition, the crypto-Jewish community of Antwerp managed to thrive. Conversos, whether sincere converts to Catholicism or poseurs in Catholic camouflage, and quite apart from any valuable skills they might offer, could be normalized by the Habsburg regime. Not so the chief religious targets of the Holy Roman Emperors in the Seventeen Provinces—those large numbers of natives who embraced Calvinism conspicuously and unapologetically. Catholicizing Philip II not only wanted to cleanse his subjects of heresy but also coveted the extraordinary wealth, based on international trade, shipping, banking, and textiles, that concentrated in Antwerp and the Lowlands. In one of the many bloody chapters of Reformation conflict, Dutch and Flemish Protestants would be notoriously brutalized between 1567 and 1573 at the command of Philip II's harsh enforcer, Fernando Álvarez de Toledo, Third Duke of Alva.[3]

Meanwhile Antwerp's conversos, fluent in Spanish and Portuguese, became indispensable agents in the hire of Dutch and Flemish trading houses or port facilities that drew the wealth of the Americas, Africa, Asia, the Baltic, and southern Germany into Habsburg coffers.[4] But Antwerp's fortunes lapsed decisively in 1586 when the masterful Alessandro Farnese, Duke of Parma, won what had been the foremost Atlantic portal for Philip, who thus consolidated Catholic control of the southern Lowlands. This conquest marked an epoch. Most Protestants in Antwerp (roughly 60 percent of the urban population) as well as a large number of conversos moved north to Amsterdam, bringing with them an abundance of intellectual and commercial capital. Besides transferring specific skills, like diamond cutting, to the city, conversos spoke the languages of commerce. This multilingualism—the Jews also learned French and Dutch—became a great asset within the orbit of Spanish-Portuguese foreign trade. Soon enough, the city on the Amstel supplanted the port on the Scheldt; at first redundantly, then at an even more magnificent pitch of achievement throughout the seventeenth century, Amsterdam dominated the Netherland's economic, scientific, cultural, and political life. At the same time, the Netherlands would become a world power whose merchant fleet, navy, and economic vitality greatly outpaced the size of the country's comparatively modest census.

The extended war for Dutch independence from Habsburg rule (1568–1648) would end with the creation of the first Dutch Republic. It was in no small part the arduous, bitter struggle against Iberian religiopolitical absolutism that inclined the Dutch to cultivate, over time, tolerance. Willingness to perceive Jews and adherents of other Christian denominations (Lutherans, Anabaptists, and eventually Catholics) as ethically mature religious communities, even though outside the reformed state church, would become a hallmark of Dutch Protestant civil society. This does not mean that the seventeenth-century republic entirely avoided doctrinal strife among its Calvinists or between its Protestant majority and Catholic minority. Yet at the beginning of the seventeenth century, when England was moving steadily toward religious division and civil war, the Netherlands had already begun to attract religious dissenters and free thinkers from more violent, polarized lands. It is hardly strange that Jews from Iberia and elsewhere sought out the Netherlands.[5]

The first records of conversos arriving in Amsterdam date from 1580. Although outwardly Christian, crypto-Jews, so many of whom had already adopted Catholicism, now took on Protestant camouflage. We must always stipulate that a small percentage converted sincerely. There is not massive documentation to describe this embryonic community. In fact a great deal of what we know derives from diarists and memoirists—writers who recount events, often years later and in changed circumstances, through the mediation of texts intended for family members, friends, and for themselves. The reliability of such accounts is (always and everywhere) qualified by the vagaries of memory—not to mention by subjective bias or unique particularity. But factual inaccuracies do not nullify emotional expressions, reflective insights, and attitudinal inclinations, nor, for that matter, the broader validity of observations whose repetition, recurring among various memoirists, points toward communal experience.[6]

These private and domestic sources show that Amsterdam's original crypto-Jewish community did not know how city leaders would react to an open Jewish presence in the city. They laid low. Twenty years on, by 1600, the crypto-Jews felt more settled, their numbers had grown, and they were confident enough to meet together for private worship. At this juncture the crypto-Jews from Iberia turned to Rabbi Moses Uri ben Joseph Halevi, an Ashkenazi who had moved to Amsterdam from Emden, in German East Frisia. Although Halevi's sermons and lessons had to be translated into Spanish, it was this non-Iberian who first led the ritually and doctrinally lapsed crypto-Jews back to traditional Judaism.

On Yom Kippur of 1603, Amsterdam authorities raided the cloistered worship of the city's crypto-Jews: their secrecy was mistaken for an effort to shield a *Catholic* service, unacceptable in the aroused Protestant environment of the moment. Set right, the city's Dutch Reformed clergy recommended that the Jews be expelled. But soon enough it became apparent that the burgomasters were not Inquisitors. When the Jews protested the proposed expulsion, they pointed out how their financial, commercial, and language skills manifestly benefited Amsterdam's growing economy—an argument that swayed the city guardians. Eventually no less a figure than the humanist and expert jurist Hugo Grotius (1583–1645), despite his faulting Judaism for willful rejection of Christian revelation, became an advocate for the Sephardim.[7] He argued in 1619 that the Jews found in Amsterdam be allowed freedom of public worship, although full civic participation should be somewhat qualified. The city's aldermen concurred: acknowledgement of a legitimate Jewish presence began in Amsterdam with its surrounding province of Holland, then, in short order, spread to other Dutch cities and provinces. In due course civic entitlements would follow. There was even a measure of respect from Protestant scholars—the brilliant linguist and historian Joseph Justus Scaliger (1540–1609)—who believed that rabbinic mastery of biblical Hebrew would help illuminate the study of the Pentateuch. This was regarded in Christendom as the "Old" Testament and its study, elucidated by exact philological knowledge of the ancient text, could only advance theological understanding among Christians. Usually toleration of a minority is a slow affair: as they settled in the Netherlands, Jews were gradually seen to serve purposes beyond the material gains associated with finance and commerce.

As time passed (c. 1620–1700), the Jewish community of Amsterdam would rise to prominence and become by far the most important in the Netherlands —a reflection of the city's economic and cultural dynamism. Their mercantile abilities in demand, Jews would soon settle in Alkmaar (1604), Rotterdam, Haarlam, and The Hague. But the gate was not open everywhere: a few cities like Utrecht and Gouda refused to admit Jews and did so as late as 1712.[8] Moreover there were definite limits to the social acceptance extended to legal Jewish residents. When two Christians converted to Judaism in 1614, Dutch Protestants were mortified: laws were quickly introduced forbidding such unthinkable conversions, not to mention prohibiting sexual relations between Jews and Christians. With mirroring tribal zeal and not a little anxiety—good fences make good neighbors—the Jewish leaders of Amsterdam quickly responded to such separatist legislation by enjoining the Sephardic community to accept similar restrictions.[9]

Still the Netherlands continued to offer feasible sanctuary and economic opportunity to Jews, be they Sephardim or, in increasing numbers that would preponderate by the eighteenth century, Ashkenazim from the Rhineland, Alsace, and Poland. Many stayed permanently; some returned; others moved elsewhere in the Atlantic World.[10] It would be non-Iberian Jews who would migrate throughout the entire Dutch nation, at least wherever they could do so, to rural as well as urban areas. As for the Sephardim, they exchanged Iberian cities for Dutch ones, concentrating in Amsterdam, Amersfoort, Kampen, The Hague, Rotterdam, Middleburg, Maarssen, Nijkerk, and Naarden.[11]

Amsterdam's importance, both for Europe and the Atlantic World, as a center of Jewish publishing has already been noted. As this activity took root within the robust flourishing of Dutch publishing in general, we should note that books for Jews were neither written nor printed exclusively in Hebrew. Texts appeared in Spanish, Portuguese, and Latin, as well as Dutch, with the Romance languages appealing to newly arrived Sephardim or (via a black market) to crypto-Jews living in Iberia or the Americas. Indeed when (c. 1649) the Inquisition arrested one Luis Mendez Chaves for Judaizing in Havana, evidence against him included six Spanish-language books on Jewish subjects published in Amsterdam variously between 1617 and 1645. The author and publisher of one of these texts was Menasseh ben Israel, who founded Amsterdam's first Jewish printing press in 1622.[12] One of ben Israel's more influential books was *Hope of Israel*, first published in Amsterdam in 1650 by his son, Samuel ben Israel. This book was of a religious genre. Besides Spanish *Hope of Israel* was also published in Dutch, English, and Latin. In summary the text claims that the Ten Lost Tribes of Israel were to be found in the Americas and that the messianic age would only come once the Jews were dispersed to the "four corners of the earth." One corner that lacked Jews was the British Isles, which was rhetoric Menasseh ben Israel used to promote the readmission of Jews, which occurred in 1655. The name, *Hope of Israel*, was also one that some congregations in the Atlantic World would later adopt as their own, such as in Willemstad, Curaçao; Spanish Town, Jamaica; Savannah, Georgia; and Philadelphia, Pennsylvania.

Another publishing pioneer was Haham Joseph Athias (1635–1700). Born in Spain, he fled with some of his family to Dutch-controlled Recife (in Pernambuco, Brazil) sometime before 1648. Among Brazilian crypto-Jews Athias was first instructed in Judaism; back in Spain, however, his father was condemned for Judaizing and died by auto-de-fé in 1665. When the Portuguese reconquered Pernambuco (1654), many Sephardim sought out Amsterdam, where Athias set up his printing press in 1658.[13] He specialized in texts on Jewish biblical topics intended for a Christian readership. This was possible because many Protestants were committed, for confessional reasons, to an exact understanding of the Pentateuch as analogue, guide, and proleptic indicator of Reformation belief. As it happens Athias's printing business was

Title page of a Book of Prophets edited by Haham Joseph Athias (1635–1700)
and Johannes Leusden (1624–99, a Calvinist Hebraist), which was posthumously
printed in Amsterdam in 1705 by Sumptibus and Mandatis Societatis. This edition
of the Book of Prophets was bilingual in Hebrew and Latin for the non-Jewish
public. On the opposite page (not depicted here) there is a handwritten notation
that Newport merchant Aaron Lopez owned the book later in the eighteenth century. K. K. Beth Elohim Collection, Special Collections, College of Charleston.

so successful that he was the first Jew admitted (1661) to the printer's guild
of Amsterdam, a status ben Israel never achieved. But fortune was fickle: in
1700 Athias died a debtor.[14]

In seventeenth-century Netherlands, only a few Jews would number
among the graphic artists and painters who made their epoch one of the pin-
nacles of Western visual culture. There were no Jews scaling the heights with
Vermeer, Rembrandt, Hals, or the Ruisdaels. But we should recognize that
this remarkable era did produce the artists Salom Italia (1619–after 1655),
Samuel d'Orta, Aaron de Chaves, Jacob Cardoso Ribeyro, and Jacob Judah

Haham Menasseh ben Israel (1604–57). Engraving by Salom Italia, c. 1642. William A. Rosenthall Judaica Collection, Special Collections, College of Charleston Library.

Leon—all Jews and capable professionals. Menasseh ben Israel's important messianic treatise *Piedra gloriosa* (1655) was illustrated by Salom Italia.[15] Still, even with minority status and Judaism's anti-iconographical traditions taken into account, demonstrably fewer Jews were involved in the making, portraying, and publication of art on Jewish themes than Christian artists treating similar subject matter for the public at large. The incomparable figure here is Rembrandt, but we should mention, if only as prognosticators of Enlightenment anthropology, Jean-Frederic Bernard (1683–1744) and Bernard Picart (1673–1733), who produced the encyclopedic, thirteen-volume *Cérémonies et coutumes religieuses de tous les peuples du monde* (1723–43). Its fine engravings of Jews and their rituals formed part of this remarkable endeavor. Drawing from Jewish, Christian, and Islamic sources—most date from the seventeenth and eighteenth centuries—the author and the illustrator undertook an investigation of the mores, beliefs, and art defining various religious traditions with careful reliance on etchings and prints as visual evidence.[16] We should mention that Rembrandt himself lived in Jodenbreestraat, Amsterdam's Jewish neighborhood. His representation of Jewish subjects, whether actual neighbors or figures used in biblical narratives, had very much to do with an artist recording his immediate environment faithfully.[17] The portrait of Manesseh ben Israel, as well as four etchings Rembrandt created for ben

Israel's *Piedra Gloriosa,* were testaments to the artist's friendship with the Jewish savant.[18]

We must also not forget the literary accomplishments of Amsterdam's Ashkenazim. Between 1644 and 1800, more than five hundred books were published in Yiddish alone, averaging three to four works per year. It is from these Dutch Ashkenazic literary works, as well as other forms of linguistic and cultural exchanges, that the Dutch language borrowed from this eastern European Jewish language, Yiddish. A Dutch-influenced dialect of Yiddish also developed among the Ashkenazim in the Netherlands.[19] From Amsterdam's Jewish Republic of Letters, in addition to the intellectual centers of Venice, Istanbul, and Prague, cultural horizons were expanded between different groups of Jews as well as with non-Jews.[20]

Nonetheless, while Amsterdam may have offered sanctuary to Jews from south of the Pyrenees and east of the Rhine, these autonomous populations literally and figuratively represented different worlds. It was only a matter of time, a decade or two, before differences in language, religious custom, and, conspicuously, socioeconomic conditions would divide the two synagogue-communities of the Netherlands. For the most part, on arrival, Rhenish and central European immigrants were neither wealthy nor expert in foreign trade as were their Iberian counterparts. In the 1630s the Ashkenazim stopped attending Sephardic synagogues, arranging their own worship services instead; by 1642, separate in death as in life, they founded their own cemetery. In 1671–72 they built their own magnificent edifice, the Grote Sjoel. [21] By 1674 the Ashkenazic influx of some five thousand souls was twice as large as resident Sephardim (known as "Portuguese" to their Christian neighbors), but this trend was growing quickly: seventy-five years later the percentage difference would more than triple (ten thousand Ashkenazim, three thousand Sephardim in 1750). In many respects, however, it was the Sephardic protobourgeoisie who made up the Jewish urban establishment, not least because the less moneyed Ashkenazim were themselves divided into smaller groups of Germans, Poles, and Bohemians. During the period between 1675 and 1725, Amsterdam's Jewish population swelled to become the largest in any European city.[22] Abroad some four thousand Sephardim had moved to the Caribbean and Dutch Surinam by 1700. But in Amsterdam itself, Jewish unity was not achieved. The social and cultural barriers that rose between the two diverging synagogue-communities calcified: Ashkenazim did not associate with Sephardim, and, emphatically Balkanizing, the rabbis of both populations forbade intermarriage.

Immigration statistics supply one reason behind the 1639 combining of Amsterdam's three separate Sephardic congregations into a single Talmud Torah. This merger became a way of preserving identity and influence as the pace of settlement by non-Iberian Jews quickened. But another social polymer for the Sephardim was their condescension toward coreligionists who, intense piety and formal knowledge of rabbinic tradition notwithstanding, appeared as parvenus and "foreign." In any case, formerly Iberian Jewry played to its strengths: consolidation made possible an authoritative Sephardic voice on matters relating to city governance as well as religious practice, established Spanish-Portuguese Jewry as a discrete stratum, and crafted both guidance and assistance for Sephardim outside the Netherlands, crypto-Jews or not, in Iberia, the Mediterranean, or the Americas.[23] Not long afterward, in 1652, the advantages of unification achieved in Amsterdam would motivate even Hamburg's Sephardim. They were a minority among far more numerous native Ashkenazim, and chose to combine their three small congregations into the far larger Beth Israel.[24]

We should not understate the achievement of Amsterdam's Talmud Torah, built 1636–39. Aside from those in the places of refuge in the Mediterranean —such as in the Italian states and Ottoman Empire—the building marked a beginning: the first purpose-built Jewish house of worship in the Atlantic World since the glorious lost days of Spain and Portugal.[25] As we have seen, this pioneer Dutch synagogue-community served as a template: even the prayer rituals marking phases of construction, not to mention architectural motifs and design plans, were copied or modified throughout the Atlantic World until the nineteenth century. And the power of example was even more demonstrable in Talmud Torah's famous second edifice, the great Esnoga (built 1671–75), which stands today as a Baroque landmark, a monument both to the Jews who built it and to the Christians who accepted them during an age of religious conflict. Indeed, connoisseurs of adversity as they had become, the seventeenth-century Sephardim recognized the tolerance shown them in the midst of the Dutch Protestant capital. A prayer composed for the city begins "Blessed art thou, O Lord our God, who has shown us your wonderful mercy in the city of Amsterdam, the praiseworthy."[26]

But as Jewish society began to thrive in Amsterdam, material achievements were accompanied by no small degree of intellectual controversy. In fact Jewish religious scholars set the stage for an epic confrontation between dogma and modernity when, in 1656, Baruch Spinoza (1632–77), one of Western philosophy's seminal rationalists, was harshly censured by the Amsterdam rabbinate for ideas deplored as heretical, dubious, or mistaken. The twenty-three year old Spinoza *had not published a word at the time;* nonetheless he was excommunicated through a rabbinic judgment, known as a writ of *cherem,* which was never removed. Here is how Stephen Nadler, an important contemporary investigator of Spinoza, accounts for this chronological anomaly: "No doubt he [Spinoza] was giving utterance to just those ideas that would soon appear in his philosophical treatises. In those works, Spinoza denies the immortality of the soul; strongly rejects the notion of a providential God—the God of Abraham, Isaac and Jacob; and claims that the Law was neither literally given by God nor any longer binding on Jews. Can there be any mystery as to why one of history's boldest and most radical thinkers was sanctioned by an orthodox Jewish community?"[27] We should note that Spinoza's radicalism was uniformly objectionable to religious authority. His works were proscribed by the Catholic Church, which consigned key texts to the List of Prohibited Books (*Index Librorum Prohibitorum*), while at the same time most of Spinoza's writings scandalized Dutch Reform clergy. Yet Spinoza, although immeasurably the most influential outrider of philosophical and theological debate in seventeenth century Amsterdam (if not Europe), was not the only Sephardic thinker condemned by the Dutch capital's Jewish leadership. Sephardic scholars Uriel da Costa (1585–1640) and Juan de Prado (b. c. 1610) shared with Spinoza not only a tendency toward heterodox, demythologizing ideas—broadly, all three questioned canonical views of divinity and elevated nature into a supreme, rationally accessible explanatory system—but, as it turned out, they garnered the same obloquy from the same confessional community: all three were excommunicated by the Talmud Torah.

It is unremarkable that a long-suppressed Sephardic rabbinate would seek to reassert hierarchy, ritual, and Talmudic authority with vigor: both rabbis and officers of the congregation (those lay leaders known as "parnassim") wanted to marginalize dissent, much less Spinozist monism equating God and Nature, while encouraging conformity with historical tradition and deference to rabbinic approval. Spinoza's *Ethics* (1677) or, for that matter, his earlier *Theologico-Political Treatise* (*Tractatus Theologico-Politicus* [1670])—it defended secular governance and rejected religious intolerance—profoundly questioned clerical authority. This challenge was reviled by a rabbinate wary of Protestant perceptions: Would the ruling Dutch oligarchy and their Reformed pastors regard the hahamim (rabbis) and parnassim as powerless to rein in Jewish apostates or, scandalously, pantheists? Here, then, an ironic dialectic becomes evident. Just as Spinoza and a small coterie of (mostly non-Jewish) philosophical radicals were exploring the boundaries of European rationalistic speculation, Amsterdam's Jewish leadership was crafting a deliberate "re-Judaizing" policy based on orthodox observance and religious education—a policy meant to normalize Jewish identity and instill respect for historical continuity. This resurgent conservative tendency reveals a Sephardic community unsure of itself and quite anxious to secure a foothold of acceptance within the first Christian society to extend Jews meaningful, if restricted, tolerance after the violent ruptures of the preceding century and a half. Nor should there be any doubt that at this delicate moment in the middle of the seventeenth century—again, Spinoza was excommunicated precisely in 1656—the forces of conservatism, religious and to a certain extent social, were incomparably more influential among Dutch Jewry than the rationalist vanguard represented by Spinoza. As far as Sephardic leaders were concerned, they wanted to make the Netherlands a beacon attracting and instructing Iberian crypto-Jews from across Europe and the Atlantic diaspora.

Baruch Spinoza (1632–77). Posthumous engraving by Étienne Fessard and Pierre Edmé Babel, eighteenth century. William A. Rosenthall Judaica Collection, Special Collections, College of Charleston Library.

The Talmud Torah agenda could never accept philosophical radicals, whatever their origin. So in the first third of the seventeenth century, we see Sephardic scholarship beginning to produce a roster of influential orthodox voices: Immanuel Aboab (1555–1628), Isaac Orobio de Castro (1617–87), Samuel da Silva, Moses Raphael D'Aguilar, and (in England) David Neito (1654–1728). All were involved in a comprehensive program of persuasion, arguing for the Talmud's validity as well as for the broad remit of rabbis, whether in religious matters or secular practices affecting Jewish-Christian interaction, to ensure the welfare of the entire Jewish community. In this affirmation of orthodoxy, Aboab's *Nomologia* (1629) and Neito's *Kuzari Ha-sheni* (1714) were landmark codifications.

As Jews thrived in their Jerusalem on the Amstel, they promptly seized commercial opportunities made possible by Dutch expansion on the other side of the Atlantic. By 1600 the United Provinces had consolidated naval, military, and mercantile forces so as to contend with Iberian (Habsburg), French, and English colonization in the Americas and beyond, such as India and the Far East. Beneficiaries of Reformed tolerance in the Lowlands, Jews played a part from the early stages of Dutch imperial enterprise. Even in the 1580s, while the Habsburg Emperors fought to control their restive

Dutch and Flemish subjects at the same time as the Portuguese were establishing dominion in Brazil, converso merchants on both sides of the Atlantic were largely responsible for Brazilian trade enriching the Dutch. [28] Certainly valuable commerce in pernambuco and brazilin, the red dye extracted from this hard wood, led the Dutch to attack Brazil in one of their first military actions against Habsburg possessions overseas. Lucrative too were Brazilian plantations producing sugarcane using methods first developed, as we noted earlier, by Portuguese conversos in Madeira and São Tomé during the early decades of the sixteenth century. Although a temporary peace (the Twelve Years Truce) intervened in 1609, hostilities resumed in 1621 when Dutch fleets attacked Spanish and Portuguese interests on a global scale—in Europe, the Americas, Africa, and Asia. What had begun as harassment or piracy against Habsburg shipping often escalated to full-scale invasion or destruction of Spanish or Portuguese territory. Dutch strategy aimed not only to gain (or seize) wealth but also to deny sources of funding for the stubborn Habsburg war against the United Provinces. [29]

So the Dutch Republic, by no means a vast entity, cast a very wide net in the first half of the seventeenth century, quite often at the expense of Iberian rulers. Besides northeastern Brazil, Dutch colonial acquisition stretched across the Atlantic from New Amsterdam to parts of the Lesser and Leeward Antilles, traced the West African coast to Cape Town, and rounded India (Pulicat, Ceylon, and Malabar) to include the East Indies (present day Indonesia). Sometimes Jews served under Dutch military commands, as in Pernambuco and the Lesser Antilles.

The Dutch West India Company, charged with administering colonies in the Americas and western Africa, had considerable numbers of Jews to supervise. Not so the Dutch East India Company—its remit covered southern Africa and Asia—which discouraged a Jewish presence in much of its jurisdiction. Although Jews had participated in the founding settlement at Fort de Goede Hoop (1652), later called the Castle of Good Hope, restrictions on Jews in Cape Town would not end until 1803. Only in India itself were Jews—who had been "indigenous" there for centuries—permitted to reside in significant numbers.[30] Very different was the policy of the Dutch West India Company. It sought out Jewish expertise for sugarcane production in Pernambuco (1630), Curaçao (1659), Cayenne (1659), and Surinam (1667); it offered liberal religious toleration as a lure; and sometimes it even paid free passage from the Netherlands to the Americas.[31] There was no comparable economic niche available to Jews who might otherwise have immigrated to East Asia. In western Africa, the Dutch focused on commerce with sub-Saharan kingdoms and tribes, from which slaves, not crops or plantations, were the object of Dutch monopoly. In any case, the number of Jews living below the Sahara remained so small that the first congregation there was not founded until 1841 in Cape Town, by then a British possession.[32]

Some Sephardim fought for the Dutch cause. During the Eighty Years' War (or Dutch War of Independence, 1568–1648), or at least during that portion of the conflict that took place in the seventeenth century, Dutch Jews took up arms against Habsburg troops. They fought the Portuguese in northern Brazil and the Spanish in various Caribbean islands, taking up anti-Iberian piracy from the 1620s through the 1640s. We thus encounter the remarkable figure of Moses Cohen Henriques, veteran of Dutch campaigns in Brazil and an active, formidable privateer. Serving with Vice Admiral Pieter Pietersen Heyn (1577–1629) in 1628, he helped the Dutch West India Company seize a Spanish treasure fleet off of the coast of Havana, Cuba. Twelve ships were captured carrying an estimated sixteen million guilders worth of cargo, equivalent today to about one billion U.S. dollars.[33]

The Dutch West India Company, modeled on the East India Company, was founded in 1621 and backed by a significant number of Jewish investors, stockholders, and merchant houses.[34] In 1624 the Dutch briefly conquered Salvador (properly, São Salvador da Bahia de Todos os Santos), then the capital of Portuguese Brazil, but were forced out a year later. About a dozen Jews took part in the Dutch invasion and occupying force, where they also served as interpreters. This brief Dutch occupation offers the first instance in which liberated crypto-Jews fought an enemy to establish freedom of conscience; some of these conversos did in fact choose to return to Judaism. When the Portuguese reconquered Salvador, five Jews were tried and executed precisely because they had thrown off the converso cloak.[35] At the same time, there were New Christians (Jewish no longer) who fought in the Portuguese ranks to defend Salvador *from* the Dutch, which shows how fully assimilated and loyal to Catholic Iberia many New Christians had become despite the harsh treatment they had long endured.[36]

Despite the loss of Salvador (1625), the Dutch, seeking total control of sugarcane and hardwood production, were adamant in their Brazilian aspirations. Through an effort mounted by the West India Company (with Jewish investors, among many others, providing capital), they decided to found the colony of New Holland. Accordingly a second Dutch campaign was launched against Pernambuco in 1630, and, at first successful, Reformed religious tolerance was extended to both the Portuguese Catholic majority as well as to Jews.[37] There were many New Christians who returned to Judaism under the Dutch regime. Thus Pernambuco could boast a Sephardic community where Jews had preceded (as conversos), then accompanied and followed, Dutch conquest.[38] By 1636 more than 130 years after Cabral became the European discoverer of the Brazilian coast, the Jews of Recife established congregation Zur Israel (Rock of Israel), the first in the New World as well as south of the equator.

The geographic situation of Zur Israel, as the first Jewish community in the *Southern* Hemisphere, immediately created a theological conundrum—an

issue of inversion. The seasonal (hence climatic) norms of Recife do not apply to the weather (hence seasonal) sequence that first inspired the prayers
beseeching agricultural fertility recited at the festivals of Shemini Atzeret and
Passover. These prayers—they appeal for the right amount of water needed
to fructify crops and soil—were conceived in the Northern Hemisphere by
Jews who lived around the Mediterranean and in the Middle East, Persia,
and Central Asia during the first centuries of the common era. Because climate and seasons are opposed in the two hemispheres, the Northern Hemi-
spheric prayer conventions (praying for when rain should fall) cannot apply
to the realities of Jews living in the south. Made up of planters and merchants
whose raison d'être was largely agricultural commerce, congregation Zur Israel consulted Salonikan rabbis for a solution to their liturgical/geographical
problem. Salonika and Venice, long established citadels of Sephardic practice, were the arbiters of halakhic and Talmudic wisdom for the newly settled
Iberian Jews of the Netherlands. Haham Hayyim Shabbetai (1556–1647) of
Salonika, one of the foremost religious scholars of his day, ruled that the
Jews of Pernambuco should either recite the traditional prayers, or, if ver-
batim northern wording led to agricultural harm in the south, the Brazilians
should omit saying the prayers entirely. Little wonder that Zur Israel's congregants chose to cull the problematic verses, a precedent followed to this day in
the Southern Hemisphere in many Jewish congregations of Argentina, South
Africa, and Australia. Whether Recife's Sephardim were motivated by piety,
a legalistic need for ritual clarity, or the desire to preserve Sephardic cultural
identity, the pragmatic solution determined by Shabbetai stands as the first
ruling on Jewish law occasioned by conditions unique to the Southern Hemisphere. Diaspora can dictate convolutions.[39]

By the mid-1640s New Holland (northern Brazil), was home to 1,450 Jews,
making up half the European population of the colony and comparable to
the number of Jews then living in Amsterdam.[40] These Sephardic colonists
were primarily merchants, sugar millers, and planters. On Antonio Vaz, an
island next to the port of Recife, Johan Maurits van Nassau-Siegen, the formidable Dutch military commander and colonial governor, built the town of
Mauritsstad (now Mauricia). First the port, then the island settlement, grew
large enough to host Jewish communities: Magen Abraham (Shield of Abraham), a satellite of Zur Israel, was built in 1648. Haham Isaac Aboab da Fonseca left Amsterdam for Pernambuco, where in 1642, as leader of Zur Israel,
he became the New World's first rabbi, seconded by another Dutch haham,
Moses Raphael d'Aguilar. Beyond Recife and Mauricia satellite Jewish communities (almost certainly without purpose-built synagogues) also appeared
in Paraiba, Olinda, Penedo, Itamaraca, Ipojuca, and Goiana.[41] This pattern of
growth was replicated elsewhere on the frontiers of the Atlantic World. Jews
in a colony's capital or major city founded a nucleus synagogue-community
that, as satellite settlements radiated elsewhere, would provide a model for

colonists in smaller settlements who needed to gather for social and religious purposes. The participants of the satellite communities were usually separated by geography from the central congregation but were full members of it. The Jews in these marginal satellites tended to meet in modest structures or rooms that were not purpose-built synagogues, though there were exceptions. During the eighteenth century, we see this same demographic and architectural trajectory in points as far-flung as Surinam, Curaçao, Barbados, Jamaica, and Pennsylvania.

In fact it is in Dutch Brazil that we find the first openly professing Jew employed in either architecture or construction. Balthasar da Fonseca, who thrived as a building contractor, had been a New Christian resident of Portuguese Brazil until the Dutch invasion allowed him to return to Judaism.[42] Despite Fonseca's success—he became one of the colony's wealthiest businessmen—we have no evidence of buildings or synagogues that bear his name—only a bridge in Recife can be assigned to him.

After 1643 the Portuguese made several attempts to retake Pernambuco; to parry these threats, the Dutch enlisted all adult males, including Jews, into the militia. Except for specific battles or pressing conflicts, Jewish soldiers in New Holland were exempted from duty on their Sabbath day.[43] In any case, the end to the Dutch Brazilian empire came quickly enough. In 1654 the Portuguese reconquered Pernambuco, and, for the Dutch, this final defeat put an end to their Brazilian venture. As for the Portuguese, who had reasserted their independence from Habsburg Spain in 1640, they exchanged Dutch Reformed tolerance for their endemic Inquisition, once again exposing Jews to existential crises—death, expulsion, and conversion. But the Dutch, who by midcentury were the arbiters of Protestant European tolerance, would not simply abandon those Jews who had enjoyed religious, civil, and economic security for the preceding three decades to Portuguese menace, at least not right away. According to the surrender terms ceding New Holland, the Jews of Pernambuco had three months to arrange their affairs and leave the colony without penalty or harm. So the Sephardim left Brazil behind, most returning to Amsterdam but others seeking Atlantic sanctuaries—Curaçao, Surinam, New Amsterdam, as well as other English and French colonies.[44] In 1658 the United Provinces granted a form of citizenship to its Sephardim. If Jewish political and social rights were still qualified when compared to the status of Dutch Protestants, state recognition was sufficiently robust to assert Dutch protection whenever Dutch Jews were subject to Iberian harassment or capture.[45] By this juncture in the still evolving social contract of the young Dutch Republic, there could be little doubt that the contributions of Jews on both sides of the Atlantic, as businessmen and colonists, had earned them the appreciation of the Dutch ruling oligarchy.

In 1634 the Dutch invaded Spanish Curaçao, soon to be followed by the acquisition of many other islands—Aruba, Bonaire, St. Maarten, St. Eustatius, and Saba—in the Lesser Antilles. Dutch strategic policy aimed to plunder Spanish and Portuguese ports and fleets, to trade with indigenes or friendly European colonies, and to experiment with resource extraction (like sea salt) or pursue cash crop production (notably sugarcane). Amsterdam Jews took part in the invasion of Curaçao; in general the Dutch West India Company, keen to cultivate so astute a commercial community, encouraged Jewish participation in island ventures. The first recorded Jew on Curaçao was Samuel Cohen, appointed chief steward with special responsibility for organizing native support during the campaign against the Spanish. Somewhat later, in 1651, another Sephardi from the Netherlands, Jan de Illan (born João d'Yllan), led a group of Jewish families to Curaçao, where they became plantation owners. By and large, Jews were accepted as a component of economic life, but not uniformly. There is a letter dated 21 March 1651, from the directors of the Dutch West India Company instructing its New Holland governor, Pieter Stuyvesant (1612–72), no friend of Jews, to make certain that Lucas Rodenborch, the company's vice-director on Curaçao, accommodate de Illan and his colonists on the island. Determinedly unhelpful, at best negligent, Stuyvesant on this occasion authorized no assistance whatsoever to de Illan's enterprise.[46]

The semi-arid environment of Curaçao, punishing to soil, could not support large-scale plantation agriculture for cash crops. Rapidly the Dutch interest in the island, with its magnificent natural harbor of Willemstad, the colonial capital, shifted to commerce, specifically the Atlantic slave trade. Simply put, Curaçao became a crucial receiving station and transshipment depot for West African slaves—many purchased in contract with Spain—who were sold throughout the Caribbean and the Americas. During the seventeenth and eighteenth centuries, the Netherlands and Great Britain would supplant Portugal and Spain as Europe's chief slave vendors and transporters. Jews certainly participated in that trade as agents, while more extensively pursuing lucrative general shipping, commodities commerce, maritime insurance, and banking.[47] Hardheaded, industrious merchants, the Sephardim sold goods, with Dutch approval, within the Spanish Atlantic market, although this trade was formally illegal because of prevailing hostility between the United Provinces and the Habsburgs. These efforts earned the Jews a firm place in the island economy. After the fall of Dutch Brazil in 1654, Curaçao's Sephardic population developed from its early refugee base to become the center of New World Jewry in the second half of the seventeenth century.

Although it did not build a synagogue until 1674, Willemstad's congregation Mikve Israel was established between 1651 and 1659. During these formative years, services were held in the homes of prominent members. As the Jewish population of Curaçao grew apace, synagogue construction expanded too: a second sanctuary appeared in 1692, a third in 1703 (it would survive until 1730).[48] The synagogues of 1674 and 1692, no longer extant, were likely small and built from wood, fieldstone, or, as was the case with many other Caribbean colonial buildings at the time, brick that had been carried from Europe—sometimes as ship ballast. In 1674 the community's first rabbi, Joseph Pardo, who had been rector of an important Rotterdam yeshiva, arrived in Curaçao, where he set up Yeshiva Etz Haim, a school that must have been housed in the new synagogue. Nine years later (1683), Pardo left Curaçao to serve as rabbi of Port Royal in Jamaica.[49]

Leaving behind northeastern Brazil after the Dutch collapse, one group of Sephardic refugees—it would be the vanguard of a population destined to command attention—sailed some four thousand miles to the north: on 7 September 1654, twenty-three Jews found their way to Manhattan island, known as New Amsterdam, and, small though their number, thus made up the largest contingent of North America's first Jewish community. The original destination of these Sephardim had been (old) Amsterdam, but travails at sea (seizure by Spaniards, rescue by a French ship, diversion to their rescuers' North American port of call) dictated their itinerary. Earlier that same year (1654), three Dutch Ashkenazic merchants, Jacob bar Simon, Asser Levy, and Solomon Pietersen, had preceded the Brazilian refugees and could thus claim priority, though only by a few months, as the pioneer Jewish settlers of New Netherlands.[50]

For a second time, more notoriously, we find a fractious relationship emerging between Pieter Stuyvesant and Jewish colonists. He had been ensconced in New Amsterdam as the director-general (de facto governor) of New Netherlands before the Brazilian Jews debarked and was angered at their intrusion. It must be said that this Dutch nativist martinet, with his constant animus toward Jews, similarly deplored Quakers, Mennonites, Lutherans, Catholics or anyone outside his own conservative Reformed communion. Stuyvesant duly urged the West India Company directors to ban the Jews, now involved in disputing transport charges demanded by their French rescuers, along with the three Ashkenazim and, presumably, any future Jewish immigrant from settling in New Amsterdam. However intolerant Stuyvesant's attitude, his goal of a Jew-free colony typified the pattern of religious Balkanization marking most early European settlement in the Americas. Let us recall that the Thirty Years' War (1618–48) conveyed, whether by proxy or counterexample, Europe's malignant religiopolitical discord to the Americas. In the seventeenth century, the Atlantic World known to Stuyvesant was made up of confessional fiefdoms congruent for the most part with the religious temper of the colonizing sponsors: English Puritan in Massachusetts, Connecticut, and New Haven; but English Catholic in Maryland; Swedish Lutheran in New Sweden along the Delaware River valley; Catholic in France's New France (Canada); and Catholic in all the Iberian territories, Portuguese Brazil as well as the Spanish Viceroyalties of New Spain (Mexico) and Peru. According to law if not categorical practice, none of these colonies allowed freedom of religious choice. In 1654 liberty of conscience as an organizing principle was to be found only in the English colony of "Rhode Island and Providence Plantations," to which Jews would find their way in 1658. The West India Company had established New Netherland, first patented in 1614, as Dutch Reformed. Yet freedom of conscience, that foundational precept of the Union of Utrecht (1579), was to be observed: faith-based penalties or persecution, at least in the eyes of the company, were obnoxious. In such an environment, Stuyvesant's 1655 expulsion appeal to company directors, who had at the same time been solicited by Amsterdam Jews on behalf of the distressed New Amsterdam Sephardim, was rejected. The directors decided in favor of the Jews not only in recognition of their longtime participation in the Dutch Brazilian endeavor, but also, good burgher businessmen, the board wanted to sustain the loyalty of the company's many useful Jewish shareholders. Consequently Jews were allowed to immigrate to New Netherlands, although this ruling in no way authorized the building of a synagogue in New Amsterdam or the public practice of Judaism.

Persistence was a Stuyvesant trait. His harassment policy continued with another order in 1655 that barred Jews from serving as soldiers on guard duty and, insult added to injury, proceeded to charge Jews monthly for the imposed exemption from military service. It was Asser Levy, joined by several others, who challenged this ostracism. Although the Jews' petition to take on militia duty was rejected by Stuyvesant's governing council, this petition when relayed to the Amsterdam authorities prevailed yet again. In an episode long regarded as seminal for religious liberty in the early colonial history of America, Levy and all Jews were granted the right of all adult males to serve in defense of New Netherland. Levy himself went on to obtain burgher rights— another first in New Netherlands for a Jew—that were required as commercial certification to pursue trade in Fort Orange (now Albany). When he died in 1680, he left behind the reputation of a respected and prosperous citizen of New York.[51] The city had been renamed to reflect English conquest in 1665, although it would take a third and final Anglo-Dutch War (1674) for Manhattan to become the pivot of an English colony. As compensation the Dutch gained Surinam, on the so-called Wild Coast of northeastern South America.

"Wild" it must certainly have seemed to Europeans at the beginning of the seventeenth century. The Spanish, Portuguese, Dutch, British, and French, all aspiring to claim one maritime access or another between 1580 and 1700, discovered a region, the Guyana Shield, whose narrow coastal plain on the Atlantic extended south into dense rain forest—an environment of great biodiversity and indigenous peoples, as well as of diseases unknown in the West, a punishing tropical climate, and a location remote from ports or assistance. Various early attempts at colonization failed, such as Dutch efforts along the Berbice, Demerara, and Essequibo Rivers, but over time Europeans established themselves in Dutch Surinam, British Guyana, and French Guyana.

To attract colonists, the nascent Protestant empires of the Netherlands and England offered religious tolerance to Jews endangered by Iberian Catholic rivals. As we might suppose, the freedom of conscience to be found in these colonial outposts was seldom absolute but frequently exceeded the norms of Protestant homelands themselves. Moreover, for their new Caribbean and South American colonies to prosper, the Dutch and English needed to find experienced plantation cultivators, especially to raise sugarcane—precisely an expertise that some Sephardim had. Thus we find that the 1657 charter drawn in the Netherlands by the Estates of Zeeland gave Jews of the Esquibbo territory in western Guyana—the colony named "Nova Zeelandia"—an array of civic sanctions: public worship, establishment of schools, jurisdiction over minor civil suits, ownership and sale of land, tax exemption for seven years to facilitate the creation of cash-crop plantations or businesses, and burghers' rights. Jews were even exempted from court appearances on the Sabbath and major holidays and, remarkably, were granted two representatives on the colony's governing board of deputies.[52] In the 1650s Dutch colonists repulsed from Brazil, including a considerable number of "Jews of the Portuguese nation," would make Surinam the first Protestant South American colonial venture to both survive and thrive.

Somewhat earlier, in 1630 and 1649, the English twice tried and failed to found a colony along the Surinam River. They succeeded in 1650 after Francis Willoughby (1614–66), then governor of Barbados, sent a three-ship expedition that launched the colony of Willougbyland. Brazilian Sephardim were probably among the Willoughby contingent that erected Thorarica as the first English colonial capital, some thirty miles south of where Paramaribo would be established on the Surinam River as the Dutch capital. In any case, we know that in 1661 England's Charles II officially allowed three Jews to live and trade in Surinam. By 1667 a colonial map indicates six Jewish-owned plantations at the town called the "Jewish Savannah." It would be called "Jodensavanne" by the Dutch, who one year later would control all of English Surinam.[53]

Meanwhile, east of Surinam, France announced its imperial ambitions on the Wild Coast by attempting to found a colony at Cayenne. The French initiative likewise failed two times—in 1604 and later in 1643. Undeterred, the Dutch West India Company in 1658 sought out abandoned Cayenne and started yet another colony there. Four years later the company signed a contract with David Cohen Nassy, a Portuguese Jew (b. 1612) who had thrived in Amsterdam, authorizing him to organize Jewish colonists for ventures throughout the Dutch Guyanese-Caribbean orbit. Although chartered to settle in Curaçao too, Nassy placed his focus across the Wild Coast—Cayenne, Berbice, Demerara, Essequibo, and Surinam. First, at the head of a large party of Jews, he went to Cayenne. Facilitated, or lured, by an accommodating company, these Jews received valuable incentives: transport, supplies—which importantly included the era's human commodity of African slaves—free land, and (as at Nova Zeeland), permission to establish religious congregations, schools, or other communal institutions.[54] But the Jewish presence in Cayenne was short-lived. In 1664, the colony yet again passed to France, so Nassy and many of this entourage rapidly moved west to Protestant Surinam. Any remaining Jews in Cayenne would have been expelled by 1685 under the Code Noir. In Surinam Nassy was a West India Company "Patroon"—an invested landholder with manorial and proprietary rights—and had the power to levy taxes on the colonists under his authority. No fewer than five of Nassy's own sons set up their own plantations around Jodensavanne. There, and in nearby Paramaribo, this wealthy Sephardic family prospered.

In 1667 the Dutch moved the capital of Surinam from Thorarica to Paramaribo, where two defensive works, Fort Zeeland and the Nieuw Amsterdam Fortress, made the city so safe that no more elaborate fortifications were needed. Most of Thorarica's Jews, who in 1671 had built a wooden synagogue off Cassipoera Creek, also went to Paramaribo. When Surinam finally passed from England to the Netherlands (1675), three English ships arrived to relocate the English colonists—a plan thoroughly disliked by the Dutch. They succeeded in persuading the Sephardic planters and merchants to remain. With Anglo-Dutch peace firmly in place, Surinam's export sugar market boomed, enriching the colony's cane plantation owners. So many Jewish families grew wealthy, and, Dutch Reformed tolerance exchanged for Anglican, they enjoyed many of the religious privileges introduced by the English. This prosperity was the fruit of an imperialism that rapidly changed the ethnic composition of Surinam. African slaves soon displaced its indigenous Ameridians as the major population group; even so, Arawaks and Caribs outnumbered European colonists, of whom Jews made up about one third. The Dutch dominated through superior military force and selective harshness, directed as needed against raiding natives, slave insurrections, and occasional attacks from European rivals. Jews participated in all aspects of Surinam's colonial defense, with some Jews becoming militia officers—a rarity in the seventeenth century.[55]

Time and again the Jewish experience in Europe and the Americas altered in degree and kind when Iberian Sephardim (soon enough joined by Ashkenazim) encountered the two mercantilist Protestant polities on the shores of the English Channel and North Sea. While the Dutch may have led the way in tolerating, then supporting, a Jewish population within the Lowlands and their Atlantic colonies, England was almost as quick to follow. Simply put, Charles II, who ruled from 1660 until 1685, sustained Cromwell's fledgling tolerance of Jews. Where Jews of the Iberio-Mediterranean diaspora had struggled to survive in the hostile century after 1492, by 1675, whether in

Amsterdam, London, or Anglo-Dutch Atlantic imperial precincts, life once again offered Jews the possibility of thriving.

During the 1650s, while still small, England's crypto-Jewish community maintained regular ties with Sephardim in Amsterdam and other parts of the Atlantic World. We see this relationship signally in the case of the Dutch Haham Menasseh ben Israel, whose mission to persuade Cromwell on behalf of Jewish readmission to England was entwined with the rabbi's own family. Rachel Abrabanel, ben Israel's wife, was a close relative of a prominent London crypto-Jewish merchant, David Abrabanel Dormido, who used his commercial contacts to assist the Commonwealth in gathering intelligence, especially on naval and maritime matters. He had also invested in Dutch Brazil, a source of considerable financial loss on the Portuguese reconquest. Circumventing the Navigation Act would greatly help Dormido recover his finances. So he facilitated ben Israel's approach to Cromwell, hoping that his good offices would allow his import business some latitude when dealing with the stricture that only English ships could transport goods to homeports.[56] In promoting an audience between Cromwell and the Amsterdam rabbi, Dormido turned to two influential figures, John Thurloe (1616–68), secretary to the Council of State, and John Dury (1596–1680) an ecumenical Calvinist minister, diplomat, intellectual, and Parliamentarian with access to Cromwell. Both favored letting Jews return to England and so advised Cromwell when he approved readmission at the Whitehall Conference in December 1655.[57] At least in prospect, robust English-based Sephardic commerce must certainly have seemed an attractive economic projection or gambit, at least if the Dutch experience were replicated in England.

After 1655, largely through Sephardic participation—including the Dormido family—the Dutch developed a new commerce in precious metals and diamonds linking London and Amsterdam in the West with Goa in the East. Indians supplied raw diamonds to Amsterdam, where the stones were cut and mounted, then sold to London jewelers. Jews often worked as skilled diamond cutters or as jewelry retailers. England's involvement with the Indian diamond trade began in 1639, when the East India Company founded Fort St. George near Madras. This settlement became a launch pad for trade and colonization, attracting a small number of English Sephardic merchants, who joined Dutch Sephardim already in the area. Soon enough this Jewish community became a destination for Jewish immigrants from Cochin and Baghdad. By 1695 Madras's diverse community had built a synagogue.[58] Between 1639, when first organized in Madras by England's East India Company, and its eventual decline in the early nineteenth century, this diamond market served as a magnet of Jewish enterprise—so much so that some of the London Sephardic community's earliest records detail a special congregational levy on diamond workers to raise funds for the building of Bevis Marks. In fact, during the industry's heyday, from 1716 until 1767, its primary work force was Jewish.[59]

Although a practicing Christian, the first person of Jewish extraction to hold Crown office was David Sollom.[60] He was a justice of the peace who served, c. 1671, in County Meath, Ireland. Regrettably most recent researchers in Atlantic studies—however malleable this young discipline may be—tend to overlook Ireland: a peculiar neglect inasmuch as British historians have traditionally regarded Ireland as the earliest significant instance of English colonization beyond island shores. In 1690 London Jews, among myriad backers of the new Protestant regime, loaned William and Mary funds to conquer an Ireland recalcitrantly Catholic and Jacobite.[61] Isaac Pereira, a recent transplant from the Netherlands to London, became King William III's chief supplier of foodstuffs and wagons for this Irish expedition. But the Pereira family was no stranger to armed intervention. Isaac's father was Jacob Periera, who joined fellow Sephardi Antonio Alvarez Machado as a *providiteur-general* to the Dutch military forces. In 1688 Jacob Periera and Machado had offered their support and expertise to William of Orange as the Glorious Revolution unfolded.

The extensive Sephardic commercial network, drawing on European and Atlantic contacts and sources, made Jews especially efficient suppliers of materiel in political and military crisis.[62] In any case, the role played deftly by Jewish merchants in advancing England's revolutionary initiative (1688–91) elevated the financial status of Sephardim at the high table of armed intervention. Throughout the eighteenth century, Jewish traders would garner military contracts. In England itself, now Great Britain upon its Anglo-Scottish political union in 1707, Jews found themselves accepted in a different, substantive, and more tolerant way. In 1700 the Jewish population of England was still small—approximately one thousand souls.[63] From the mid-seventeenth century, worship had been confined to rented quarters or homes only: in 1657 London's first Sephardic congregation, Sha'ar Hashamayim (Gates of Heaven), rented a Creechurch Lane house owned by the Church of England and would met there until 1701.[64] But by 1699 steady population growth led this congregation to lease a vacant lot at Plough Yard, off the road still called Bevis Marks, providing the name to England's oldest purpose-built, active synagogue-community.[65] The building, completed in 1701, was the work of Joseph Avis, a Quaker carpenter trained by Robert Hooke, who was himself a student of Wren. Stylistically the interior owes a great deal to Amsterdam's Esnoga, while the synagogue as a whole expresses Wren's late-Baroque sensibility. Both Bevis Marks and the Esnoga provided models for synagogue construction throughout the Anglo-Dutch Americas.

Even though Bevis Marks held historical priority in the British Isles, this impressive London achievement could not have been the first purpose-built synagogue in the British Empire. That structure, whichever it was, would certainly, and portentously, have been in the Caribbean. But precise identification remains difficult, if not impossible, because the survival of archaeological sites and supporting documentary evidence is tentative at best. Aesthetically we can infer that the earliest Caribbean synagogues must have conformed to Jacobean vernacular or English Baroque conventions found in surviving buildings of the colonial period.[66] The English began colonizing Barbados in 1625, their goal to expand into a sphere that had been exclusively Iberian. There is some evidence that this island in the Lesser Antilles could have received Jewish settlers as early as 1629. When Dutch Brazil fell in 1654, Pernambuco Sephardim began to resettle in Barbados, where they joined a small quasi-crypto-Jewish community. Following Cromwell's legitimation policy, Nidhe Israel (Scattered of Israel) was officially founded at Bridgetown in 1656, although this congregation may have been the legal avatar of an existing crypto-Jewish community. The earliest mention of the Nidhe Israel synagogue is from a surveyor's record dated 1664 that describes the building as already constructed. Its Torah scrolls came from Amsterdam, which shows that the congregants were in the orbit of Dutch Sephardim before the rise of London's own Sephardic community. Unsurprisingly Amsterdam produced Nidhe Israel's first rabbi, Eliahu Lopez, who arrived in 1679, moving later (1693) to Curaçao, where he was appointed haham.[67] Toward the end of the seventeenth century—the exact date is not known—a second Barbados synagogue, Semah David (Branch of David), arose in Speightstown, although it was not an autonomous congregation but rather a branch of Nidhe Israel meant to accommodate a growing population. In a sad incident, an anti-Semitic mob destroyed Semah David after a dispute between a Jew and a Christian escalated.[68] Almost one hundred years later, Nidhe Israel itself, along with many of its historic records, disappeared when a hurricane struck in 1831, and the only known surviving image of the building is in the background of a painting that hangs at the Barbados Museum called *Governor Robinson Going to Church*, that depicts Bridgetown from c. 1740. No description survives of Semah David. In 1833, a second Nidhe Israel synagogue was built, this time designed in au courant Gothic Revival. This building remains in active use by the congregation, though it has not done so continuously.[69]

Jamaica was one of the very earliest outposts of European Atlantic colonialism. The island was discovered by Columbus in 1504 and was for a time ruled by his descendents. The English raided the Spanish capital, Santiago de la Vega, in 1597 and 1643, while the entire island fell to the English admirals William Penn (1621–70) and Robert Venables (1613–87) in 1655. Under Spanish rule, there were crypto-Jews who had settled on the island, but we know little of their lives. Not so the Jews who arrived in the wake of English conquest, some of whom were among the earliest English colonists, followed in turn over the next forty years by even more Jews since the conquest of the island coincided with Cromwell's decision to readmit them into the Commonwealth.[70] As had been the case when the Dutch displaced Portuguese rule in Pernambuco, some Jamaican conversos returned to Judaism under the more tolerant Protestant policy. Indeed both Captains Campoe Sabbatha and Simon de Caceres were New Christians, possibly even crypto-Jews, who helped the English in their conquest of Jamaica. Caceres, not without conquistadorial appetites, also proposed to Cromwell a plan—it never materialized—for invading Chile.[71] Another early Jewish Jamaican was Jacob Jeosua Bueno Enriques, who sought permission from Charles II to explore Jamaica's copper deposits and share a percentage of profits with the Crown. Tellingly Enriques also petitioned the king "to naturalize me and my brothers Josef and Moise Enriques so we can use our [Jewish] law and to have synagogues confirmed by Parliament."[72]

The first synagogue in Jamaica was built in Port Royal, the new English capital, during the seventeenth century. Neither date of construction nor designer is known, but the structure was mentioned as part of the townscape by the 1680s.[73] It's possible that the Enriques brothers participated in the original synagogue project and helped guide the nascent Jewish community. As Port Royal developed into a center for trade forbidden by the Spanish Crown in the Americas, this black market absorbed Jews into a world of piracy and privateers. So we find one Moses Cohen Henriques, plausibly same person as the Port Royal worthy known as "Moise," in a role quite uncommon for Jews—that of dedicated privateer. He was pardoned and granted citizenship in 1681 by Admiral Sir Henry Morgan (1635–88), who chameleon-like had left behind his own privateer days to become governor of Jamaica.[74]

However various or violent the consequences of the European Reformation, its splintering of Catholic hegemony that gave rise to relatively tolerant Protestant mores proved providential for Jews. By 1675 Sephardim in parts of the Atlantic World were in more advantageous positions than they had occupied for some two hundred years. There were setbacks, as we see in one tenet of France's comprehensively repressive Code Noir of 1685 that expelled Jews from the French Americas. In any case, time was not on France's side in North America: Canada became a British possession in 1763, and Louisiana became Spanish. But the decisive changes had to do with the ascendant Protestant colonial powers, not with the Catholic empires of the Habsburgs or Bourbons. In the Dutch and English polities, Jews began to prosper. They could practice their religion with little restriction, accumulate property, and in the great urban centers of Amsterdam and London rise to a level of substantial wealth. The Jews of the Dutch and British colonies were generally shopkeepers, shippers, traders, and servants, with a minority of wealthy sugar producers and rich commercial houses.[75] By some counts the Dutch Republic's numerically small Jewish population of approximately eighty-four hundred in 1690 accounted for a remarkable 8 percent of the Netherlands' overseas trade.[76] After their readmission to England in 1655, Jews there rapidly established themselves as profitable traders not only with European partners, but also with distant new colonial markets opening up in the Americas and Asia.[77]

The architectural record tells a similar tale. Within a seventy-five-year span, two great synagogues arose in Amsterdam (Esnoga, 1675) and London (Bevis Marks, 1701), radiating an influence, at once aesthetic, social, theological, and ritual, throughout the Dutch and British colonial spheres. As with religious structures in any place or time, the Atlantic World synagogues double as symbols of developing community prosperity. Dutch control would give way to British power during the seventeenth-century contest between two vigorous Protestant states—there is that signal moment of convergence when William of Orange became King William III in 1688—making inevitable an English Jewish displacement of Dutch Sephardic priority in the Americas. This narrative is recorded architecturally as new synagogues appear in what soon enough would be a Greater England peopling the Atlantic seaboard of North America and the Caribbean. And it is a narrative in which Jews, no longer incognito, play an overt part.

CHAPTER 4

Jewish Prosperity in the Protestant Atlantic World, 1675–1775

On 11 March 1669, the eight Lords Proprietors of Carolina—a province then encompassing a great swathe of land between Virginia and Florida—published *The Fundamental Constitutions of Carolina*. The chief Lord Proprietor, Anthony Ashley Cooper (1621–83), wrote it with the assistance of no less a contributor than John Locke (1632–1704). The political remit of this text, with its peculiar amalgam of nascent liberalism and feudal restrictions, was limited and soon abandoned by the colonists. But what concerns us is the two authors' strong endorsement of religious freedom, which had a far more lasting trajectory in American experience. While the *Fundamental Constitutions* officially established the Church of England, "Jews, heathens, and other dissenters from the purity of Christian religion" were guaranteed tolerance in Carolina. Article Ninety-Seven declares that "any seven or more persons agreeing in any religion, shall constitute a church or profession, to which they shall give some name, to distinguish it from others."[1] This tolerance was seen as an inseparable element of the familiar Lockean pursuit of "life, liberty, and property." In a sense the Cooper-Locke headcount ("seven . . . shall constitute a church") was less stringent than Judaism's *minyan* (specifying ten congregants to begin a prayer service). The colonial assembly never ratified the Fundamental Constitutions. Nevertheless, as aspiration, Article Ninety-Seven lived on, with religiopolitical tenets eventually permeating the civil society that would emerge not only in the Carolinas, but in many of England's Atlantic colonies.

England's tolerance, we have seen time and again, was preceded by that of the Netherlands. Starting with the Union of Utrecht (1579), the Republic of the Seven United Provinces asserted freedom of conscience as axial despite state confessional policy: this was notional. In practice Dutch Reformed Protestantism was frequently empowered to the disadvantage of Catholicism. Yet in an age of religious wars, the seventeenth-century Dutch were increasingly committed to accepting personal religious conviction as unassailable. In the event, far across the Atlantic, it would be the projection of precisely this Anglo-Dutch tolerance that provided a bedrock for Jewish settlement in the

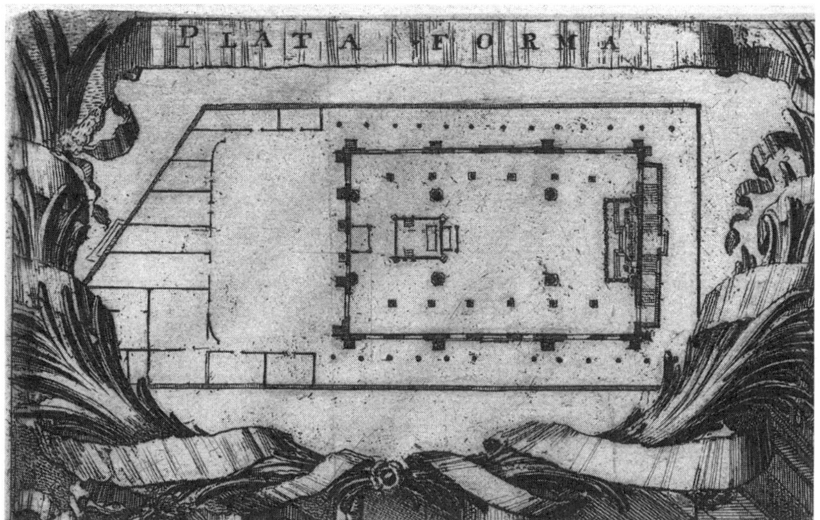

The floor plan of the Esnoga and its dependencies, designed by Elias Bouman,
as it appeared in the late seventeenth century. This plan was copied for synagogue
design across the Atlantic World. This floor plan is a detail from the etching *The
Inauguration of the Esnoga in 1675,* by Romeyn de Hooghe. William A. Rosenthall
Judaica Collection, Special Collections, College of Charleston Library.

Americas. We have only to look at the fine synagogues built on both sides of
the Atlantic, notably in Amsterdam, London, Rhode Island, and Curaçao, to
appreciate the power and permanence of this new, inclusive social contract.

Jewish Life in the Dutch Empire

In 1675, when architect-builder Elias Bouman completed the Esnoga, that
luminous Baroque monument of Amsterdam Jewry, the aesthetic achievement was quickly prized in a city of great churches—that is, in a society
for which mature religious architecture must express piety, praise, and grati-
tude before the divine transparently and convincingly. Upon completion, the
Esnoga stood as one of the largest synagogues in the world. Its design would
offer a template for synagogue construction throughout the Sephardic Atlantic World, whether in Dutch or English territories, for almost 150 years.

After decades of military (often naval) conflict, the Anglo-Dutch convergence of 1689 under William III of Orange and his wife, Mary II (of the House
of Stuart), meant that colonization and economic development in the Americas could coexist, if competitively, between the two maritime Protestant powers. In any case, the great era of Dutch expansion into the New World was
waning. It would be France that rose to contest Britain for dominance, especially in North America, during the eighteenth century. But in precisely this

period, as far as Jews were concerned, neither Canada, nor Louisiana, nor the Atlantic seaboard figured as the center of settlement. That—quite unexpectedly from any rigid Anglo-American historiographic perspective—was located on the distant northeastern coastal shelf of South America—in Dutch Surinam. Its capital, Paramaribo, on the Surinam River, flows into the Atlantic only nine and a half miles away. The city's Jews were mostly traders, transatlantic shippers, skilled craftsmen, and absentee landowners with plantations further south, along the alluvial river system that extended into central Surinam. During the seventeenth and eighteenth centuries, these cash-crop plantations multiplied and were worked by African slaves. Historical property maps show plantations laid out in long narrow parcels that front onto riverbanks for ease of access and transport. On early land surveys of Dutch Surinam, a distinctly Jewish character marks many plantations, bearing names like "Sukkoth," "Carmel," "Hebron," and "Aaron's Staff."[2] At the end of the seventeenth century, 104 Jewish families (ninety-two Sephardic, twelve Ashkenazic) were counted in Surinam. By 1737, Jews owned 115 of Surinam's 401 plantations: all were profitable (or at least debt-free) and produced sugarcane, cacao, and cotton, as well as other crops for domestic consumption. During the height of Surinam's economic prosperity in the first half of the eighteenth century, the colony's Jewish population reached two thousand—more than all the Jews residing on the North American continent at this time.[3] Even though Paramaribo was the governmental administrative seat, each of Surinam's five jurisdictional districts achieved a certain autonomy given the sheer geographic scale required by plantation agriculture. Significantly it was lucrative, large-scale sugarcane cultivation that made the "District of the Jewish Nation" the colony's most profitable in the eighteenth century.[4]

Beginning in 1669 each district was placed under the direction of a "jurator" appointed by and answerable to the colonial governor. This jurator presided over local trials or disputes. In 1684 Samuel Nassy, a son of the patriarch David Nassy, became the first jurator of the District of the Jewish Nation, whose administrative seat was the town of Jodensavanne. Both there and in Paramaribo, the Dutch gave the growing number of Jewish colonists even greater autonomy and privileges than the English had granted earlier. By 1700 Surinam's Jews resembled a quasi-state within the colonial state structure: there was a Jewish jurisprudence, applicable to all Jews, with a code based on both Dutch secular and Jewish religious legal principles, while the Jodensavanne jurator represented the entire Jewish community in relations with the general civil government. At the same time, the jurator, as controlling legal authority, had the power to impose fines, arrange for shunning, and excommunicate.[5] The Paramaribo-Jodensavanne lay religious leadership, assisted by the rabbinate, also oversaw synagogue maintenance, schools, cemeteries, and social services. Only in 1825, when Surinam passed from Dutch West India Company governance to the Crown, was the office of jurator retired.

Jodensavanne, Surinam, as it appeared c. 1800. Engraving of *Vue de Savannah—le Juif* (Jew's Savannah), by John Gabriel Stedman. William A. Rosenthall Judaica Collection, Special Collections, College of Charleston Library.

Jodensavanne was situated thirty-one miles south of Paramaribo on a hill overlooking the Surinam River. (This important settlement burned down in 1832 and has, archaeological remnants apart, disappeared.) The town had a well-planned gridiron street pattern with a single synagogue, Berakha ve Shalom (Blessing and Peace), built in 1685 and set on a hilltop at the center of a spacious rectangular plaza.[6] Next to the town was a small fort, Gelderland, which defended the settlement from raids by natives and bands of escaped African slaves. Despite its small size, Jodensavanne was recognizably urban: there were a coffee shop, a billiard hall, a fire station, a wharf for shipping, and some eighty houses built within the town limits. Nearby and stretching south for miles along the river were numerous plantations. In 1797 the Philadelphia-educated jurator was David de Isaac Cohen Nassy (1747–1806), a descendent of the community's founding family, who tried to establish in Jodensavanne a college of humanities open to all, though affecting, quite obviously, the Jews of Surinam.[7]

Coffeehouses and billiard halls, not to mention an active river trade, connote a rather robust socioeconomic environment.[8] As in Europe, so in the New World, coffeehouses of the seventeenth and eighteenth centuries provided popular meeting places for merchants, bankers, and businessmen to conduct affairs. Newspaper advertisements announcing professional or commercial engagements were a commonplace in the Atlantic colonies.[9] Obviously coffee, becoming ever more available on both sides of the Atlantic from the onset of the early modern period, has a different stimulant effect than alcohol—one that promotes rational exchange in a social milieu quite different from

the tavern or inn. Sixteenth-century Italian and Ottoman Empire Jews—
Istanbul's first coffeehouse appeared in 1473—had drunk coffee early on,
while Jewish scholars, like their academic incarnations ever since, were quick
to recognize the benefits of coffee. Is it any wonder that the peculiarly ener-
gizing plant first discovered by Ethiopians would go on to be widely cultivated
in the Arab world, then to become a mainstay of plantation agriculture in the
congenial tropical climate of Central and South America? As for Jodensavanne, the billiard hall must have supplemented the socially and profession-
ally active coffeehouse. Because the Surinam River is navigable between the
ocean and the town, the Jodensavanne wharf would have been a conduit for
the district's plantation exports and imports, not to mention news from Paramaribo. Thus, for the better part of a century, Jodensavanne figured as one of
the most thriving Jewish communities in the Americas. But by 1770 the economic winds had shifted, Surinam's agricultural advantages had been supplanted by other Atlantic colonies, and Jews had begun to leave Jodensavanne
for Paramaribo and Amsterdam, where the economy fared better.

Now only a distant memory, Jodensavanne in its prime incorporated certain Jewish-utopian traits. These, as with any aspirationally idealized project,
must be qualified. The town was, for all practical purposes, an exclusively Jewish domain that was granted an unusual degree of autonomy by the Dutch.
The Jewish residents placed a synagogue at the center of their community
design plan as an overt religious, social, and civic statement. According to two
recent expert investigators, Aviva Ben-Ur and Rachel Frankel, "Jodensavanne's
town plan was remarkably similar to that described in [Lutheran theologian]
Johann Valentin Andreae's (1586–1654) utopian *Christianopolis,* published in
1619": for these scholars the Jewish community on the banks of the Surinam
demonstrated the messianic worldview conceived by Andreae for certain seventeenth-century Protestant communities. On this scholarly reading is New
Haven, Connecticut, though a distant continent away; the town's gridiron
plan partially embodies the Puritan theocratic nature of that settlement as it
took shape between 1638 and 1640.[10] While Ben-Ur and Frankel do not conflate Jewish messianism with its Christian analogue, they only remark the
eschatological character of both. Typically insightful, these two researchers
may well be correct when they infer some utopian intention from the name
"Blessing and Peace" (Berakha ve Shalom) given to the synagogue-community in Jodensavanne, but the view that its town plan conveys a full-throated
messianic ideal raises problems. Based on the extant ruins of Jodensavanne
and historical records, the extended Greco-Roman classical tradition seems
the more plausible source for Surinamese Jews' development of their town
plan for this river settlement.

Long centuries after the decline of Rome, her genius for urban design, efficiency in pairing functionality with social requisites, and rational land usage survived, however modified, enriched, or admixed with barbarian (later

national) elements. In this broadest sense, it is the evolved Romano-European heritage that significantly articulates the design projects of Spain, England, and their colonial projections into the Americas during the seventeenth century. Ancient Britannia and Hispania, with many characteristically Roman contributions like a gridiron street pattern, refract over a millennially distant span the towns that later European empire builders—sometimes cultural mediators of Rome—were erecting in the early colonial Atlantic World. For that matter, as far as the Romans were concerned, the gridiron plan was of fifth-century B.C.E. Hellenic origin and was transferred to the Italian peninsula through trade and colonization. That is why we can compare seemingly disparate traditions like Renaissance or Baroque Spanish architecture with the geometric austerity expressed in that quasi-avatar of Andraes's Christianopolis, Puritan New Haven.[11] Of course, it was the Italian Renaissance—discharging an intellectual momentum that spread the perspectival discoveries of Brunelleschi, Alberti, and subsequent like-minded innovators through Italy and much of western Europe—that gave this evolutionary process its greatest impetus since the fifth century: we see a self-consciously classicizing artistic sensibility flourish, supported in turn by elite scholarship committed to retrieving Greco-Roman principles.

So when we observe Euclidean proportionality, symmetry, and balance defining the gridiron design on the banks of the Surinam, there is an identifiable if articulated continuity linking Roman aesthetics and engineering with Jodensavanne's town plan. In fact the linearity and pragmatism of the gridiron should be understood as pan-Romanic. When New Orleans was founded in 1718, the city was similarly plotted on a gridiron, and no one attributes the French Mississippi Company's determined commercial venture at the mouth of the great river to the messianic impulses of colonial New Haven. Andraes's idealized Christianopolis may well have followed a proximate biblical "model": "[each Hebrew tribe should] encamp by its own standard, three tribes each on the north, south, east, and west sides of a square in the center of which was the tent [synagogue] of meeting" (Numbers 2:1–31).[12] But whatever degree of literalism or symbolism may be involved here, such an arrangement hardly seems unique, neither when applied to the centrality of the place of worship, nor especially to the utilitarian and normalizing perspective that laid out streets at right angles to each other with a forum at the town center. It was a deliberate choice of many Atlantic World colonists to adapt the Roman grid to their urban designs: at one level, no doubt ethnocentrically, Europeans must have seen themselves as transforming the state of nature, conferring on a wild and strange terra incognita the orderliness of civilization. How else can we account for similar, far-flung initiatives elsewhere—say, those of the colonizing Dutch, who used the grid plan for their cities across hemispheres and continents, in the Americas, Africa, and Asia.[13] Seen in this light, and in such ubiquity, the intersecting axes found in

Andrae's Christianopolis suggest or embody the general practice of European city planning every bit as much as the symbolism of a missionary Protestant theology.[14]

There are differences, too, between Jodensavanne and the idealized Christianopolis plan. According to *Essai Historique sur la Colonie de Surinam* (1788), whose chief author was David de Isaac Cohen Nassy, the dimensions of Jodensavanne's central plaza were originally 450 feet in length by a width of 300 feet. We must bear in mind that the Surinam town was founded by Sephardic Jews from the Netherlands, Iberia, and Italy, which is to say, by settlers thoroughly versed in Spanish practices. As it happens, the Spanish Law of the Indies—that amalgam of statutes and decrees dating from 1512— specifies that a town's central plaza length should be one and half times the width, just the proportions we find in Jodensavanne and, perforce, rectangular. Not so seventeenth-century New Haven, whose central space was bounded by a square in conformity with the Christianopolis scheme. Moreover another Law of the Indies regulation required the building of a strong palisade around a central plaza to defend against enemy (frequently indigene) attack. On each side of Jodensavanne's synagogue plaza there remains sets of brick columns serving as the gates of a rectangular palisade. This was probably wooden and has long since decayed away. The Christianopolis town plan—so much for the peaceable kingdom—indicates defenses around the *periphery* of the settlement, as was common English practice of the period; Andraes does not propose fortifications to guard the central square alone.[15]

Finally, architectural details aside, we must acknowledge what seems self-evidently true. The Sephardic founders of Jodensavanne, however much the inquiring and educated among them might have been aware of Andraes and his "Christianopolis" text, would almost certainly deprecate a book with this explicit confessional title or purpose. Nor would they accept as a literal model any built environment posited on Protestant millenarian thought. These once-Iberian colonizers in the Americas, whose own speech and cultural memory were steeped in Spanish-Portuguese traditions, would almost certainly have been drawn to a Spanish vocabulary of town planning, codified to a degree in the Law of the Indies, when they gave form to a community meant to express their Sephardic Jewish values.

Yet there is a convergence in what we might call the religious predisposition of the three communities, whether proposed or realized, that we have been examining: the millenarian believers of Andraes, the Connecticut Puritans, and the Sephardim of Jodensavanne all were inspired by messianic conceptions. Influential within early colonial New England, the town plan of New Haven embodied certain theological and social ideas espoused by the colony's Puritan founders.[16] Because eschatology was so keen a force in post-Reformation Europe, it is unremarkable that Christians and Jews would express, though in separate hermeneutic narratives, a powerful messianic preoccupation. This attitude informed seventeenth-century town planning—whether in Europe itself or the brave new worlds opened up through exploration, religious fervor, or commerce. What makes Jodensavanne unique is not its messianic or utopian character but rather the political context in which the Sephardic community emerged: first England, then the Dutch sponsored a nearly autonomous Jewish initiative on the Surinam River.

We can only infer, but the early settlers of Jodensavanne must have consciously adopted relevant Jewish precepts in executing their town plan. For example Judaism's normative legal code, the *Shulcan Aruch*, prescribes (150:1–154:15) that the primary house of worship be situated at the highest elevation in a settlement. Or again: not only did Jodensavanne's location provide ample fresh water and ready commercial access, but also a supply of what Jewish law defines as "living water"—not pumped from the earth but in visible continuous flow—for the ritual bathhouse known as a *mikvah*. We do not find Jodensavanne's Jewish imprint elsewhere in European settlements on either side of the Atlantic. In relatively tolerant, developed cosmopolitan environments, such as Amsterdam, London, or Venice, Jews functioned within an existing Christian context and were forced to accept a lowered or restricted posture—the life of a ghetto or some discrete district, hardly the New Jerusalem.

We cannot leave this small settlement on the Surinam River, etched by its suggestive plan and resonant remains, without remarking on the manifestly Dutch vernacular style of the buildings, almost as if we had encountered a town in rural Holland.[17] Replace Jodensavanne's central synagogue with a Reformed church; retain, almost completely, the external features of the place of worship, and this modest South American colonial community would not be out of place in a painting by Jacob van Ruisdael (1628–82). Unavoidably so: many of the Sephardim who founded the town were from the Netherlands; so too those who raised its buildings—all fully conversant with Dutch architectural models. Why does such a genealogy or architectural gestation matter for so small a place, now almost forgotten, lodged on an edge of the colonial plantation economy? First, we should note that in the early modern period, extending well into the eighteenth century, Jodensavanne's Jewish community was among the most influential and prosperous in the nascent Atlantic World. More important, however, there is what we might call a controlled experiment in cultural dynamics. In Jodensavanne's amalgam of Hebraic, Hispanic, and Dutch motifs, we detect a unique, now-muted, expression of how seventeenth- and eighteenth-century Sephardim, left to their own devices, would conceive a Jewish urban environment on a remote tabula rasa of the Atlantic World. Grafting religious and secular elements, this vanished town invokes a baroque Zionist imagination, *avant la lettre,* on the threshold of the Enlightenment.

During much of the seventeenth and eighteenth centuries, Paramaribo thrived as a colonial capital exporting sugarcane, cacao, and cotton to the Netherlands and Europe. As long as the sugarcane market stayed profitable, Sephardim from Amsterdam made their way to Surinam. The capital also attracted many Ashkenazim, Jodensavanne hardly any. In 1719 Paramaribo's Jews built a synagogue, Neve Shalom (Abode of Peace), but it was regarded as a satellite of Jodensavanne's Berakha ve Shalom, rather than as a separate congregation. Because of religious and social discord between Sephardim and Ashkenazim—non-Iberian Jews were becoming more populous as Paramaribo grew larger—Neve Shalom was effectively ceded to the Ashkenazim in 1735. But, almost oddly, the intra-Jewish divide was not categorical, since Neve Shalom's Jews, central European background and languages notwithstanding, substantively accepted Sephardic minhag, thus continuing to acknowledge Berakha ve Shalom's authority. This Sephardic aura was so prestigious, at least in the Americas sought out by Jewish refugees and conversos from the time of Columbus, that as late as 1835, when the Ashkenazim ambitiously replaced Neve Shalom with a larger building, its overall design scheme remained Sephardic. Paramaribo's Sephardim, still affiliated with the founding Jodensavanne congregation, built their own synagogue, Zedek ve Shalom (Justice and Peace) in 1735. But such Iberian prestige definitely had limits: throughout Surinam's colonial era Ashkenazim and Sephardim insisted on maintaining separate cemeteries.[18]

In fact there was always tension between Sephardim and Ashkenazim in Surinam—as had been true earlier in Amsterdam. However much Dutch-speaking Sephardim carried the early banner of colonial achievement into Jodensavanne and the colonial capital, over half of Surinam's Jewish population was Ashkenazic by 1800. The two Jewish communities were in many senses balkanized, with sociocultural differences so sharp that intermarriage was frequently tantamount to marrying outside the faith. This makes Neve Shalom's acceptance of Berakha ve Shalom's ritual priority in 1735 all the more extraordinary. Couples (hence their families) that intermarried were often ostracized, no small barrier for those seeking appropriate partners in so distant, isolated, and relatively underpopulated a territory as Surinam. By the mid nineteenth century, after some two hundred years of Jewish residence, this kind of discrimination meant that cousins would marry each other sooner than transgress the balkanization. In the event, Surinam's days of wealth would fade, first as the price of sugar declined gradually during the eighteenth century, then as the Napoleonic Wars disrupted markets, and finally as slavery, so necessary for sugarcane production, officially ended in 1863, when the Dutch abolished the practice. As we have seen, in 1832, reduced by slave rebellion and fire, Jodensavanne fell to ruins. Its wealthier

Jewish residents left for the Netherlands, the less prosperous headed for Paramaribo, and the plantation economy beckoned no more.[19]

Around 1693 the Dutch founded Tucacas, a port on the northern Venezuelan coast opposite Curaçao. This became a base for raiding Spanish South America, principally Venezuela and Colombia, as well as for trading contraband—goods legally forbidden by Spain but tolerated as needed by local authorities throughout the Caribbean. Curaçao's Jews were much involved in this black market. As for Tucacas, its Jewish population, which came via Curaçao, had grown enough by 1715 to establish the congregation Santa Irmandade ("Holy Brotherhood" in Portuguese): unusual as it may seem, there are no documents of any kind specifying a Hebrew name for this synagogue-community, which would have been "Chevra Kadisha." In 1720, goaded by illicit trade, a senior Spanish commissioner planned to invade Tucacas by land and sea. The Dutch, warned in advance, withdrew, first burning down the entire settlement, which included the synagogue.[20]

Rivaling Jodensavanne's congregation Berakha ve Shalom by the mid-eighteenth century, Mikve Israel in Willemstad, Curaçao, eventually became the most significant Jewish congregation in the Americas. Regular population increase can be gauged by the replacement of the house of worship into larger, more durable quarters three times—in 1674, 1692, and 1703. Though the first two structures were rather small, the third (1703) must have been larger, as we can infer from the number of ritual artifacts that survived for later use and display. Curaçao's first architecturally impressive mikveh appeared in 1728, and as growth continued, a completely new synagogue was built (1730–32), ever since known as the "Snoa," or synagogue in Papiamento. This creole language, with complex, disputed origins, is now spoken by those of African descent on the Dutch islands of Curaçao, Aruba, and Bonaire. During the eighteenth century, however, Curaçaoian Sephardim surely contributed to the linguistic development: the oldest extant document in this pidgin dates from 1775 and belongs to the correspondence between two Jewish merchants from Curaçao.[21] By 1746 the Snoa could no longer accommodate the population. So yet another sanctuary was built, called Neve Shalom, but it was an affiliate of Mikve Israel rather than a new synagogue-community.[22]

Between 1650 and 1710, the Jews of Curaçao became an essential part of the Dutch colony's economy. Five times as many Jews as non-Jews were traders or financial brokers, while Sephardic merchants owned at least two hundred ships.[23] Little wonder that the opulent residential district of Punda became a preserve of Willemstad's Jewish commercial elite. They also favored elegant mansions or "landhuizen" in the countryside outside the capital.[24] The island's rabbinate produced such notable scholars as Eliahu Lopez (1648–1713), Raphael Jesurun (b. 1678), and Samuel Mendes de Sola (b. 1699), all of whom served on or guided the Beth Din (court of Jewish law) and Vaad (committee to oversee Jewish affairs).[25] Here we find a flourishing

Jewish culture, defining Curaçao as the most vital, dominant, and emulated Jewish community in the Atlantic World until New York's emergence in the second quarter of the nineteenth century. For it was Curaçao's Sephardim who offered the most desirable model for other congregations in the Americas, assuming an important role besides the Amsterdam and London synagogue-communities by providing religious tutelage, social organization, and, at times, financial assistance.

In the northern islands of the Lesser Antilles lies St. Eustatius, a small Dutch possession called *Statia* by its inhabitants. Jews began migrating there in the 1660s from neighboring Caribbean islands, but a significant Jewish community did not take hold until 1730, when Amsterdam's Sephardim petitioned Dutch authorities in the Netherlands for more extensive Jewish privileges. At least in its earlier days, the Jews of St. Eustatius received help from Curaçao. Then, in 1737, congregation Honen Dalim (Charitable to the Poor) was founded and allowed to build a synagogue. This was given financial support from Curaçao. In 1739 the structure was completed, an achievement recognized by Amsterdam's Sephardim through the gift of a Torah scroll.[26]

Unfortunately little material on Jewish women in the Dutch Atlantic World survives. One of the earliest examples are two sisters, Rachel and Clara Belilhos, in late seventeenth- and early eighteenth-century Amsterdam, who ran a small printing establishment that produced Jewish wedding contracts, called *ketubot*. Their father, Daniel Belilhos, who was a teacher of rabbinical and biblical literature, most likely, trained the Belilhos sisters.[27] From Curaçao we have a late eighteenth-century account by Ester Alva Rodriguez Nunes, owner of Berg Sinai plantation. Like her there were other women involved in commerce at this time; all inherited their property.[28] There is, too, the instance of one Rachel Mendes Meza who lived in Jodensavanne during the late eighteenth and early nineteenth centuries. From her gravestone in the Jewish cemetery, we know that Mendes Meza was, quite unusually, a precentor, or prayer leader, a role she must have filled for those at Berakha ve Shalom. This was a rare thing, considering that Jewish law's rigid gender separation rarely allowed for a female "chazzan" (the transliterated Hebrew word for precentor) and given women's passive status in public religious observance during this era.[29] The only other place where this phenomenon is recorded in the Sephardi diaspora, during the seventeenth century, was Ottoman Istanbul and Salonika. Here female cantors lead a second prayer service apart from the one organized by men, as well as taught their fellow women certain aspects of Jewish law relevant to them and the home.[30] At the very least, Mendes Meza was almost certainly aware of her Ottoman counterparts, if not actually a witness to their work on the far opposite side of the Atlantic World.

Scenes of Jewish Life in Eighteenth-Century Netherlands and Her Empire

The brit milah, or circumcision, is performed on a male newborn on its eighth day and is the sign of God's covenant with the Jews that was first made with Abraham the Patriarch (Genesis 17:1–14). The mohel performs the ceremony with the assistance of the sandek. The sandek holds the baby while the mohel performs the minor operation. Engraving by Bernard Picart, *Cérémonies et coutumes religieuses de tous les peuples du monde,* Amsterdam, 1723. William A. Rosenthall Judaica Collection, Special Collections, College of Charleston Library.

The pidyon ha-ben, or redemption of the firstborn son, is a ritual that applies to a firstborn son of any Jew except a member of the tribe of Levi. That child (not descended from the priestly tribe) is released from the obligation to serve in the Temple. This ritual is done twenty-nine days after the birth of the newborn and only for those born naturally (as opposed to by caesarean section). Levites and the sons of Kohanim (plural of Kohen) and (part of the tribe of Levi), however, cannot be released from the obligation to serve in the Temple according to Jewish tradition (even after the destruction of the Temple). Engraving by Bernard Picart, *Cérémonies et coutumes religieuses de tous les peuples du monde*, Amsterdam, 1723. William A. Rosenthall Judaica Collection, Special Collections, College of Charleston Library.

BOTTOM FACING: The mikvah, a small pool of water fed from a spring or groundwater well, is still used by traditional Jews, for ritual purification. The reservoir is frequently drained to allow new water into the pool. Bathing remains an important observance by married women who thus satisfy the rules of family purity (*taharat ha-mishpacha*), especially in relation to menstruation. Men occasionally use the mikvah for purification before a major holiday or the Sabbath. Water from the mikvah is also used to purify kitchen utensils for Kosher dietary purposes. Drawn by P. Wagenaar and engraved by C. Philips Jacobsz, 1783. William A. Rosenthall Judaica Collection, Special Collections, College of Charleston Library.

A Dutch Sephardic wedding ceremony. Engraving by Bernard Picart, *Cérémonies et coutumes religieuses de tous les peuples du monde*, Amsterdam, 1723. William A. Rosenthall Judaica Collection, Special Collections, College of Charleston Library.

Cleaning the home for the Passover holiday—by searching for chametz, that is, bread, grains, and other leavened products—is done every spring. The prohibition on consuming chametz is specified in Exodus 12:15–20 and 13:3, and Deuteronomy 16:3–4. Engraving by Bernard Picart, *Cérémonies et coutumes religieuses de tous les peuples du monde*, Amsterdam, 1723. William A. Rosenthall Judaica Collection, Special Collections, College of Charleston Library.

BOTTOM FACING: Sukkoth, also known as the Feast of Booths, is a festival marking both the Exodus from Egypt and the fall harvest. Observance requires the construction of a temporary booth, called a sukkah, in which, according to traditional practice, one dwells during the holiday. These booths serve as dual symbols: for the temporary shelters used by Israelites during their forty years of wandering the Sinai; and for the general bounty of nature as farmers harvested their fall crops. Engraving by Bernard Picart, *Cérémonies et coutumes religieuses de tous les peuples du monde*, Amsterdam, 1723. William A. Rosenthall Judaica Collection, Special Collections, College of Charleston Library.

The Passover seder is the festive meal during which the Israelite flight from Egypt as recounted in the book of Exodus is celebrated. Engraving by Bernard Picart, *Cérémonies et coutumes religieuses de tous les peuples du monde*, Amsterdam, 1723. William A. Rosenthall Judaica Collection, Special Collections, College of Charleston Library.

Shmira is the vigil for the deceased held just after death and before burial. This custom allows the deceased to be attended, never alone, before burial. One or more attendants, or shomrim (plural), normally members of the (holy) burial society, or Chevra Kadisha, conduct the vigil and recite psalms. In some Sephardic communities, shomrim circle the deceased seven times during the shmira. Only then can the memorial service and burial take place, usually at the gravesite. It is this circular movement that is most likely represented in this engraving. Engraving by Bernard Picart, *Cérémonies et coutumes religieuses de tous les peuples du monde*, Amsterdam, 1723. William A. Rosenthall Judaica Collection, Special Collections, College of Charleston Library.

A Jewish burial, most likely at the Beth Haim Cemetery at Ouderkerk aan de
Amstel, where Amsterdam's Sephardic cemetery is located. Engraving by Bernard
Picart, *Cérémonies et coutumes religieuses de tous les peuples du monde*, Amsterdam, 1723. William A. Rosenthall Judaica Collection, Special Collections, College
of Charleston Library.

The Dutch golden age, a period falling between the late sixteenth and
eighteenth centuries, ushered in a renaissance, or in some instances a first
birth, of synagogue architecture. To the degree that the Atlantic World traced
a dialectic between Europe and the Americas, there can be little doubt that
Dutch material and aesthetic culture informed Sephardic synagogues in the
New World more rapidly than in the Dutch Republic itself. For Europeans,
though obviously and tragically not for American indigenes or enslaved Africans, both western continents and the Caribbean islands presented a blank
slate, where imperial development and exploration became a template for
economic gain, religious experiment or orthodoxy, and sociopolitical initiative. We have seen that the constraints or punishments visited for so long on
European Jewry markedly diminished throughout the seventeenth century
in the Protestant territories across the Atlantic. In this newly discovered, or
newly conquered, world Sephardim built their synagogues anew—just as they
forged new, better lives in ever greater numbers. The architectural record is
statistically and sociologically revealing. For the Dutch Sephardim—the Ashkenazic experience was utterly different—the construction of Amsterdam's

two impressive Portuguese synagogues, the first in 1636–39 and the great Esnoga in 1671–75, marked a term, or at least a hiatus. Only three additional purpose-built Sephardic synagogues appeared in the Netherlands before the Patriot Revolt of 1787—the crystallizing event that links the Netherlands to the Euro-American revolutions. In fact nearly a half century had to pass before there were any Sephardic successors to the Amsterdam achievements: Neve Shalom was built in Maarssen (1720), Honen Dal (or the Snoge) in The Hague (1726), and the Portuguese Synagogue in Naarden (1759). There were few other Dutch Sephardic communities. Even the relatively significant ones in Rotterdam and Middleburg had developed only schuilkerken.[31] But this is no mystery, only demography. By 1700 it was Ashkenazim who constituted the majority of Dutch Jewry, thus the scores of synagogues that dot the towns and villages across the Netherlands were built by Jews of central and eastern European origin. But the Dutch overseas acquisitions tell us a different story—one of diasporal momentum. Between 1640 and 1787, the Sephardim in the Atlantic colonies erected no fewer than sixteen purpose-built synagogues, often when climate, site locations, or distances from sources of supply made construction difficult. With perhaps the exception of Curaçao's Snoa, the Sephardic synagogues of the Netherlands in use as of 1787 were architecturally more substantial than those in the colonies. The New World synagogues, the Snoa excepted, cannot bear architectural comparison with the larger, more ornate, and more elegantly designed Sephardic synagogues to be found in the Netherlands. The colonial houses of worship were most often utilitarian, built on a small scale to serve small populations. Still we can detect from the geographic range of these religious structures, a span that encompassed the Caribbean and both American continents, a Sephardic advance into the New World that prepared the ground for Jews of the Americas to thrive in a non-European future.

Jewish Admission into Denmark and the Danish Empire

Denmark's role in the Atlantic World was relatively minor when placed beside the imperial projects of Spain, Portugal, Great Britain, France, and the Netherlands. Yet that role nevertheless attracted the attention of Jews. Between 1619 and 1630, King Christian IV (1577–1648) invited Sephardim from Hamburg and Amsterdam, as well as other German Ashkenazim, to settle in Denmark, a land where Jews had previously been unwelcome. In fact the royal invitation provides the earliest record of Jewish settlement in Denmark. When King Fredrick III (1609–70) formally opened Denmark to Jews in 1657, it took some time for Jews to respond: first Frederica (1682) and Copenhagen (1684), then other commercial centers, received Jewish immigrants, although the Copenhagen community quickly became the largest. This nascent presence was reinforced by close ties, at once economic, religious, or even familial, with English and Dutch Jews. Danish congregations during the

TABLE 2. The Sephardic synagogues built in the Dutch Empire
before the Patriot Revolt in 1787

Synagogue	Years Extant	Location	Notes
Talmud Torah / Portuguese Synagogue (I)	1636–1931	Amsterdam, Netherlands	
Zur Israel	1640–1900s	Recife, Brazil	Used as a synagogue until 1654
Magen Abraham	1648–1653	Mauricia, Brazil	Satellite synagogue of Zur Israel
Unknown	1661–1667	Cayenne (French) Guyana	
Unknown	1671–after 1685	Thorarica, Suriname	
Mikve Israel (I)	1674–1692	Willemstad, Curaçao	
Talmud Torah (II) / Esnoga	1675–present	Amsterdam, Netherlands	
Berakha ve Shalom	1685–after 1832	Jodensavanne, Suriname	
Mikve Israel (II)	1692–1703	Willemstad, Curaçao	
Mikve Israel (III)	1703–1730	Willemstad, Curaçao	
Santa Irmandad	1710s–1720	Tucacas, Venezuela	
Neve Shalom	1719–1835	Paramaribo, Suriname	Ashkenazic satellite synagogue of Berakha ve Shalom
Neve Shalom	1720–1839	Maarssen, Netherlands	
Honen Dal / Snoge	1726–present	The Hague, Netherlands	
Mikve Israel / Snoa (IV)	1732–present	Willemstad, Curaçao	
Zedek ve Shalom	1735–present	Paramaribo, Suriname	Sephardic satellite synagogue of Berakha ve Shalom
Honen Dalim	1739–after 1800	Oranjestad, St. Eustatius	
Neve Shalom	1746–after 1864	Willemstad, Curaçao	Satellite synagogue of Mikve Israel
Portuguese Synagogue	1759–1935	Naarden, Netherlands	
Darkhe Yesharim	1779–1800	Paramaribo, Suriname	Mulatto satellite synagogue of Berakha ve Shalom
Unknown	1783–before 1828	Philipsburg, St. Maarten	

seventeenth century were housed in vernacular buildings, such as Copenhagen's first modest synagogue, and resembled the *schuilkerken* of the Lowlands.[32] Not until 1766 would Denmark have its first purpose-built Jewish house of worship, the Great Synagogue of Copenhagen, which, lasting hardly three decades, burned down in 1795.[33] But another Great Synagogue, this time designed by the distinguished Danish architect Gustav Friedrich Hechst in a hybrid Egyptian-Greek revival style, was built in 1833 and stands to this day.

Beginning in the ninth-century C.E. then proceeding with ever more boldness, Norsemen and Vikings were the first North Atlantic mariners to settle the Faroe Islands, Iceland, Greenland, and Newfoundland. Our concern here is not with Scandinavian medieval navigators or colonizers but rather with the post-Columbian voyagers of early modern history. The Danes, as lineal descendents of Norsemen, remained occupants of the Faroes and Iceland continuously; by the 1730s Denmark would once again recolonize Greenland. Yet there is no time before the eighteenth century when this very old Scandinavian record reveals any Jewish presence—though more scrupulous to say *significant* Jewish presence. By the early eighteenth century, however, some Sephardic Jews from Copenhagen had begun trading with Iceland and the Faroes, notably in tobacco. The nicotine-rich plant, originating in the Americas, was an increasingly popular export crop grown by Sephardic planters in the New World and traded by Jewish merchants in Europe. During the seventeenth and eighteenth centuries, Jewish involvement with Danish North Sea or Atlantic colonies was limited to this tobacco market.[34]

But the Caribbean in this era was another matter. In 1671, under the aegis of the Danish West India Company set up the same year, the Danes founded their first permanent Caribbean colony on St. Thomas. To this island came not only Danish Jews, but also Jews from the Dutch, British, and French Empires during the 1670s and 1680s. In 1684 Gabriel Milan (1631–89), a Sephardic convert to Lutheranism whose commerce with Denmark and the Netherlands thrived, became governor of St. Thomas—a post held for five years, until he was removed for abuse of power.[35] By 1796 there were Jews enough to erect at Charlotte Amalie, St. Thomas, a first synagogue, Beraka ve Shalom ve Gemilut Hasadim (Blessing and Peace and Acts of Piety). Because many Jewish immigrants to this Danish territory came from Dutch St. Eustatius, the new congregation, as so frequently was the case throughout the eighteenth century Atlantic World, accepted the bylaws and practices of the Amsterdam Esnoga. Beraka ve Shalom ve Gemilut Hasadim burned down twice: in 1804, to be replaced by an 1813 building, then again in 1831. A third sanctuary was promptly completed in 1833 and still graces St. Thomas.[36]

After long dispute Denmark gained St. John from Great Britain in 1717 and St. Croix from France in 1733. Although St. John had many sugarcane plantations, few Jews settled there. It took a generation for the Jews of St. Croix to build a synagogue (in 1764), but the house of worship burned only two years later without any successor. Even the name of this early synagogue-community has vanished. Nonetheless this lost St. Croix sanctuary should be considered the first purpose-built synagogue on Danish territory since it predated Copenhagen's Great Synagogue by two years.[37]

At the end of the eighteenth century and in the first decades of the nineteenth century, the Enlightenment had permeated Lutheran Denmark. One result was as to relax various restrictions on Jews. They could and did join guilds, attend Danish universities, and own real property. During the Napoleonic Wars, after the British bombardment of Copenhagen (1807), Denmark became a French ally. In 1849, after Europe's second cataclysm of attempted liberal revolutions, all Danish Jews were categorically emancipated and received the same citizenship rights as the general populace.[38]

Jewish Life in the Age of British Empire Building

If Denmark represents a minor (though interesting) marker on the map of the Europeanized Atlantic World, Great Britain stands at the opposite point on the imperial scale, attaining the full measure of military and socioeconomic dominance. Gradually but inexorably an environment would develop in the English-speaking lands between the early modern period and the Enlightenment that let Jews thrive materially and culturally. We should recall that only two decades passed between Cromwell's readmission policy for Jews— a mixture of realpolitik and tolerance—and the general freedom of worship granted Jews by Charles II in 1674. This royal command meant that Jews during the latter half of the Restoration could attend synagogues rather than recite prayers at home. Later, after the 1688 revolution, Jews were excepted by indirect parliamentary sanction from penalties under the Blasphemy Act (1698): all Christians, especially nonconformists, who denied the Trinity were blasphemous; not so Jews, who denied Christ's divinity in the first place and were thus perceived as *hors de combat*.[39] Indeed this was an issue Jews had to be weary of. As early as 1658, in colonial Maryland—only a few years after readmission—we find the unfortunate Jacob Lumbrozo in front of the Provincial Court for blasphemy, having denied the divinity of Jesus, since Lumbrozo was Jewish. Fortunately he was given clemency. The governor, Josias Fendall (1628–87), issued a mass pardon in celebration of Richard Cromwell (1626–1712) becoming the second Lord Protector. Lumbrozo's case was dropped before sentencing.[40]

In 1705, four years after Bevis Marks was completed, London was the site of England's first Jewish-owned and -operated printing press in Hebrew— that is, with fonts set in Hebrew letters. This matters. During the seventeenth century, there had been several English Protestant presses producing publications in Hebrew. The consumers of these works were Christian Hebraists. But both literally and symbolically, as the Enlightenment took shape, England's Jews had achieved a prerequisite of cultural dissemination: they could now prepare and publish texts in their ancient language while relying on historical, scholarly, and intellectual sources that were undilutedly Jewish.[41]

Over time Jewish "citizenship rights"—a convenient if anachronistic usage in an age of monarchy—were also being realized in the colonial arena. In 1740 Parliament passed the Naturalization Act, often known as the Plantation Act, allowing Jews and nonconformist Protestants (though not Roman Catholics) in British America to become subjects of the Crown after seven continuous years of proven residence. Previously a colonial alien had to apply to the monarch, the colonial governor, or Parliament for naturalization rights, a process that was often tedious, daunting, and expensive. So we encounter one Luis Gomez (b. 1660), a Jew who emigrated to New York City in 1703, who spent more than £57 (roughly £7,400 today) to obtain a "patent of denization" (naturalization) from Queen Anne in 1708.[42] Likewise there is the Sephardi Simon Valentine. He not only purchased burgher's rights from New York in 1682 but, having moved south, fifteen years later received formal naturalization from the Carolina assembly and Carolina governor Joseph Blake.[43] In fact Valentine would become the first Jew to purchase land in South Carolina. It's likely that his redundant acquisition of British colonial status was meant to cover any possible legal, financial, or bureaucratic hurdle that might face an émigré merchant at the turn of the eighteenth century.

The Naturalization Act also recognized the dignity of the Jewish faith in certain matters of legal procedure. Jews were exempted from being bound by oaths "upon the true faith of a Christian" and were allowed to swear truthfulness on the Hebrew, not the Christian, Bible. It must be said that ambiguity in the relevant portion of the 1740 Act also allowed anti-Semitic administrators to nullify such tolerance and consideration. In some instances, notably in Jamaica, Barbados, and Bermuda, there were officials who penalized Jews out of bias or in pursuit of personal interests. In 1753 Parliament passed the Jewish Naturalization Act, commonly and with no subtlety designated the "Jew Bill." This law naturalized Jews who lived in England, Scotland, Wales, and Ireland—the homeland polities not covered by the earlier Naturalization Act—but was repealed because of Tory anti-Semitism only months later. Moreover this followed an earlier attempt by Ireland's House of Commons in 1746 and 1747 to naturalize "persons professing the Jewish religion in Ireland."[44] At the time only Protestants were eligible to vote. Catholics, the majority of the island's population, were disfranchised. Naturalizing Jews would have enticed more to settle there; however, Ireland's attempt at Jewish naturalization never received the royal assent. So Jewish colonists in the Americas, at least in legal form and often in practice, were more enabled than Jews in the British Isles.

Regrettably, deplorable as were the bias and hostility that so rapidly assailed the Jewish Naturalization Act, the population balance between Jews resident in the British Isles and those in overseas possessions was not the same between 1655 and 1800 as would be the case subsequently in the nineteenth and twentieth centuries. Invariably more Jews lived in the British Isles, primarily London, than abroad. Moreover the importance of colonial Jewry was well understood among Jews who lived in Great Britain. In 1688 Daniel Levi de Barrios (1635–1701) wrote in a poem: "Now, in six English cities, made known is the light of six sacred lights of Israel [congregations]: three in Nevis, London, Jamaica; the fourth and fifth in two parts of Barbados; and the sixth takes place in Madras Patan [India]."[45] To verify, the emphasis of de Barrios's informative poem was on congregations, not purpose-built synagogues. However, the number of colonial synagogue-communities, especially in the Americas, was hardly trivial either. In the forty years after Cromwell's 1655 readmission of Jews, no synagogues were built in England, while three—two on Barbados alone—had appeared in the Caribbean. Great Britain's first synagogue was Bevis Marks (1701), and two more London sanctuaries would follow it before 1740; at the same time, across the vastness of British America, six synagogues, three on Jamaica alone, were built.[46] On the eve of the American Revolution, eight of the thirteen purpose-built synagogues in the empire were to be found outside of Great Britain. This geographic range should not hide the fact that Britain's eighteenth-century domestic Jewish population was considerably larger than its dispersed analogues overseas. Nor should we suppose that the modest, occasionally quite plain colonial houses of worship could stand architectural or aesthetic comparison to sanctuaries in Great Britain proper. Although British synagogues may have taken longer to build, the pace of construction comports with the size, elegance of design, and imposing materials used, not to mention the sheer cost of construction and decoration in Great Britain. For that matter, from eighteenth-century illustrations, we know that the majority of British Jewish houses of worship, whether in London, Portsmouth (1740s), Birmingham (1740s), or Liverpool (1750s), were inconsequential architecturally.[47] Most English Jews of the time worshipped in rented or provisional quarters, structures displaying only the most basic architectural motifs. In nondescript appearance though not perforce, such congregations seemed close to the anonymity of Dutch schuilkerken.

Certainly the Naturalization Act of 1740, coupled with British ascendency in the Atlantic World, determined where European Jews emigrated. Aside Curaçao and St. Eustatius, as the Dutch Empire slowly began to decline during the middle eighteenth century, it would be British possessions that presented to Jews their colonial destinations of choice and opportunity. We see synagogues appearing throughout the British sphere of settlement—not least in the thirteen Atlantic seaboard colonies that cohered in 1776. But a reverse demographic trend, evident from the synagogue census among other economic measures, affected the American ventures of the Dutch. Their colonies had seen thirteen Jewish houses of worship erected between 1640 and 1739. In the subsequent fifty years (1740–1830), only three synagogues were built.[48]

Front entrance to London's New Synagogue: its location on Leadenhall Street was leased from the 1760s to the 1830s. The New Synagogue congregation shared this building with another tenant, the General Literary Institute.[49] Engraving by J. Nixon, *European Magazine*, London, 1 August 1811. William A. Rosenthall Judaica Collection, Special Collections, College of Charleston Library.

TABLES 3 AND 4. The synagogues built in the British Empire before the American Revolution in 1776

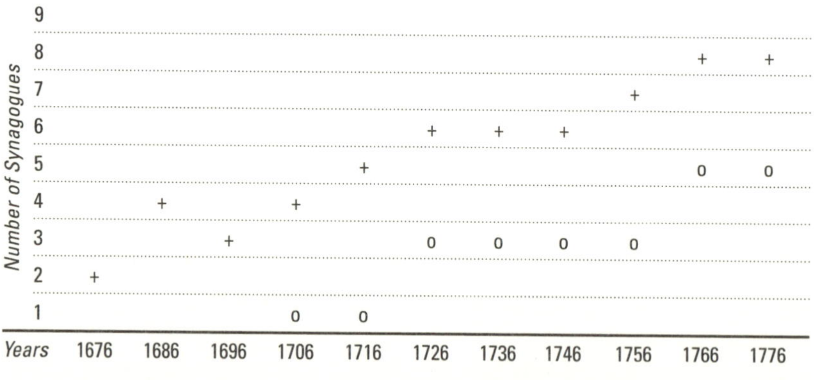

TABLE 3 AND 4. (CONTINUED)

Synagogue	Years Extant	Location	Notes
Nidhe Israel	1660s–1831	Bridgetown, Barbados	
Semah David	1660s/70s–1739	Speightstown, Barbados	Destroyed by riot
Neve Zedek (I)	c. 1684–1692	Port Royal, Jamaica	Destroyed by earthquake
Unknown	c. 1684–1772	Charlestown, Nevis	Destroyed by hurricane
Sha'ar Hashamayim / Bevis Marks	1701–present	London, England	
Neve Shalom	1704–1907	Spanish Town, Jamaica	
Shaar Ha Shamaim (I)	after 1704–1744	Kingston, Jamaica	Replaced by 1744
Neve Zedek (II)	c. 1719–1815	Port Royal, Jamaica	
Great Synagogue / Duke's Place	1722–1790	London, England	
Hambro Synagogue	1726–1893	London, England	
Shearith Israel	1730–1818	New York, New York	
Shaar Ha Shamaim (II)	c. 1744–1882	Kingston, Jamaica	
Shaar Hashamayim (I)	1749–1766	Gibraltar	Destroyed by storm
Plymouth Synagogue	1762–present	Plymouth, England	
Jeshuat Israel / Touro Synagogue	1763–present	Newport, Rhode Island	
Exeter Synagogue	1763–present	Exeter, England	
Shaar Hashamyim (II)	1768–1781	Gibraltar	

Notwithstanding thwarted naturalization in 1753, eighteenth-century Great Britain provided Jews with a tolerant, socioeconomically stable environment that fostered settlement. Besides London, Plymouth (1762) and then Exeter (1763) gained purpose-built synagogues, which testifies both to population growth as well as a sense of broader economic potential for a minority. But, as with so many aspects of English urban society, London remained the epicenter, its small population of 750 (in 1700) growing over the century to fifteen thousand, mostly Ashkenazim (in 1800). In 1678 the familiar tension between Spanish-Portuguese Jews and those of central European origin was already evident at Bevis Marks. By the 1690s this strain led most Ashkenazim to leave Bevis Marks. Even earlier some central European Jews had already begun to pray in small, makeshift locations, often private residences. While documentary evidence is secondhand or virtually nonexistent, despite, too, the malleability of early eighteenth-century place names when applied to maps, a group of London's Ashkenazim founded a congregation, north of Aldgate in an area called Duke's Place, c. 1690. Not until 1722 did they erect a purpose-built house of worship, upon which they called themselves the Great

Synagogue.[50] Three smaller Ashkenazic synagogue-communities—they were named Hambro, New, and Western—were also active by the end of the seventeenth century or soon after Queen Anne's reign began (1702). The expanding Great Synagogue congregation chose the gifted architect James Spiller to build a much larger, classically inspired, and quite beautiful sanctuary in 1790, which lasted until destruction by Nazi bombing in 1941. As for the Hambro Synagogue (built 1726), it was torn down in 1893, while the New and Western congregations did not occupy purpose-built houses of worship until the nineteenth century.[51] But numerous as were London's Ashkenazim, their influence with Jews abroad remained marginal until the end of the Napoleonic era. Before then, as we have seen time and again, Atlantic World Jewry was far more likely to maintain contacts with the Sephardic community of Bevis Marks. Only when very large numbers of Ashkenazim arrived in Great Britain after 1815 did the religious authority and economic strength of London's central and eastern European Jews disseminate among Jewish communities in the British Empire. By then these colonial Jews were largely Ashkenazic too, some settling in Canada, but others in places far away from American or Caribbean shores—in South Africa, Australia, and New Zealand.[52]

In 1704 a joint British-Dutch invasion force captured Gibraltar, which Spain soon ceded to Great Britain through the Treaty of Utrecht (1714). Although this peace agreement ending the War of the Spanish Succession forbade Jewish or Muslim settlement in Gibraltar, the British ignored this stipulation—a policy that, when joined with other concerns, goaded Spain twice to mount unsuccessful campaigns (1727, 1779–83) against Europe's Mediterranean gateway. Yet, given British naval power, the Utrecht peace effectively meant that more than two centuries after the great Iberian racial expulsion, Semites could, and did, return to the peninsula, officially so in 1727, when the British agreed with Morocco's sultan to let Muslims and Jews cross the straits and live on Gibraltar. However, some Jews had entered the territory before the formal British policy of acceptance. During the eighteenth century, Gibraltar would thrive as an entrepot linking Europe, Africa, the Americas, and the Mediterranean. Sephardic Jews from Great Britain, the Netherlands, and Morocco, as well as crypto-Jews from Spain and Portugal, sought out British Gibraltar for its mercantile advantages and religious tolerance. By midcentury, one-third (575 people) of the colony's civilian population was Jewish; they even owned 20 percent of Gibraltar's private property.[53]

In 1749 Haham Isaac Nieto (1702–74) traveled from London to Gibraltar, where he became the founding rabbi of Shaar Hashamayim (Gates of Heaven). This synagogue, dating from Nieto's arrival and the first to be built in Iberia since the expulsions of 1492–98, must have posed a manifest religiopolitical affront to the Spanish, themselves no longer masters of this strategic enclave. Shaar Hashamayim itself was destroyed in 1766 but was rebuilt only two years later. Another somewhat cryptic Jewish organization, Etz Chaim (Tree of Life), appeared in 1759, but without any relevant documents or records, it's unclear whether this name referred to a yeshiva, a religious congregation, or both. As for Isaac Nieto, he seemed destined for the rabbinate as son of no less a figure than David Nieto, rabbi of London's Bevis Marks and a leader whose intellectual distinction and institutional acumen were greatly admired. So it was hardly unusual for Isaac Nieto to be recalled to Bevis Marks, where he succeeded his father from 1751 until 1757. Back in London Isaac Nieto was even named *av bet din*—head of the rabbinical court.[54]

Not only in the Atlantic World but also in the entire empire, Jamaica was the British colony whose population grew fastest. Under the Spanish the island had been sparsely populated—a forgotten backwater. Following the English conquest, Jamaica became a hub first for privateering and then for lucrative sugarcane plantations. An earthquake destroyed Port Royal's synagogue in 1692, but it was rebuilt in 1719 as Neve Zedek (Abode of Justice).[55] Presumably the destroyed building had also been called Neve Zedek; this name certainly was given to the second structure and to its congregation, which in any case disbanded by midcentury as Jews preferred the thriving communities of Spanish Town and Kingston.

From surviving cemeteries are known various small Jewish settlements in Jamaica: Lacovia, Savanna-la-Mar, Buff Bay, St. Ann's Bay, Port Maria, Annotto Bay, Longwood, Lucea, and Falmouth. But synagogues were another matter. These were built only in larger, successful communities like Spanish Town, Kingston, or Montego Bay. So we find Neve Shalom (1704), Spanish Town's first synagogue, in use for almost two hundred years, closing in 1900. At the time of the 1907 earthquake, which caused significant damage to the building, it was the oldest extant synagogue in the British Empire outside of London. Although Kingston Jews built Shaar Ha Shamaim in the early eighteenth century, almost no records remain; not so the successor structure (built 1744), which survived until the Great Fire of 1882. Beth Jacob, Montego Bay's synagogue, was not built until 1845 but suffered that same tropical fate—destruction by hurricane in 1912.[56]

The synagogue of Nevis, one of the Leeward Islands, is the least known of all the British Caribbean synagogues. Jews inhabited this small outpost from the last quarter of the seventeenth century until the early nineteenth century. When the synagogue was built, when it disappeared remain conjectural, although construction toward the end of the seventeenth century seems likely. We know that the island's Jewish community was in decline by the 1760s, and there is reason to believe that the synagogue did not survive a hurricane in 1772. Nevis was the birthplace of at least one great Enlightenment figure, Alexander Hamilton (c. 1755–1804), whose birth from an illegitimate marriage closed the doors of Anglican schooling to the young student. But the island's Jewish school, almost certainly housed in the synagogue, admitted the future revolutionary and foundational economist of the early American republic to classes. This inclusiveness Hamilton never forgot. His favorable opinion of Judaism and its adherents remained constant in a man not known for intellectual sloth or wayward enthusiasms.[57]

Another English possession, not in the Caribbean but lodged below Cape Cod on the East Coast of North America, would likewise attract Jews from afar. In 1658 some fifteen Sephardic families from Dutch Brazil arrived at Newport, Rhode Island. These Jews had been wandering in the Caribbean since 1654. Rhode Island was the first colony in the empire to allow freedom of religious conscience as well as the separation of church and state—both positions advocated by Roger Williams (c. 1603–83). There should be no understating Williams's radical tolerance in this age of European confessional barriers. Williams was a nonconformist theologian and minister whose profound objections to state Anglicanism, then Puritanism, eventually led to his banishment from the Massachusetts Bay Colony (1635) and his resettlement in Providence, Rhode Island (1636). Even though he professed Protestantism, Williams soon insisted that freedom of worship should be given to all, specifically mentioning Jews, "Turks," and other "Antichristian consciences."[58] As for Newport, established in 1636 on Aquidneck Island in Narragansett Bay, the town actualized the new tolerance: the Brazilian Sephardic immigration (1658) meant that Rhode Island became the first English North American colony to accept a discrete Jewish population. Four years earlier some Jews had arrived in Dutch New Amsterdam. Even though the first Newport Jewish community dispersed, a second group of Caribbean Jews arrived in the 1690s, until yet more Jews came in the eighteenth century—finally forming a stable community.[59] But we are still talking about quite small numbers. At its height before the American Revolution, the Jewish population in Newport numbered two hundred.

As we have seen so often in the Atlantic experience, Jewish mercantile skills carried economic benefit. Traders like Aaron Lopez (1731–82) and his father-in-law, Jacob Rodriguez Rivera (1717–89), thrived in Newport. Lopez, a crypto-Jew born in Lisbon as Duarte Lopez, fled Portugal, accompanied by his first wife Abigail and infant daughter. He was determined to make a full return to Judaism and to join his well-established older half-brother, Moses Lopez (1706–67). Once in Newport Duarte was circumcised and took the name Aaron.[60] Lopez traded throughout the rim of the Atlantic World, with far-reaching connections. Though his business success was impressive, it was not unusual within the Atlantic World's Sephardic mercantile network. From Newport Lopez exported spermaceti candles, furniture, axes, flour, and salted fish. Among the exports, too, were African slaves bound for the Caribbean as well as North America.[61] Lopez was an indefatigable entrepreneur who constructed both buildings and ships. We do not know about particular buildings he designed, but Lopez's construction methods amounted to what we might call prefabrication. In one location workmen would make frames or housing sections, which were then assembled elsewhere. Customers for such prebuilt structures came from as far away as Jamaica, and Lopez would also supply carpenters for final assembly.[62] David Lopez Sr. (1750–1811), Aaron's nephew, was a merchant in Charleston, South Carolina, where architectural ornaments were sold from his store.[63] Even though the British colonies made possible the prominence of the extended Lopez family, naturalization did not come readily before the American Revolution. Rhode Island's freedom of worship would not translate into citizenship rights for colonial Jews—at least a nominal hindrance to commerce. Aaron Lopez, with his formidable resilience, became naturalized in Massachusetts, the Bay Colony in this instance showing more tolerance than Williams's own project.[64]

In 1756 the Jews of Newport formed congregation Jeshuat Israel (Salvation of Israel), purchasing land for a synagogue three years later. The synagogue, designed by Peter Harrison, was the first in North America to have been done by a professional architect. Building costs were shared by Jews spread across the Atlantic World, as Newport Jews turned to communities in New York, London, Curaçao, Jamaica, and Surinam for assistance. By then the French and Indian War had intervened, so construction was delayed. Among contributors to the Jeshuat Israel project was Aaron Lopez, whose generosity and efforts earned him the distinction of laying one of the synagogue's cornerstones. Lopez also purchased other ritual objects for the sanctuary.[65]

Almost all cities, even the most imposing, begin modestly. At the start of the eighteenth century, Manhattan provided a port and a splendid harbor but otherwise must have seemed poised precariously at the portal of a vast green frontier. We have already seen the first Jews to arrive in New Amsterdam were Sephardim who made their way north as refugees from Dutch Brazil. Before 1695 the small Jewish contingent in New York—the city having passed from the Netherlands to England between 1664 and 1674—were required to practice their religion, privately and unobtrusively, in homes. This changed sometime between 1695 and 1704 when congregation Shearith Israel lifted the veil and rented a building where services were held. It was in 1730 that this same congregation built a synagogue, which thus became the first structure erected for Jewish worship in North America.[66] Two years earlier the property itself was purchased on Mill Street, in lower Manhattan. Stanley Holmes, a local bricklayer, became the contractor and builder for a fee of £100, plus a loaf of sugar and a pound of (black Chinese) Bohea tea.[67]

Typically the Sephardic Atlantic network made financial donations for this project. As it happens, one Stanley Holmes was a juror in the famous John Peter Zenger (1697–1746) libel trial (1735), the case synonymous with its jury's resounding decision to protect press freedom in America. We do not know if this was the same Holmes who built Shearith Israel. But if so, then he might well be regarded as an early advocate for liberty, whether in the cause of religious tolerance—Jews surely being unpopular—or for civil society, given the Zenger jury's defiance of both judge and colonial governor. [68]

Included in *A Plan of the City and Environs of New York* (1813 by cartographer David Grim) is an illustration, though with little detail, of the synagogue.[69] Shearith Israel survived both the Revolution and the War of 1812, until demolition in 1818 made way for a larger synagogue, one that in turn gave way to an even larger Greek Revival structure on Crosby Street (built 1834).

For much of the eighteenth century, Boston and Philadelphia were larger cities than New York. Its population in 1750 was about twelve thousand. For much of the eighteenth century, New York's Jewish population was quite small. Many Jews were merchants often away from the city on business. At the time of the Naturalization Act (1740), the New York census counted only thirty-four adult Jewish men, all except eight listed as merchants. These businessmen were frequently away as they handled trade in the Caribbean and Europe. In the event, where Sephardim and Ashkenazim were so fractious elsewhere in the colonial orbit, they tended to cooperate in British North America. Small wonder. With such an extremely small population, American colonial Jews were in effect forced to coexist, whether for religious, social, or political reasons. During the second half of the eighteenth century, Ashkenazim began to outnumber Sephardim in British North America. But these colonial congregations, whether central European or Iberian in composition, so relied on the financial support and religious guidance of Bevis Marks, the Esnoga, and the larger Caribbean communities—the Sephardic hegemony—that cultural differences were never given free rein to alienate or displace.[70] Cadets, despite private reservations, for the most part salute officers. This situation meant that Sephardim, either in New York or throughout Britain's Atlantic colonies, were often positioned to control religious or community affairs.

Among prominent New York Jews were families with the surnames Franks, Seixas, Pacheco, Levy, and Gomez. We should note Abigaill Franks (1696–1756), married to the successful merchant Jacob Franks (1688–1769). Her correspondence (1733–1748) with her son Naphtali, who lived in London, not only describes the particularities of a Jewish mother and wife but also documents, from a vantage at once domestic, personal, and not bound by religious concerns, the bourgeois experience of a colonial woman.[71] Occasionally Jewish women did become merchants, almost always on the death of a spouse. So we find here an unusual female cohort: Esther Pinheiro of Nevis, whose business made her travel as far away as New York and Boston; Abigail Minis (1701–94), a Savannah plantation heiress with control of more than a thousand acres and seventeen slaves; Katey Hays Sarzedas, the manager of a kosher boardinghouse in Savannah; and Rachel Pinto of New York, who was an important supporter of Shearith Israel's Talmud Torah school.[72] Moreover a small number of Jewish women achieved an element of equality during marriage. Rachel Lazarus of South Carolina was declared a "sole trader" by her husband, Marks Lazarus, in 1785 so that she could run the family store.[73] Charlotte Hart David of Windsor, in Upper Canada, had a prenuptial agreement when she married her husband, Moses David, in 1811 that, quite exceptionally, enabled both of them to conduct business and own property independently of each other.[74] We also find Rachel Luis (d. 1737), a trader in her own right and never married, who specified in her will that her property be sold following her death and the proceeds used to purchase a Torah scroll for New York's synagogue.[75] Property and commerce were not the only freedoms Jewish women were coming to enjoy: Richea Gratz (1774–1858) of Philadelphia became the first Jewish woman in the United States to study as an undergraduate, in her case at Franklin College in Lancaster, Pennsylvania, during the late 1780s.[76]

During the eighteenth century, small Jewish communities lived in South Carolina, Pennsylvania, and Georgia, but none had a need or the capacity to build a synagogue until after the American Revolution. Elsewhere individuals, extended families, and small clusters of families moved to Connecticut, Delaware, Massachusetts, New Jersey, North Carolina, Virginia, and, a great distance indeed, the Michigan territory. Their lives often passed strenuously in frontier exploration and settlement, though not always: Benjamin Levy, presumably a London Jew, figured as one of the thirty-two proprietors of West Jersey (1674–1702), but he never visited the colony he invested in.[77] Daniel Nunez, who settled in New Jersey around 1720, was no anonymous toiler. He was Piscataway's town clerk and became a justice of the peace in Middlesex County before fleeing to Delaware to avoid debtors' prison.[78] Nunez was possibly the first Jew to hold public office in North America, two to three years before Mordechai Gomez's term as tax collector in New York City's East Ward in 1723.[79]

During the French and Indian War, the British captured Montreal in 1760; shortly after, the city's first Jews, no longer under the Bourbon ban, arrived to engage in the valuable fur trade. Aaron Hart (1724–1800), who served as a commissary officer to the British Army during the war was among these first Jewish settlers. Somewhat earlier, in 1749, a small number of Jews settled in British Nova Scotia and thrived as merchants. Though they bought land and built a cemetery, the fledgling Jewish community died out in the 1760s. Only a few Jews remained in the colony throughout the eighteenth century.[80] Some rare intrepid souls traveled Canada's northern frontiers under the authority of the Hudson Bay Company: one was Ferdinand Jacobs (1713–83) at Fort Prince of Wales, now in Manitoba. The majority of Jews settling in Canada, however, chose Montreal, with its trading posts that turned furs, insatiably demanded by Europeans, into great wealth. Thus we find at Fort Michilimackinac, on the shore of the Straits of Mackinac in present-day Michigan, the records of one Ezekiel Solomons, from Montreal to make his fortune. Archaeological excavations (c. 1960–90) have revealed Solomons's house as well as various artifacts, rare surviving examples of material culture related to early North American Jewish heritage.[81] Yet Solomons was not alone in this distant imperial outpost during the eighteenth century. He belonged to a mercantile consortium that included Chapman Abraham (c. 1723–83) in Detroit, Benjamin Lyons in Albany, Levy Solomons (1730–92) at Fort Niagara, and Gershon Levy, also at Fort Michilimackinac, whose enterprise bore the name Gershon Levy and Company.[82] Solomons and Abraham were taken hostage during Chief Pontiac's rebellion in 1763, were ransomed, and remained in Montreal for the duration of the conflict. By 1768 the Jewish community in Montreal had grown large enough to found its own Shearith Israel, which was also the first non-Catholic congregation of worship in Quebec.[83] Jews also settled in Quebec City and Trois-Rivières.[84] Due to challenging terrain and difficulties of access, the few Jews who lived in the U.S. portion of the Great Lakes–St. Lawrence River watershed following the Revolution were more oriented to Montreal than New York. Not until 1825, with the completion of the Erie Canal, did this change, making New York the more viable cultural and economic connection.

As we have seen, the eighteenth century introduced significant prosperity for Jews who settled in Protestant Atlantic territories, those colonies owned by the Netherlands and Great Britain, and, on a much smaller scale, by Denmark. This economic stability can literally be seen from the architecture and decoration of synagogues built at the time. Yet by the 1770s, European empire as such was under enormous, existential pressure: 1776, 1789—the epochal revolutions, both liberal and radical, consolidated into a political juggernaut that would alter everything on both sides of the Atlantic. The Old World orders of royalty and hereditary aristocracy were turned on their heads, crucially in America and paradigmatically, in France—wherever the rights of man and civil liberties were seen as necessary or inevitable solvents to the unrepresentative, predatory, oppressive powers of an ancien regime. Although the unleashing of such forces—they were nurtured on Enlightenment thought and concurrent with a comparably important revolution in material production taking place in Great Britain—would create modern Western society as we conceive it, this decisive historical momentum affected Jews too. If citizenship in civil society was replacing, whether at the point of a gun or guillotine, the status of being subject to some compact of authoritarian and religious dominance, then enfranchisement of Jews was understood as natural and desirable. By the last quarter of the eighteenth century, both Jews and Christians began to believe that Jews should cease to function as a separate or alien group within a state, and should instead be considered members of general society. Economic prosperity had proved a harbinger, if not the sole catalyst, of civil empowerment. So La Nación, that Portuguese name used ubiquitously by Sephardic Jews of the Atlantic World to refer to themselves for well over a century, gave way to a heterogeneous, democratic reality: the idea that nation-states contained ethnic and religious groups with common political and legal rights. Henceforth there would be American, British, or French Jews just as there were American, British, and French Catholics. Moreover the Spanish-Portuguese Sephardim were no longer the only Jews to settle in either European or New World communities and frontiers. Gradually, over the course of the eighteenth century—especially in the British Isles, the Netherlands, and North America—Sephardim were joined and then outnumbered by an influx of Ashkenazim from central and eastern Europe. These demographic movements in turn launched conflict among Atlantic World Jewry. As always, there was a material record of all this change: the actual design and architecture of synagogues in the period between 1775 and 1825. These buildings register the great political upheaval transforming Europe and the Americas.

CHAPTER 5

Jewish Enfranchisement in the Atlantic World after 1775

Caught up in the American and French Revolutions, then the Napoleonic Wars, the Jews of Europe and the New World rapidly encountered a condition they had not known before—enfranchisement as equal citizens. This status followed from the recognition of freedom of conscience as inalienably linked to the practice of republican liberty.[1]

Often it was the acceptance of religious pluralism that preceded, or in some instances catalyzed, crucial debates on related issues, like the abolition of slavery or the redefinition of women's rights. From this perspective changing the status of Jews during the era of democratic revolution and royalist counterrevolution, represented an early extension of human rights by Western society as it sought to become more just and heterogeneous. Whether Sephardic or Ashekenazic, Caucasian Jewry seemed less alien to eighteenth- and nineteenth-century Christians than African slaves, Amerindians, Asians, or the more proximate Muslims of the Ottoman Empire, which threatened the hegemony of Christian Europe. Ironies abound when we consider that Enlightenment-informed followers of Voltaire, Hume, Hegel, and Kant, those who intellectually deprecated confessional rigidities and irrational biases, continued to label monotheistic Islam infidel and implacably hostile. In the event, it was acceptance and the granting of full political rights that brought an end to the Sephardic Atlantic World. In an enlightened democratic age, Jews would identify with the nation-states that made them citizens, not with La Nación of colonialist dispersion. First in the United States and France, then elsewhere in Europe and the Americas, Jews entered civil society as equals. So it seemed to erudite Jewish reform leader Isaac Harby (1788–1828) of Charleston, South Carolina, who explained to Secretary of State James Monroe in 1816 that Jews "are by no means to be considered as a Religious sect, tolerated by government . . . [but rather they] constitute a portion of the People. They are, in every respect, woven in and compacted with the citizens of the Republic. Quakers and Catholics; Episcopalians and Presbyterians, Baptists and Jews, all constitute one great political family."[2]

By 1775 the Dutch presence in the Americas had been effectively erased by the British. All that remained was a handful of islands in the Caribbean and Surinam. Dutch holdings in Asia continued to grow and develop; however, only a small number of Jews went to these colonies. But while we have just examined the consequences of European westward projection across the Atlantic, this world bridged continents on either side of the great ocean. Fronting the Atlantic northward from Gibraltar, European states often provide a part—from one vantage the essential part—of our account. During the revolutionary epoch we must look at the interaction between Europe and the Americas. Let us stipulate here that our discussion neither quantifies nor prioritizes speciously: for our purposes, the American and French Revolutions are twin profound fault lines precipitating one epochal tectonic shift in Western history.

That said, internal revolutionary forces, who called themselves Patriots, emerged in the Netherlands during the 1780s. The Dutch, like most European peoples, were quite obviously aware of the American rebellion. In 1787, the Patriot Revolt broke out against William V of Orange. For some two years, the country was torn by civil strife eventually brought to an end after Frederick William II of Prussia, William's brother-in-law, invaded the Netherlands to restore William, quelling the revolt by 1789. During the Patriot Revolt, rumors spread that rioters would enter Amsterdam's Jodenbreestraat to attack the synagogues. The Sephardim mustered sixty men to guard the Esnoga, the Ashkenazim another thirty to protect their synagogues across the street. The Jewish guards succeeded—no synagogues were damaged. Rioters also threatened to attack the home of Deputy Chief Constable Papegaay, who hired nearly forty Jewish men to protect his property instead of using his own retinue. We know of no other instance when Jews were specifically chosen to protect an Amsterdam city official. Spreading beyond Dutch borders to outposts of the dwindling empire, the Patriot movement inspired rebels not only in Curaçao and Surinam but also at the tip of Africa in Cape Town.[3]

The Prussian intervention of 1787 was by no means the last phase of struggle between Dutch revolutionaries (Patriots) and monarchists (Orangists). At the end of 1794, Napoleon marched into the Netherlands, setting up the Batavian Republic in 1795 and forcing stadtholder William V to flee a second time to England for sanctuary. In response the British invaded Dutch colonies to prevent their becoming French. But in Europe the Batavian regime quickly instituted (1796) radical reforms, often in the image of revolutionary France: the creation of a representative National Assembly, separation of church and state, and emancipation of Jews. This revolutionary momentum was welcomed by an Amsterdam organization, Felix Libertate, which had a high Jewish membership and wanted to establish a new democratic order in the Netherlands, including Jewish emancipation. Oddly enough,

Amsterdam's parnassim, unlike a large number of their congregants, opposed enfranchisement. The traditional religious leaders feared loss of authority and control, or at least they perceived measures normalizing Jews as citizens. This tension would have repercussions over the next decade for the Jewish community. Yet the Dutch Assembly, lobbied by Felix Libertate and other Jews, acted decisively, so on this essential issue we might say that Rousseau and revolution won.

In 1797 Moses Moreseco was elected to Amsterdam's Municipal Council. But more notably, that same year, when the Batavian Republic held elections for the National Assembly, Harmannus L. Bromet (1725–1812) and Hartog de H. Lemon (1755–1823) were elected delegates. These two Jews were the first of the revolutionary era to participate in a representative European legislative body. Bromet was a coffee merchant who had spent twenty years in Surinam. During the 1770s, as someone who staunchly supported the American rebels, he was well on the path to being radicalized. His colleague Lemon was a physician who had studied medicine in Leiden. By the 1790s both men had become wealthy members of Amsterdam's Ashkenazic community. In 1795, when the population of Amsterdam was 217,000, the city was home to 20,300 Ashkenazim and only twenty-eight hundred Sephardim—the two together forming the largest urban Jewish community in Europe. Given these numbers, it seems inevitable that an Ashkenezi would be the first to become an Assembly member. It was also in this period that Jews were recruited into the Batavian Civil Guard and Navy: they were few indeed, nor would their military eligibility long outlast the regime.[4]

But the revolutionary Netherlands proved as unstable as the revolutionary lodestar radiating from Paris. The Batavian Republic was under constant turmoil, its radicals, liberals, moderates, and conservatives struggling for power. Effective governance was elusive and disrupted: a Radical Patriot regime lasted for six months during 1798, replaced by an Executive Authority (until 1801), a National Authority (until 1805), and in the final year of the Republic (1806) the rule of a Grand Pensionary. Napoleon, at least, had had enough. The new emperor installed his brother Louis (1778–1846) to rule the Kingdom of Holland, which eventually was absorbed into the French Empire in 1810 after Napoleon sent an army to enforce his will. So although, in broad terms, the Netherlands, under compulsion, imitated the French in a movement from republic to empire (but a Napoleonic, not a Dutch one), the emancipated Dutch Jews, after recognition by the National Assembly, had little role to play. They were, in effect, *hors de combat*. At Napoleon's insistence, his imaginative system of organizing Jews into representative administrations (or *consistories*) from a regional to a national level—created in France but extended throughout Bonaparte's remit—was introduced to Holland in 1806. According to this organizational plan, at least during the Napoleonic period,

Dutch Ashkenazim and Sephardim, those often recalcitrant partners, were combined into a centralized governing bureaucracy.

Meanwhile Dutch Ashkenazic communities fractured from within—a small microcosm of the assaults on entrenched power unleashed by 1789. The nomenclature here suggests a certain Jacobinism: there was a minority "New" congregation, that emerged in Amsterdam to oppose the authoritarian governance of all status quo "Old" synagogue-communities dating from the mid-seventeenth century. In an age of revolt, democracy, and universal rights, the top-down dictates of parnassim and rabbinate struck many as intolerable. The spiritual leader of the New Congregation, as it was called, embodied this volte-face: Rabbi Yizhak Graanboom (1738–1807) had been acting chief rabbi of Dutch Ashkenazic Jewry before his self-recruitment to the liberal cause.[5] He was often assisted by leaders or congregants drawn from the ranks of Felix Libertate, many of whom regarded themselves as *maskalim,* followers of the Jewish Enlightenment or *haskalah.* This is the name given to the late eighteenth-century intellectual movement most famously associated with the philosopher Moses Mendelssohn (1729–86). He and like-minded thinkers were guided by reason, fervid rejection of superstition, and the goal of making Judaism responsive to the contemporary, non-Jewish world. As with any new cultural formation taking root in different societies, the haskalah had innovators more and less bold. Eventually, during the first half of the nineteenth century, modern Reform Judaism would develop from the chrysalis of haskalah as interpreted by German Jewish intellectuals or those from such a background. The phenomenon was not entirely without irony: central European Jews guided by Mendelssohn were in effect the encyclopaedists and Voltaires here; the maskalim of the Netherlands, beneficiaries of their country's early, open embrace of the Enlightenment, did not undertake to reform Judaism radically. Instead Dutch Jews tried to normalize Enlightenment thought and democratic institutions, when feasible, by appealing to the existing framework of Jewish law.[6] This more modest, Thermidorean posture of Dutch maskilim would have affected Jews in the Dutch colonial arena, especially in the Caribbean and Surinam. It would take fully a half-century after the end of the revolutionary epoch before Reform Judaism—well established in North America by central European Jews—penetrated the Dutch bastion of Curaçao. Temple Emanuel, a Reform congregation, was established there in 1864.

Louis Napoleon, despite having begun his reign (1806–10) as Napoleon's puppet, tried to rule the Kingdom of Holland on behalf of Dutch interests, a policy not congenial to his masterful brother. So, in regard to the emancipated Jews, we find Louis objecting to the directives of the French Grand Sanhedrin (the highest Jewish authority in France) as inappropriate for the Netherlands, insisting that Dutch Jews should be guided by their own consistory.

By 1810 Napoleon, thwarted in revenue collection and military administration, had forced his brother to abdicate, thus annexing Holland into France. Only after defeat at the crucial Battle of Leipzig (1813)—it was the preface to Napoleon's downfall—did the emperor withdraw his army of occupation from Holland.

In 1814 William VI of Orange (1772–1843), who had been exiled to England with his father (whom he succeeded), became King William I of the Netherlands, ruler of a nominally constitutional monarchy that granted the king extensive powers. According to the Constitution of the Netherlands of 1815, Jewish emancipation as decreed in 1796 was retained. William I, who wanted to adopt Napoleon's goal of integrating Jews into Dutch society, insisted that official synagogue minutes or correspondence be written in Dutch, not Portuguese or Yiddish. But he also abolished the Jewish High Consistory, thus allowing the divide between Ashkenazim and Sephardim to reappear. On balance the post-Napoleonic constitutional arrangements were a setback for the Netherlands's recently emancipated Jews. Though legally equal under William I, Jewish citizens saw their freedom somewhat curtailed in practice until the 1870s. No doubt this regression can be attributed to the resurgence of conservative Jewish religious attitudes—a return of the ancien regime under the de facto control of parnassim. Their powers had once been *dirigiste*—until the revolutionary winds swept the Dutch Empire. Now, in an environment that to some degree reflected Metternich's absolutist reactionary settlement at the Congress of Vienna (1815), in a Europe traumatized by over two decades of revolution, war, and Napoleon, Dutch Jews turned again to the conventional organization that had served so well before 1789.[7] But the rabbinate and communal leadership were vitiated. Neither Amsterdam's Sephardim (from 1822 to 1900) nor Ashkenazim (between 1838 and 1874) could produce chief rabbis for their congregants, surely leadership vacuums that bespeak exhaustion and accommodation, consequently acculturation and assimilation. Nostalgia aside, the era of Dutch prominence in a Sephardic Atlantic was irretrievably lost.[8]

Small wonder that the revolutionary epoch dissolved the Dutch West India Company (in 1771) and the Dutch East India Company (between 1796 and 1800). These were quintessential organs of empire that could have no second birth in the post-Napoleonic peace crafted by the victors—Great Britain, Austria-Hungary, Russia, and Prussia. The naval might of the Netherlands had been eclipsed, its mercantile supremacy diluted. After 1815 some territories once controlled by the two quasi-national Dutch companies reverted to the Kingdom of the Netherlands. The British gained formerly Dutch colonies in southern Africa, Guyana, Ceylon, and parts of southern India. But a contracted empire did not leave the Netherlands entirely without profitable Atlantic assets. St. Eustatius, an island in the northern Leewards, was located at a geographic intersection of American, European, and African trade, precisely the kind of commercial nexus that attracted Jewish immigration. Hosting a free-trade port near major shipping routes across the Atlantic and within the Caribbean, the island serviced British, French, and Danish colonial commerce, besides Dutch. By the 1750s Oranjestad, capital and port city of St. Eustatius, was second only to Curacao's Willemstad for West Indies trade volume. By 1775 the island's population had risen to a remarkable thirty thousand—larger than the fourth largest British North American city, Charleston, South Carolina. There was a plantation economy, too, but it paled in value when compared to the port's commercial ventures. For example the island's eighty-odd sugarcane plantations produced six hundred thousand pounds of sugar in 1775; five years earlier, twenty million pounds of sugar were exported. Even given the different years involved, 19.4 million pounds of sugar (that is, 1770 export weight minus 1775 domestic weight) could never have been accounted for by increased agricultural yield. What does explain this vast discrepancy is smuggling. Neighboring islands, possessions of Great Britain, France, Denmark, and Spain, all sent their sugarcane under wraps to Oranjestad, that gateway so conveniently unencumbered by any European colonial tariff, for transshipment. Moreover, in the late 1770s, Statian merchants were already involved in a black-market weapons trade that would supply the thirteen rebel American colonies at war with Britain. Sharp Dutch practice indeed: the profit on gunpowder alone, smuggled through St. Eustatius, amounted to 120 percent.[9]

In the event, Dutch-ruled St. Eustatius was the first international entity to recognize American independence, a diplomatic entree that followed from naval protocol. On 16 November 1776, the American brigantine *Andrew Doria*, flying the colors of the Continental Congress, fired an eleven-gun salute to greet the island's Fort Oranje, whose commander and Dutch governor, Johannes de Graaf (1729–1813), fired a return salute as a courtesy to the American vessel. Decorum thus observed, the *Andrew Doria* proceeded to load munitions, and then returned through the British blockade to the fledging United States.[10] This amiable contraband relationship between the Dutch enclave and the embattled American colonies continued for five years until finally provoking the British. They invaded St. Eustatius in 1781, commanded by Admiral George Rodney (1718–92), cutting off weapons traffic and occupying the island until the end of the war. In turn Rodney's action angered the Dutch, neutral at the start of the American Revolution though friendly to the rebels' cause. Thus began the Fourth, and last, Anglo-Dutch War. Great Britain, besides wanting to block the Netherlands from a neutral northern European league (Russia, Sweden, and Denmark) inclined toward the Americans and their French and Spanish allies, also tried to thwart a Dutch commercial treaty with the rebellious colonists. The war was widespread. Naval battles stretched from the West Indies and Brest to the Cape, Bengal, and as far east as Sumatra. In the end (1784), however, Dutch interests were fundamentally compromised as Britain's star rose higher—a compensation of sorts for Great Britain's loss of her thirteen North American colonies.[11]

Albeit small, St. Eustatius was home to a large Jewish community. Its four hundred Jews were more than could be found in any North American settlement before the Revolution.[12] Admiral Rodney keenly disliked Jews, whom he treated as severely as the few actual (non-Jewish) Americans on the island—certainly more cruelly than any French or Spanish nationals under his control. Shortly after the British occupation, a hundred Jews lost their property in land and goods while some twenty were deported to neighboring islands.[13] The anti-Semitism was pervasive. Even the Rhode Island Tory, Jacob Pollack, a Jew twice imprisoned by American revolutionaries and an immigrant to St. Eustatius because of his deep attachment to the Crown, was out of luck. He, too, lost his wealth and was deported: so Rodney esteemed Jewish loyalty.[14]

The Continental Army purchased much of its gunpowder and materiel by way of Statian merchants, who numbered Jews among them. Indeed army supply was often the responsibility of Haym Solomon (1740–85), a major broker dealing with the U.S. government's Office of Finance. As a resident of both New York and Philadelphia and with a thriving financial business, Solomon used his commercial connections and especially his bills of exchange, tendered between St. Eustatius and Europe, to help supply the Continental Army. Most likely Solomon knew Statian merchants personally.[15] By the Treaty of Paris (1783), ending the Revolutionary War, St. Eustatius reverted to the Dutch, who quickly allowed deported Jews to return. But the fruits of peace were not evident, at least not at first. Both Great Britain and France invaded St. Eustatius several times during the French revolutionary–Napoleonic era. Not until 1816 was the island permanently restored to Dutch rule under William I. But constant strife, war taxation, and French and British maladministration had gutted the wealth of St. Eustatius, forcing large numbers of merchants and inhabitants to leave. Those Jews who remained did not prosper, and during the nineteenth century their once fine synagogue, Honen Dalim (Charitable to the Poor), built in 1739, fell into ruin.[16]

There was only one other Dutch Jewish community in the Caribbean that, however briefly, emerged during the epoch of revolution. St. Martin, partitioned between the French and the Dutch in 1648, lies 190 miles east of Puerto Rico. In the island's Dutch territory (Sint Maarten) is the capital, Philipsburg, where in 1783 a synagogue was built, which was by 1828 in ruins. The name of the congregation with any documentary records are lost.[17] As is so often the case in the great hurricane corridor of the Caribbean, storm and flood most likely erased the memory of a colonial settlement, in this case, a short-lived Dutch Sephardic outpost.

When the twin revolutions erupted, that is in 1776 and 1789, Great Britain found itself in a state of more of less constant warfare that would not end until Waterloo. But outside of the obvious conflict zones of North America and France, the rest of the Atlantic World would also be caught up in the struggles—a condition that would not least affect Jews. Gibraltar, gateway to the Atlantic, presents certain unique features, all geographically determined. Here we have a fortress-port that controls the straits, access to the Mediterranean, and consequently all exchange between the sea and the ocean. In the age of sail, of Nelson's navy parrying French, Spanish, and Dutch fleets, Gibraltar was a prize of inestimable value, at once strategic and financial. For eighteenth-century Jewish merchants, Gibraltar offered the only safe harbor in the mid-Atlantic where they could stop, settle, conduct business, or move between Europe and the Americas.

Some historical context must be mentioned here. Besides driving Sephardim into the perils of exile or subterfuge, the Spanish and Portuguese Inquisitions had paralyzed western Mediterranean Jewish commerce: after 1492–98 the twin Catholic monarchies had not only closed Iberia and its North African colonies to Sephardic merchants—crypto-Jews aside—but also denied Jews any use of trade routes proximate to Portugal and Spain. Other hazards travelers faced in the Mediterranean of early modern Europe were the Knights of Malta and, on the Muslim side of the religious divide, Barbary pirates based in Morocco: both groups kidnapped for ransom. Although masters of Gibraltar after 1713, the British provoked Spain by their Anglican tolerance of Jews on territory so long Iberian. During the Great Siege (1779–82), sustained, menacing Spanish attempts to conquer Gibraltar by sea or marine-launched assaults ultimately failed. Allied to the American rebels, Spain meant to defeat an overstretched Great Britain so as to regain lost colonies. Typically, however, war makes for strange partners—a truth not lost on Atlantic World Jews. Inquisitorial Spain, the iconic anti-Semitic empire still committed in the age of democratic revolution to ridding the peninsula and all Hispanic overseas possessions of Jews, was briefly the supporter of American revolutionaries, surely among the most religiously tolerant people of European descent in the world at the time. However that may be, we should note that Gibraltan Jewish merchants, using their extensive trade connections, helped supply Nelson's fleet at Trafalgar (1805), in Britain's decisive naval engagement with France. In a sense Gibraltar's economy at this time showed many features of an Atlantic colony like St. Eustatius, lacking productive capacity but a critical commercial enclave. The population depended largely on imports for domestic consumption and defense.

Warfare scarred Gibraltar's oldest synagogue. Shaar Hashamayim, rebuilt in 1768, was destroyed at the beginning of the siege, though it was almost immediately replaced (1781–83), and extensively remodeled in 1812 with a synagogue architecturally inspired by the Esnoga and Bevis Marks. Two other synagogues appeared during the revolutionary period: Etz Chaim (Tree of Life) in 1783 and Nefusot Yehudah (Dispersed of Judah) in 1799. Nefusot

Yehudah shares some striking design elements with the Snoa of Curaçao and has often been called the Flemish Synagogue because of its Dutch gables. After Napoleon's downfall, a Gibraltar congregation built the synagogue with the unusual name Abudarham in 1821, after one of the colony's most distinguished eighteenth-century rabbis.[18]

It was not only the Jews of Gibraltar—they lived, after all, under tolerant Protestant rule—who experienced the anomalies of European conflict. This was also the case for Jews far away from the front lines of American revolutionary struggle. Let us look at Hesse, in west-central Germany, a contingent of whose able soldiers Washington famously defeated at Trenton. Near the Hessian city of Marburg an der Lahn is the small town of Rauschenberg, where Isaak Katz (1713–90), a cattle and horse trader, and his wife, Rewecka (d. 1806), raised a barn just outside the town precincts in 1779. However marginal an event at first glance, that the Katzs built their barn does indicate a sociopolitical shift, showing Ashkenazim overcoming the prohibitions of many preceding centuries in central Europe where they had lived isolated, precarious lives. In fact almost invariably Jews did not, and could not, own nonresidential buildings, much less any building dedicated to commerce or the agricultural economy. For Jews even legally authorized improvements or renovations applied solely to residences.[19] So we now have one of those unusual moments, when a precise historical marker expresses the achievement of little people, the vast majority of humankind born into neither wealth nor power: the Katzs proudly declared on the lintel above the entrance to their new building, "This barn was built by Isaak Katz and Rewecka his house wife in anno 1779." The simple inscription, written in both Hebrew and German, with a carved Star of David flanking each side of the text, announced to all comers that here was a monument to ordinary people who regarded themselves as Jewish *and* Hessian.[20] Most likely the actual builder would have been Christian—no records attest to any Jews in the local building trade at the time. Given that many young male Hessians—they formed the largest contingent of some thirty thousand German troops hired by the British to fight the American rebellion—were posted abroad, strict enforcement of traditional anti-Jewish ordinances in remote, rural places might well have proved difficult. Manpower and constabularies were hard pressed. As it happens, in 1779, the same year when the Katz barn appeared, a large number of Hessian soldiers were camped on the Stono River in South Carolina—far from the River Lahn that flows past Marburg.[21] They would go on to fight in shifting alliances during the Dutch Revolt, the French Revolution, and the Napoleonic Wars. When Hessian veterans returned home after Waterloo, the existence of Jewish commercial property was fait accompli.

Meanwhile, across the Atlantic, Jamaican Jews were building synagogues to accommodate growing numbers and changing settlements. In 1796 the Ashkenazim of Spanish Town built Mikveh Israel, in use until 1860: many of the congregants had moved to Kingston. Similarly Spanish Town Sephardim had to close the venerable Neve Shalom (built 1704) at the turn of the twentieth century because its congregants, too, had moved to the capital city. In the end this synagogue succumbed to an earthquake in 1907. In the same year the Bastille was stormed, Kingston's Ashkenazim founded a congregation and built as their sanctuary Shaare Yosher (Gates of the Upright), the first purpose-built Ashkenazic synagogue in the Americas. By the end of the eighteenth century, Jamaica itself, with four active congregations, had more synagogues than any other colony in the British Empire. The original Shaare Yosher had to be replaced in 1837 with a larger structure. Clearly the island's Ashkenazim were prospering, a trend that can be seen throughout British North America. By 1800 the Sephardim in these areas had been supplanted in numbers and influence by Central European Jews, a demographic change that would have important consequences.[22]

And what of Canada, Britain's second great dominion in North America? With a landmass of more than half a continent, stretching between two oceans from the Arctic to what would become the American border in 1783, Canada was no trivial entity. There too, as had been the case with both Gibraltar and Jamaica, new British sovereignty enabled Jewish settlement. Jews first arrived in Montreal in 1760, shortly after British forces defeated the French on the Plains of Abraham during the Seven Years' War. By 1778 the Jews of Montreal had built their first synagogue, Shearith Israel (Remnant of Israel), whose Torah scrolls were a gift from Bevis Marks. Although mostly Ashkenazic, the original Montreal congregation decided to follow Sephardic minhag and practices. This would seem peculiar until we consider the likely motive—generous philanthropy and active support from the wider Sephardic Atlantic community, by then dispensing a veritable proto-Judaic development fund.[23] The first Shearith Israel building, in fact, survived until 1824, when, much dilapidated, it was demolished, to be followed in 1838 by a second structure built in the Egyptian Revival style. During and after the American Revolution, Canada was a haven for Tories, among whom there were a certain number of Jews. Most went to Montreal, the dominion's only city with a synagogue; others settled elsewhere. So we find Moses David, a loyalist from Detroit, simply crossing the Detroit River in 1797 to settle in adjacent Sandwich, later renamed Windsor.[24]

At the end of the eighteenth century, Canadian Jews were frequently either related to or involved with coreligionists in the thirteen colonies (after independence, in the United States). Prominent Montreal Ashkenazic families were named Hart, David —Moses David of Windsor was a relative—and Franks, most of whom had cousins, friends, or business contacts in New York, Newport, and Philadelphia. Aaron P. Hart (1724–1800), Canada's first known Jewish immigrant, arrived in Montreal quite soon after the British victory (13 September 1759).

However universal the freedoms asserted in the American Bill of Rights or the French Declaration of the Rights of Man, oaths of office proved continued problematic for Jews of the British Empire. In 1807 Ezekiel Hart (1767–1843) was elected to the Quebec Legislative Assembly from the district of Trois-Rivières. Yet he was not seated because he refused to swear "upon the true faith of a Christian" as a prerequisite of office. In fact this oath violated the Naturalization Act (1740), but Hart's protest went unheeded by the Assembly, as happened a second time, when, defiantly, Trois-Rivières reelected Hart and the legislature still would not admit him. Anti-Semitism may well have been a secondary factor in this situation. The Parti Canadien, representing (as its name specifies) Francophone Quebec in political contest with English-speaking Canadians, had no wish to accept Anglophone Hart, despite the enthusiastic embrace by the otherwise characteristically French Québécois of Trois-Rivières. We can understand why Hart refused a third invitation from his would-be constituents to stand for office. The entire affair had emboldened or calcified the Quebec Assembly, whose overwhelmingly Catholic majority tried to pass a bill, very ancien regime, excluding not only Jews but, more importantly in actual numbers, all Protestants. Angered and distressed by such chauvinism, the dominion's chief executive, Governor-General Sir James Craig (1748–1812), temporarily dissolved the Assembly ruling that the initiative unconstitutionally infringed the Naturalization Act. Not far away, on the Atlantic coast, there was a somewhat similar situation in a different social environment. At the same time that Ezekiel Hart was struggling in Quebec, another Jew who shared his surname, but not his family, was elected to the Nova Scotia assembly. Samuel Hart (1747–1810) had been a Tory in Newport, Rhode Island, during the American Revolution, who came to Nova Scotia after the war. But upon his election to the maritime colony's legislature, Hart became Anglican and could thus take an oath of office that required him to be Christian.[25]

By the late 1820s the situation for religious minorities had changed. French political parties in Quebec were seeking minority support to strengthen their hand against traditional English rivals. During 1831–32, Jews finally gained equal civil rights with other Canadians across the dominion. Fittingly it was Samuel B. Hart (1759–1859) of Trois-Rivières—*not* from Nova Scotia but rather the son of Quebec's Ezekiel Hart—who petitioned the colonial assembly, now Lower Canada, to remove the obnoxious oath excluding non-Christians from the elected body. When the Declaratory Act was passed there was neither dissent not amendment. But though this last parliamentary hurdle barring Jewish equality collapsed, it would take another quarter century before George Benjamin, in 1857, was elected to the Ontario Assembly.[26]

War can often provide an incubator for citizenship, and so it proved when the War of 1812 arrived. Jewish citizens fought on both sides. While the role of American Jews—Uriah P. Levy (1792–1862) and Judah Touro (1775–1854)—in this conflict has long been known, Jewish Canadian participation remains obscure. And on Canadian soil, at least, there was certainly the motive of protecting property and sovereignty from American depredation or annexation. The Quebec legislator Ezekiel Hart showed typical combativeness as he rose to become a lieutenant in the Eighth Trois-Rivières Battalion. Samuel David (1766–1824), of the Second Montreal Battalion, became a major and fought at the Battle of Chateauguay.[27] Then there is the rather chameleon example of Jacob Franks, Wisconsin's first Jewish inhabitant, who lived in Green Bay during the 1790s. In 1812 he joined the Canadian militia that helped British troops seize Fort Michilimackinac on Mackinaw Island (now in Michigan) in the first land battle of the war. After peace and the return of Mackinaw to the United States, Franks moved to Canada, where in 1816 he married Mary Solomons of Montreal.[28] She was the daughter of Levy Solomons (1730–92), no kind of Tory, who, when the American Revolution broke out, assisted the American forces under General Richard Montgomery. It was Solomons who supplied Continental Army troops and hospitals in Canada during the brief American invasion and occupation (1775–76).[29] During the Revolution, some one hundred Jews fought on both sides, although none as officers in the British Army. Onward soldiers indeed: the Crown required its ranks to be led only by professing Christian officers.[30]

Among all British colonies in the Americas, population growth notwithstanding, Jamaica proved the most challenging for Jews. Simply put, white English Jamaicans, that is, the class made up of plantation owners, merchants, and traders—we must for obvious reasons exclude the large African slave population—were markedly anti-Semitic. From the seventeenth until the nineteenth century, Jamaican Jews were marginalized, subject to punitive taxation, and barred from entering local government. Yet, as we have seen, their numbers grew. Before the mid-eighteenth century some other English territories, notably Bermuda and Barbados, did not extend Jews the same civil rights and economic freedoms granted to the Christian majority. As a matter of law and often of practice, however, the Naturalization Act (1740) eliminated most of these disabilities or impositions across the English colonial map. Bermuda ended up not having a permanent Jewish community, and in Barbados Jews received their rights in the eighteenth century.[31] Not so Jamaica. For a possession of a dynamic seafaring empire cognate with islands, Jamaica remained uncannily steeped in a kind of microculture—a place where Jews remained subordinate and unpopular. There can be no doubt that legal, political, and economic handicaps suppressed Jamaican Jews. Although they were as numerous as the communities in either Surinam or Curaçao, Jamaican Jewry seemed detached from the wider Atlantic diaspora, at least in respect to cultural or religious contributions. Not until 1831, roughly half a century after the great democratic revolutions, were they enfranchised. This is not to say that these Jews were either silent or unaware of the broader political environment. So we find this trenchant assertion from a letter published by a Jew in the *Kingston Chronicle* during 1820:

> With regard to the British Parliament recognising the right of Jews to vote, I can confidently assert, that at Westminster and Middlesex the rights of those Jews who have voted have never yet been disputed. In Canada, they not only vote, but also sit in the Provincial Parliament; as in 1808, at the election for the town of Three Rivers, which was sharply contested, Mr. Ezekiel Hart, a Jew, was chosen to serve for the town by a large majority. Here [in Jamaica], nothing has as yet been produced against the eligibility of a Jew's voting, but . . . resolutions and customs.[32]

Nor, when Jamaican Jews were allowed to vote, was this enlarged franchise a product of enlightened thought: at the time, with notable exceptions, the European continent, quite unlike Bolivar's South America, was permeated by reaction. As for the Jamaican sugarcane planters, a veritable colonial fronde whose profits depended on slave labor, their interests could no longer withstand the British Parliament's campaign (c. 1816–36) to abolish African slavery in Jamaica (1833, Abolition of Slavery Act). For plantation owners and businessmen faced with dominating a new, legally emancipated African majority, more white faces and bank accounts were needed to exercise control. So, ironically, and very much against the typical instincts of the sugar barons, the local Jewish community, its idea of freedom millennially based in Exodus, not commodities, was at last turned to by Jamaica's patriciate—and for the wrong reasons. Jewish enfranchisement became entwined with African liberation, or more accurately, with the policy of diluting that liberation. The Jews were seen as a lesser evil, a white-skinned ally who could be counted on to keep former slaves in their exploited place. Whatever the vagaries of social bonding—long-embraced anti-Semitism could hardly disappear overnight— Jews quickly moved into Jamaica's political echelons. Alexander Bravo of Kingston was elected Jamaica's first Jewish Assembly member in 1835. He later became a member of the Council of the Island and a receiver-general.[33]

The final maneuvers that let Jews vote in Jamaica reveal a retrograde colony, at least in respect to human and civil rights, belatedly trying to sanitize the past. In 1831, when the Jamaican Assembly proposed special legislation to Westminster that would enfranchise Jews, the Privy Council, let alone Parliament—since London's legal ratification was essential in colonial affairs— would have none of it. According to the Council, Britain's Naturalization Act, passed ninety years before, was the controlling statute and Jamaican anti-Semitic policies or laws were illegal, unfortunate, and groundless. Rebuked, the island assembly then hastily repealed (1831–32) all existing local laws that penalized Jews, most of which dated from the eighteenth century.[34] It must be said that enfranchisement and constitutionalism were pressing throughout the North American and Caribbean sphere of the British Empire at this time. Canada, too, with its very different history of slavery and anti-Semitism, legally gave its Jews full equality in 1832. For that matter England in her own right was struggling with similarly complex civil rights issues and socioeconomic pressures: Catholic Emancipation (1829) as well as the passing of the first great Reform Bill (1832). Meanwhile, across the channel, Orleanist reaction in France crumbled at the barricades of the July Revolution (1830).

As we have seen time and again, for more than two centuries (c. 1650–1860) Jews under English colonial rule frequently circumvented a colonial policy that, de jure, disabled them because of religion. De facto, life was quite different. English colonists would turn a blind eye, so that any number of Jews prospered, even though Jews were indeed barred from admission to assemblies—starting with the Westminster Parliament itself—Crown offices, and some professions or corporations, because all these bodies required an oath using the words "upon the true faith of a Christian." Or to demarcate: religious liberty (freedom of conscience) began in 1673; full civil and legal liberty came in 1858–60, when Parliament abridged, then abandoned the exclusionary oath. Success could be quite substantial. In 1700 Solomon de Medina (c. 1650–1730) became the first English Jew to be knighted.[35] By the standards of early modern Europe, England in the mid-seventeenth century had treated Jews tolerantly. But the twin revolutions in America and France seemed to leave large parts of English society hobbled by a traditionalist and clerical mindset. In the event, we see great Enlightenment-defined advances toward religious freedom in the Atlantic World—the American Constitution prohibited any religious discrimination—and parts of western Europe and Italy similarly inspired by Republican then Napoleonic France, while English laws remained restrictively complacent. However, despite the relative civil and legal advantages offered elsewhere, British Jews remained loyal to the Crown during the postrevolutionary era. There were no large-scale emigrations from either Great Britain or its colonies.

In 1847, forty years after Ezekiel Hart's collision with the Quebec Assembly, Lionel de Rothschild (1808–79) was elected as one of four members of Parliament representing the City of London. Lionel was no typical British subject. His father Nathan established the English branch of one of Europe's most powerful banking enterprises in 1798. Like Hart, Rothschild was denied his seat because he refused swearing "upon the true faith of a Christian" in order to assume office. We should note that Benjamin Disraeli, who became an MP in 1837, was baptized (name notwithstanding) Anglican at the age of thirteen and could thus start his parliamentary career without overt objection to the exclusionary oath. But his philo-Judaism remained an unassailable force, literary as well as political.[36] In 1850 the reelected Lionel de Rothschild was again denied his seat because of the oath, as happened the next year to another Jew, David Salomons (1797–1873), voted in from Greenwich.

Subsequent reelections by Rothschild's constituents were thwarted until 1858, when Parliament passed the Jews Relief Act, at last allowing Rothschild to take office by his assent to an oath "so help me Jehovah." He thus became England's first Jewish MP.

British military service posed similar conflicts for Jews. Captain Sir Alexander Schomberg (1720–1804) was born Jewish but later converted so as to receive promotions requiring the Christian oath. An officer in the Royal Navy, he became a decorated hero during the French and Indian War.[37] The 1858 Relief Act applied to Jews in British colonies too, enabling parliamentarians or administrators to take an alternative oath that no longer violated Jewish religious identity. Times were changing indeed. When the final restriction on Jewish civil liberty under English rule was removed, it was virtually the same moment America was approaching its seminal Civil War by confronting a crisis in human rights at the most elemental level. That said, and Great Britain's sluggish emancipation of Jews aside, attitudes toward Jews in England were far more tolerant and socioeconomic opportunities immeasurably greater than could be found in the vast areas of Europe controlled by the czar or the Holy Roman Emperor.[38]

Yet the fact remains that decades before the attempts of Ezekiel Hart and Lionel de Rothschild to assume their parliamentary seats, a Jew in South Carolina did so successfully and without hindrance from his Christian peers. Francis Salvador (1747–76) was elected to the Provincial Congress of South Carolina, but not as an Englishman. The year was 1775, with South Carolina in rebellion, and Salvador was a revolutionary. He later encouraged South Carolina's delegation at the Second Continental Congress in Philadelphia to support the proposed Declaration of Independence. He was the first Jew to be elected to a legislative seat anywhere in the English-speaking world.

Before 1776 the Jewish population of British North America, numerically insignificant, relied heavily on larger, more established Jewish communities in Amsterdam, London, and the Caribbean for financial support and religious guidance. We should also make an effort here to reject anachronism. New York, for us so long regarded as a global epicenter of Jewish culture, was anything but that during the eighteenth century. In 1700 the entire urban population of New York was roughly five thousand, growing to sixty thousand by 1800. The great waves of Jewish immigration into North America from eastern Europe would fall between 1880 and 1924. During the American Revolution, Philadelphia became North America's principal Jewish community, while Jewish colonists, along with many others from various religious or national backgrounds, relocated there as the British took control of territory on the Atlantic seaboard. At the beginning of the nineteenth century, the Jewish population of the United States numbered approximately twenty-five hundred. New York, the new nation's largest city, was home to four hundred Jews, and

Philadelphia—America's second largest city in 1800 with a census of forty-one thousand—almost the same. After the Revolution, the economy of Charleston, South Carolina—the fifth largest American city, its 1800 population about nineteen thousand—grew impressively, as did the Jewish community there—disproportionately so. In the early decades of the nineteenth century, Charleston had five hundred Jews, while radiating from the port city across rural areas there were an additional five hundred, so that as a state South Carolina claimed about 40 percent of the Jewish population in the United States, more than any other of the original states.[39] In all of North America, only New York and Newport had synagogues; between 1776 and 1800 three more appeared, in Philadelphia (1782), Charleston (1794), and, across the Canadian border, Montreal (1777–78). The Jewish population in Federalist and Jeffersonian America (c. 1800–1825) grew steadily if modestly, enough so that Savannah's Jews built a synagogue in 1820, and two years later, Richmond's congregation did the same. In New York the venerable Shearith Israel rebuilt its Mill Street synagogue (1730) as a larger, more substantial structure in 1818.

In settler societies demography is virtually defined by immigration. Not until the nineteenth century do we see the first phase of the American Jewish population pattern that has existed ever since: central and eastern European immigrants arrived in New York and made it decisively the numerical and cultural center of Jewish settlement; from New York in turn Jews inhabited every region of the United States. Before this it was primarily Sephardim who had founded North America's first Jewish communities. But throughout the eighteenth century, the descendents of Iberian Jews were constantly joined by ever-greater numbers of Ashkenazim, who eventually made central Europeans a majority of the total census of Jews. Even though Ashkenazim were numerically predominant by the time the Revolution began, all congregations practiced the Sephardic minhag—both in the colonial period and during the early republic. For once, the sociocultural differences between Sephardim and Ashkenazim did not alienate or disable communal life, at least in comparison with the rancorous intra-Jewish divisions in Europe and the Caribbean.[40] Why not? Arithmetic matters: whatever disagreements there were to be negotiated, or contained, if only because the actual number of Jews extant was so small, and religious life required cooperation. Jews needed each other, to satisfy, first, the ritual requisite of forming a minyan—consisting of ten Jewish men over the age of thirteen—the quorum without which a formal worship service cannot be held—and in the larger social sense of offering mutual support in an overwhelmingly Christian, though legally tolerant, environment. If, as so often happens, the disposition of discrete cultural groups is to quarrel, then balkanize, that was factionalism the Jews in British North America could not indulge.

In fact, for American Jews the Sephardic-Ashkenazic compact was sometimes—quite unlike relations in Amsterdam or Surinam—productive, respectful, and advantageous. In 1790 we find the president of Philadelphia's Mikveh Israel, a Jew of German background as were most in his congregation, soliciting funds from the Ashkenazim at Neve Shalom in Paramaribo.[41] At the same time, Mikveh Israel, which had adopted Sephardic minhag, could appeal to Sephardic communities in London and the Caribbean for assistance. This was hardly unusual. The inclusive action of the American melting pot was already evident: central European Jews from North American congregations following the Iberian tradition often sought support from Sephardic and Ashkenazic congregations elsewhere. As for Mikveh Israel, founded in 1740, it was small until the Revolutionary War brought an influx of refugees from neighboring areas, when its size grew rapidly. This internal migration applied conspicuously to far larger numbers of non-Jews. New arrivals to Philadelphia might or might not take up arms but were certainly pro-American; Tories reversed the movement, leaving cities and communities in revolt for British-controlled territory in North America, the Caribbean, or England itself.

To the city where the Declaration of Independence was signed came Myer Myers (1723–95), Haym Solomon, and the New York chazzan Gershom Mendes Seixas (1745–1816). Myers was a silversmith who also came from New York, where he had been president of the city's Gold and Silversmiths' Society during the 1770s and, after independence, would resume his position in the 1780s. Here we see American social tolerance already in play. It would have been unthinkable for a Jew to lead a (non-Jewish) professional organization in Europe before the French Revolution. Along with other members of Shearith Israel, Myers left British-occupied New York after Washington's withdrawal but returned after the war to take up his profession.[42]

There were Tory Jews too. One was Alexander Zuntz, a Hessian émigré who as a capable merchant helped supply local Hessian troops under British command and served as interim president of Shearith Israel during the war years. When peace came he was briefly exiled, but he returned with vigor, not only to the presidency of Shearith Israel but also to become a founding member of the New York Stock Exchange. Another Shearith Israel congregant, Benjamin Seixas (1747–1817), also was a founder of the exchange. The political sympathies of American Jews during the Revolution varied. For the most part, Sephardim favored rebellion, while Ashkenazim were divided, some fervent American patriots, others remaining loyalist.[43]

Philadelphia's Jews needed a purpose-built synagogue (a rental space was being leased instead) to accommodate the larger community that came to the city for political reasons during the revolutionary period. Hayman Levy (1721–89), Isaac Moses, Benjamin Seixas, and Simon Nathan (d. 1822) purchased a parcel on Sterling Alley in the late 1770s but found a better site on Cherry Street in 1782, where Mikveh Israel was built.[44] It was the first synagogue to appear in the new republic, not unfitting for a city so identified with American independence. During the dedication of Mikveh Israel we have the first recorded Jewish blessing for the government and officials of the United States, as opposed to the British royal family, spoken by chazzan Gershom Mendes Seixas. Those Jews who left Philadelphia and returned to their homes after the war took with them the prayer for the United States they had learned at Mikveh Israel, a practice subsequently disseminated wherever Jews settled. When chazzan Seixas returned to New York and Shearith Israel, he had the blessing translated from Portuguese to English. By so doing Seixas underlined the American identity of his congregants, who would worship as equal citizens in a free land.[45]

In 1795 a group of Philadelphia Jews established Rodeph Shalom (Pursuer of Peace), North America's first permanent Ashkenazic congregation, although it remained relatively small until the 1830s.[46] Mikveh Israel built a new synagogue in 1825 on Cherry Street. This new structure, designed by William Strickland (1788–1854), was conceived in the Egyptian Revival style, recently fashionable and very much a response to the newly discovered antiquities unearthed and displayed by French and British archaeologists. However ephemeral Napoleon's sovereignty in Egypt had been, his imperial venture had stimulated a new level of acquisitive Egyptological research. Objects thus discovered would be sent to the museums of London and Paris—and later to Philadelphia, New York, and Berlin—trophies of bourgeois dynasties that dazzled those who viewed them and created a new aesthetic. Moreover Strickland's Mikveh Israel—despite the Portuguese-Iberian heritage of its founders—bore no resemblance to any other synagogue in the Americas, the result of a different historical, or rather historicized, sensibility, utterly unlike the Sephardic vocabulary that had for so long defined synagogue architecture in the Atlantic World. For instance, besides its exterior architectural style, this building also broke from long-standing tradition by not utilizing the Sephardic open central-aisle plan in its interior, having a theater orientation instead.[47] We should note that during the end of the eighteenth century and the first decades of the nineteenth, Pennsylvania was home to other, smaller Jewish communities, in Lancaster and Reading, but neither had a purpose-built synagogue at the time. [48]

Jews first settled in Charleston, South Carolina, at the end of the seventeenth century. Throughout the eighteenth century, the city's economy was deeply connected to the Caribbean, as were its Jews who made their livelihood through trade. In 1740 Charleston received a boost in its Jewish population from those who fled Savannah (Georgia) at the onset of the War of Jenkins' Ear (1739–48) with Spain. Nine years later the small Jewish community living in South Carolina's major port established a congregation, Beth Elohim, which would become the largest in North America by 1800. It wanted to build a synagogue in 1775, but the Revolution intervened. In 1794 the South Carolina legislature authorized a lottery to raise construction funds.[49] The building itself was a hybrid, with an external steeple and pitched roof suggestive of the city's Georgian-style Episcopalian churches, but containing a detailed Sephardic interior based on the Esnoga and Bevis Marks.[50]

That Beth Elohim was completed at all during the 1790s represents no casual compromise between its Ashkenazim and Sephardim. In fact construction, ritual, and administrative disagreements had briefly split the Charleston community into two camps—Beth Elohim (Ashkenazic) and Beth Elohim Unveh Shalom (Sephardic)—with both asserting credentials as the rightful heir of the original 1749 congregation.[51] Once reunited, they achieved consensus to move the tebah closer to the center of the sanctuary. This design alteration meant that the floor plan was a kind of entente, allowing some merger between the open central aisle plan, used by the Sephardim across the Atlantic World, and the central bimah plan, favored by the Ashkenazim across central and eastern Europe.[52] While the split lasted—it was evanescent but slightly before Philadelphia's Rodeph Shalom—Beth Elohim found itself notionally the first Ashkenazic congregation in North America. That said, the Federalist-era Ashkenazim who proudly claimed their connection with mid-eighteenth-century Beth Elohim tended to overlook how the founders of Charleston's synagogue community practiced the Sephardic customs so prevalent then in the Atlantic World. Disputes over minhag were moderated by the need for a synagogue, and cooperation prevailed: when the building was dedicated in 1794, the two sides reunited.

Although Tory opinion was strong in parts of South Carolina, most Jews there supported the Revolution. Probably the most famous was Francis Salvador, elected to the state's General Assembly in 1776. Having taken up arms in a revolutionary militia, Salvador was killed later that year in a Loyalist ambush. There were many Jews fighting in the various Carolina militias, often in small units (three soldiers or fewer). But one militia, commanded by Captain Richard Lushington, counted fourteen Jewish soldiers in its mostly Christian roster, a proportion large enough to earn this group the sobriquet "Jews' Company."[53]

It was not only as revolutionary soldiers or, for that matter, as citizens insisting on equal rights and religious liberty that South Carolina Jews made a notable contribution to both American society as well as the norms governing Great Britain's larger Atlantic World. Women's rights were also on the docket. There is the singular case of Elizabeth Chapman, surname notwithstanding, a Jewish woman married to Mordecai Lyon (also Jewish). In 1788 she became the first woman to have a divorce recognized in South Carolina, although divorce was not legalized in that state until 1868. A Jewish religious court, however, granted her divorce; the court's ruling, a *get* (certificate of divorce), was considered by state authorities to be a free practice of religion. The religious court, organized by Charleston's congregation Beth Elohim, found the couple to be incompatible. After the ruling each would go on to marry a second time, and it was in fact these second marriages, permitted by the state and not deemed bigamous, that, ex post facto, validated the earlier get divorce.[54]

Congregation Beth Elohim split for a second time in 1824, and this division proved to have lastingly important consequences. A group of forty-seven congregants (almost half the total membership) appealed for changes to the order and method of worship with the goal of making services "Americanized" or "reformed." The rest of the congregation refused, and so the forty-seven broke off to form the Reformed Society of Israelites, led by Isaac Harby (1788–1828), Abraham Moïse (1799–1869), and Jacob Cardozo (1786–1873). The Reformed Society thus became the first reformed congregation in the Americas, and it fostered notable innovations. Most strikingly, while services retained Hebrew prayers, many—this became standard practice—were recited in English translation to instruct those without the ancient language, just as the sermon itself was delivered in English. Prayer books too were written in English and soon distributed. It will always be argued whether assimilationism caused these changes; this question seems myopic. Clearly Charleston Jewish reformers observed, adopted, or modified certain confessional practices that could be seen in any number of local churches. At the same time, the reformers were intent on creating ritual practice that both responded to contemporary experience and preserved the core of familiar Jewish worship. So in one edition of the reform prayer book, we find greater prominence given to women. This included actual reference to women—previously rarely made—in marriage or burial rites, and most conspicuously, the naming ceremony for baby girls (*Zeved ha-Bat*).[55] Women even recited a new Sabbath prayer. It may well have been written by Caroline Harby (1801–76), Isaac's sister. The Reformed Society undertook a campaign to build a new synagogue in 1826, but the money was not forthcoming.[56]

But by far most meaningful change introduced by the reformers was theological, affecting the Jewish reform movement throughout the Atlantic World and beyond. This was eliminating the last three principles, out of a canonical thirteen, advanced by Maimonides. For traditional or normative Judaism, the prestige and authority of this multivolume medieval work cannot easily be overstated. The three principles excised by the Beth Elohim reformers all deal with the Messiah.[57] American Jews, in common with evangelical Protestants who arrived in North America to settle what was for them a new land, would regard their settlement as a notional realization of biblical promise— if not the Zion of prophecy, then a credible approximation that no longer required so active a messianic intervention. Building Zion on American soil seemed to offer real possibilities for spiritual fulfillment and the creation of social relations that would embody religious precepts. However that may be, in American history, while Charleston would subsequently be perceived as a bastion of states' rights and conservatism—epicenter of the slave trade, nullification, Civil War, and the collapse of Reconstruction—the city's place in

American Jewish history is quite different, at least in the first third of the nineteenth century. Jews there were free, imaginative, and bold enough to adapt (or innovate) the contemporaneous European Reform movement, a force for religious modernity that originated in Germany. In short order, reform thought and worship would grow to dominate Judaism in the United States until the last quarter of the twentieth century.[58]

By 1832, after well more than a decade of separation due to several core issues, members of Charleston's Reformed Society decided to rejoin Beth Elohim. Not long after the synagogue burned down, to be replaced in 1841 by a famous, beautiful structure in which American Reform Judaism established its first permanent home, one that still stands today on Hasell Street in the city's downtown district. Like Jeshuat Israel in Newport, Beth Elohim benefited from the efforts of the Lopez family. Indeed the construction of the 1841 structure was the work of David Lopez Jr. (1809–84), owner of a prominent Charleston building firm as well as a pillar of the Jewish community at the time.[59] The principal architect, however, came from New York: Cyrus L. Warner conceived an elegant Greek Revival design for the exterior, its regular Doric columns and precisely proportioned pediment making the sanctuary resemble an Athenian temple, one of the first buildings of this kind in the city. This project was completed with the assistance of Tappan and Noble, a local firm.[60] But the disagreements between reform and traditionalist camps within Beth Elohim continued. Disputes over liturgy, observance of holidays, and, especially, the use of an organ, appropriated from Christian worship services, set traditionalists members against reformed congregants. Because orthodoxy forbids any playing of music on the Sabbath, traditionalists deplored the proposed use of an organ to complement services as sacrilege. Soon enough the issue came to a vote that was won narrowly by the modernizing reformers. This proved to be the last straw for conservative members, who broke away in 1843 to found the distinctly orthodox congregation named Shearit Israel.

The struggle for control of Beth Elohim would legally be adjudicated through *State vs. Ancker,* with the rival camps led by the congregation's president, a reformer, and the mostly orthodox board of trustees. From the bench of the South Carolina Court of Common Pleas, Judge Andrew Butler (1796–1857) ruled that the government should not intervene in vexed religious or theological problems; hence the congregation must resolve such issues internally. This decision has long been regarded as precedent for limiting state interference in matters of religion. But at the same time, the Butler decision did find against Beth Elohim's traditionalist board for supervening the congregation's constitution once the organ installation vote had been approved. As a result of this procedural violation, the court awarded the synagogue building itself to the reformers.[61] So for the first time, Beth Elohim reformers had both a sanctuary to call their own and Reform Judaism to guide their worship as they consolidated a new identity. It was this Charleston community that became the first in the Atlantic World to split along denominational lines and in so doing became the first Reform Jewish congregation outside of Europe.

We have grown used to Atlantic World congregations rebuilding synagogues that fell victim to tempest, fire, or conflict. But the more pedestrian and voluntary rebuilding of a synagogue because of the need for larger quarters or aesthetic wishes—that did not happen in America until the nineteenth century in New York. The original Shearith Israel Synagogue there was built in 1730, used until 1818, demolished after serious deterioration, then reconstructed on the same site to house a much larger community. During the nineteenth century, Shearith Israel would raise three more synagogue structures, in each instance because of a growing membership.[62] Almost counterintuitively we must bear in mind that until 1825, the Sephardic Shearith Israel was New York's *only* synagogue. Only after midcentury would the floodgates of Ashkenazic immigration open, soon making New York home to the world's largest Jewish population, one replete with dozens of congregations from across Europe.[63]

It is significant that 1825 marks the year a contingent of Ashkenazim split away from Shearith Israel to found B'nai Jeshurun (Children of the Upright), New York's second congregation. In point of fact, for several decades Shearith Israel's Ashkenazim had already outnumbered the Sephardim. They had reached both a demographic as well as a sociocultural critical mass by the early nineteenth century: ready acceptance of Iberian rituals—once advantageous because of support from the Sephardic diaspora—no longer made sense or satisfied Jews shaped by a central or eastern European religious experience, Jews who were now numerous enough to track their own path. Then too there was the pervasive influence of America's democratic environment. Ashkenazim in New York had never lived in a society that allowed for freedom of conscience or the constitutional separation of religion from the state. Central European Jews were free to adopt rituals and practices without fear of interference, either from secular authorities or intrusive Sephardic officialdom, as had happened from time to time elsewhere under British and Dutch rule.[64] In general, after the first quarter of the nineteenth century, Atlantic World Jews, whether in the United States or in any number of polities throughout the Americas, were free to form congregations following the traditions of their own choosing. The earlier synagogue-community model that existed under colonial conditions was superseded by variety and, depending on demography, even multiplicity. A dualistic control of Judaism (either Sephardic or Ashkenazic), though prevalent, was no longer absolute in the United States.

As the fifth American president, James Monroe, took office (1825), western New York state would become home to the modern world's first proto-Zionist Jewish community. Five years before, American-born Mordecai M. Noah conceived of a Jewish haven, part colony and part utopia, on Grand Island in the Niagara River. This amalgam would be of particular value for persecuted Jews fleeing religious intolerance and in need of a homeland. It would be nothing less than the biblical archetype of a port after storm, appositely named Ararat by the New York Noah who, unlike his Genesis forbear, sought funds from Jews and Christians alike in America and Europe—including an approach to the Parisian rabbinical Consistory.[65] In 1825, amidst pomp and ceremony, Noah erected a monument on Grand Island, the legend announcing "Ararat, a City of Refuge for the Jews." But Ararat was a failure from the very start. Noah had appointed himself governor and judge of the community, a despotic act that discredited him and made the plan seem capricious and un-American.[66] Since they had already achieved equality in the United States, few American Jews felt any need to move to Grand Island, then a backwater on New York's upstate frontier, on the border with Canada. Most American Jews of this generation wanted to find stability within mainstream society, not seek out ways to be differentiated. The only people interested in Noah's vision, philo-Semites from a Christian background, were ineligible because they were not born Jewish. So Ararat was abandoned after only a few years, its cornerstone monument the lone witness to a miscarried experiment.[67] There was a simultaneous attempt to form another utopian Jewish community. During the 1820s Moses Elias Levy (1782–1854) mounted a second project, this time in the newly acquired Florida Territory, but it failed too. Levy sought financial backing from donors in Great Britain and Gibraltar, where he had passed much of his childhood, although in the event his main advocate was the like-minded Mordecai M. Noah, despite the New Yorker competing for similar support. It came to neither man.[68]

More grounded if less idealistic settlement took place on the southeastern Atlantic coast, where Jews joined James Oglethorpe (1696–1785), founder of the Georgia colony. It was established in 1733, and Jews were there from practically the beginning. During the colony's early years (c. 1732–40s), leaders of Bevis Marks in London had approached Georgia's trustees as well as the Board of Trade for permission to settle Jewish paupers in the vicinity of Savannah, though it came to naught. When the *William and Sarah* arrived near Savannah, the ship debarked forty-two Jews, and they encountered the original group of colonists battling a cruel fever epidemic. Among the Jews was a fine physician, Samuel Nunes (1667–1741), who immediately dispensed with the medieval medical treatment (bleeding veins, purging) that he encountered, prescribing instead cold fluids and baths. His patients survived. Although Jews and Catholics were barred from entry by the first colonial charter, Governor Oglethorpe reconsidered this restriction, soon granting Jews the same right to settle as Protestants. (Catholics, however, were still excluded.) In persuading the other Georgia trustees to accept Jews, Oglethorpe pointed to the exemplary services of Nunes in the recent epidemic, not to mention the need to replace colonists who had died from fever. The Jewish colonists quickly formed their first congregation, Mickve Israel (Hope of Israel) but would have to wait until 1791 and the ratification of the Bill of Rights before receiving full civil and legal rights.[69]

By the 1770s the Jewish community of Savannah began to revive. Mordechai Sheftall (1735–97), a leading figure at congregation Mickve Israel, was widely respected for his abilities. Besides being involved with own congregation, Sheftall served as Georgia's commissary general during the Revolutionary War and was ably assisted by his son, Sheftall Sheftall (b. 1762). But, as happened not infrequently during the Revolution, families divided: Mordecai's brother Levi (1739–1809) sided with the British, the two reconciling when peace came. There is, however, some evidence to suggest that the Sheftall division was strategic, part of a scheme to make sure that family interests were associated with the victor. By 1820 the Savannah Jewish community would build their first synagogue, a structure fated to survive a mere nine years and not be soon replaced. But the city's Jewish population continued to grow and became a fixture of the port's social and commercial life.[70]

Fittingly enough, Virginia, where Jamestown provided the cradle for permanent English settlement on American soil, also hosted the first English Jew to visit American shores. But the Ashkenazi Joachim Gaunse, who arrived in 1585, stayed with the lost Roanoke Colony only temporarily before his return to England. Before the Revolution—this span in Virginia covers nearly two hundred years since Gaunse—Jews would occasionally make their way to the colony but not until the founding of the republic did they come in large enough numbers to form a congregation.

Among early Jewish Virginians, the best known is probably Moses Myers (1753–1835) of Norfolk, a successful entrepreneur whose fine brick Federal-era home, built c. 1787, is now preserved as a museum. It would be the new capital of Richmond where Jews would build the state's first synagogue, Beth Shalome (House of Peace), which dated from 1822. This building's architecture was hybrid, combining the Georgian conventions of Bevis Marks with the later, ancillary Federal style developed in America.[71] This Virginian house of worship was the last essentially Atlantic World Jewish religious structure to be built. Put differently, synagogue architectural models after 1822 reflected a non-Sephardic dispensation. A new period had begun in the Americas—which set new aesthetic boundaries—where either Ashkenazim used their ancestral traditions or American reformers introduced their own innovations into the design of synagogues.

During the American Revolution, the British captured Newport, Rhode Island, destroying much of the small city. One of the few buildings to survive was Jeshuat Israel's synagogue. As Newport declined economically, Jews sought out better prospects in New York, Charleston, and, soon enough, in New Orleans. The synagogue's doors, built only twelve years before the outbreak of the Revolution, were closed for the last time in 1822. Moses Lopez, the nephew of Touro Synagogue's leading founder Aaron Lopez, was the last Jew to leave for New York, where he lived until his death in 1830. Jeshuat Israel's six Torahs, emblem of Sephardic bounty and support before the twin democratic revolutions on both sides of the Atlantic, passed to New York's Shearith Israel, along with title to the synagogue and the Rhode Island's congregation's property.[72]

While Jefferson's insistence that the young United States purchase the Louisiana territory from France stands as an indelible marker of American expansion, less well known is how briefly the French tricolor flew over that vast territory (eight hundred thousand square miles) on either side of the Mississippi River. Not until 30 November 1803 did Spain, which effectively controlled the great parcel of land, formally convey Louisiana to France. On 20 December of that same year—not even a month later—France transferred the territory to the United States, although the treaties specifying these arrangements date to 1801.[73] So ended for Jews the dangers, prohibitions, or exclusions enacted by Spain in Louisiana. Cities like New Orleans, perched on the Gulf of Mexico, and Cincinnati, on a bend of the Ohio River, soon attracted Jews from the eastern seaboard and, in formidable numbers, central European immigrants, among whom there were many Jews too. By the 1820s Jewish congregations were established in booming cities of what was fast becoming America's Midwest. That encompassed the western periphery of America's original thirteen states, as well as areas that now belong to Ohio, Indiana, Kentucky, Missouri, and Louisiana.

Even though New Orleans was founded in 1718, Jews settled there in consequential numbers only from the time of the purchase. Yet the city's organized Jewish life developed slowly. Not until 1828 does the first congregation, Shaarai Chesed (Gates of Mercy), appear, largely at the instigation of New York businessman Jacob S. Solis. He was visiting New Orleans as Passover approached, found no forum for collective observance, and urged local Jews to act together promptly: the result was Shaarai Chesed. In the beginning this New Orleans congregation followed Sephardic minhag—and for precisely the same reasons that influenced earlier East Coast synagogue-communities. Because trade with the Americas, Europe, and the Caribbean provided the economic raison d'être for the port of New Orleans, its Jews benefitted from relations with Atlantic World Sephardic merchants, relying on friendships, family ties, and familiarity of worship. By 1842, however, the mostly central European membership of Shaarai Chesed adopted Ashkenazic rituals instead (though a constituency did withdraw to form a second Sephardic congregation, Nefusot Yehudah [Dispersed of Judah]). The necessity of following Sephardic traditions for purposes of commerce was no longer essential. The bylaws of Shaarai Chesed were written in both English and French, reflecting the members' active participation in Louisiana's specific social and cultural milieu.[74] Revealingly this bilingualism was not adopted by Montreal's

Shearith Israel—whose bylaws were written only in English—after French Canada became British. At the time Montreal Jews identified with Quebec's Anglophone Protestant minority, not the dominant Catholic population.

For some thirty years, from 1795 until 1824, no new Jewish congregations appeared in the United States. In its first generation, the American republic saw congregations (like Newport's Jeshuat Israel in 1822) close, not open. The year 1824, however, marked a change in this communal hibernation: Charleston's Reform Society of Israelites (as noted) and Cincinnati's congregation Bene Israel (Children of Israel) were founded in that year. Thereafter almost all new congregations founded in the United States before the Civil War would be Ashkenazic or Reform, in close correlation with the population growth of Central European Jews, who by far outnumbered Sephardim.[75] During this same period, Jews of Spanish and Portuguese origin loss control of the congregations they had founded and witnessed the passing of Sephardic minhag in synagogue worship. The year 1838 stands as the first when there were more Ashkenazic than Sephardic congregations—Beth El (House of God) in Albany and B'nai Yeshurun in Cincinnati were founded then—and this trend line would never alter. However, the numbers of Jewish Americans at the time remained small—in 1840, only some fifteen thousand out of a national census of 17,069,453. By 1838 New York was home to three congregations, while Philadelphia and Cincinnati each had two.[76] It was also shortly after this (early 1840s) that the first permanent resident rabbi in North America, Abraham Rice (1800–62, who was Ashkenazic), took his pulpit position in Baltimore. All previous spiritual heads of Jewish congregations, including Gershom Mendes Siexas in New York, were chazzanim (plural for chazzan) and did not have official rabbinical ordination.[77]

TABLES 5 AND 6. The breakdown of formal Jewish congregational life according to tradition, or minhag, in the United States, up to 1838. The split between Beth Elohim and Beth Elohim Unveh Shalom in Charleston, South Carolina, during the early 1790s was not counted because it was so brief.

TABLES 5 AND 6. (CONTINUED)

Sephardic	Ashkenazic	Reform
Shearith Israel, New York, circa 1695/1704	Rodeph Shalom, Philadelphia, 1795	Reform Society of Israelites, Charleston, 1824–1838 (rejoined with Beth Elohim, which became Reform in 1841)
Mickve Israel, Savannah, 1733	Bene Israel, Cincinnati, 1824	
Mikveh Israel, Philadelphia, 1740	B'nai Jeshurun, New York, 1825	
Beth Elohim, Charleston, 1749	Anshe Chesed, New York, 1828	
Jeshuat Israel, Newport, 1756–1822 (Closed in 1822 and reopened in 1883)	(Nidche Israel) Baltimore Hebrew Congregation, Baltimore, 1834	
Beth Shalome, Richmond, 1789	Beth El, Albany, 1838	
Shaarai Chesed, New Orleans, 1828 (changed to Ashkenazic minhag in 1842)	B'nai Yeshurun, Cincinnati, 1838	

A different historical period was emerging in American Jewish life, one that reflected the expansion of the United States itself. Before the Civil War, Reform and Orthodox communities organized themselves across the boundaries of the growing nation. When Jews set up congregations in Albany, Cincinnati, New Orleans, and Baltimore, they were settling in cities and towns that had few Jews to speak of in the eighteenth and early nineteenth centuries. Ashkenazim—mainly central European in origin, but after midcentury, increasingly eastern European—would build either Orthodox synagogues or Reform "temples" architecturally distinct from the modest Sephardic structures of the colonial, revolutionary, or early republican epoch. The Reform use of the word "temple" instead of "synagogue" reflected a theological movement, evolutionary rather than revolutionary, away from traditional Jewish belief in a future messianic reign—the dogma that had animated Jews, not least the Sephardim of the Atlantic World, for so much of their history. Certainly "temple" was an innovative compound signifier. The term conspicuously denotes the ancient Temple of the Hebrew Bible but inevitably implies acceptance of a broader cultural, historical, and political reference, one associated with the ascendant republican mythos that grew out of the twin democratic revolutions in Europe and America. "Temple" in this second sense connotes Periclean Athens and republican Rome as key referents in a contemporary, politicized symbolic vocabulary. Put another way: for Americans generally, including Reform and traditional Jews, Greco-Roman architectural attributes bespoke a political ideology that excluded, or in any case displaced, pagan polytheism.

The Federal era enshrined Demosthenes and Cicero, not Apollo and Jupiter. In fact the European classicizing aesthetic—it unfolds from the Renaissance and Palladio to Winckelmann and the Enlightenment—received authoritative and typical American treatment in Jefferson's Virginia state capitol (built 1785–92, which imitates the Maison Carrée, built c. 16 B.C.E.), a design that came to signify democracy. Perforce these attitudes affected Jews in the United States. Especially for Reform Jews, rabbinic Judaism was embraced as an age-old, vital, and coherent belief system, yet one whose messianic vision left little psychological or intellectual space for a Jewish faith rooted simultaneously in familiar Jewish practice and an awareness that would comport with secular democratic society. Respect for tradition in balance with a new, democratic sociopolitical ethos was precisely what the Reform movement in the United States aimed to create—a process that, beginning in the 1820s, required several generations to achieve. According to this aspiration, Zion was less a dream of messianic futurity, more a condition to be realized by engaging civil society while accommodating an ethically robust, historically informed religious consciousness. In any case, the Reform designation for a Jewish house of worship predicates the increasing socioeconomic stability Jews achieved in the first half of the nineteenth century. They were confident, wealthy, and free enough to gradually create a new religious posture in what for them was a new land.

But for all Jews, whether reform or traditional, the age of democratic revolutions made investment in liberation, that archetypal Exodus-forged yearning, more pressing and timely. And so at this juncture, we see the early emergence of a recognizably modern problem of Jewish identity: how to combine being Jewish with the nationalist, civic idea of being an American or German. Even though Reform Jews would respond first to such pressures by incorporating modern languages as a necessary complement to their ritual practice and social participation, traditionalist Jews would, after a fashion, follow a similar, though not identical, path. In the nineteenth century, Orthodox Jews would never surrender or vitiate biblical messianism but to it (much like the reformers) would add the sense of America as a land of opportunity—those who came from Yiddish-speaking origins called it *Die Goldene Medina* (the Golden Land)—where Jews could express themselves freely and contribute as informed members of a modern state.

How did Jews fare in the other Atlantic World societies formed in the crucible of an epochal revolution? Although the seminal names associated with the French Revolution are hardly Jewish, that does not mean Jews were absent from the ferment or foment that erupted in France during the latter eighteenth century with its Napoleonic sequel. Voltaire's "Des Juifs" (1756), later included in the famous *Dictionnaire Philosophique* (1764), criticized Jews—the clarion philosophe, for all his insistence on religious tolerance, was ambiguous in his views on Judaism—and elicited from the Sephardic scholar Isaac de Pinto a sharp reply in the form of a pamphlet (*Réflexions critiques sur le premier chapitre du VIIe tome des oeuvres de monsieur de Voltaire au sujet des Juif*, 1762).[78] Although Hebrew biblical scholarship had been approved in the seventeenth century, this attitude changed as the Lumieres advanced the Enlightenment agenda. Studies of the Hebrew Bible, whether by Jews or Christian Hebraists, were seen derogatorily—for all of Spinoza's pioneering textual methodology—as products of a narrow provincial scholasticism. In this reductive light, there was debate in Paris and other enlightened centers on the merits of extending equal civil rights and protections to the Jews.[79] So "Des Juifs," and recall that elsewhere Voltaire's views on Jews were more favorable, formed part of a wider discussion, one that became loud indeed in 1789. Another voice, very much in the accents of a nation that had just witnessed the fall of the Bastille, can be heard in *Les juifs d'Alsace doivent-ils être admis au droit de citoyens actifs? Lisez et jugez* (1790).[80] In the event, Jewish emancipation came quickly—1790 for the Sephardim (who primarily lived in Bordeaux and Bayonne), a year later for the Ashkenazim (centered in Alsace and Lorraine). This burst of tolerance also coincided with the revolutionary emancipation of Protestants in 1791.[81] As it happened, the actual response to the pamphlet's title question about Alsace and Lorraine was: extend rights limitedly, grudgingly, and slowly. Perdurable anti-Semitic views toward French Ashkenazim held more sway among those provincial authorities than the dictates of the Legislative Assembly in Paris.[82]

The difference between the French enfranchisement that liberated Jewish citizens during the revolutionary era and the freedoms previously granted Dutch, British, and Danish Jews hinges on the vital difference between "privileges" and "rights." In the first instance (privileges), a condition or action (volitional worship or voting) is in the gift of the state and may be modified as the state chooses; in the second (rights), the condition or action is an irreducible attribute of citizenship, not subject to state preference or caprice.[83] As we have seen, after 1603 the Jews of Amsterdam were allowed to settle in the city and worship unobtrusively, almost without restriction. Such freedoms were, however, privileges that the governmental authorities could reduce or take away. Moreover Jews were not the only religious minority treated in this way. Through a more combative, complicated relationship, Catholics and dissenting Protestant groups sometimes enjoyed a similar privilege in the seventeenth-century Dutch republic. But neither Jews nor Catholics nor dissenting Protestants had a *right* to worship as they chose. Equality for all Dutchman—though first experimented with in 1796—would have to wait until the passage of constitutional guarantees in 1815, reinforced by subsequent amendments (notably in 1834 and 1848).

When we look at the other revolutionary Atlantic World society ideologically committed to civil liberties in the age of democratic revolution,

America's record is somewhat checkered. The Bill of Rights was ratified in 1791 but, besides originally protecting only white male property owners, applied exclusively to the federal government. State governments, on the other hand, followed their own, later trajectories toward endorsing the freedoms enshrined in the Constitution's first ten amendments. The extension of the Bill of Rights to all citizens as an inalienable prerogative—for many a work still incomplete—would require, besides Supreme Court jurisprudence, Civil War, Reconstruction, and the passage of the Fourteenth Amendment to the Constitution (1868). This uneven history created certain anomalies for Jews in the early years of the American republic. A Jewish citizen could hold high federal office yet be barred from holding the lowest state position. It was New York that became the first state to extend Jews comprehensive equal rights constitutionally, a provision most other states emulated by 1830. Not so New Hampshire, which waited until 1877 to recognize Jewish civil liberties: presumably so few Jews lived in this corner of New England that the exclusion went unattended until the spirit of the times cued the conscience of the state assembly.[84]

Conversely, both as model and reality, France's emancipation of Jews had a far more profound effect on Jews everywhere than did the American recognition of religious liberty. France itself had a relatively small Jewish population in 1789—perhaps forty thousand—mostly concentrated in Alsace and Lorraine with far smaller numbers in Paris, Bordeaux, Bayonne, and Avignon. At least initially Napoleon's wars and conquests, both before and after Bonaparte became emperor, served as conduits—some more porous than others—through which French revolutionary ideas and political practices permeated. For the Jews and New Christians of Europe, the revolution meant liberty, equality under the law, the end of the Inquisition, and freedom from the ghetto. In 1806 Napoleon assembled in Paris the leading rabbis and Jewish religious laymen in France and Italy. Called the Grand Sanhedrin after the ancient biblical assembly, it would meet for approximately a year and consisted of seventy-one men charged with determining the role of Jews in Napoleonic Europe. The writ of this body's rulings on religious law was confined to Napoleon's empire—hardly a small area. As far as French-ruled lands were concerned, the Grand Sanhedrin normalized the status of Jews, whose newly defined republican citizenship was retained under the empire. Within France and her dependencies, a system of "consistories" was also established in 1808—in emulation of the centralized Napoleonic civil bureaucracy—that regulated Jewish communities on the local, regional, and national levels, the principal authority radiating from Paris. This structure of governance had recently, in fact, been developed as appropriate and effective for relations with the far more numerous French Protestant population.[85]

After Napoleon's final defeat, it was left to his Bourbon "successors" to restore the French monarchy while consolidating revolutionary-Napoleonic achievements. This legerdemain meant accommodating the irreversible rise of the bourgeoisie under the increasingly atavistic royal authority. In general, as far as Jewish relations with the French state are concerned, constitutional forms replaced the absolutism of the ancien regime. So France under the last Bourbon kings (1814–48) accepted a bicameral legislature, the Code Napoleon, and the civil bureaucratic and departmental structures developed by Napoleon. In 1830 the Rabbinical Seminary of Metz was founded, while the next year the government started paying the salaries of pulpit rabbis, an arrangement that already applied to Catholic and Protestant clergy. As France began to colonize Algeria, Morocco, and Tunisia in the nineteenth century, a process that started—Napoleonic ventures aside—in 1830, native North African Jews were added to the overall census of French Jewry.[86]

When 1848, that year of so many promised and balked European revolts, arrived in Paris, the Bourbons, in the person of their pedestrian avatar Louis Philippe, would at last fall. There ensued the turbulent Second Republic, ending with the coup of Louis Napoleon, nephew of the great Bonaparte, promulgator of the Second Empire (1851–70), and object of Marx's paradigmatic Eighteenth Brumaire judgment—"history repeating itself as farce." In the midst of such turmoil, with the French capital by no means replicating the anti-Semitism of Alsace and Lorraine, Jews were actors: briefly (Jewish) Michel Goudchaux (1797–1862) served as finance minister of the Second Republic. Then too, under Napoleon III, France was led by someone who, whatever Marx's strictures, did not discriminate against Jews. Although frequently an opponent of the coup-installed emperor, the trenchant liberal Adolphe Cremieux (1796–1880) was appointed minister of justice in 1867, while Achille Fould (1800–67) served as minister of finance between 1861 and 1867. Both Cremieux and Fould were Jews.[87]

The Napoleonic Wars took place on the global stage and were some of history's first true "world wars." Because European colonization and imperial conquest had redrawn the politicoeconomic map since 1500, campaigns to unseat French power inside and outside Europe became inevitable after 1789, even before Bonaparte became First Consul and Emperor. So when France conquered the Netherlands in 1795 and made it a puppet state, the Batavian Republic, Great Britain responded by striking at Dutch overseas possessions, such as St. Eustatius, Curaçao, and parts of India, to prevent France from gaining control of them. The British overtly wanted to deprive France of any colonial resources or spoils and, at the same time, to increase their own strategic power and war-making capacity. By and large the British treated Jewish merchants in colonial territory seized from the Batavian Republic (as briefly we must call the Netherlands) in the same way the Dutch had done. Although this treatment by Anglican rulers was fairly liberal, full emancipation for Jews would have to wait until the Netherlands regained its possessions after Waterloo.

When Napoleon invaded Portugal in 1807, he began the Peninsular War (1807–14), a series of campaigns involving regular and irregular forces that would last until his downfall six years later. French armies periodically controlled a great deal of Portugal and Spain, waging increasingly difficult battles against *guerrillas* (the name was coined during this very conflict) and the maneuvers of invading British troops led brilliantly by Arthur Wellesley, the Duke of Wellington. How did this fighting affect Iberian Jews, or rather the remnant that had lived as conversos for the preceding three hundred years? During the troubled interlude of Napoleonic rule, under the direction of Napoleon's older brother Joseph (1768–1844), named king in 1808, the Inquisition was (temporarily) abolished in Iberia. With the restoration of the Portuguese and Spanish monarchies after 1813, France's revolutionary social program, articulated by the Declaration of the Rights of Man with its concomitant emancipation of Jews, was annulled. But this did not mean that the spirit of freedom that Napoleon had unleashed (or conveyed), even as an occupier, disappeared utterly—whether in respect to Jews or, more profoundly, to society itself. In a broad sense the Peninsular War, as an expression of nationalist fervor animating Iberian patriots joined Wellesley in driving French forces from the Peninsula, helped set in motion liberal ideas that would end the Spanish Inquisition forever in 1834.

The French Revolution and Napoleonic rule began to have decisive political effects on Latin America in 1804, when Haiti successfully rebelled against France. Along with a majority of the white population, the few Jews in the colony formerly known as Saint-Domingue fled the racial crucible that attended Toussaint Louverture's revolt with its bloody abolition of slavery. Across the Atlantic World, one epoch had ended, and another began. Between 1810 and 1825, nearly all Spanish possessions in the Americas—except Cuba and Puerto Rico—fought and eventually won wars of independence from their imperial sovereign. Bolivar was only the most famous of the Libertadores. As for Brazil, so long Portugal's infinite Atlantic cornucopia, it became independent in 1822. We should note that in all this great new stratum of American republics, none had an openly professing Jewish community at the moment of independence. That distinction had been achieved only by the United States a generation earlier. Inevitably so: the "Jews" living in the Latin American republics were conversos, joined by a certain far smaller number of itinerant Dutch, British, or American Jews who had slipped into the Catholic colonial territories to conduct illegal trade.

During the Venezuelan War of Independence (1811–23), the Jewish community of Curaçao supported Simon Bolivar, as did the Liberator's personal friend Mordechay Ricardo (1771–1842). Some Curaçaoan Jews fought alongside Bolivar, notably Juan de Sola (1795–1860), who as a lieutenant colonel commanded the cavalry at the decisive Battle of Carabobo, which led to Venezuelan independence. Later in his career, he attained the rank of general.[88] By 1825 only Cuba and Puerto Rico remained Spanish possessions, though later Santo Domingo for a period (1844–65) returned to Spanish rule. As independence came to each Latin American republic, its Inquisition was quickly abolished, an anticipation of Spain's own ending, on 15 July 1834, of the once-mighty ecclesioroyal office that defined Jewish survival in the Atlantic World. This termination also applied (after 1834) to Spain's remaining loyal colonies—Cuba, Puerto Rico, Guam, and the Philippines—although these islands had almost no Jews before 1898, when the United States launched the Spanish-American War.[89]

Conflicts between Latin and Anglo America were hardly a novelty. A half century before the war with Spain, the Mexican-American War (1846–48) had secured Texas (not to mention California and New Mexico) for a United States motivated by Manifest Destiny fervor. Slightly earlier, in 1836, during the first stage of American imperialism above the Rio Grande, the Texas Revolution had carved Tejas away from Mexico. In this conflict we know Jews participated. Both Moses Albert Levy (1800–48) and Isaac Lyons served as surgeons in the Texan Army under Sam Houston. In any case, a small number of Jews were among the Anglo-American and central European settlers who participated in *empresario* Stephen F. Austin's (1793–1836) colony during the 1820s and 1830s, before the revolt.[90]

Portugal dissolved its Inquisition in 1821, Brazil declared independence in 1822, and Lisbon recognized Brazilian sovereignty in 1825—so in the broad wake of Napoleon's defeat the Portuguese imperial era with its anti-Semitic apparatus came to an end in South America.[91] At the same time, in 1824–25, British treaties were negotiated with Brazil, Venezuela, and Argentina, securing religious tolerance for non-Catholic British businessmen working in those countries (Catholics needed no such insulation). Even though protection of British Protestants was the overt goal here, Jews benefitted too. The environment was a favorable one. For the most part, the new South American republics were titular heirs of the French Revolution in their early constitutions: these, at least notionally, established religious and civil liberties as foundational. We know that Jews in the Dutch Antilles had been trading in contraband with Venezuela since the last quarter of the seventeenth century. Mostly from Curaçao, West Indian Jews settled in Coro and Maracaibo, Venezuela for purposes of trade, invited by Bolivar himself as an acknowledgement of their support during the war for independence.

Belém is a major river port sixty miles inland from the Atlantic on Brazil's northern coast. To this important commercial center, soon after Brazilian independence came Jews from Morocco. By 1828 they had built their first synagogue, Shaar Hashamaim (Gates of Heaven), which, given their origins, could not but differ stylistically and culturally from any other religious structure then seen in the Americas. Yet on this Brazilian riverine delta a distinctively North African Jewish sensibility and ritual orientation would emerge. Indeed a veritable Moroccan Jewish network spread from Belém into the Amazon basin, linking Santarém and Manaus, in Brazil, to Iquitos and Tarapoto in Peru. From North Africa, too, a trickle of Jews also sought out Portugal's Atlantic Islands, with an Azores congregation established in Ponte Delgada by 1836.[92] Everything had changed with the 1830s. The Atlantic World of the Sephardim, that diasporic realm inaugurated by the great Iberian flight from intolerance and Inquisition, had gestated almost beyond recognition.

Who can say how quickly the twin revolutions in France and America would have disseminated their doctrines, including the assertion of universal religious freedom, absent the thunderbolt of Napoleon and the Enlightenment attitudes his rule, even in imperial dress, stimulated in Europe and the New World? We can only guess. But a genie (or as Hegel proposed, a *Geist*) had been released into western and parts of central Europe as well as the Americas. What we do know is that the terms of European society, politics, and economy—for industrial and agricultural production were also revolutionized in the British Isles during this era—had crossed a critical threshold during the last quarter of the eighteenth century. After 1814, for all Metternich's efforts, restored monarchies would bear the imprint of the great struggles that had toppled so many thrones or seen Bonaparte control so much territory. Across the Atlantic, slightly later, the examples of the French and American revolutionaries would bring on the downfall of the centuries-old Iberian empires too. In the midst of such tumult and change, Jewish enfranchisement played a limited but ideologically significant part. Jews in lands opposing Bonaparte were often first committed to showing patriotic allegiance, either as warriors or government supporters, feeling secure enough to pursue full equality only after Waterloo. This was notably the case in Great Britain, whose campaigns against Napoleon effectively retarded Jewish enfranchisement. The advanced parliamentary nation that produced and embraced Locke, Hume, Edinburgh's Adam Smith, and industrial manufacturing would wait until practically the outbreak of the American Civil War before granting full civil rights to Jews in 1858. If we were to posit a close date for the main narrative of the Sephardic Atlantic World, 1822 offers as good a marker as any. In that year the post of Amsterdam's chief rabbi went vacant and would so remain until 1900—precisely the rabbinate that had spoken for some two centuries to the Sephardim of Europe and their settlements or colonies in the New World with the single most authoritative voice. In that same year, when

Beth Shalome was founded in Richmond, the Sephardic congregation there had no successor ritually, socially, or architecturally. Or, to be more exact, we should regard Beth Shalome as a mostly Ashkenazic congregation that nevertheless followed Sephardic minhag, but for the last time.

But that world, its material and ideological lineaments, had virtually disappeared. On one level cash crops like Caribbean sugarcane, the slave labor that made them profitable, and the colonial commerce linking European markets to American producers were in varying degrees of decline—precipitous in Haiti, less rapid but inexorably in the United States and Brazil. Nonplantation agriculture worked by free labor would set the next stage of economic development. However, it was in the political and social realm that new ideas had caused the most evident and rapid cataclysm. The revolutions ignited at Lexington and by the storming of the Bastille, then the Napoleonic geopolitical system and its sequitur after the Treaty of Paris, forever changed the status of Jews in the Americas and much of Europe where Bonaparte had prevailed. Again Jews form part of a larger, more complex whole here, but that part was a key litmus test of religious tolerance in the new age of republican democracy, civil rights, and industrial capital. Though there would be relapses into ancient regime anti-Semitism, Jews had left the ghetto and internal exile to engage a more inclusive civil society. If the Atlantic World had been marked by concealment, wariness, and sanctuary, the post-Napoleonic dispensations would allow Jews to align their traditions with dominant social forces in a forthright, uninhibited way. There was variation and differentiation: the Jews of France did not live in exactly the same political or moral culture, as did those in Denmark, the United States, or Brazil. But the default environment of tolerance, citizenship, and empowerment was fundamentally changed, nowhere more so than in the Americas and decisively so in the United States.

For American Jews, beginning in the 1820s, there would be permanent changes not just in their attitude toward tradition or religious practice, but in the deeper sense of belonging: America became home itself, not a sanctuary or way station. Buildings, like language, gauge social experience. So we find synagogue architectural forms altered to register this changed consciousness. At the dedication ceremony of the second Beth Elohim synagogue in March 1841, the reverend-chazzan, Gustavus Poznanski, spoke to his Charleston congregation as someone perspicuously aware of place and time: "This synagogue is our temple, this city our Jerusalem, this happy land our Palestine, and as our fathers defended with their lives that temple, that city, and that land, so will our sons defend this temple, this city, and this land."[93]

By the 1840s New World congregations were mostly Ashkenazic or Reform. Nor was the older Sephardic minority as rigidly bound to its own past. In the United States many helped create Reform Judaism and became advocates of non-Sephardic designs whenever a new synagogue was needed. In any case, with almost no population growth, Sephardic congregations would replace or replicate aging synagogues rather than build new structures. As the Caribbean economy passed into doldrums after the mid-nineteenth century, many Sephardic Jews left the West Indies for brighter prospects elsewhere, notably the United States, Great Britain, the Netherlands, Venezuela, Colombia, and Panama. The Caribbean homeland of the Atlantic World era was in steady decline: its synagogues and cemeteries pointed to a once-prosperous past, never to reappear with such stability or significance. At best the Sephardic synagogues built in the Caribbean during the halcyon days of the eighteenth and early nineteenth centuries were maintained, abandoned, or lost without replacement because of "acts of God." The venerable Jeshuat Israel (built 1759–63) in Newport, now called Touro Synagogue, also suffered a virtual Caribbean fate: it lapsed into dormancy, and the congregation dispersed, very much because Newport during the Federalist era waned with the decline of Caribbean maritime commerce. Only in 1882 would the congregation revive for a period, this time with an Ashkenazic constituency. Just the reverse happened in the rest of North America and Europe, however, where newer and larger synagogues replaced older buildings as their respective Ashkenazic congregations thrived.

As for the new religious structures that would increase numerically and vary stylistically as Jewish populations became rooted in their new nineteenth-century abodes, we must recognize that, pragmatic construction concerns aside, the aesthetic forms adopted by the Ashkenazim expressed what a given Jewish community aspired to be—its imagination of itself in history and society. That is why Jews of central European origin did not employ the Sephardic vocabulary of the Esnoga and Bevis Marks. No longer defined by or beholden to the Iberian diaspora, Ashkenazim—especially in North America— saw themselves as citizens who participated in a broader, more inclusive social contract. North American Jews in particular—although this was more or less true in any nation with an elected government—understood that their needs and values were subject to new forces: democracy and a rapidly industrializing economic system.

Or we might say that a world shaped by universal human rights and industrial capitalism produced a social order that allowed Jews to thrive far from the sanctuaries of early modern Europe and its overseas projections. Here we encounter a brave new world indeed. In this altered environment, new opportunities became manifest, even pressing; immigration, freedom, and upward mobility moved hand in hand. Before the American and French Revolutions, the typical Sephardic community in the colonial Americas, whether island-bound or on the mainland, was small and would support a single synagogue designed by non-Jews. But by the mid-nineteenth century, in the United States and elsewhere, relatively large Jewish urban populations would establish several congregations, each with its own synagogue. By 1900 New York and London would rival Warsaw and Vilna as the most populous Jewish cities in the world. Given the new access to civil rights, enfranchisement, and education propagated by the great revolutionary epoch, nineteenth-century Jews could and did design or build synagogues of their own choosing. In the new era, what was to stop a congregation from hiring a Jewish architect or construction firm director, as did Charleston's Beth Elohim with David Lopez Jr.? Such professions had been unthinkable if not illegal for Jews in Stuart, Cromwellian, or Hanoverian North America, Bourbon Canada and Louisiana, or the colonies of the United Provinces, and Iberian Viceroyalties. So the posture of Jews in what we have framed as the Atlantic World of Sephardic survival and adaptation transformed, gradually at first, radically after 1776. This we know from a wide range of documentary sources and records. But it is conspicuously from synagogues themselves, buildings that would rise in ever-increasing numbers after 1825, that we receive the most palpable and vivid impression. We should stipulate that change per se does not determine aesthetic merit. There were reasons the Esnoga or Bevis Marks proved paradigmatic for so long: their rational proportions, interior elegance, and spiritual integrity reached out to encourage imitation across distant oceans and borders. Yet however beautiful or imposing, these structures remain artifacts of an Iberian exile marked by monarchy and oligarchy, of a time when Jews adopted, somewhat reticently as dictated by their tentative social position, a dominant postclassical idiom. There is a telling contrast with the synagogues that American Jews or the Jews of a largely Ashkenazic modernity would build later. In fact never again would a single synagogue architectural style stand as uniquely prestigious. The world after Jefferson, Danton, and Napoleon had become multiform and too filled with possibility for that.

CHAPTER 6

Jews and Non-Caucasians in the Atlantic World

The history of Jews in the Atlantic World has unfolded thus far as the experience of a religious minority. From this perspective, very small Jewish populations were sometimes persecuted, often penalized, and occasionally tolerated by Christian majorities. But from 1500 until 1800, the exploration and imperial forays within the region disclose another narrative in which white colonialists, including Jews, encountered Native Americans whose homelands were conquered and often made to serve as depositories for transported African slave labor. We need, if briefly, to consider how Jews figure in this second Atlantic World historical frame, one where Europeans' white skin was almost always color coded for dominance and oppression.

For comparative purposes, however, it is useful to begin outside the specific boundaries of the Atlantic World. By so doing we can get a sense of how greatly the status of Jews in non-European precincts could vary. In parts of India, for example, certain Jewish communities do date from ancient times. More than two thousand years ago, Jews arrived in Cochin, on the subcontinent's Arabian Sea coast, 170 miles from where India's southernmost tip juts into the Indian Ocean. The Hindu population accepted this Jewish presence, so much so that Indian Jews became an integrated, though infinitesimal, element of the larger society, practicing the faith of Moses among the many millions who worshiped the Vedas. When fifteen hundred years later some Sephardic Jews fled to Cochin after the expulsion from Iberia, they were received as a newer variant of a known religious phenomenon, thus entitling them to trade and do business, not least with indigenous Cochini Jewry. But commerce did not lead to social integration: European Jews had their own congregations, becoming another strand (eventually known as Paradesi) in the vast ethnic fabric of India. Other Indian-Jewish communities, notably in Mumbai (Bombay), would follow a different chronology and conditions of contact. The point is comparative: one of the world's great non-Caucasian civilizations was relating to Jews not as aliens but as socially viable agents who were culturally worthwhile. This was hardly the case in sub-Saharan

Africa (where only a small number of Jews traveled) and emphatically not so in our area of primary concern, the Atlantic World.

Luis de Torres, a converso who served as Columbus's translator on the 1492 expedition, was almost certainly the first European to speak with Native Americans since Viking encounters nearly five centuries before. It follows that he was the first person of Jewish heritage—Torres had become Catholic only shortly before the explorers left Palos de la Frontera—to accomplish this feat as well. As time passed in the Spanish and Portuguese Americas, there was some degree of intermarriage between conversos and Amerindians, part of the larger melting pot that produced Latin America's varied mestizo population. One fascinating instance of this rather incongruous cultural and biological linkage can be seen in the territory that later became New Mexico.[1]

According to views advanced in the 1500s, Israel's Ten Lost Tribes—no mention of them can be found in biblical texts after references to the Assyrian conquests in the eighth century B.C.E. (I Chronicles 5:26; II Kings 15:29–18:12)—were identified with Native Americans. The Caribbean's indigenous peoples or, for that matter, those native to the Americas, were at first considered descendents of biblical Israelites. This particular confusion can be attributed to Columbus, who, bound for India, famously supposed that he had reached islands near his goal—hence the emergence of the world-famous misnomer. That San Salvador's or Puerto Rico's "Indians" had descended from lost Hebrew tribes that at one time had migrated from northern Israel to Asia joins mistaken geography to mistaken history—but mistakes fully consonant with a Bible-saturated culture shaped, too, by Herodotus and Pliny. Nor would the Amerindian-Jewish identification disappear right away among explorers of the era, even though Amerigo Vespucci quickly grasped that the Brazil he encountered was not Asian but wholly new to the Western mind.[2] Such unscientific attempts at provenance make up a long and colorful list from the Middle Ages to our own time. Judeo-Christian historiography in the sixteenth and seventeenth centuries was not about to jettison the Bible as a sound basis for understanding the past or its consequences. In any case, Christians did not have copyright on this species of conjecture. In Amsterdam, Menasseh ben Israel produced his *Hope of Israel* (1650), which contains the best known Jewish example of this false idea about indigenous Americans. Myths die hard. As late as the 1820s, the inventive proto-Zionist Mordecai M. Noah would open to Native Americans his utopian Ararat in upstate New York because of the Columbus-inspired genealogy.

For the most part, interactions between Jews and Native Americans in the Atlantic World were limited. While intermarriage and reproduction between these groups did take place, such relationships were more prevalent in the Spanish and Portuguese colonial spheres than in non-Iberian North America. Nevertheless, from a strictly demographic vantage, the numbers involved throughout the Americas were not large, and social relations, such as they were, developed only where the predominantly commercial activities of Jews were situated, so little relevant historical information, documentary or otherwise, survives. We know that during the mid-seventeenth century the Dutch colonial government appointed the translator Samuel Cohen chief steward of the aboriginal population in Curaçao, but precisely what this title entailed remains unclear. A Captain David C. Nassy (mid-eighteenth century) also employed indigenous tribes in Dutch Surinam for campaigns against mixed-race Maroon raiders.[3] Far away on another continent, we know that Ezekiel Solomons in the 1760s traded with Native Americans and Métis at Fort Michilimack, near where Michigan borders Canada. Even archaeological excavations at the fort reveal little—only a few Solomons artifacts remain, providing a glimpse of what life was like for a merchant at a frontier trading post before and shortly after the American Revolution.[4] Many of his customers belonged to Great Lakes tribes, who exchanged lucrative furs for European manufactured goods.

However, Jewish interaction with Africans, especially those mounting millions who were enslaved and transported across the Atlantic to the Americas after 1500, is a better-known history. This is contrast to places such as the Ottoman Empire, where slavery was multiracial. There are accounts of conversos and Jews from the Iberian and Dutch empires settling in Istanbul, bringing with them their slaves from Africa and the West Indies; but most slaves in the sultanate were Caucasian.[5] Additionally any comprehensive treatment of slavery in the Atlantic World cannot be our focal concern here, but we can refer to certain measurable phenomena that involve Jews. (Of course there are relevant documents, mostly of commercial origin but including letters as well as birth and death records, that shed important light on this topic.) For instance synagogues can be concrete, revealing indicators of social and material developments. For any community where people of African origin formed a significant percentage of the work force, black people, whether slaves or free—and the free component was comparatively trivial—almost certainly contributed significantly toward construction and repair as carpenters, masons, or general laborers. Sometimes, though seldom so credited, people of color erected buildings; among the structures raised were churches (and a few synagogues). But if much of Christian society in colonial America can be said to have raised its material culture on the backs of slave labor, this was proportionally less true of Jews, who constituted so small a demographic unit at the time. As far as we know, except at the remove of financing or planning, Jews in the Americas did not build houses of worship for a very long time. Not until 1841, when a congregant, David Lopez Jr., supervised the construction of Charleston's Beth Elohim, was a Jew responsible for building a synagogue in the United States. That is, as a class phenomenon, it was nearly the mid-nineteenth century before American Jews were established enough to control every aspect of synagogue construction.

But as a race phenomenon, given the slave economy of the American South, the physical effort of construction probably was exerted by black people in addition to waged white laborers. According to the 1850 Charleston census, Lopez owned fourteen slaves (six were men), two of whom, Kit and George, were designated carpenters.[6] There were Jewish congregations that arranged for slave labor to help with maintenance and custodial work in synagogues. Occasionally a congregation owned slaves outright, as did Berakha ve Shalom in Surinam during the early eighteenth century; more frequently, slaves were rented from or "donated" by masters.[7] So we find in the official Minute Book of New York City's Shearith Israel several entries between 1728 and 1730 compensating owners for slave labor.[8] This serves as a reminder that far from the traditionally labeled slave zone of the Atlantic World—the American South, the Caribbean, and parts of Latin America—slavery was an active presence, relied on by Jews and Christians alike. There were proportionally far fewer slaves in the north of the United States, but the peculiar institution's economic tentacles ran deep. Too often slave labor, whether in building or caring for a synagogue, has been dismissed as mundane—manual labor, no matter how excruciating, is subject to many prejudices, especially from those who never perform it. But occasionally there is evidence of slaves recognized as skilled workers. In Beth Elohim's Minute Book from 27 December 1840, we find this mention of a slave, newly hired after the fire of 1838: "a colored man, who works with Hayden & Gregg [Jewelers], recommended by Mr. [?] Levy, had offered to repair the [silver] rimonim [Torah scroll finials], and he would ask the sanction of the Board to employ him."[9] Such finials, called *rimonim* and usually made of silver, are quite delicately crafted works of art, apposite for decorating the holiest text of Judaism. In this instance the enslaved Charlestonian would have had skills as a silversmith, one who could be entrusted with the congregation's most prized cultural possession as well as valuable materials.

After the American Revolution, the first state government to seek some measure of freedom for its slaves was Pennsylvania, whose Act for the Gradual Abolition of Slavery passed on 1 March 1780. If Quaker conscience had spoken—Philadelphia also had a visible Jewish community, some of which was abolitionist—its voice was deliberately retarded or politically guarded: the law emancipated only slaves born in 1780 or later—despite the Revolution, all of Pennsylvania's adult slaves would remain in bondage for a long time. Complete abolition in the state where the Declaration of Independence was announced would have to wait until 1847. Pennsylvania's gradualism was copied by Rhode Island and Connecticut in 1784, and New York in 1799. Even colonial Canada, whose slave population was trivial compared to that of the United States, also adopted a staggered approach in the 1790s and 1800s. Total abolition across the British Empire did not come until 1834. This inspires the curiosity as to whether Philadelphia's Mikveh Israel, built in 1782, as well as subsequent synagogues built in the abolitionist North, may have been constructed with the assistance of slave labor during the antebellum period.

But Britain's abolitionists, who upended the institutional bondage and brutality of centuries with the great Abolition of Slavery Act (1833), most likely spared the Crown's Atlantic World appalling trauma of the kind soon to befall the United States: literally hundreds of thousands of enslaved Africans were freed across the British Empire.[10] As for Jews, their religious building projects followed prevailing political winds. While congregations before 1834 drew on slave labor to create synagogues, those synagogues that came later, like Beth Yaakob (built 1845) in Jamaica's Montego Bay, were built without it—even though the reality of low wages paid to the earliest liberated workers cannot be overlooked.[11] As it happens, the Netherlands would end Atlantic colonial bondage in 1863, the very year that Lincoln's Emancipation Proclamation (decreed on 1 January) liberated slaves in states controlled by Confederate forces. Some synagogues in the American South were built proximate to, but still on the wrong side of, this temporal boundary of freedom: in 1861–62, builder George M. Figh used slaves to construct Alabama's Kahal Montgomery (Montgomery congregation).[12] Nonetheless Figh's addition to the city was the last synagogue on American soil to have been constructed with slave labor.

If we widen our focus to include the Jewish posture within the Atlantic World's slave economy and its concomitant culture before the mid-nineteenth century, we find unsurprisingly that Jews were involved much in the same ways as non-Jews. This is meant as description, not exculpation or justification. Some Jews were agents participating in the slave trade, some planters and merchants who owned slaves, some abolitionists who deplored bondage —taken altogether, Jews followed these paths to much the same degree as did the Christian majority.[13] Bear in mind that the history here—or rather histories, linking different populations that trace a tangent from the eastern Mediterranean to large portions of West Africa over several centuries— remains complex, multifaceted, and morally painful enough to task any tragic writer. To mention only one key relationship, there is the compact between slave suppliers and slave purchasers, with the suppliers responsible for capturing and selling Africans into the voracious demand market of New World servitude. Those involved in the slave trade came from a plethora of backgrounds: Catholics, Protestants, Muslims, and pagans, besides the handful of Jews. Profit was all, dissolving kinship and custom alike, as European facilitators and entrepreneurs gained far greater wealth once enslaved Africans were transported to Caribbean or American ports of destination, from there to be sold yet again. Where do Jews figure in all this getting and spending? Evidence varies, with some colonial communities better documented than others.

We know that by the late eighteenth century, most Jews in North America were Ashkenazim working as traders in goods, peddlers, or shopkeepers.

Ownership of a large, slave-worked plantation, as some wealthy Sephardim had managed to acquire in Jamaica or Surinam before 1800, represented an economic stratum unimaginable for most of the central or eastern European Jewish petite bourgeoisie who settled in British North America.[14] When Jews did own slaves, these were, unsurprisingly, exposed to a different dominant subculture and consequently, they experienced slight behavioral variations from slaves owned by Christians. Because Sabbath observances, holidays, and dietary practices of Jews were not shared by Christians, bondage to Sephardim or (occasionally) Ashkenazim meant conformity to the preferences of the masters. This by no means suggests that African slaves were more inclined to adopt Jewish mores than Christian ones: domination by definition extinguishes choice. That said, Jewish slave owners sometimes differed, albeit not in essential ways, from their Christian counterparts.[15]

In Britain's Atlantic colonies and in the United States, Jews—unlike Protestants or Catholics, both of whom would press slaves to go to church—did not impose synagogue attendance on those in bondage. In any case, slaves in churches were restricted to the balcony. This area was occupied by women and girls in synagogues, gender's caste system having priority, so that one could find a male slave seated in the main sanctuary, a female slave above with her mistress. Nor did Jews teach their religious faith to their slaves—Christians did so—even when a child had a Jewish father. The progeny of a miscegenistic union remained enslaved. There is little record of miscegeny between a Jewish woman and an African, although such relationships were naturally not unknown. Both Moses Nunes of Savannah in 1797 and Samuel Simons of Charleston in 1824 emancipated and gave property to their "negro housekeepers" and their children by these women. In these two cases, the mixed-race children showed little interest in their Jewish heritage, which may have been a reflection of paternal indifference or inattention to religion.[16] But among the Dutch, whether in the Netherlands or in Surinam, there were, if exceptionally, instances of biracial children being raised as Jews.

This began with Jewish traders of European origin who traveled south, some as far as the major cultural and commercial center of Timbuktu. Evidence here, whether archaeological or documentary, remains—Egypt and Morocco excepted—sparse for so early a phase of Jewish experience on the African continent away from the Mediterranean coastal region. The earliest reliably identified Atlantic World encounters between Sephardim and sub-Saharan Africans took place during fifteenth-century Portuguese expeditions down the West African coast, such as the one that attracted Joseph Vecinho in 1485. Indeed early European maps designate the pristine area now named Loango (at the mid-point of the Atlantic coast in western Gabon) as the Gulf of the Jews.[17] By the sixteenth century, once-Jewish conversos had traveled to the Portuguese island of São Tomé in the Gulf of Guinea, and, if we look momentarily from Africa back across the Atlantic, we see that Iberian conversos had, as mentioned earlier, settled in Brazil as well as the Spanish viceroyalties of New Spain and Peru. In all these places, Jews met Africans not as equals but as enslaved laborers on plantations.

One of the less visible (or unforeseen) perquisites that Jews gained along with admission to Amsterdam (1603) was another settlement option: the Petite Côte, Senegal's Atlantic coast between the Senegal and Gambia Rivers. As legal residents of Amsterdam, Jews were allowed to follow the banner of the Dutch West India Company in settling the republic's West African colonies (corresponding now to Mauritania, Senegal, and Gambia)—a first Dutch projection into the Atlantic World meant to counter the powerful Spanish and Portuguese Empires. From the second decade of the seventeenth century, European merchants, Jews among them, bought from Senegambians slaves and goods, which were then resold in Europe. No permanent Jewish community was ever established; one Jacob Peregrino, however, served as an itinerant Jewish spiritual leader in the Dutch settlement area and carried with him the medical instruments for ritual circumcision, or *brit milah*. But there was another legacy we should mention. These Dutch colonies gained a small, recondite mulatto community, one born specifically of Sephardic men and African women.[18] This was an increment to be added to the larger mixed-race population with Christian fathers.[19]

As long as Senegambian Judeo-mulattos were isolated from any organized Jewish community—the nearest was in Morocco—mixed parentage seemed unremarkable. But on European soil, given normative Caucasian racism, problems emerged. In the records of Amsterdam's Talmud Torah we find as early as 1644 rulings prohibiting Senegambians, raised as Jews by their fathers, from reading the Torah in synagogue services. This exclusion was followed by a 1647 ruling that designated a separate area in Amsterdam's Sephardic cemetery (called Beth Haim, located in the Ouderkerk aan de Amstel district) for the interment of Jewish mulattos. Although different issues were involved, the Talmud Torah ban against converting Christians to Judaism was extended to mulattos and African slaves. Yet Beth Haim records for the cemetery reveal that at least forty freed African slaves and mulattos were buried there before 1716. Despite adverse conditions then, Jews with black African ancestry must have remained in Amsterdam during the early eighteenth century. But they were subject to increasing penalties that affected their religious and civil rights. In 1658 Jewish mulatto boys were no longer allowed to enroll in the Talmud Torah yeshiva.[20] Based on a 1665 declaration, mixed-background (European African) Jews were designated mulatto until the third generation, when they were emancipated and could be accepted within the Jewish community. The Dutch hahamim recourse to biology here can seem chillingly contemporary and purblind enough—even though the particular religious precedents controlling this seventeenth-century ruling dated back to Deuteronomy's treatment (23:8–9) of Edomite and Egyptian converts.[21] Various editions of *Sefer Berith Yitshak*, the instruction manual on circumcision published in Amsterdam between 1709 and 1824, specify prayers appropriate for a convert to Judaism with African familial connections. Such prayers must have been recited rarely. [22]

It is never easy to decipher prejudice across the divide of centuries. What seems conspicuously discriminatory or unfair to us would have been "natural" to a white-skinned Dutch Jew (as well as his or her compatriots) in the Atlantic World centuries years ago. Thus, when examining the Jewish treatment of African Caucasian Jews in the seventeenth and eighteenth centuries —a process that analytically must *begin* with historical awareness, not moral assessment—we should recognize that concepts of race and religious affiliation evolve, albeit not neatly or synchronously. That said, in an anthropological categorization authorized by religious dogma and social practice over millennia, Jewish identity is determined matrilineally.[23] In Judaism, religious identity (a *cultural* datum) is transferred through mothers, material wealth through fathers. From this age-old perspective, despite having a Jewish father, a mulatto with a non-Jewish mother would not have been regarded as Jewish at birth. By and large, Christian European culture differed: it operated patrilineally, with kinship, social, and material inheritance conferred through the father. Moreover Judaism has rarely been historically predisposed, or even friendly, to active proselytizing on the part of Jews. Nor were Jews alone in their need to assert religious boundaries. As early as 1614, Amsterdam's secular authorities declared conversion to Judaism illegal for the city's Christians—a prophylactic against complications coming from the Jodenbuurt (Jewish quarter) east of the Amstel. The Sephardim responded in kind, condemning the error of conversion to Christianity.

Before the Talmud Torah prohibition regime of 1650, some Judeo-mulattos became converts and joined Amsterdam's Jewish community. But the numbers involved here were trivial, and Judaism very much remained a faith focused on its ancient, biblically declared exclusivity. Dutch-African cohabitation during the seventeenth and early eighteenth centuries in the Netherlands was hardly a model for things to come. But outside the Caucasian citadels of Europe, across the colonial diaspora, people of color would cohabit with white settlers, and, depending on the overseas empire involved, those of mixed race would become a more evident social presence.[24]

Eighteenth-century Surinam is a case in point. As we have seen, the colony, its economy dependent on large plantations worked by a comparably large African slave labor force, would attract Jewish settlers who by the mid-eighteenth century grew to constitute some 25 percent of Surinam's European population. This fact needs emphasis here because of particular demographic factors: Jamaica aside, no other American or Caribbean colony, over such a stretch of time, had so high a proportion of slaves in relation to Jews as Surinam. With constant interaction between Jews and their slaves, no trivial mulatto community emerged; generally speaking the mulattos with Jewish fathers were not raised as Jews. Even though there were Jews and Africans in Dutch Brazil, its duration (1630–54) was too fleeting and ridden with conflict for a meaningful Jewish mulatto demographic to appear. Curaçao too had both groups, but interactions were limited: Jews formed a merchant class of importers and exporters rarely involved with daily plantation cultivation or management of cash crops; African slaves there lived in another stratum, working large estates mostly owned by Christians. In seventeenth-century St. Domingue, there were numerous African slaves but few Jews.

To the west, while the Protestant empires were displacing their Catholic rivals, Jamaica featured certain anomalies. The island, when compared to all the rest of the British or Dutch Americas, attracted Jews in large numbers, although always a small minority of Jamaica's general European population. Still there were Jews enough to yield an identifiable Jewish mulatto community. Perhaps because Jamaican anti-Semitism was virulent enough to alarm Jews with the stigma of mixed-race parentage, or perhaps because antiblack feelings were so powerful among the Jamaican elite, there is no record of mulattos practicing Judaism on the island.[25]

Colonial Surinamese society saw the growth of a large Judeo-mulatto population whose fathers were Jewish and mothers African. Not only did Jewish planters own slaves for agricultural and household labor, but Berakha ve Shalom, the congregation formed in Jodensavanne, also bought slaves as an investment.[26] In Atlantic World annals, some characteristics of this mostly mixed-race community are unique, differing from other Protestant (whether English or French Huguenot), Dutch mulatto, or exclusively African slave populations. For one, the Surinamese creoles admitted a certain number of slaves or former slaves of both sexes—people who were identifiably black. Moreover some Jewish slave masters culturally embraced their mulatto children, although not their adult African slaves, by practicing circumcision and, as important, by giving their children a basic education that included knowledge of Judaism. Often Surinamese Jews—again, this was almost always the decision of a Jewish father—freed mixed-race children. By 1762 twenty-seven members of the Jodensavanne settlement were free people of color, a third under the age of ten.[27] Sometimes free Judeo-mulattoes inherited property, as did Joseph Pelegrino's children Simcha, Jacob, and Mariana.[28]

In 1754 congregation Berakha ve Shalom allowed the Judeo-mulattos to become part of the religious community as *congregantes* whose ritual rights were qualified. Unlike Jews with full membership rights—designated *jahid,* the Hebrew word for "member"—people of color were required to perform certain critical religious services, such as marriage and burial, in the afternoons; whites had the option of choosing any time for these rites. Deprived, too, of full honorific privileges during the Sabbath or holidays, mulattos, in another sign of their secondary status, were excused from the categorical

Sabbath injunction not to work; they were allowed to perform certain minor activities. There were still other limitations: a separate synagogue door and a separate area of the Jewish cemetery were the lot of mulatto Jews. To these strictures we must add a most telling deprecation. Berakha ve Shalom's white *jahidim* (plural) could be demoted to the congregante status if they married an African or mulatto—lèse-majesté indeed.[29]

In 1759 Jodensavanne's Judeo-mulattos organized Darkhe Yesharim (Path of the Righteous). This was an auxiliary of Berakha ve Shalom—not per se a congregation—formed with the help of several native white Jews on the understanding that no sectarian splinter develop. Its leader was the creole Joseph de David Cohen Nassy, whose name almost certainly registers some prior familial or genealogical slave relationship with Surinam's ubiquitous Nassy clan, leaders of the Sephardic Jewish community. Twenty years later there was an expansion of the Darke Yesharim project, again facilitated by white Jews, into Surinam's coastal mercantile center, Paramaribo. In 1779 a synagogue was built there for Jewish mulattos who could practice their faith with no ritual restrictions, as long as formal affiliation with the Jodensavanne Jewish community was sustained. But what seemed to augur an increasingly tolerant Sephardic attitude toward creole Jews was quickly checked. Only a year later, in 1780, the white parnassim ruled that mulattos unable to prove both manumission and Jewish paternity were barred from synagogue worship. This meant that slaves or those without a recognized Jewish father—people who had previously regarded themselves as accepted believers—had lost any claim to the public practice of Judaism. In fact Paramaribo's Darkhe Yesharim stands as the only instance of a synagogue built for Judeo-mulattos and African ex-slaves. In the event, Darkhe Yesharim was torn down in 1800—whether as matter of policy or physical decrepitude we cannot say.[30]

During the nineteenth century, Surinam's Judeo-mulatto community gradually dispersed, assimilating into general Caucasian society with its very large number of mixed-race people, though a minority of Judeo-creoles were absorbed into the white-skinned Jewish creole population. There are records of several Surinamese mulatto women having converted to Judaism—Jeudith Hava Robles in 1819, Ribca Louise de Leon in 1832, and one Wilhelmina in 1841. After 1841 new, more rigid regulations on conversions were announced. A requirement specifying more substantive knowledge of Judaism and full conformity with ritual practice was introduced, but in turn, the congregante/jahid distinction disappeared: there would no longer be class distinction among Surinam's Sephardic Jews.[31] We know of one mulatto from Barbados who moved to Surinam in order to convert.[32] Those who most frequently converted were children or women connected with Jewish men. Most often such conversions were preludes to manumission and, in the case of single men with de facto wives, marriage. The circumcision pain factor certainly deterred adult male conversions. Thus we find a Jewish marriage between a Surinamese Sephardi and a free Jewish woman of color as early as 1817, only six years after Surinam's first marriage between a Sephard and Ashkenazi—both were white, but came from distinct European traditions. Then in 1820 came the first marriage between a Jewish man and a Christian woman, the bride having converted to Judaism. Clearly it is in the early nineteenth century that barriers between Jews and the general population began to topple, an easing of exclusion that affected Jews in their relations among themselves too. Intermarriage with Jews over a long history dating from the seventeenth century became so continuous that today's Surinamese regard this Jewish component as fundamental to their multicultural identity.[33]

Blacks and mulattos who assimilated with the white Jewish community literally left their mark. The West African *sankofa* and *akoma* symbols decorate some of the tombstones in Paramaribo's Jewish cemeteries, often superimposed on Judaism's graphic archetype, the six-pointed Star of David. This Surinamese Judeo-African mortuary adornment is unique in the New World and bears witness to one of colonialism's more unforeseen cultural intersections.[34] Appropriately enough the Judeo-mulatto population developed their own dialect, Djoe-tongo, or "Jew tongue."[35] But however remarkable the Jewish encounter with Africans in Surinam, we should not see it as typical or fantasize about human propensities for exchange in unequal situations. Throughout most of the Atlantic World, slaves owned by Jewish masters were a subjugated, deprived labor force, utterly removed from and untutored in Judaism. European Jews who settled in the Americas, the Caribbean, or Africa were not given to impressing an alien subject race with the majesty of their faith.

There is also the story of Billy Simons (1780–1859) of Charleston, South Carolina. Extraordinarily Simons is the only known person in the Anglophone Atlantic World recorded to have shown a deep interest in Judaism as an expression of his own faith and beliefs. Considering that 83 percent of Charleston Jewish households owned slaves in 1830, the Simons case seems only more remarkable. For most of his life, Simons did manual labor for local newspaper companies where he became a fixture, given the typological deprecatory nickname "uncle" by those around him. During this time he became familiar with Charleston's Jewish community. He attended Beth Elohim, especially on Yom Kippur, and essentially became part of Charleston's Jewish community. Even though Beth Elohim stipulated in its 1820 bylaws that people of color could not belong to the congregation, the congregants seemed to have looked the other way in the case of Simons presence, so much so that, according to an 1859 obituary, Simons had been provided a front row seat, truly an honor within the congregation. At the time of his death, Beth Elohim's spiritual leader, Maurice Mayer, said that Billy Simons had been "the most observant of those who go to the synagogue."[36]

Conclusion

In retrospect there is an almost uncanny homogeneity governing Atlantic World synagogue-communities during the seventeenth and eighteenth centuries.[1] So vast a geographic space, such embryonic settlements touching "new" continents, seas, or islands, so small a number of Sephardic colonists—and yet the far-flung Jews were identifiably bound to the Spanish-Portuguese religious tradition. All congregations followed the paradigm set by Amsterdam's Sephardic Talmud Torah in 1639, a pattern that would, until the second decade of the nineteenth century, provide religious, administrative, and material support to Jews who settled across great arcs of the Atlantic. There was seemingly a cart-before-horse development of new Jewish communities, if the cart stands for a colony and the horse for the imperial center. So we find in the Dutch and Danish colonies more Sephardic purpose-built synagogues than in, respectively, the Netherlands or Denmark. Recall that "purpose-built" differs as both a physical and a sociological category from the numerous provisional, unobtrusive religious meeting places that Jews first used when first allowed to live and worship in a polity.

As for Britain, its Atlantic possessions had more purpose-built Sephardic synagogues than did the combined total (Sephardic plus Ashkenazic) of synagogues in the home islands. It was the Caribbean periphery, not the European homelands, that saw the first appearance of British and Danish synagogues. Nor were disembodied artificers at work here. It is people who construct buildings: synagogues are the visible signs of a population. The French, too, were prepared to confer rights on Jews abroad that the monarchy would deny within the kingdom itself. According to the 1664 agreement by which the French regained Cayenne (Guyana) from the Dutch Republic, the Bourbons recognized the nascent Sephardic community and its rights (already granted by the Dutch) to maintain a synagogue—that is, to worship publicly. It was not until 1723 that the Jews of Bordeaux and Bayonne received the official sanction that allowed them to officially put aside their Catholic convert status. During the seventeenth and eighteenth centuries, Protestant countries joined somewhat by France, were havens for Jews. But it was the European imperial project, especially in the Caribbean (including Surinam), that provided the forward momentum for Sephardic settlement in the Atlantic World.

Wherever Jews thrived synagogues appeared. Seldom did these modest structures aspire to anything besides utilitarian efficiency: they were small, simply designed, and built as economically as possible. Larger, more aesthetically ambitious synagogues—mostly Ashkenazic—would find a place in later nineteenth-century architecture, both in Europe and the Americas. But with the notable exceptions of Amsterdam, London, and a few extraordinarily tolerant outposts (such as Curaçao and Charleston, South Carolina) Jews between c. 1600 and 1825 lacked the financial means, political power, and demographic concentration to assume a more enduring posture—in either the socioeconomic, cultural, or the built environment. During the nineteenth and twentieth centuries, this posture would change substantively and exponentially. However formulaic, the bromide that modernity was the creation of three Ashkenazic Jews—Marx, Freud, and Einstein—still touches a historical nerve. By looking at the origins of the gestation, so much of which took place in the Atlantic World and specifically the Americas, the scope of Jewish development in the modern era can be gauged.

If the Sephardic template set in Amsterdam and London was maintenance of a single sanctuary by a single Jewish community in a single locality, it must be said that England and the Netherlands were precisely where such a template first eroded, and quickly. In the larger urban areas or towns of both Protestant countries, once major prohibitions against Jews were removed after 1655, multiple synagogues, almost always Ashkenazic, appeared: there was not a cohesive community inasmuch as Iberian and central European Jews worshipping in separate spaces according to different ritual traditions. This segmentation happened in the mid-seventeenth century in the Netherlands, during the eighteenth century in Great Britain.

Among the Sephardim religious and lay leaders worked hard, for the most part successfully, to control their members within the unitary synagogue-community. Conformity often required a measure of discipline or, alternatively, benevolent co-option. On the one hand, to name the most notorious instance, there was the harsh rejection of the heretic Baruch Spinoza; on the other, focused attentiveness to congregants in matters personal, ritual, and financial. Hence pressure was exerted on matters of doctrine (Spinoza again) or institutional organization (rooting out potential cults, as with Jewish mulattos in Surinam). If such control strikes us today as heavy handed—it was—recall the undeniable benefits available to an Atlantic World Sephardi: participation in a religious, economic, and social network traversing a great ocean, multigenerational associations often based on kinship and common friends, confidence in a shared culture, spiritual uplift—the powerful resonances of tradition and familiarity. Moreover secular authorities as well as Christian governments preferred the Sephardic organizational model, with its simplicity of one official voice representing one group: uniformity so often pleases bureaucracies most. During the seventeenth century, with any number of dissenting Christian denominations in Europe and its colonies abroad, state governments and authorized churches were used to addressing the leaders of religious minorities. The Sephardim fit this pattern of governance through relationships firmly in place in the Netherlands, England, Denmark, and, to a lesser extent, in France. So Atlantic World parnassim could indeed claim that their control over Sephardic congregations was effective and efficient when dealing with secular authorities.

The migratory character of Atlantic World Sephardic life cannot be overstated. Someone born in Europe could live in Gibraltar or cross the ocean to settle in the Caribbean, North America, or South America. Permutations of these settlement options multiplied. Moreover, for Ashkenazim, their birth tradition was not indelible. Even when outnumbering Iberian Jews in a given community, central European Jews were willing to adopt Iberian minhag—we saw this particularly in North America during the eighteenth and early nineteenth centuries—as long as tangible social and economic benefits attached to the more established Sephardic presence. Yet again the Spanish-Portuguese identity provided a safe port, if not from a storm then in the vicissitudes presented by shifting conditions on both sides of the Atlantic.

However authoritarian the parnassim were in Amsterdam's Talmud Torah framework, some flexibility was required of leaders as well as congregants. The synagogue-community of Dutch Pernambuco, lodged in Recife's Zur Israel since 1636, when the congregation was founded, understood that. By 1648 the Jewish population had spread across the colonial territory: attendance of services had become logistically and financially untenable for Jews far away from Recife. That is why another synagogue, Magen Abraham, was built in the neighboring town, Mauricia, with the understanding that the newer entity was a satellite only, to be guided by Zur Israel in all significant religious or administrative matters. And so it went elsewhere, in Curaçao, Surinam, and Barbados, with a central synagogue controlling its appendages. In such instances the unitary synagogue-community definition is stretched, or must be qualified, even though the original goal (cohesion under a single recognized authority) survived in spirit, at least for a time. This arrangement, however, did not ensure the peaceable kingdom. There was no dearth of conflict between Jewish congregations and their affiliates in Curaçao and Surinam—so much so that Crown authorities would sometimes intervene. Colonial governors might be indifferent to religious or organizational disputes, but they were committed to the steady flow of commerce. Jews were too important economically to let communal misunderstandings interrupt profits.

As it happens there were two affiliate synagogues named Neve Shalom or Oasis of Peace, one in Paramaribo (Surinam), the other in Willemstad (Curaçao). This poetically resonant Hebrew name—without any appeals to elaborate deconstruction—signifies. It could very well have revealed a need to put aside quarrels in an arduous world, or, more concretely, in a situation where intracongregational disputes could paralyze. It is within the Sephardic orbit the words *shalom* (peace) and *mikveh* (hope) appear very frequently in the names of both unitary synagogue-communities and, as circumstances required, of authorized satellites too. Why? The ground remains speculative, but surely an all-too-human impulse can be detected from ubiquitous nomenclature. It must have centered on some common aspiration toward attaining what was so often absent from the fractious experience of Jews spread across the Atlantic World: peace.[2] Neither place nor time offered easy solutions. Settling and commerce seemed precarious, a pawn of economic vagaries; nations were at war; social conflicts abounded, whether among Jews or non-Jewish majorities with whom relations were periodically tense: such endemic uncertainties would have injected anxiety, frustration, and impermanence into the lives of Sephardim and Ashkenazim on both sides of the Atlantic, especially before 1700, but during the next century too. So Jews hoped for shalom: sometimes we give a name to our dearest wish, especially when fulfillment seems ephemeral. Perhaps there might even have been a messianic usage connoted through the words *hope* and *peace*. This was certainly a preoccupation of the Amsterdam savant Manasseh ben Israel, whose *Hope of Israel* (1650) expressed a millenarian vision that seemed fittingly providential for Jews wandering yet again, this time through an Atlantic wilderness.[3] Temporal or sempiternal, whether forged by women and men, or spiritually charged with the Messiah's redemption, no promise could have beckoned more to Atlantic World Jewry than peace.

The case of Surinam tells us a great deal great about how disagreements between Sephardim and Ashkenazim, as well as their synagogue satellites, played out during the 1710s through 1730s. Simply put, Spanish-Portuguese and central European Jews could have plagued each other with disabling quarrels. Bitter sectarian feelings had erupted elsewhere, even in Amsterdam; tropical Surinam, with slow transit corridors between the coastal region (Paramaribo) and the riverine interior (Jodensavanne), not to mention the colony's entirely novel mixed-race issues, could have become a veritable incubator for friction. But somehow the conflicts were contained, and at least some of the credit must be given to institutional moderation. The colony contained a single synagogue-community, Berakha ve Shalom in Jodensavanne, while two subordinate synagogues of this primary congregation were built in Paramaribo (Neve Shalom for Ashkenazim, Zedek ve Shalom for Sephardim). By so doing, Surinam's Jewish presence figured as the most heterogeneous Jewish community in the New World. Berakha ve Shalom bridged not only two European cultural traditions (Iberian and central European), but also the far more radical, potentially schismatic racial divide between Jewish Europeans and their African or mulatto families. To be precise, between 1779 and 1800, Paramaribo was the site of three satellite synagogue buildings: Neve Shalom, Zedek ve Shalom—as mentioned—and, chronologically the last to appear, Darkhe Yesharim, for the Judeo-African creoles. All these affiliates followed the customs and directives of Berakha ve Shalom.[4] But, by the late eighteenth century, it seems likely that, given the larger Jewish population in Paramaribo than in Jodensavanne, the former subordinate groups had actually supplanted Berakhva as Surinam's most authoritative Jewish voice. However that may be, Berakha ve Shalom still remained a significant counterweight vis-à-vis other congregational units, not least because Neve Shalom (Ashkenazic) and Zedek ve Shalom (Sephardic) chronically quarreled. No doubt Darkhe Yesharim was less of a factor here; racial tolerance probably met its limits when the European Jews asserted themselves.

After 1775 the satellite extension model began to fracture. First in Jamaica and then in North America, the unitary synagogue-community gave way to a new reality: several independent synagogues together constituting the Jewish community of a given locality. As always such a structural institutional shift among Jews was linked to profound forces changing the very character of the Atlantic World. Looking at settlement patterns throughout the Americas after 1825, demographic changes hardly seem remarkable: populations moved west, away from Atlantic corridors and the Caribbean basin, into continental interiors. Over time North Americans came to the Pacific coast—such as San Francisco or Victoria—the natural boundary for nationalist expansion. For the United States, this westward movement carried in its vanguard and its wake American Jews, as well as Ashkenazim more recently en route from Europe. But in the Jewish experience, the pull of the West was still subject to a counterpressure from the East: Ashkenazim increasingly fixed New York City as their lodestar after 1850. Do not forget that the peopling of North America with the kind of density and diversity that surged exponentially throughout the nineteenth century—obviously more so in the United States than in Canada—owed everything to political dynamism.[5] The radical revolutions of America and France enabled the subsequent great transatlantic emigrations from Europe. Quite apart from issues of religious liberty, especially in North America, colonial commerce (whether British, French, Dutch, Spanish, or Portuguese) provided the material platform for civil society and economic growth to flourish in the new democratic age. The hour of Caribbean wealth (sugarcane-based on the backs of slaves) had passed. As the concentration of capital shifted decisively to the United States—whose fatal flaw of slavery would erupt in 1861—Jews benefitted, as did so many millions of others.

In all this remarkable gestation, as far as Jews were concerned, Jamaica proved unusual. In fact, rather than adopt the satellite plan used everywhere else (as in Curaçao and Barbados), we find in Jamaica the only Atlantic World colony to host several autonomous synagogue-communities before 1776. The reasons here concern the particular history of Jamaican Jews. After the 1655 British conquest of the island, Sephardim concentrated in the southeast, where they built a synagogue (c. 1684) in Port Royal, some fifteen years before

London's Bevis Marks. But a ruinous earthquake in 1692 destroyed all of Port Royal, including its synagogue. In nearby Kingston and Spanish Town, however, Jewish communities soon developed, at a time when Port Royal Jewry was prostrate. So, in short order, there were three Jamaican synagogue-communities—Port Royal slowly recovered—though none connected or predominated as had happened at Jodensavanne.

In 1787 a group of Ashkenazim split from Kingston's Sephardic Shaar Ha Shamaim and in so doing created the first dissenting congregation in the Americas to establish itself on a permanent basis: Shaare Yosher. Its members built their own synagogue two years later; Kingston's Jewish population thus became the first community of permanently unaffiliated synagogues in the New World. By 1790 Ashkenazic and Sephardic divisions had spread to Spanish Town, where central European Mikveh Israel separated from Iberian Neve Shalom and, only six years later, the Ashkenzis built their own synagogue. Nor, by the end of the eighteenth century, were such intra-Jewish disputes, based on minhag and memories of European origins, confined to Jamaica. Although documentation remains scanty, during the early 1790s a controversy seemed to have emerged in Charleston, South Carolina, involving Beth Elohim and a temporary offshoot, Beth Elohim Unveh Shalom.[6] Almost certainly, quarrels over Ashkenazic versus Sephardic minhag were the source of the disagreement. Similarly the Philadelphian Ashkenazim formed their own group in 1795, later called congregation Rodeph Shalom. Its departure from the firmly established Sephardic Mikveh Israel proved final.[7]

At the eastern margin of the Atlantic, Gibraltar's Jews had similar experiences. Before the Great Siege (1779–83), Shaar Hashamayim was the only synagogue in the colony. When the siege lifted, large-scale reconstruction began, which meant not only rebuilding Shaar Hashamayim but also breaking ground on a new synagogue, Etz Chaim (1783), a congregation that could well have served earlier as a yeshiva or chevra (prayer group). Then, in 1799, congregation Nefusot Yehudah built the magnificent Flemish Synagogue. So at the dawn of the nineteenth century, there were three distinct, unaffiliated synagogues, though, understandably for the cornerstone of Iberia, all were Sephardic (unlike the growing communities in Jamaica or the United States that put aside Spanish-Portuguese authority). But the Dutch Baroque architecture of the Flemish Synagogue should not deceive us. Since most of Gibraltar's Jews came from across the Straits, it was North African traditions rather than the Bevis Marks or Amsterdam practices that shaped worship and identification. The last synagogue built on the peninsular outpost was the Sephardic Abudarham (1821).

The Napoleonic epoch for the most part put an end to internecine feuding within Jewish communities on both sides of the Atlantic. It was an age when energy and intellect focused on political and social upheavals, cataclysms that may well have made Sephardic and Ashkenazic communal concerns press less urgently. The wars, naval battles, and blockades associated with France's catalytic emperor effectively disrupted the maritime commerce that was the lifeline for New World Sephardim. Put differently, for fifteen conflict-ridden years (1799–1814), the initiatives crafted by France and its European allies were parried by the countermeasures of Great Britain, Russia, and (eventually) Prussia. This was the age when Enlightenment ideas were disseminated—in a dialectical pivot Hegelians still savor—through the force majeure of an enlightened hierarchic tyrant. When the dust settled after Waterloo, the ideological contours of Europe, along with the extensive Atlantic colonial structures built by Great Britain, the Netherlands, France, Spain, and Portugal, had effectively dissolved. Even the reactionary coda of Metternich would struggle fitfully to contain revolutionary and liberal ideas. In the event, the repercussions on the Atlantic World—first of the American and French revolutions, then of Napoleon's hegemony and downfall—was the transformation of two American continents into polities more or less reliant on republican governance. For Latin America the 1810s and 1820s broke the system of exploitation and conquest imposed by Renaissance and seventeenth-century rulers or their mercantilist viceroys, that socioeconomic system enabled by slavery, missionary religious dogma, and military power. The Caribbean too was fundamentally changed by the conflicts brought on by Napoleon and the political rearrangements that followed from the Treaty of Vienna (1815). As sugarcane and slaves no longer remained primary engines of wealth, the very concept of an imperially subservient Atlantic World became irrelevant. Is it any wonder that crypto-Jews—made so to escape the Inquisition, constantly adapting in pursuit of provisional tolerance—would be almost unrecognizable after 1825?

With the founding of Cincinnati's Bene Israel (1824), we find a congregation without any pretense of allegiance to the Sephardic London-Amsterdam nexus, as was the case, too, with Gibraltar's Etz Chaim and Nefusot Yehudah. So at virtually the same time, but at opposite poles of the Jewish world between western Europe and the American frontier, the once-pervasive synagogue-community model had broken down.[8] This development was no doubt inevitable given the rapid and diverse demographic expansion that surged in the United States after the Civil War. Central and eastern European Jews helped build a large-scale industrial economy that would have had little in common with the more settled but far outnumbered Sephardim who had functioned in a colonial, less urbanized world.[9] America was rapidly becoming the "shining City on a hill" for Jews too, a nation where, by the criteria of population, social integration, and cultural achievement, Jews would rival the far older central and eastern European centers of Austria-Hungary, Prussia, and Russia.

Five of the original synagogue-communities of the United States—those in New York, Philadelphia, Richmond, Charleston, and Savannah (since

Newport folded in 1822)—were subject to the great winds of change set loose by democratic politics. Just as the American Revolution led to the Constitution and the Bill of Rights, so Jewish congregations on the eastern seaboard emulated the nation's foundational texts, at times literally, in organizing their religious affairs. Gone were omnipotent parnassim; in their stead some congregations drafted an institutional constitution for its bylaws (sometimes copying Jeffersonian diction).[10] Previously these documents, called by their Hebrew name *hascamoth,* emulated the originals drafted by the congregations in Amsterdam and London; and they, in turn, had copied their predecessors in the Mediterranean. Adopting democratic governance American Jews established religious and communal affairs on a new basis. Two new congregations reflected this ethos. Although New York's Ashkenazic B'nai Jeshurun (established 1825) and Charleston's Reform Society of Israelites (established 1824), a composite of Americanized Sephardim and Ashkenazim, approached ritual somewhat differently, both were committed to democratic practice as that was conceived before the Civil War. Adult white men were allowed to determine congregational policy under majority rule—a gesture toward Jacksonian inclusiveness, although the same gesture excluded women. (With the one known exception of Billy Simons in Charleston, "Jewish" African Americans, let alone Native Americans, were unheard of in North America at this time.) In any case, as American democracy evolved, the ideological and cultural environment of the United States after the Monroe presidency (1817–25) affected Jews profoundly. Existing congregations, as well as new ones appearing in tandem with America's westward growth, posited the idea of citizen suffrage within a given congregation. Here we see Jewish acceptance of Emersonian self-reliance: congregations should function as self-governing entities, responsive to the needs of members, no longer accountable to some distant organizational or doctrinal authority. In this more complex, decentralized social environment, the unitary synagogue-community of the Atlantic World had no place. In Jacksonian America, with its emphasis on the scope and worth of the common citizen as a necessary caustic to elitist entitlement, we can understand the multifaceted career of Mordecai M. Noah. However grandiose, exceptional, or illusory his Ararat scheme might seem, the utopia he envisioned in 1825 was the product of a mind open to republican experiment and a belief that Jews could invent their own future. But it would be a mistake to think of Noah as only a dreamer. On a more mundane level Noah, as a capable New York City politician, led Tammany Hall when it first backed Jackson for president in 1828.[11]

After 1825, but starting a generation before as Ashkenazim began to outnumber the Spanish-Portuguese Jewish population in North America, Sephardim gradually came to represent something of an ancien regime in the eyes of newly arrived émigrés or young native-born Jews of central European background. The congregations just mentioned, Bene Israel, B'nai Jeshurun, and the Reform Society of Israelites, as well as the unusual Ararat project, were all predicated on arrangements then perceived to be democratic. This flourishing of largely Ashkenazic institutions was evident at a time when westward settlement was changing the consciousness of Americans, even those easterners in New York or Charleston, who witnessed the growth of their country made possible by Jefferson's visionary, acquisitionist gambits of 1803–4, the Lewis and Clark Expedition and the Louisiana Purchase. Similarly, a continent away, postimperial politics and increasing inland economic activity during the 1820s led to the founding of congregation Shaar Hashamaim in Belém, an old Brazilian port sixty-two miles from the Atlantic on the Para River, the Amazon's northern outlet to the ocean, where a synagogue was constructed in 1828. Jews would also settle in Coro, Venezuela, in the 1820s, shortly after its independence was secured.

By the 1820s the United States had become, incommensurably, the chief destination for transatlantic Jewish immigration. Here was a vast nation, in need of labor, and, as steam replaced sail, no longer unthinkably distant from Europe. America was a republic that consciously regarded religious tolerance as a foundation of civil society: not absolute tolerance but sufficiently robust for worship without hindrance. Nor did America with its constitutional separation of religion and state have anything that resembled the Napoleonic consistory, the emperor's dirigiste method of designating a government apparatus to deal with religious minorities. As for Latin America, Brazil, the largest newly independent country, became a monarchy with a liberal constitution (1822–24) and offered a template of sorts for relations with non-Catholics. There had been relatively few Jews in Catholic Latin America, both conversos and pseudo-Christians having been unwilling to risk the Inquisitor's suspicions. That centuries-old form of oppression, sanctioned by church and state, whether in its Portuguese or Spanish variant, at last died under revolutionary pressures. For Latin America the initial tendency between 1825 and 1840 was to build a society responsive to the Declaration of the Rights of Man. Catholicism remained either officially (as with Brazil) or de facto (as with some new republics) a state religion, but this prominence merely expressed the reality of a huge landmass where few non-Catholics were to be found. Among Bolivar's revolutionary progeny, during that first heady generation after liberation, the Church was institutionally less assertive. The old dispensation of a powerful ecclesiastical authority linked to an aristocratic colonial ruling class retreated. Yet, mutatis mutandis, there would effectively be a revival. Conservative reaction to democratic precepts did occur sporadically throughout the nineteenth century, as political parties representing oligarchic wealth gained pace even as like-minded generals used the military to dominate legislatures. An example was the reign of Maximilian I (1832–67), emperor of Mexico from 1864 to 1867, who invited German Jews to settle in Mexico. So the new republics would dissolve, giving way to governments almost incurably ruled by strong caudillos, as one dictator replaced another through chronic coups.[12]

The geography of settlement in South America paralleled that of North America. It could hardly be otherwise: cities were founded first on the Atlantic; economic and demographic expansion then proceeded into the continental interior. But Jews played a distinctly minor role in this growth. Brazil's pre-Inquisition Jewish population was trivial, almost nonexistent, and throughout the nineteenth century, immigration would never remotely approach what was happening in the United States. The North African Jews who came to Belém in the late 1820s and afterward did not adopt the synagogue-community model, whether there or in their later movements into the Amazon basin. For their part, neither the American nor Brazilian governments—nor anywhere else for that matter—in the postcolonial era (if ever) encouraged Jews to adopt this unitary religious organizational system. In the period after independence, a Jewish presence was a matter of ideological indifference (worship was a matter of conscience), or, in the case of Brazil, that a small, law-abiding Jewish community posed no problems.

After 1825, as American Jewry became increasingly Ashkenazic, synagogue architecture evolved from its earlier, modestly utilitarian aesthetic. This was so even within established Sephardic congregations, as some once-dominant Iberian Jews chose to embrace new ways rather than insist on familiar designs. So we find Philadelphia's Sephardic Mikveh Israel building its second synagogue (1825) in the fashionable Egyptian Revival style. Actual results in this instance may not have been especially successful, but the architect hired was the distinguished William Strickland—a sign that the congregation meant to be adaptive rather than conservative. These Sephardim were quite prepared to let their new structure bear the stamp of contemporaneity, especially given the rapid growth of a newer Ashkenazic congregation, Rodeph Shalom. Purposely replacing the Sephardic open central-aisle plan with the theater one instead was also part of this statement. Strickland himself was a prolific and popular practitioner whose name commanded attention in an era when architecture was becoming increasingly professionalized.

New York City's Shearith Israel, the storied Sephardic congregation with a plausible claim to being America's oldest (1654), modernized in 1834 by building its third synagogue, on Crosby Street, in the Greek Revival style. By then New York's Jewish population had (at least) three other congregations, all Ashkenazic, to draw new members: B'nai Jeshurun, Anshe Chesed, and Shaaray Tefila. Beyond American borders we find Nidhe Israel of Barbados (rebuilt 1831) and Beraka ve Shalom ve Gemilut Hasadim of St. Thomas (rebuilt 1833), both in different architectural styles from the originals. A hurricane felled Nidhe Israel, while Beraka ve Shalom ve Gemilut Hasadim was lost to fire. Nidhe Israel's new design was Gothic Revival, whereas Beraka ve Shalom ve Gemilut Hasadim is an unusual hybrid of Greek *and* Gothic revivals.

Across the Atlantic, France during the July Monarchy (1830–48) saw synagogue construction proliferate, permanent buildings replacing clandestine houses of worship that had served Alsace, Lorraine, Bordeaux, and Bayonne. In Paris itself, from which Jews had been banned for centuries, an officially sanctioned congregation was permitted in 1788. Similarly, between 1825 and 1850, as more Jews emigrated to or were born in Great Britain, the Netherlands, Denmark, or their colonial territories, more and larger synagogues were built in styles that tended to acknowledge the diverse national fashions of the day. In the end, after the mid-nineteenth century, the final architectural marker would register as socioeconomic rather than aesthetic: a Jewish bourgeoisie took hold in parts of northern and western Europe. Consequently it would be Jews themselves, as architects and owners of construction firms, who created their own houses of worship, controlling every phase of design, planning, building, and decoration. What we might call synagogues of confident authenticity, given shape by Jewish citizens with their hearts, minds, and (often) hands, became, irrespective of minhag, the hallmark of an evolving modernity. Here is evidence not only of acceptance by secular and Christian majorities, but also of a diverse social landscape in which various Jewish congregations were free to coexist in a given community.

How striking a contrast with the more constricted Atlantic World of the eighteenth century. In preindustrial Europe, comprehensive anti-Semitism meant that Jews were banned from guilds, the traditional organizations of skilled workers that trained and supplied builders, ironmongers, or decorators —those who executed public and private commissions. During the Middle Ages, Jews were sometimes allowed to form their own guilds (such as for butchers, tailors, and others), but for medieval Jews living in confined districts of cities or small rural villages, a career as a building contractor would have been economically limiting and rare.[13] Jewish builders must have existed at the margins of socioeconomic acceptance, but it is probably fair to say that synagogues built by Jews were few, far between, and very likely inconspicuous, not intended for public identification as Jewish places of worship. There is no Jewish equivalent to Chartres, not in Iberia, nor in all Christendom. In early modern or Enlightenment Europe (c. 1600–1800), even in those Protestant lands where Jews, at least within the letter of the social contract, could have legally pursued architecture or building arts, not a single Jew is known to have designed or physically constructed a synagogue. Their contribution was limited to providing a ceremonial cornerstone or engaging in a ritual sod-turning. Among Jews who might have been but were not involved in building synagogues, in what was a presumably tolerant setting, was the active and ambitious Aaron Lopez, of Newport, who as a successful contractor made houses and ships.[14] We must wonder why, and at least two feasible conjectures beckon. The first concerns the historical situation: Atlantic

World Jews were formed by loss and exile, driven from Iberia, and, even when tolerated by more benevolent regimes, Sephardim and their Ashkenazic cohorts lived in frequent motion, traveling between continents, nations, and ports bordering the Atlantic, the Caribbean, and the Americas. To the degree that architecture is an art of permanence bespeaking secure social entitlement, an art expressed through artifacts made by those who stay and prosper rather than those who wander, Atlantic World Jewry could not be overly concerned with the work of permanence. Contingencies and external dangers— an intolerant governor or colonial assembly, failed crops, trade disrupted by war—were too near. So for most Jews during the seventeenth and eighteenth centuries, as members of a recently vilified minority, social relations and material well-being must have seemed provisional. Non-Jews must have felt similarly exposed to the vicissitudes of colonial life and economy in climates and regions new to Europeans.

The second conjecture concerning this total absence of Jewish architects or designers in synagogue construction—while not entirely unrelated to the first—is cultural. Judaism, the religion and its traditions as practiced by dispersed groups of people without a nation-state for nearly two thousand years, is preeminently fixated on and guided by texts—the meaning of the Bible, of commentary, of faith, of ethical problems, all to be explored through a knowledge of rhetoric, historical example, and formal literary study. Simply put: words not things are at the archetypal center of Jewish consciousness. Call it the genius born of dispossession with its corollary defects. The intellectual disciplines of architecture and engineering, the vocation of physical construction, were not major concerns of Jews anywhere, including the Atlantic World. In a culture of conversos, of subterfuge and denial, who would erect monuments to an anathematized faith? When the Dutch and English rulers extended tolerance to Jews in the seventeenth century, the vocation of building must have seemed alien to those Jews first drawn to Amsterdam, London, and Barbados. However that may be, Jews with limited roots in the early modern society of Western Christendom needed generations before conceiving of themselves as sufficiently established or invested to take up architecture as a profession and calling. Remember, during the eighteenth century and later, Jews turned to non-Jews for the expertise to design and build synagogues. It seems clear that the requisite learning curve for Jews to appropriate architectural skills was determined by internal communal conditioning as much as by external pressures. What was needed was a different sense of identity to function in a different kind of society.

For instance, the ambitious young Mordecai M. Noah became an apprentice "carver and gilder" around 1800, contemplating a career as a master artisan engaged to build furniture and decorate homes for the rich. But this path, highly regarded in the young American republic, was soon abandoned.

Instead Noah went on to became the lawyer, journalist, diplomat, and utopian whose influence we have chronicled.[15] Although actual motives are hard to assess here, there remains the great weight of historical precedent. Jewish upward mobility was seldom a matter of perfecting a craft. Noah might well have decided that mastery of the law, writing, scholarship, and the negotiating skills appropriate to an ambassador formed the natural avenue open to an ambitious young Jew in antebellum America.

It was not until 1833 that a Jewish architect would design a synagogue in what we have been calling the Atlantic World: David Mocatta (1806–82) and Montefiore, in Ramsgate, England. Atlantic World Jewry constituted, or emulated, as was the case with so many Ashkenazim, a Sephardic cultural and socioeconomic entity in a predemocratic political era that cannot plausibly extend beyond the first quarter of the nineteenth century. The hour of Sephardic dominance had passed. By way of historical differentiation, however, and as a lens into the future that Sephardic settlement in the Atlantic World made possible, if briefly, consider synagogue architecture and nineteenth-century socioeconomic developments after 1825. That is, we ought to look at Jews when they encountered a more politically diverse and tolerant civil society, whether in the Americas or Europe, precisely in those lands that once demarcated the Atlantic World.

In the 1830s David Mocatta became one of the first members of the Royal Institute of British Architects (1833), eventually serving as its vice president. Slightly older than Mocatta, George Basevi (1794–1845) was a Jew who, like his first cousin, Benjamin Disraeli, converted to Anglicanism at a young age but instead of entering politics went on to become an accomplished architect.[16] Both Mocatta and Basevi were students of the eminent John Soane (1753–1837), receiving tutelage that helped launch their careers. In the event, Basevi would never design a synagogue. Two other synagogues were Mocatta's work: the Devonshire Place Synagogue (built 1836–38, sometimes called the Brighton Regency Synagogue) in Brighton and the Reform congregation's Burton Street Temple (built 1842) in London. Mocatta's Montefiore combined the Regency style with elements of Soane's preferred neoclassicism. It was designed as a private synagogue for the estate of one of Victorian England's most influential Jews, Moses Montefiore (1784–1885), a powerful banker, philanthropist, Sheriff of London, and baronet. Although Montefiore opened with an impressive public ceremony in 1833, it was in fact the family's private synagogue, an extraordinary phenomenon in any era.[17] Nevertheless, as family patriarch and financial patron for the house of worship to be constructed under his own roof, Sir Moses Montefiore was definitively in a position to choose his architect cousin as the designer for his synagogue. However unusual the Montefiore may have seemed in its origin, the synagogue in effect was a harbinger. After the private initiative of Sir Moses, English Jews received commissions from Jewish communities and were deeply involved in designing new synagogues in Great Britain and abroad.

In the Americas, it was David Lopez Jr., builder of Beth Elohim (1841) in Charleston, who figured as the first Jew whose firm built a synagogue—a design plan created by New York architect Cyrus L. Warner. His father, David Lopez Sr. (1750–1812), owned a store that sold architectural ornaments among other imported goods.[18] Whether it was his father's pursuits or those business skills learned from another family merchant, his great uncle Aaron, notably successful importer of varied materials, David Jr. received the orientation, amounting to an apprenticeship in relevant building practices, that launched his career as owner of a construction company. Besides numerous residences in Charleston, the younger Lopez's firm was responsible for such commercial and religious buildings in Charleston as the Farmers' and Exchange Bank (1853–54), Institute Hall (1854), and Zion Presbyterian Church (1858–59). (It was Institute Hall in which the signing of the crucial political instrument precipitating the Civil War, South Carolina's Ordinance of Secession in 1860, took place.) As for Zion Presbyterian Church, whose black congregation was under white administration Lopez's commission was the second church completed by a Jew in the Americas.[19] The first, St. John's Episcopal in Savannah, a white congregation, must be assigned to Lopez's nephew, David Lopez Cohen in 1851–53.[20] Increasingly successful, the Charleston-based Lopez went on to become South Carolina's general superintendent of works during the Civil War: he built the state's armory in Greenville.[21]

When Beth Elohim decided to follow the reform program (c. 1841, the Lopez family remained traditionalists, joining Charleston's splinter congregation (Sephardic-orthodox), Shearit Israel. So David Lopez did not personally worship in the fine synagogue he had so painstakingly built. After the Civil War (1866), the two congregations merged and the Lopez family once again was Beth Elohim congregants; David Lopez himself, steadfastly orthodox and unwilling to accept reform innovations, soon resigned (1868).[22] But as a builder, Lopez must have been exemplary—his sons John and Moses, as well as his nephew David Lopez Cohen, all took up the profession. The sons joined and maintained their father's firm, though Cohen later operated his own. It was Cohen who built Charleston's Shearit Israel in 1847, thus emulating his uncle's achievement by constructing the second synagogue attributable to a Jew in the Americas.[23] He also renovated Savannah's Mickve Israel (1841) in 1852–53.[24]

The initial Jewish authorship of synagogues during the 1840s would precede a second phase, one favoring monumental design for ever-larger buildings. These synagogues were made possible by using the most recent technological advances in iron and steel framing—that is, by relying on the most advanced techniques used for major urban structures in nineteenth-century Europe and the Americas. Notable Jewish architects of this era included Leopold Eidlitz (American, 1823–1908), Nathan S. Joseph (British, 1834–1909), Alfred-Philibert Aldrophe (French, 1834–95), and Leon Winkel (Dutch, 1822–84). Smaller Jewish communities would, whenever constraints of budget and local preference allowed adopt or adjust to scale the grand architectural idiom found in New York, Chicago, and London.[25] Architecture, so often a vital expression of an era's sociocultural milieu, would in effect reach out and help bind together the great waves of European immigrants—mostly arriving in the United States but elsewhere in the Americas too—who would be absorbed into Jewish-American life. Moreover those Jews who came from eastern European villages or rural poverty could recognize in the substantial, impressive synagogues constructed in the second half of the nineteenth century, and later, a material condition that seemed to link the American dream—here was a gold-paved country where wealth could be earned by all—to a social environment that affirmed Judaism. The persecutions of shtetl and pogrom belonged to the past, to another land. It was imposing places of worship like Temple Emanuel on East Forty-Third Street in New York (1868), which created a secure sense of religious identity.

Leopold Eidlitz was arguably the most remarkable of the nineteenth-century Jewish architects who flourished in the United States. Born in Prague, educated in Vienna, he immigrated to the United States at the age of twenty (1843). In New York Eidlitz was apprenticed to Cyrus L. Warner and the famous master of Gothic Revival, Richard Upjohn (1802–78). Though Eidlitz married Warner's daughter, Harriet, in 1845, he did not work on Charleston's synagogue—that commission had already been completed. Notwithstanding, Eidlitz became the first Jew to design (as opposed to build or contract to build) an American synagogue, New York's Wooster Street Synagogue (1847). It was a Romanesque Revival building housing congregation Shaaray Tefila. A decade later Eidlitz became one of the founding members of the American Institute of Architects.[26] His important projects included P. T. Barnum's house in Bridgeport, Connecticut (1848), New York City's Temple Emanuel Synagogue (built 1866–68, destroyed 1927), and the New York County Courthouse (1876–81). He then joined with two famous colleagues, Henry Hobson Richardson and Frederick Law Olmsted, to create the controversial renovation New York's state capitol in Albany (1876–81). Eidlitz's achievement with Temple Emanuel was noted for eclectic grandeur—it combined Moorish revival and various Islamic motifs-while the architect took on his younger brother Marc, a builder, and Henry Fernbach (a respected younger Jewish architect) to help design and complete the project. An argument can be made that this synagogue represents the finest accomplishment of any of these men. Nor were the successful, versatile Eidlitz brothers in any way confined to a Jewish clientele: they built the Broadway Tabernacle, an impressive church, between 1857 and 1859.[27]

Crossing the Atlantic for a last time, Jewish architects in the United Kingdom followed in the footsteps of Mocatta. By the late nineteenth century, as far as the home islands were concerned, the United Synagogue, an organization founded in 1866 by three London orthodox congregations that received full legal sanction in 1870, centrally administered synagogue design. This parliamentary authorization bears a certain comparison with the hierarchic structure familiar to us from the Napoleonic consistory. Over time, dozens of Great Britain's orthodox congregations would affiliate with the United Synagogue. Its first "architect-surveyor" was Nathan S. Joseph, answerable to an authoritative building committee that specified what synagogues should look like and who would build them. Nor did he attain such a position entirely on merit. Joseph belonged to the family of Rachel Joseph Adler, who happened to be the wife of Nathan Marcus Adler (1803–90), the chief rabbi of the British Empire (1844–1890) for much of the Victorian era. Joseph himself was involved with architectural designs for many projects—such as the Garnethill (1879–81), New West End (1877–79), and Hampstead (1892) synagogues, all built in the popular Romanesque Revival style. But, however well connected, the official architect-surveyor always occupied a secondary role, assisting other architects from various backgrounds. For instance, the lead architect for the Garnethill Synagogue in Glasgow was John McLeod (1838–88), as Presbyterian as his name suggests. The design team for London's New West End Synagogue was by another Scotsman, George Audsley (1838–1925), although Jewish architect Edward Salomons (1828–1906) also contributed.[28] On the other hand, and unlike the American experience, a Jewish construction firm or builder has *yet* to produce a synagogue in Britain. Though there have been a handful of Jews in the building trades, such as Abraham Davis and his brothers who constructed flats and workshops in London's East End during the early twentieth century, a synagogue project was never an opportunity for them.[29]

What was the situation across the English Channel? French synagogue architecture was governed by the consistory system for much of the nineteenth century. The main Jewish practitioner of the era was Alfred-Philibert Aldrophe (1834–1895), architect for the Consistory of Paris. His most significant projects were the Grand Synagogue of Paris (1867–74), the Versailles Synagogue (1884–86), and Baron Gustave de Rothschild's elegant Hôtel de Marigny (1873–83). But Aldrophe had a progenitor: Abraham Hirsch (1828–1913) was France's first Jewish architect to have designed a Jewish house of worship, the Grand Synagogue of Lyon (built 1864). Hirsch was probably better known as the honorary chief architect for Lyons, a city where he designed many buildings, as well as where he served as director of the School of Fine Arts.[30]

Yet France did not typify all European nations in respect to synagogue projects. In the Netherlands, the tolerant country that had decisively allowed Jews equality in 1796, extraordinarily a small number are known to have designed synagogues the entire nineteenth century. This included Leon Winkel, a civil engineer by training, who designed Delft's synagogue (1862) in a neoclassical style, and Emanuel Rood, a builder by profession, who designed Amsterdam's Dutch Renaissance Gerard Dou Synagogue (1891-92).[31]

Clearly Jews in western Europe and the Americas had achieved a different posture, created almost a different identity, by the mid-nineteenth century. Their entry into civil society, their upwardly mobile socioeconomic status, indeed their growing political voice given the nature of democratic representative government, rendered the Sephardic Atlantic World of early modern Europe distant, even archaeological. As we have seen architecture is a primary signifier of human experience, conversing through a public, tangible language available to all: the built environment represents what hearts and minds can make possible given existing material, technological, and sociopolitical norms. Buildings often relate who we were, are, and aspire to be. Zadoc Kahn (1839–1905), chief rabbi of France, was filled with this kind of awareness when he declared at a synagogue dedication in Boulogne-Sur-Mer: "if Judaism benefits today from full and complete freedom, then for these same reasons, like all religious and philosophical doctrines that demand respect and admiration, it has, I will not say the right, but the duty to recognize and show itself."[32]

A brave new reality then, far removed from the exigencies or deprivations of the Atlantic World: Kahn speaks with the accents of modernity, although no one could then have imagined the tragedy of the Holocaust or the establishment of modern Israel. Still the statement of the French chief rabbi seems familiar enough to us and utterly unlike what any seventeenth-century Sephardic Jew could have conceived. In Kahn's polity Jews take hands-on responsibility for the buildings in which they pray. But we should not forget the evolution that made possible this more substantial, rooted Jewish presence. In fact, as a record of that lost Sephardic presence that peopled Atlantic coasts and Caribbean islands, synagogue design and, where extant, the surviving religious structures themselves, provide a critical narrative thread between a colonial past and subsequent Jewish life in the age of democratic pluralism. This story should not be ignored.

Survey of Atlantic World Synagogues

Portuguese Synagogue (I) | Amsterdam, Netherlands

Built 1636–1639
Years Extant 1636–1931

The front elevation of the Portuguese Synagogue (I), of the Talmud Torah congregation in Amsterdam, built 1636–39. Engraving by Romeyn de Hooghe. William A. Rosenthall Judaica Collection, Special Collections, College of Charleston Library.

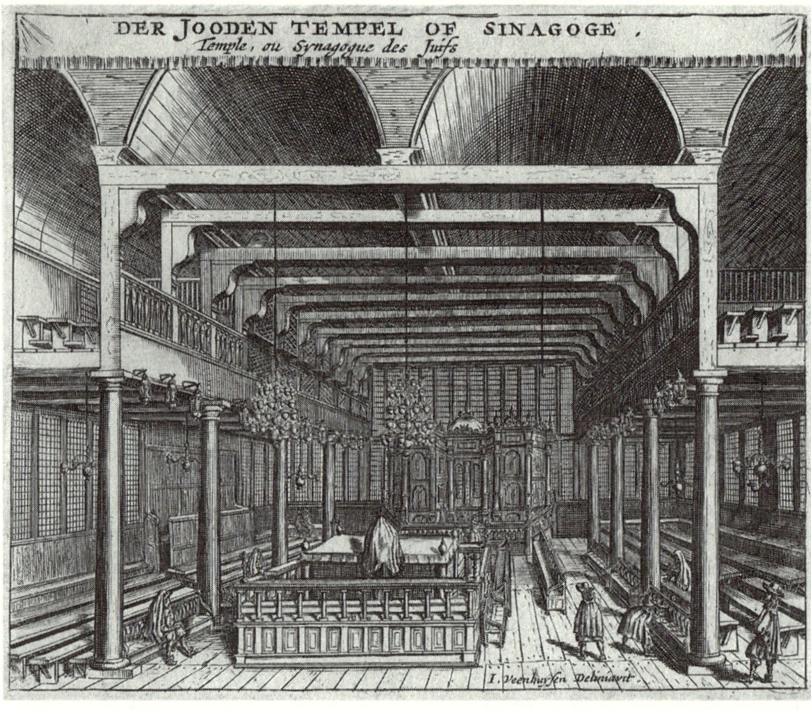

Interior of the Portuguese Synagogue (I), of the Talmud Torah congregation, Amsterdam built c. 1636–39. Engraving by Johannes Veenhuysen, c. 1662. William A. Rosenthall Judaica Collection, Special Collections, College of Charleston Library.

The synagogue was the first purpose-built in Amsterdam and had some features that were reminiscent of the schuilkerken that were common across the Lowlands during this period. The preceding synagogues of congregations Beth Israel, Beth Jacob, and Neve Shalom in Amsterdam had also been schuilkerken. The Portuguese Synagogue (I) construction was initiated by the Beth Israel congregation for its own use; however, with the merger that took place with Beth Jacob and Neve Shalom congregations between 1636 and 1639, a larger edifice than originally intended was completed to accommodate the additional congregants. After 1639 the schuilkerken that Beth Israel, Beth Jacob, and Neve Shalom had used were sold. The first synagogue of the merged Talmud Torah congregation was used until 1675, when it was replaced by a new and larger building. After 1675 the old synagogue was renovated on numerous occasions and used as an auxiliary synagogue, banquet room, and warehouse. In 1931 the building was demolished to make way for new construction.[1]

Based on the extant exterior illustrations of the synagogue the building was two-stories tall with a hipped roof. The front elevation was divided into seven bays with each bay separated by a Corinthian pilaster. The first and second stories were visually divided by a belt course decorated with garlands. The center bay had a small second story balcony with an elliptical window or fan above it. Throughout the exterior, Palladian ornamentation was used. A description of the interior survives from this period by Tobias van Domselaer in *Bechrijvinge van Amsterdam,* when he visited in 1665:

> below one enters a forecourt or large empty place where there is a Water Butt which is opened by a tap, with a towel beside it, for the Jews wash their hands before entering the Church; on each side there are stairs leading to their Church; The Women sit in the gallery above, separate from the Men unseen by them; at the one end is a great wooden box with two doors in which many precious objects are to be seen, among them the Books of Moses hung with costly embroidered mantles: their Teachers stand on a raised platform, above three foot above the rest: over their Hats the men wore a white shawl which hangs down over their shoulders and body, and each holds a Hebrew Book in his hands.[2]

Zur Israel | Recife, Pernambuco, Brazil

Built 1640
Years Extant 1640–1900s

In 1640 the congregation Zur Israel built the first synagogue in the Americas, which was a two-story building constructed of rock with a plaster exterior. After the fall of Recife to the Portuguese in 1654, Zur Israel Synagogue came into the possession of João Fernandes Vieira as a gift from the Portuguese authorities due to his assistance in retaking Brazil. Later the Vieira family donated the property to the congregation of the Oratory of St. Philip Neri in 1679, who used it for more than a century. In 1835 the former synagogue was used as an orphans' school and then an asylum in 1862. At the turn of the twentieth century, the building was demolished to build a bank, which later became an electronics store.

Arising in Brazil during the 1950s, there was renewed interest among historians in the former Dutch colonial history of the country as well as the Jewish presence that was once there. One of these historians of note was Arnold Witznitzer, president of the Brazilian Jewish Historical Institute, in Rio de Janeiro. Witznitzer published articles in the *American Jewish Historical Society Journal* as well as a book, *The Jews in Colonial Brazil,* in 1960. A Portuguese translation of *Jews in Colonial Brazil* was published in Sao Paulo six years later. In 1962 Professor Jose Antonio Gonsalves de Mello, an archaeologist at the Federal University of Pernambuco (UFDP), made a startling rediscovery of Zur Israel's former location through historical documents. However, this study was not published until 1988. A bronze plaque was also placed on the façade of the electronics store by municipal authorities and the state's archaeological institute recognizing the historical significance of the site.

The year 1992 not only marked the five-hundredth anniversary of Christopher Columbus's "Voyage of Discovery" but also the expulsion of the Jews from Spain. This anniversary resulted in numerous publications on Sephardic-related history. In addition the Jewish Center of Pernambuco received permission from Recife's Mayor, Gilberto Marques Paulo, to install a hand-painted, ceramic plaque on the façade of the electronics store, which read, "Street of the Beneficent Jesus formerly Jews Street 1636–1654." This small act of commemoration set many others in motion. Two years later Germano Haiut, Ernesto Margolis, and Boris Bernstein established the Association for the Restoration of Jewish Memory in the Americas (ARMAJ), which was recognized by the Brazilian Institute of Historical Heritage. The leaders of ARMAJ and the Recife Jewish community also signed an agreement with Mayor Roberto Magalhaes Melo, the president of IPHAN, and Brazil's minister of culture to preserve the Jewish heritage at the Zur Israel Synagogue site. In 1993 the municipal authorities of Recife began to revitalize its historic urban core, or barrio, where the former Zur Israel Synagogue site was located.

In 1998 Professor Marcos Albuquerque of UFDP began archaeological excavations beneath the present commercial building on top of the site. The synagogue site was also designated a National Monument by the Ministry of Culture. In 1999 the city transferred the title ownership of the former Zur Israel Synagogue site to the Jewish Federation of Pernambuco. After 345 years the Zur Israel property was again in Jewish possession. The Ministry of Culture in partnership with the Inter-American Development Bank's Monuments Program, the Safra Bank Foundation, the Recife municipal government, the Jewish Federation of Pernambuco, and the Jewish Confederation of Brazil financially supported the excavations that continued through 2001. The archaeological excavations removed over 750 metric tons of earth and debris. At the bottom was found the remains of a stone-lined Jewish ritual bath, or mikveh. This mikveh is believed to have both have been part of or adjacent to the Zur Israel Synagogue and had once been fed by a local stream. The mikveh was small, suggesting that it was most likely used only for the immersion of kitchen vessels for kashrut purification purposes followed in Jewish tradition. In 2001 architects Jose Luiz Mota Menezes and Luciana Menezes and engineers Bernardo and Amir Schwartz were contracted to adaptively reuse the commercial building at the site into a museum. The ground floor was designed to provide views of the excavation and exhibits of the recovered artifacts. On the second floor is a theorized recreation of Zur Israel sanctuary. This recreation was developed based on studies of the Esnoga and Snoa.[3] No images or descriptions of the original synagogue could be identified.

Magen Abraham | Mauricia, Pernambuco, Brazil

Built 1648
Years Extant 1648–1653

The synagogue was built c. 1648 in Mauricia, a town built by the Dutch near Recife. Though a separate synagogue, Magen Abraham was an extension of the Zur Israel congregation in Recife. In 1653 the synagogue was destroyed during the Portuguese campaign to reconquer Brazil from the Dutch. No images or descriptions of this synagogue could be identified.[4]

Unknown | Cayenne, French Guyana

Built 1661
Years Extant 1661–1667

Built around 1661 during the brief occupation of Cayenne by the Dutch, the synagogue was most likely a small makeshift structure but built specifically for use as a synagogue, which qualifies it as applicable for this study. In 1664 the Dutch colony was surrendered to the French, and the Jews were allowed to maintain their religious liberties. Three years later the English sacked the colony, and the synagogue was destroyed. No images or descriptions of this synagogue could be identified.[5]

Nidhe Israel | Bridgetown, Barbados

Built 1660s
Years Extant 1660s–1831

Close-up of the painting *Governor Robinson Going to Church* (1740), showing the city of Bridgetown, centered on what is believed to be Nidhe Israel Synagogue's exterior. Artist unknown. Barbados Museum and Historical Society Collection.

It is not known exactly when the first synagogue in Barbados was built, but evidence suggests sometime in the 1660s. According to a surveyor's record from 1664, the synagogue is mentioned as having already been built.[6] The building may have exhibited late English medieval or Jacobean vernacular architectural detailing, as is found in surviving buildings in the colonies from this period. A possible depiction of the synagogue survives in the skyline of a painting depicting Bridgetown c. 1740, called *Governor Robinson Going to Church*. The synagogue is small within the illustrated landscape but provides an idea of what the building looked like.[7] This detail within the painting is possibly the oldest surviving image of a synagogue built in the Americas.

In 1831 a hurricane hit Barbados and devastated much of the island, including the synagogue and its historical records, and a replacement was built on the same location two years later. Beginning in 2008 archaeological excavations were initiated on the Nidhe Israel property by the University of the West Indies. A mikveh dating from the seventeenth century was uncovered on the site.[8]

Semah David | Speightstown, Barbados

Built 1660s/70s
Years Extant 1660s/70s–1739

Built in the 1660s or 1670s, shortly after the construction of the Nidhe Israel Synagogue in Bridgetown, Semah David was built in Speightstown to cater to the Jews that lived there on the opposite side of the island. The synagogue was not a separate congregation but an extension of Nidhe Israel. In 1739 the synagogue was destroyed by an anti-Semitic mob after a misunderstanding between a Jew and a non-Jew. It is one of the rare instances of a pogrom to take place within the tolerant British and Dutch Atlantic World empires. No images or descriptions of this synagogue could be identified.[9]

Unknown | Thorarica, Suriname

Built 1671
Years Extant 1671–c. 1685

Built in 1671, along Cassipoera Creek, near Thorarica, the synagogue served the Jews of Surinam until 1685, when it was abandoned for a new building at Jodensavanne. It too was most likely a vernacular, makeshift structure made of wood. Nonetheless, there is debate as to what flag the synagogue was originally built under. In 1671 Surinam was an English colony under Dutch occupation since 1667 as part of the Second Anglo-Dutch War (1665–67). Not until the Treaty of Westminster of 1674 did the English permanently relinquish their claim to Surinam to the Dutch. No images or descriptions of this synagogue could be identified.[10]

Mikve Israel (I) | Willemstad, Curaçao

Built 1674
Years Extant 1674–1692

In 1674 Mikve Israel built the first of many synagogue buildings that served as the home for the congregation. It was most likely a small vernacular building. No images or descriptions of this synagogue could be identified.[11]

Portuguese Synagogue (II), Esnoga | Amsterdam, Netherlands

Built 1671–75
Years Extant 1675–present

The exterior of the Portuguese Synagogue (II), often called the Esnoga, in Amsterdam, built 1671–75. Engraving by Willem Hendrik Hoogkamer, *Vue D'Amsterdam No 26.*, *De Portugeesche Jooden Kerk*, early nineteenth century. William A. Rosenthall Judaica Collection, Special Collections, College of Charleston Library.

Haham Isaac Aboab de Fonseca initiated the building of the second Portuguese Synagogue in 1670. He was also the chief Sephardic rabbi in Amsterdam and formerly the chief rabbi in Dutch Brazil during the 1640s and 1650s. The architect, Elias Bouman, designed the building in the Dutch Baroque style. Bouman had also worked on the Ashkenazic synagogue, the Grote Sjoel, which was completed in 1670. Construction on the Esnoga began in 1671 and was scheduled to take a year to complete but took four years due to the Third Anglo-Dutch War. Since the completion of the building in 1675, the synagogue has experienced several alterations and additions, but they have done little to affect the historic character and integrity. One of the earliest took place in 1690 and was due to a visit by Stadtholder William III. Apparently the four large Ionic columns were originally wood, and during his visit, William III decided that stone columns would be better suited for the building. With his assistance the wood was replaced with the stone columns that are still seen today. In 1773–74 sharply slanting buttresses were added to the rear elevation of the Esnoga. The buttresses were added based on an interpretation of King Solomon's Temple in Jerusalem by Jacob Juda Leon dating from 1667. It was the intent of the Talmud Torah congregation to render their synagogue more like this interpretation of the Temple. Two projecting mezzanines were removed and two staircases were also added as part of the project.

Between 1852 and 1854, a significant restoration project was conducted that replaced the small leaded glass windows with cast-iron frames. New sills were also added but used matching material. The overall result was a greater amount of natural light entering the sanctuary. In addition an interior vestibule was added at the front entrance and the hinges on the front doors were altered so that they could no longer open outward. Within the building wood paneling was installed on many of the walls, and benches with backs were placed in the women's section of the sanctuary.

The interior of the Portuguese Synagogue (II), often called the Esnoga, in Amsterdam, built 1671–75. Engraving by Bernard Picart, *Cérémonies et coutumes religieuses de tous les peuples du monde*, Amsterdam, 1723. William A. Rosenthall Judaica Collection, Special Collections, College of Charleston Library.

In 1875 the Esnoga celebrated its two-hundredth anniversary, and marble memorial tablets were placed at the two sides of the hechal. On the tablets are listed the names of the architect (Elias Bouman) and the building committee members at the time of the building's construction. Within the synagogue complex some changes were also made, among these the building of a new mikveh as well as a new apartment for the chazzan in 1891, which were later replaced in 1939 by newer apartments. At the end of the 1890s, restoration work was done on part of the exterior façade facing Muiderstraat, including the replacement of the congregation's coat of arms, which depicts a pelican feeding its three young. The pelican represents the united congregation, and the three young are represented of the three prior congregations, Beth Israel, Beth Jacob, and Neve Shalom. Together they are a united family. There is also a second coat of arms of the congregation that depicts a phoenix rising from the ashes.

In commemoration of the 250th anniversary of the Esnoga in 1925, the congregation planned to install an amud—an extra pulpit—within the sanctuary. The Esnoga had just been listed as a national monument, and the Amsterdam Office of Monuments and Archeology rejected the proposal. Their reason for doing so was that the "Portuguese Synagogue is a building of such beauty, in its lines, proportions and sober ornament, that no change whatsoever which might be made to the interior could improve it."[12] This stance on the historic character of the synagogue has remained unto the present and is why electricity was never installed throughout the building, though it was attempted more than once.

With the outbreak of World War II, plans were made by the Dutch government in conjunction with the congregation to protect the synagogue. The attic was sprayed with fire-resistant paint and covered with a material that could withstand incendiary bombs. Fire-extinguishing systems were installed as well as two rear fire escapes. A special protective scaffold was built over the hechal, which consisted of walls made of sand-filled boxes and fire-resistant netting. The Dutch government covered the expenses for the wartime retrofitting, while the congregation supplied firewatchers. Worship in the synagogue continued until May 1943, three years after the Nazi German invasion of the Netherlands. In June 1943 the ritual artifacts, records, and other important treasures of the congregation were hidden in one of the architraves supporting the vaulted ceiling. Surveillance of the Esnoga by the congregation continued until 1944, when non-Jews had to take over the work since too many of the congregants had been deported to concentration camps. The synagogue remained unscathed through the end of the war thanks to these firewatchers. It is presumed that the Nazis did not touch the synagogue because of plans to turn the building into a museum on the lost civilization of the Jews, similar to one planned for the Altneuschul in Prague. However, the Etz Chaim Library at the Esnoga was raided and its collection sent to

Germany. Fortunately the collection was recovered and returned after the War. In May 1945 the synagogue was reopened with a special joint service held with Amsterdam's Ashkenazic community.

Significant repair work was first conducted on the Esnoga in 1955–59 by consulting architects J. S. Baars and J. W. Kuipers. The project was not completed according to their plans because of lack of funding. Work that was accomplished included the exterior façades, balustrade, and roof. Windowpanes were also replaced, and the windows above the hechal were shortened. The windows above the main entrance were replaced with wood panels. The floor within the Esnoga was slightly raised, and the paint on the banca from the nineteenth century was removed. Similar restoration work also took place on the surrounding outbuildings that housed classrooms and other supporting facilities. The Etz Chaim Library's auditorium was also converted into a small sanctuary for use during winter, and a heater was installed. The most recent changes include a renovation to the mourners' room during the 1970s.[13]

In 1990–93, a more thorough restoration project was undertaken on the Esnoga. This project included many repairs from years of mild wear, tear, and neglect. The ceilings beneath the women's balcony and the balustrades were restored to their original shade of blue. The women's section in the winter sanctuary was enlarged, and an open section of the outbuildings was converted into a reception and video area. During the middle 1990s, interest arose to have the historic core of Amsterdam placed on the UNESCO World Heritage List (which occurred in 2010), to which the Esnoga is considered a contributing building. In 2000 a restoration project was done within the Etz Chaim–Livraria Montezinos Library, which included the installation of climate-control devices to help maintain and preserve the collection of manuscripts and books that date from the late thirteenth century. In 2003 UNESCO listed the Etz Chaim–Livraria Montezinos Library onto the Memory of the World Register for its unsurpassed collection of Judaica.[14]

The Esnoga is a large two-story, cubed brick building with stone trim. The synagogue complex includes the surrounding outbuildings that fill a city block. The building has a barrel-vaulted brick foundation that rests on top of approximately three thousand timber pilings sunk below the water table. The exterior elevations of the synagogue are relatively unadorned. On the front façade there are five bays and four pilasters that reach almost the full height of the building. The windows are composite with those on the second story, having elliptical tops. There is a hipped roof that is crowned by a brick-and-stone balustrade. Centered within the balustrade is a circular dormer window. The front entrance has rusticated architrave trim that is framed by Tuscan columns and a lentil entablature with classical details. There is also a sconce on each Tuscan column to illuminate the front entrance. Within the frieze of the front entrance is a sign with a quote from Psalm 5:8, which translates into "I will come into thy house in the multitude of thy mercy." Within the quote is encrypted the initials of Haham Isaac Aboab da Fonseca, the first chief rabbi of the synagogue.

Within the sanctuary there is seating for over twelve hundred in the men's section and 440 in the women's. Besides the natural light that comes through the many windows of the sanctuary, artificial light is still provided by twenty-six brass chandeliers that hold approximately three hundred candles. It is believed that the older chandeliers may have come from the previous synagogue. These chandeliers, divided into three rows, are suspended from the ceiling by rods. The largest of the chandeliers are located in the central row over the open central aisle. Where the rods meet the ceiling are blue and gilded wooden rosettes. The lack of more light made studying the interior difficult since the chandeliers were not in use at the time of the site visit. The tone of the interior is also affected by the dark wood barrel vaults that span over the aisles as well as by the four massive Ionic stone columns that support the nave in the center of the sanctuary. Flanking the open central aisle on the north and south walls of the sanctuary are the women's balconies, which are screened off by grilles. Beneath these balconies is the men's seating area with benches placed lengthwise on the north-south axis—characteristic of the open central aisle plan. The most prominent seating is the banca on the north wall.

On the eastern wall, facing toward Jerusalem, is the hechal. The hechal is extravagantly decorated in the Dutch Baroque style and is made of Brazilian jacaranda wood. This hechal is a testament to the prosperity that the Sephardic community of Amsterdam knew during the seventeenth century as well as its ties within the Atlantic World since Brazilian jacaranda is an exotic New World hardwood. Inscribed on the hechal is a biblical excerpt from Malachi 4:4, translated as "Remember the law of Moses my servant which I command unto him at Mt. Horeb for all Israel." Crowning the hechal is an ornate lukhot inscribed with the Ten Commandments and "Crown of the Torah" in gilt Hebrew letters. A balustrade, with rounded ornaments and brass candlesticks, encloses the hechal. Hanging in front of the hechal is the ner tamid lamp.

On the opposite side of the sanctuary from the hechal is the tebah, which is also of the Dutch Baroque style and made of jacaranda wood. Enclosing the tebah is another balustrade that also has brass candlesticks and large brass ornaments to hang the Torah mantels. At the head of the tebah is the seat reserved for the hacham. Behind the tebah is an enclosed vestibule from which one enters the main floor of the synagogue's sanctuary.

Neve Zedek (I) | Port Royal, Jamaica

Built 1684
Years Extant 1684–92

It is estimated that the congregation built Neve Zedek Synagogue around 1684, but this could have taken place a few years later. The historical record is not exactly clear on the issue; however, it is known that the synagogue was destroyed along with most of the rest of Port Royal by an earthquake in 1692. Because of the earthquake much of the city was inundated when it sank below sea level. No images or descriptions of this synagogue could be identified.[15]

Unknown | Charlestown, St. Christopher and Nevis

Built 1684
Years Extant 1684–1772

This synagogue was built around 1684, but its appearance and its name have been lost. During the eighteenth century, Nevis fell into economic decline, and much of its European population left the island, including many of its Jews by the 1760s. The synagogue was possibly destroyed by a hurricane in 1772. In 1993 Michelle Terrell embarked to study the former site of the synagogue in Charlestown, Nevis, for her doctoral dissertation in archaeology at Boston University. The Nevis Historical and Conservation Society had initiated the project in order to develop an interpretive program on Nevis's former Jewish heritage. The islanders led her to a spot that had traditionally been identified as the site of the seventeenth-century synagogue, located near an alley named "Jews Walk" that connected the site with the Jewish cemetery. Following four seasons of excavations, Terrell had unearthed a significant number of artifacts; however, none of them was characteristic of synagogues or other forms of houses of worship. Upon further research, the site revealed itself to be a private residence belonging to an English planter from a significantly later period in history, which had never been inhabited by Jews. Highly determined to identify the actual location of the vanished synagogue, Terrell was able to sift through layers of oral tradition and archived historical records to recreate the distribution of the entire Jewish community during the eighteenth century as well as find the original location of the synagogue. To her dismay the site of the former synagogue's location was beneath a more recent building only a short distance from the location where she had been digging. Excavations at this location were therefore impossible for her dissertation; however, it is hoped that at an undetermined time in the future, excavations will be made under the newer building in order to uncover any possible surviving remnants of the synagogue.[16]

Berakha ve Shalom | Jodensavanne, Suriname

Built 1685
Years Extant 1685–after 1832

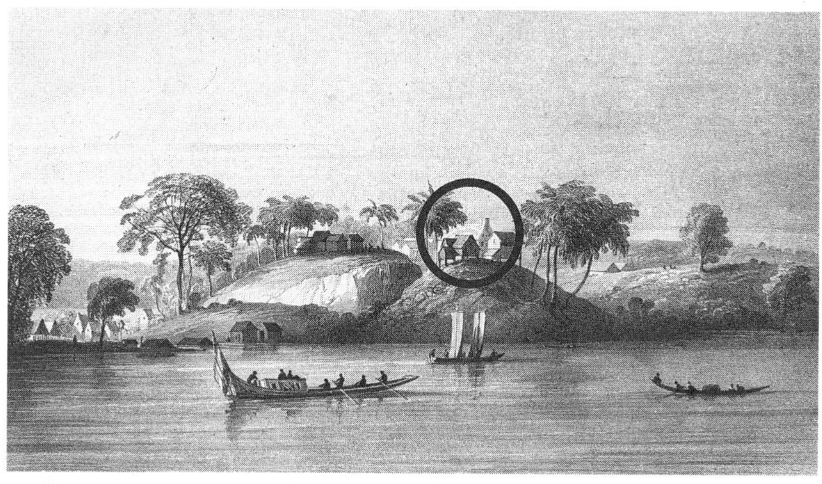

Very few images survive of Berakha ve Shalom Synagogue (within the circle)
of Jodensavnne, as shown in the illustration by Pierre Jacques Benoit, c. 1830.
William A. Rosenthall Judaica Collection, Special Collections, College of
Charleston Library.

The ruins of Berakha ve Shalom Synagogue of Jodensavanne. This view faces east,
where the hechal would have stood against the wall. Photo from the personal
collection of Barry Stiefel, picture taken by Lori H. Stiefel.

Berakha ve Shalom Synagogue was completed in 1685 after much of the Surinamese Jewish community had relocated from Thorarica to Jodensavanne. This coincided with the Dutch transfer of the colony's capital from Thorarica to Paramaribo. The synagogue was used for almost 150 years, and on the occasion of the hundredth anniversary in 1785 a great celebration was held to commemorate the event. In 1832 a great fire devastated the town but left the synagogue untouched. It was saved because of its position in the middle of Jodensavanne's central plaza, which acted as a firebreak. The town's population had been in decline for several decades, and after the last residents found themselves homeless owing to the fire, they relocated to Paramaribo. The synagogue essentially remained abandoned to the elements and slowly fell into ruin during the nineteenth century.

According to travelers' accounts, the remnants of Jodensavanne were visited and observed on numerous occasions, but little if any intervention work was conducted. In 1906 Pincus Hilfman became the first to conduct significant clean-up work at Jodensavanne and noted that the synagogue had collapsed. The primary threat to Jodensavanne since the fire of 1832 has been the never-ceasing encroachment of native vegetation. With the outbreak of World War II, the Dutch authorities incarcerated all German nationals and sympathizers of the Nazi regime in order to prevent them from creating a fifth column. In 1943 an internment camp was established near the Jodensavanne site and their labor included the cleaning, maintenance, and inventorying of Jodensavanne's synagogue and cemetery. There is a sense of irony in this considering the events taking place in Europe in regard to the Holocaust at the same time. At the conclusion of World War II, work at Jodensavanne nearly ceased; however, there was still civilian interest in the site as late as the middle 1950s, as indicated by a plaque dated from 1954 installed at the Berakha ve Shalom ruin jointly by American and Surinamese Jews. This work included a partial reconstruction of the ruin using the materials present at the site in order to provide a better idea of what the synagogue once looked like.

The site was again abandoned for a number of years and overtaken by the jungle until 1968, when Suriname's government took an interest in Jodensavanne and issued three postage stamps in order to promote awareness and celebrate Suriname's cultural diversity. In 1971 the Foundation for Jodensavanne was established to attend to the preservation and heritage interpretation of the site. Reclaiming the ruins began again in 1972 and was included in Temminck Groll's study on Suriname's historic architecture, *De Architecture Van Suriname, 1667–1930* (1973). Jodensavanne was managed as an open-air museum until the fall of the democratically elected government in the 1980s. Preservation efforts slowly resumed at Jodensavanne in the 1990s once democracy was reestablished. International attention was brought to Jodensavanne in 1996 and 2000 when it was placed on the World Monuments Fund Watch List. In 1998 Rachel Frankel and Aviva Ben-Ur conducted an in-depth historical study on the ruins, with an emphasis on the Berakha ve Shalom Synagogue and the cemeteries. Since these most recent projects at Jodensavanne, the Foundation for Jodensavanne has erected bilingual interpretive signage in Dutch and English on the historical significance of the site and manages the place as an open-air museum.

Berakha ve Shalom Synagogue appears in several historical illustrations of the skyline of the town from the Suriname River. Not much detail is given other than it had a brick exterior, a vernacular Dutch Baroque architectural design with a steep Dutch-gabled roof, and a rectangular floor plan. The ruined foundation of the synagogue is still extant and reveals that there were two main entrances, one on the north elevation and the other on the south. A secondary entrance was also located on the west elevation. Iron hardware still remains for wood shutters that once flanked the windows. According to archaeological excavations, the interior of the synagogue had a wood floor. Within the ruins were also found deposits of sand that once covered the floor. Along the western section of the sanctuary there was a balcony, most likely the women's section. In the *Essai Historique* (1788) there is brief description of the interior, which describes there being an ornately decorated hechal made of cedar in the sanctuary, with the room illuminated by brass chandeliers. The hechal was supposedly large enough to house eighteen torah scrolls. On the opposite side of the sanctuary (west) of the hechal was the women's balcony. Beneath the balcony were a series of rooms used for meetings and storing community records.[17]

Mikve Israel (II) | *Willemstad, Curaçao*

Built 1692

Years Extant 1692–1703

Owing to immigration, the congregation Mikve Israel outgrew its synagogue by 1690 and thus required a new building. This second synagogue was built c. 1692 and served the congregation for ten years, but it too proved to be inadequate because of the steady congregational growth. No images or descriptions of this synagogue could be identified.[18]

Bevis Marks | *London, United Kingdom*

Built 1699–1701

Years Extant 1701–present

Bevis Marks Synagogue was designed by Joseph Avis and completed in 1701. After the Esnoga in Amsterdam, Bevis Marks is the next most significant synagogue within the historical context of the Atlantic World. The synagogue exhibits a high level of integrity of its historic character with only a minimal degree of alteration. Known alterations to the interior of the synagogue include the installation of four extra pews in 1746, a choir stall behind the tebah in 1840, and a new ner tamid that was donated as gift to the congregation in

Front elevation of Bevis Marks Synagogue, of congregation Sha'ar Hashamayim, in London, United Kingdom. Photo from the personal collection of Barry Stiefel, picture taken by Kathy and Gilbert Stiefel.

Interior of Bevis Marks Synagogue, of congregation Sha'ar Hashamayim, in London. Watercolor by I. M. Belisario, c. 1812. William A. Rosenthall Judaica Collection, Special Collections, College of Charleston Library.

1876. On the exterior a clock was installed in 1858, and the tile-hipped roof is now covered with slate. In 1929 electricity was wired into Bevis Marks to provide additional lighting. Historical threats to Bevis Marks include a fire in 1738, which caused damage to the roof and burned several adjoining buildings. In 1885 plans were made to demolish the synagogue and build a new edifice elsewhere because of rising property values. The Bevis Marks Anti-Demolition League was organized and successfully rallied to save the building. Another threat was the Nazi German bombing of London during World War II, called the Blitz. The synagogue was unharmed, but the congregational records, ritual silver, and chandeliers were sent away for safekeeping. In 1992 shockwaves from an IRA bombing near Bevis Marks (the target was the nearby Baltic Exchange) shattered the windows of the synagogue.[19]

Bevis Marks is a two-story building situated at the end of an alley. The façade is divided into three bays, with the main entrance in the central bay having segmental arched windows on the first floor, and Roman arched windows on the second. The trim for all window types has a keystone detail. Perched on the second story central bay window is a black clock with gold-colored Roman numerals on the face, dating from 1858. Visually separating the first and second floors is a white stringcourse. The main entrance has a classical-style surround capped by a segmental pediment. Within the frieze and architrave of the pediment are two signs, one with the name of the congregation in Hebrew (Sha'ar Hashamayim) and the other with the date the synagogue was built in the Hebrew and Gregorian calendars—5461 and 1701, respectively. Above the entrance is a sconce that provides the sole exterior source of illumination. On both sides of the entrance are wrought-iron foot wipers for cleaning shoes.

The Bevis Marks sanctuary has cream-colored plaster walls and flat ceiling, and stained wood furnishings. Clear leaded windows, seven large chandeliers, and several small sconces and candlesticks illuminate the room. Unlike the Esnoga, electricity has been installed in the sanctuary of Bevis Marks, but it complements the wax candles kindled on special occasions. Chandeliers hang from the ceiling by rods that terminate at ornamental rosettes. Running along the north, south, and west walls is the women's balcony, which is screened of by a grille. These balcony areas are supported on Tuscan columns, decorated with painted timber shafts. On the main floor are rows of wood benches that face north and south, typical of the open central aisle plan. The most prominent seating is the Banca platform along the north wall. Along the east wall is the oak hechal, which is decorated with Baroque detailing. The cabinet doors of the hechal have been painted to look like mahogany, and the columns and bases to imitate marble. Crowning the hechal is a lukhot with the Ten Commandments in gold block Hebrew letters. Also inscribed within the lukhot in Hebrew is the phrase "Know before whom thou stands" from Pirke Avot 3:1. The platform upon which the hechal stands is fenced off with an ornate wood balustrade. Six brass candlesticks are also attached to this. On the opposite side of the room, by the west wall, is the tebah. A balustrade, with twisted balusters, square posts, and molded rail detailing; encloses the rectangular tebah. Brass candlesticks are affixed to the four front posts, which illuminate the desktop. Six other posts have brass acorn-shaped ornaments.

Mikve Israel (III) | Willemstad, Curaçao

Built 1703
Years Extant 1703–30

The construction of the third Mikve Israel Synagogue was lead by Haham Eliau Lopez, who was very involved with the community. The synagogue was used until the congregation outgrew its capacity and was replaced by a newer one in 1732. The third synagogue was thus torn down to make room for the fourth in the same place. Some of the furnishings from the older synagogue also were transferred to the new one. No images or descriptions of this synagogue could be identified.[20]

Neve Shalom | Spanish Town, Jamaica

Built 1704
Years Extant 1704–1907

Front elevation of Neve Shalom Synagogue of Spanish Town, Jamaica, drawn from surviving historical photographs. Drawn by Lori H. Stiefel. Personal collection of the author.

Neve Shalom was the first synagogue built in Jamaica following the catastrophic 1692 earthquake that destroyed the synagogue in Port Royal. Built in 1704, Neve Shalom Synagogue was modeled off of London's Bevis Marks. Shielding the front entrance was a triangular pedimented portico. Based on surviving documentation, the interior of Neve Shalom had brass chandeliers and candle sconces similar in shape and style to Bevis Marks illuminated the synagogue. The hechal was made of mahogany with a damask curtain. On top of the hechal was a richly decorated centerpiece with a pediment, carved pilasters, and scrolls framing the lukhot. The tebah was a raised platform made of mahogany with a balustrade and on which a brass candlestick was placed at each corner. The banca was also made of matching mahogany.

During the 203 years that the Neve Shalom Synagogue stood, it most likely underwent a significant history of maintenance and alteration; however, the knowledge that survives about the building is scant. It was recorded that repairs were made to the synagogue in 1844 and 1863, both of which were partially funded by appropriation bills from the Jamaica House of Assembly. In 1900 Neve Shalom Synagogue was closed because of the small size of the congregation, and the ritual objects were sent to Shaar Ha Shamaim in Kingston. Seven years later an earthquake severely damaged Neve Shalom. In 1932 interest arose in restoring the decrepit synagogue but to no avail. Over the course of the twentieth century, the building collapsed into complete ruin. The site remained undisturbed until the 1990s, though the local inhabitants occasionally used it as a dumping ground for household garbage.

In 1997 Ainsley Cohen Henriques, chairman of the Jamaica National Heritage Trust, proposed that the Neve Shalom Synagogue site should be archaeologically studied and excavated. Coincidentally Henriques was an active member of Jamaica's Jewish community with ancestry residing on the island for a considerable period of time. The Neve Shalom Institute was also created at the time for the purpose of studying this synagogue ruin. Work began with participants from the Caribbean Volunteer Expeditions program. The Jamaican National Heritage Trust partnered with the University of the West Indies and the Archaeological Survey of Jamaica to conduct excavations in 1998–99, exposing the foundations of the Neve Shalom Synagogue. Members of the Spanish Town Historic Preservation Commission and District Steering Committee also took interest in the excavations taking place at the Neve Shalom Synagogue site. The materials that were recovered from the excavation were analyzed at the University of the West Indies and then transferred to the Jamaican National Heritage Trust for conservation and storage. A substantial quantity of the artifacts that were recovered dated from the eighteenth century, including smoking pipes, glass vessels, and ceramics, as well as artifacts dumped at the site from later periods. Conservation work was also performed at the Jewish cemetery in Spanish Town in conjunction with the project.[21]

Shaar Ha Shamaim (I) | Kingston, Jamaica

Built after 1704
Years Extant after 1704–44

A redrawing of a building depicted in the painting titled the *Spanish and Portuguese Synagogue,* purportedly the first synagogue in Kingston. The painting portrays a rectangular Georgian-style building from an oblique angle, revealing the north and west elevations. Drawn by E. Megan Funk.

Very little is known about this synagogue other than it was built after 1704 when Jews started settling in larger numbers in Kingston and that it was the first synagogue in the city, with the second having been built 1744–50 by the same congregation. There is a painting of the first Spanish and Portuguese Synagogue in Kingston; however, there are doubts as to whether or not the synagogue actually existed. By 1750 it is presumed that this first synagogue was demolished and had been replaced by a newer building. Many of the records pertaining to the Jews in Jamaica have been lost to hurricanes, fires, and earthquakes during the eighteenth, nineteenth, and early twentieth centuries, so research on these early synagogues is very difficult.[22] The building is one story, made of brick, and capped by a hipped roof and cornice. At each corner of the building are stone quoins. There are three bays on the west elevation and five on the north. The center bay for both elevations comprises an entrance instead of a window, and by appearance, the north elevation seems to be the front. The tall, full-story windows have an arched lintel and a keystone detail. An entablature and Doric pilasters frame the west elevation entrance. The north elevation entrance has an entablated portico supported at each front corner by Doric double columns.

Santa Irmandad | *Tucacas, Venezuela*

Built 1710s
Years Extant 1710s–20

At the end of the seventeenth century, the Dutch established a trading settlement on the Venezuelan coast. Among the Dutch colonists were Jews from Curaçao. The Jewish population was significant enough to establish a congregation, and it is reported that there was a synagogue there in 1720. In November 1720 the Spanish raided the settlement in order to eliminate Dutch encroachment but found the settlement already destroyed. The Dutch had received word of the impending Spanish invasion and decided to abandon it. Prior to their withdrawal, it is believed that the Dutch set fire to the town in order not to leave anything of use or benefit to the Spanish, and hence the loss of the synagogue. No images or descriptions of this synagogue could be identified.[23]

Neve Zedek (II) | *Port Royal, Jamaica*

Built c. 1719
Years Extant c. 1719–before 1816

It is recorded that a synagogue was rebuilt in Port Royal after the devastating earthquake of 1692. Since the building existed during the eighteenth century, it is believed that the synagogue was built after 1704, the year Port Royal was destroyed this time by fire. Port Royal was struck a second time by fire in 1815, and if the building was still extant in that year there is no record of it having survived. Following the fire of 1704, many of the inhabitants of Port Royal, including the Jews, relocated to the growing towns of Spanish Town and Kingston. Records pertaining to Jews in Jamaica have been lost to hurricanes, fires, and earthquakes during the eighteenth, nineteenth, and early twentieth centuries. No images or descriptions of this synagogue could be identified.[24]

Neve Shalom | *Paramaribo, Suriname*

Built 1719
Years Extant 1719–1835

Neve Shalom was built by master carpenter Abraham van Edam and completed in 1719. The building was made of wood and underwent a series of renovations, with the most significant one taking place in 1780, when it was enlarged to accommodate a total of two hundred seating places in the men's section. The Neve Shalom Synagogue was originally built as a satellite of the Berakha ve Shalom congregation in Jodensavanne. Shortly after its completion, conflict arose between the Sephardim and Ashkenazim in Paramaribo, which persisted for many years. The conflict was not resolved until 1735, when the Sephardic members of the community offered the building to the Ashkenazim. The Sephardim then took the money from the sale of the synagogue to build their own separate synagogue elsewhere in Paramaribo. However, the sale of the synagogue was made on the condition that the Ashkenazim remain attached to Berakha ve Shalom in Jodensavanne and maintain the Sephardic minhag already in use at the building. The Ashkenazim accepted the offer of the Sephardim, and the Sephardim built their new house of worship, called Zedek ve Shalom. When the c. 1719 building was replaced in 1835, the Sephardic-Ashkenazic hybrid was maintained. This building is still used by the Jewish community of Suriname today. Brass fixtures and wood furniture from the 1719 synagogue were also reused in the second Neve Shalom Synagogue that was built in 1835. In the 1990s synagogue membership at both buildings in Paramaribo had dwindled so significantly that the two decided to reunite after more than 260 years of separation. The 1835 Neve Shalom building is the one used by Suriname's Jewish community. No images or descriptions of the c. 1719 synagogue could be identified.[25]

Shearith Israel (I) | *New York, New York, USA*

Built 1730
Years Extant 1730–1818

The thumbnail sketch of Shearith Israel Synagogue (I), built in 1730, from *A Plan of the City and Environs of New York*, by David Grim, 1813. William A. Rosenthall Judaica Collection, Special Collections, College of Charleston Library.

In 1730 congregation Shearith Israel contracted with Stanley Holmes to build the first synagogue in North America. Holmes built the synagogue thirty-five feet long by thirty-five feet wide, and twenty-one feet in height with hewn stone, with the flooring using square Bristol stones.[26] Within the congregation's Minute Book is record that slaves were used on several occasions to build the synagogue.[27] Historic images of the Shearith Israel Synagogue reveal that the building was one story, made of stone, with three bays, and had a hipped roof. The middle bay was the front entrance, and it and the two flanking windows were arched. In the following years, a spring-fed mikveh

The "Little Synagogue" at Shearith Israel (V), built in 1895, with its collection
of authentic period furnishings arranged as they may have been in the eighteenth
century. Photo from the personal collection of Barry Stiefel, picture taken by
Lori H. Stiefel.

outbuilding, school building, and housing for the chazzan were built on the
property. Numerous references and descriptions of the synagogue were made
over the course of the eighteenth century; however, the most detailed description found was that by Lieutenant Isaac Bangs written in his journal on
8 June 1776, at the onset of the American Revolution:

> This Day being the Jewish Sabbath, I went into the City in the After-
> noon with Insign Bryant to observe the Method of the Jewish Wor-
> ship. The Synagogue is a small Square Building, having a Gallery all
> around, though no Person sat therein. At the Heith of the lower Part
> of the Gallery in the corners are 4 Candlesticks of Brass hanging from
> the Roof, each having 16 Candles of Wax; in the Centre of these is
> another, having twice that Number. At the East End of the Synagogue
> is a large Closet, which serves as a repository for the Law and (I sup-
> pose) other holy things. This is encompassed with Banisters, and the
> Ascent thereto is by 3 or 4 Steps. Upon the Corner Posts of the Banis-
> ters are standing large Brass Candle Sticks, about 1 Feet long, & pro-
> portional in Magnitude. In these are Wax Candles of about 4 Inches
> Diameter and about 3 Feet Long. In the Middle of the Synagogue

is the Rostrum or Pulpit looking to the Repository, to which the Ascent is by 3 Steps. On this is a large Table covered with Red Tapestry, fringed with Silver Lace. On each Corner of this also is a Candlestick and Candle like the Former. None of the Candles are alight in the day Time, but a Glass Lamp hangs from the Roof, facing the Repository, which is kept constantly burning both night & Day. The Priest was a handsome Young Man of about 25, dressed in a black Gown, such as is worn by Bachelors of Arts. When he entered the Synagogue, he first walked to the Repository and unlocked the Door, then came down & went into the Rostrum & began to read, or what we should call sing, and soon after the People all joined with him, tho they did not observe good Time in their singing (as I then thought it to be, tho afterwards I was informed it was the proper way of their Reading). Sometimes this singing would alter into jabbering, & the Priest would mutter his Hebrew much faster than I could read or speak English. This was done all sitting. Afterwards the Priest arose, and stood still singing with his Eyes fixed on the Repository of the Law, and leaning on the Table in the Rostrum; in about a Minute he went out of the Rostrum, & several others followed him to the Repository, & one of them brought out the law written on a Roll of Parchment. At each end of the Roll was a Stick or Staff, over which the Law Rolled in two Rolls. On the Top of the Sticks were a great Number of small Silver Bells, & over the Bells a Silver Crown. They carried the Law into the Rostrum, when they Pawwayed a little Time over it; then the Priest took it, & opening it, he lifted it up by the two sticks and turned it around to all the People, at the sight of which they all Bawled out again. After much Ceremony, the Law was carried back again; the Priest, both in taking out the Law, in carrying it back, continued singing. After this they Prayed, all standing, faced eastward with their Eyes cast upward, &c., &c., which I cant remember, & then all dispersed, except a Few whom we left behind. It is worthy of observation that during the whole Ceremony, even in Praying, none took off their Hats, but sat and stood with them on.[28]

In 1785 new windows had to be installed because of the deteriorated state of the originals. The previously mentioned outbuildings were also in dilapidated condition, with some repairs made, but eventually they had to be taken down. The synagogue was used until 1818, when it was replaced by a newer and larger building in the same location.

Within the current Shearith Israel Synagogue (V), the congregation set aside a small room as a chapel for daily worship. This is a common practice within many synagogues as a practical measure. The larger, main sanctuary is usually used only on Shabbat and holidays, when attendance is typically higher. However, what is unique about the chapel, called the Little Synagogue, is that the room was furnished in the style of the first building from 1730 and with many of the original artifacts, as well as a few remnants from the 1818 synagogue. This colonial interior rendition was developed from surviving historic descriptions. The current building dates from 1897 and was designed by American Jewish architect Arnold Brunner in the neoclassical style when the congregation moved to Seventieth Street and Central Park West, making it their fifth house of worship. Louis Comfort Tiffany designed the building's interior and stained glass windows, and it is considered to be one of his finest masterpieces. The building is a significant historical and architectural landmark within the City of New York.

The Little Synagogue measures thirty-one by twenty-four feet, which is very close in size to the original 1730 interior. The walls are painted white with gold trim, and a sky-blue ceiling in keeping with the colonial atmosphere that once decorated the first synagogue in North America. The tebah in the center of the room is the original one from 1730, and it is covered with a replica crimson silk-damask cloth. The railing and spindles around the tebah are also original. Attached to the railing are the original brass candlesticks that were used in the 1730 synagogue; however, these candlesticks are believed to date from the fifteenth century, before the first synagogue was built. The brass Hanukkah Menorah was also made in the Netherlands before 1730. The hechal is not historic, but the lukhot on top is from the 1730 synagogue. Within the hechal are stored Torah scrolls that were used by the congregation during the eighteenth century with original silver rimonim. Colonial-era congregant and silversmith Myer Myers designed two sets of Shearith Israel's rimonim. Two of Shearith Israel's Torah scrolls were sacrilegiously damaged by British troops during the American Revolution and to this day still bear the scars as a testament to this history.

The interior of the hechal is also lined with replica crimson silk-damask just as it was during the eighteenth century. In front of the hechal hangs the ner tamid from the 1818 synagogue. On the opposite side of the room from the hechal, in front of the west window, hangs the Sabbath Lamp of the Seven Wicks from the 1730 synagogue. Along the side of the room there are three mahogany pews that date from 1730. An antique Rosh Chodesh tablet and Omer board are also found in the room, both of which were used for keeping track of the Jewish calendar and holidays. Furnishings from later periods include additional pews, ceiling lamps, and candlesticks. Many of these furnishings are from the 1834 synagogue on Crosby Street.

Mikve Israel (IV), Snoa | Willemstad, Curaçao

Built 1730–32
Years Extant 1732–present

Mikve Israel Synagogue, also known as the Snoa, built in 1732 and designed by Hendrik Schielach. Photo from the personal collection of Barry Stiefel, picture taken by Lori H. Stiefel.

The fourth Mikve Israel Synagogue, more commonly known as the Snoa, was completed in 1732. The architect-builder was Hendrik Schielach, who was brought to Curaçao from the Netherlands specifically to build the edifice and it remains as the oldest surviving synagogue in the Americas. Because of its age, there is a substantial amount of history associated with it. The building has undergone some changes over the centuries, but it retains a high level of its historic character and integrity. Many of these changes have also acquired historic significance over the years.

Major historical events in the history of the congregation after the Snoa's completion started with the construction of a second building in 1746, called Neve Shalom. The Neve Shalom building served as a satellite to the congregation in another neighborhood of Willemstad until 1818 when membership in that area declined sufficiently to warrant its closure. In 1750 conflict arose within the congregation that was so disruptive that it affected commerce on Curaçao. Its resolution did not come about until Prince William Charles

The interior of the Snoa, looking toward the tebah, built in 1732 and designed by Hendrik Schielach. Photo from the personal collection of Barry Stiefel, picture taken by Lori H. Stiefel.

Henry Friso personally intervened and concluded the discrepancies with an edict. Beginning in 1839 conflict again divided the congregation between different parties that wanted reforms within religious ritual. In 1864 the reformers broke with Mikve Israel and formed a separate Reform congregation, called Emanuel, named after New York's Reform congregation on which it was modeled. Temple Emanuel was also built later that year. By the 1960s membership at both Mikve Israel and Emanuel had shrunk considerably and the issues that had divided the community a century earlier were no longer important. In 1964 the two congregations reunited and are now known as congregation Mikve Israel—Emanuel. A compromise was made that the congregation would follow the Reconstructionist movement within Judaism. Temple Emanuel was sold in 1989, and the merged congregation uses the Snoa building.

Despite the long history of the Snoa, the preservation of its heritage has been a relatively recent phenomenon compared to the other synagogues. This is not to say that the building was neglected. The building is adored by its congregation and has been well maintained over the centuries with no significant instances of man-made threats having been recorded. In a certain sense, the lack of a lengthy, controversial history over its preservation is a testament to the high degree that the congregation has appreciated the historic resource that is their inheritance. To a certain degree, the non-Jewish citizens of Curaçao are aware of the historic significance of the Snoa for it is a recognized landmark within the cultural landscape of the island. Historic preservation at the Snoa officially began in 1970, with the establishment of the Jewish Cultural Historical Museum in a restored building from the eighteenth century within the synagogue complex. This museum is currently open to the public and exhibits the long history and artifacts collected over the centuries by the congregation. In 1974 the Snoa underwent a long-overdue restoration that included a historical study of the building's development.

Not only was the Snoa in better condition following the project, but a greater understanding and appreciation was also achieved.

In 1982 the Netherlands Antilles government honored the Snoa on a postage stamp and festivities were also conducted in 1992 remembering the five hundredth anniversary of the Spanish expulsion. This event included the attendance of the Dutch royal family, which was commemorated on a special plaque. In 1995 the Snoa received official recognition as a National Monument. This was reiterated in 1997 when the historic center of Willemstad was placed on the UNESCO World Heritage List, for the Snoa was listed as a contributing building within the nomination. Presently the Snoa is a popular point of interest for tourists that visit the island from all over the world.

The Snoa measures approximately eighty feet in length, sixty feet in width, and fifty feet in height. A wall encloses a courtyard around the synagogue and encircles the periphery of the property. The entire exterior is covered by yellow-painted stucco with white trim accents. This scheme is typical of building traditions and workmanship in Curaçao and other areas of the Caribbean region. The east and west elevations nearly mirror each other in appearance, as do the north and south elevations. All four elevations are divided into three bays by classical style pilasters that encapsulate rainwater downspouts. Within each bay are sub-bays of identical styled windows. A glazed fanlight crowns each of the windows. Also on the south elevation is a staircase to the women's balcony. On top of the building is a clay tile roof with three gables that correspond to the three vaults on the interior. Along the east and west elevations are ornamental Dutch gable ends that characterize the style of the synagogue. The east elevation is the primary visual façade; however, it is the portal at the southwest corner on the rear elevation where the main entrance for public access is located.

Across the lintel on the east façade courtyard wall of the central portal is a wood plaque with the following verse from Deuteronomy 28:6 inscribed in Hebrew: "Blessed will you be when you come in"; on the inside of the same portal the second half of this verse, there is another wood plaque with brass letters that says: "and blessed will you be when you go out." On the west elevation of the Snoa inscribed in Hebrew on a plaque across the lintel is: "May

God enlarge Jafeth and may he dwell in the tents of Shem." According to the tradition at the Snoa, this statement has multiple significances. The letters in the word "Jafeth" have a mark above them, which indicates that they should also be interpreted as Hebrew numbers for a specific date, with the value corresponding to 490. In Jewish tradition the first number corresponding to the number of millennia, is often left out of an inscription because it is assumed. In this instance the missing number is "5," from the Hebrew calendar date of 5490. The Hebrew calendar year 5490 corresponds to 1730, which was the year the synagogue was built.

Like the Esnoga in Amsterdam, the Snoa too has a barrel-vaulted ceiling that spans over the aisles as well four massive, central columns that support the roof. It is possibly not a coincidence that this "daughter" synagogue of the Esnoga chose the Doric order for these columns, as they are one order lower than the Ionic ones in Amsterdam. Unique to the Snoa is that these four columns of the matriarchs are labeled in Hebrew block letters Sarah, Rebecca, Leah, and Rachel. The hechal within the Snoa, like the other synagogues, is also positioned in the middle of the eastern wall toward Jerusalem. Hanging from the ceiling are four large, triple-tiered, twenty-four-branch brass chandeliers that date from the first three decades of the eighteenth century—some originally having been used in the previous 1703 synagogue building. Joining the chandeliers in illuminating the interior are twenty-three brass wall sconces. Each chandelier branch and sconce end has a glass hurricane shade on top of a drip dish.

Made from richly carved red mahogany, the hechal is crowned by a lighter colored mahogany lukhot, which is inlaid by silver block Hebrew lettering listing the Ten Commandments. Below this is the cabinet section that contains the Torah scrolls. The cabinet section is covered by paneled doors, which are divided into bays with Doric pilasters. Hanging in front of the central bays from the top of the hechal is the brass ner tamid. The entire hechal rests on a mahogany platform, which is enclosed by a balustrade. At the corners of the balustrade are brass candlesticks, and in the center section are brass ornaments. In front of the west entrance to the sanctuary is the tebah, also made of dark red mahogany and carved Dutch Baroque detailing. A balustrade encloses the table on top of the platform. At the head of the tebah is the chair reserved for the hacham, which dates from 1858. At each corner of the table are silver ball ornaments, and at the four corners of the tebah are affixed tall brass candlesticks to the balustrade in a similar fashion as found at the Esnoga in Amsterdam.

Running along the north and south walls of the sanctuary, framing the open central aisle, are mahogany benches and chairs. Several different types appear representing different periods of style of the synagogue's history. The most prominent seating is the banca on the north wall. Covering the concrete floor throughout the synagogue is white sand. Originally wood was used beneath the sand, but after centuries of wear and tear it was replaced in 1965. Above the main floor seating area is the upper level balcony. In 1964 the congregation became Reconstructionist, and seating between men and women was integrated. Originally balconies were only on the north and south walls, but a third one was added onto the west wall in 1866 in order to accommodate a choir area and pipe organ. The mahogany organ is also ornately decorated.[29]

Zedek ve Shalom | Paramaribo, Suriname

Built 1735
Years Extant 1735–present

The front elevation of Zedek ve Shalom Synagogue, Paramaribo, Suriname, built in 1735. Photo from the personal collection of Barry Stiefel, picture taken by Lori H. Stiefel.

Zedek ve Shalom Synagogue was built by the Sephardim in Paramaribo following the mutually agreed on split with the Ashkenazim who stayed in the Neve Shalom Synagogue that they purchased. Just like Neve Shalom, Zedek ve Shalom was also a satellite building for Berakha ve Shalom in Jodensavanne; however, as the Jewish population shifted from Jodensavanne to Paramaribo over the course of the eighteenth century, Zedek ve Shalom rose in prominence. After the fire of 1832 that burned Jodensavanne, the Berakha ve Shalom Synagogue was abandoned, and Zedek ve Shalom became the sole Sephardic synagogue in Surinam. The building's layout is modeled after the Esnoga, though the Zedek ve Shalom Synagogue is much smaller and originally had no women's balcony. After the synagogue's completion in 1735, it was altered in 1754, 1774–77, 1788–91, and 1854. The women's balcony was added to the interior in 1813.

The interior of Zedek ve Shalom Synagogue exhibit at the Israel Museum, Jerusalem, Israel. Israel Museum and Elie Posner, photographer, with special thanks to Tania Coen Uzzielli.

During the early 1970s, renowned Dutch architectural historian Temminck Groll conducted an extensive study on Suriname's historic architecture, which included drawings of Zedek ve Shalom, Neve Shalom, and the ruins at Jodensavanne. Prior to 1999 Zedek ve Shalom was a functional synagogue used by Suriname's Jewish community. Because of the shrinking size of the Jewish community and its decreasing ability to maintain two historic synagogue buildings, arrangements were made with the Israel Museum in Jerusalem to lend the interior eighteenth century furnishings for exhibit as a period room. As part of the arrangement, the Israel Museum documented the synagogue and took on the responsibility of providing material conservation work on the interior furnishings in order to ensure their longevity.

The empty Zedek ve Shalom Synagogue is presently lent out to a computer store. While not considered an ideal reuse of the building, the installation of the store has had only a small impact on the historic fabric of the synagogue. In fact its daily use provides a certain element of protection from the elements, including the constant battle with termites that would otherwise devour the wood building if left unattended. The rent collected by the Surinamese Jewish community from leasing Zedek ve Shalom is also a source of income for the impoverished community. Much of the money is used to maintain the Neve Shalom Synagogue (1835) that the community uses for worship.

Zedek ve Shalom Synagogue is a one-story, hipped-roof building with white clapboard siding. The entire building rests on a brick foundation, which appears to mirror the Berakha ve Shalom foundation ruin in Jodensavanne. The north and south elevations are nearly identical to each other, with both defined by seven bays with the central bay as the primary entrance. At the entrances on the north and south elevations are black-and-white paneled double doors with casing and crown trim. Above the entrance is a decorative fanlight. The same fanlight also appears over the casement windows throughout the exterior of the building. In front of the north and south entrances is a front step that is decorated with marble, stone, tile, and brick. On the west elevation, there are three secondary entrances as well as two bays of windows. Only the central secondary entrance and the windows have an ornamental fanlight. On the east elevation there are two bays of windows as well as two floating transom lights. This is because the hechal is located on the inside of this wall elevation.

The Zedek ve Shalom exhibit in Israel mirrors what the interior looked like in Suriname as a reconstructed period room. According to the Israel Musesum, Zedek ve Shalom had a wooden rectangular interior defined by high vaulted ceilings, and a nave and two lateral aisles divided by two rows of columns. The hechal, on the eastern wall, was made of cedar and mahogany, with the tebah made of similar materials on the opposite side of the room. Against the north wall was the banca for the congregation's officials, and regular benches for the rest of the congregation along the north and south walls. The balcony addition was built only on the western end. The wood floor was covered with sand according to Jewish Caribbean tradition.[30]

Honen Dalim | Oranjestad, St. Eustatius

Built 1739
Years Extant 1739–after 1800

Honen Dalim Synagogue was built in 1739 and is recorded as having undergone significant restoration work in 1772 following hurricane damage. In 1781 Admiral George Rodney invaded St. Eustatius to end the illicit weapons trade that was taking place between the island and the thirteen rebelling British North American colonies. Many of the Jews on St. Eustatius were involved in the trade, and the community was disproportionately singled out among the rest of the island's population, resulting in expulsion of many of the men from St. Eustatius. After the conclusion of the American Revolution with the Treaty of Paris, St. Eustatius was returned to the Netherlands, and the Jews that had been deported were allowed to return. The British and French invaded St. Eustatius on several other occasions during the Napoleonic Wars until 1816, when it was permanently restored to the Netherlands. Because of the constant strife and administrative mismanagement by the French and British, St. Eustatius's economy suffered, and many left for

The ruins of Honen Dalim Synagogue, built in 1739. Photo from the personal collection of Barry Stiefel, picture taken by Lori H. Stiefel.

elsewhere. It is believed that the Jewish community had all but disappeared shortly after 1800, and thus the synagogue fell into ruin.

From the nineteenth century, Honen Dalim sat undocumented and in a ruinous state. Official interest in the site began again in 1966 when Dutch architectural historian Temminck Groll acknowledged the synagogue as one of the more significant sites in the historic core of Oranjestad and recommended it for restoration. Unfortunately not until 1983 did a team from the College of the William and Mary in Virginia undertake archeological investigations inside the ruins of Honen Dalim. This team of archaeologists found the synagogue roofless, with four badly deteriorated walls, and exterior brick stairs to the women's balcony on the second floor. Excavations resumed in 2004 by the St. Eustatius Center for Archaeological Research (SECAR) and uncovered the Jewish ritual bath, or mikveh, as well as architectural evidence that revealed details about the synagogue's original configuration.

Not much is left of Honen Dalim Synagogue, but as a ruin it is the most intact compared to the other Atlantic World synagogue archaeological sites. Unfortunately no known descriptions or images exist of Honen Dalim Synagogue from its original state. Based on archaeological evidence, it can be determined that it was a two-story, rectangular brick building. The exterior dimensions are forty feet long and twenty-six feet wide. The brick walls are nearly two feet thick. There were a total of twenty-five windows for the first and second stories, which were arranged into three bays on the west elevation, two bays on the east elevation, and four bays on the north and south elevations. The first-floor entrance was located in the center bay of the west elevation. On the northwest corner of the building are the remnants of a brick stairway that lead to the second-floor women's balcony. The corners exhibit ashlar quoins, and the window and portal openings are finished with locally worked volcanic basalt with arched lintels. On some of the windows are remnants of iron hardware that was used to attach wood shutters. The ruins of a mikveh were also uncovered near the synagogue. Based on archaeological excavations, it has been surmised that the interior of Honen Dalim primarily consisted of wood and plaster. Deposits of sand were also found, indicating that sand once covered the wood floor. Indentations on the eastern wall and in the adjacent floor were uncovered, as well as the lack of a third central bay for the eastern wall indicate the placement and approximate size of the hechal. Within the interior walls are joist holes from where supports were attached to hold the women's second floor balcony. Pieces of brass lighting hardware, possibly from chandeliers, sconces, or even the ner tamid, were also found during the excavations.[31]

Shaar Ha Shamaim (II) | Kingston, Jamaica

Built 1744–50
Years Extant 1744–1882

A historic illustration of the Shaar Ha Shamaim Synagogue (II) following the Great Fire of Kingston in 1882, which destroyed it. From the *Illustrated London News*, 20 January 1883, William A. Rosenthall Judaica Collection, Special Collections, College of Charleston Library.

The second Shaar Ha Shamaim Synagogue was built in 1744 for Kingston's growing Jewish community. Much information was lost on the history of this synagogue. It was destroyed during the Great Fire of Kingston in 1882, which incinerated much of the town as well as the congregation's records from prior to 1809. Based on surviving records, it is known that the synagogue underwent some repairs in 1839, which were partially financed by the House of Assembly of Jamaica. Additional repairs were made in 1878. Following the fire of 1882, a new synagogue was built in 1884 that was destroyed by an earthquake in 1907.

The second Shaar Ha Shamaim Synagogue no longer exists; however, a description survives from *The Handbook of Jamaica*, printed in 1882.

> The synagogue occupied a space of ground fronting west on Princess Street . . . it was capable of seating five hundred persons. It was built of bricks and stone . . . its beautiful cupola being a modern addition. . . .
>
> The gallery for ladies, of rich old mahogany, the entrance to which was a flight of granite steps on the east side, ran round three sides of the building. The fourth side was occupied by the Echal (or Ark) the receptacle of the Sacred Scrolls of the Law. The Echal was one if the finest specimens of art on the island. The interior was lit by seven large brass lamps suspended from the ceiling, each lamp bearing the name of its donor engraved around (its base). Rich crimson carpets covered the floor of the Tebah as well as the raised platform on which the Echal was placed. The ladies gallery was supported on pillars which were painted to represent marble.[32]

Neve Shalom | Willemstad, Curaçao

Built 1746

Years Extant 1746–after 1864

In the early 1730s, Jews began to settle in the Otrobanda neighborhood of Willemstad, which was too far away for them to attend the Snoa in the city center. In response a branch of the Mikve Israel congregation was established to attend to the needs of the Jews living in Otrobanda, called Neve Shalom. In 1746 a synagogue was built whereas prior they had used space in the houses of its members. By the early nineteenth century, the Jewish population in Otrobanda had significantly declined, and in 1818 the Neve Shalom Synagogue was closed. In 1864 the building was sold to raise funds for the organ that was installed in the Snoa, and Neve Shalom was eventually lost. No images or descriptions of this synagogue could be identified.[33]

Shaar Hashamayim (I) | Gibraltar, United Kingdom

Built 1749
Years Extant 1749–66

Founded in 1749 by Haham Isaac Neito and built shortly after, the congregation's first synagogue was heavily damaged by a storm in 1766 and rebuilt two years later. No images or descriptions of this synagogue could be identified.[34]

Jeshuat Israel, Touro Synagogue | Newport, Rhode Island, USA

Built 1759–63
Years Extant 1763–present

The front elevation of Touro Synagogue, built 1759–63. Photo from the personal collection of Barry Stiefel, picture taken by Lori H. Stiefel.

Work began on Jeshuat Israel in 1759; however, its completion was delayed by the French and Indian War and was not completed until 1763. The architect for the synagogue was Peter Harrison, with Joseph Hammond working as the builder and Naphtali Hart & Company assisting with financing the purchasing of supplies. Construction for the synagogue was £2,000 sterling with another £1,500 for the land. According to purchase records from 25 August 1760; 196,715 bricks were bought to construct the synagogue in addition to brown sandstone. The building epitomizes the Georgian style and

The interior of Touro Synagogue from the vantage point of the women's balcony, looking down on the tebah and west entrance. Photo from the personal collection of Barry Stiefel, picture taken by Lori H. Stiefel.

is considered one of the best examples of North America's first professional architect. Based on architectural studies of the synagogue, it is believed that Harrison may have used the architectural pattern books of *Rules for Drawing* by James Gibbs (1739 edition), *A Treasury of Design* by Batty Langley (1740 edition), and *Designs of Inigo Jones and Others* by Isaac Ware (1735 edition).

During the American Revolution, the British captured Newport and destroyed much of the town. Being a brick structure, Jeshuat Israel was one of few buildings that survived. Following the war the synagogue briefly housed the Rhode Island legislature and the state supreme court. It was during this period (1781 and 1790) that George Washington visited Newport and the synagogue (he is presumed to have visited in 1790, though documentation is unclear if he entered the building a second time). The 1790 visit coincided with a letter on freedom of religion by Washington, where he stated: "the Government of the United States, which gives to bigotry no sanction, to persecution no assistance, requires only that they who live under its protection should demean themselves as good citizens in giving it on all occasions their effectual support."[35]

At the beginning of the nineteenth century, Newport's economy fell into substantial hard times and many of its inhabitants relocated elsewhere, including its Jews. Jeshuat Israel was officially closed by 1822 and the congregation's six Torahs as well as ownership of the synagogue were transferred to New York's Shearith Israel. This was done so that Shearith Israel could oversee the safeguarding of the building until the synagogue could be reopened. Abraham (1774–1822) and Judah Touro (1775–1854) also participated in this effort. Their father, Isaac Touro (1738–83), had served as Jeshuat Israel's first chazzan. In 1822 Abraham Touro of Boston paid for a brick wall around the cemetery and a caretaker and also bequeathed $10,000 to the congregation. Rhode Island's General Assembly and Newport's town council oversaw this trust. Two years later, in commemoration of Abraham's bequest to repair Griffin Street (on which both the synagogue and cemetery were located), the town changed its name and the synagogue's to "Touro." Extensive restoration work and maintenance were later performed on Touro Synagogue in 1827–29. Newport's town council also used a portion of Abraham's trust in the 1840s to erect a granite wall around the synagogue in order to provide some security. For most of the nineteenth century, tourists used Touro Synagogue on various occasions. During the early 1880s, an influx of Ashkenazi immigrants settled in Newport, and the synagogue was reconsecrated in 1883 under Shearith Israel's supervision, maintaining the Sephardic minhag of the synagogue.

In 1946 Touro became the first synagogue designated a National Historic Site by the U.S. government through the Historic Sites Act of 1935. The nomination for Touro Synagogue was largely owing to the efforts of Arthur Hays Sulzberger (1891–1968). Sulzbeger published newspapers and was president of the *New York Times* between 1935 and 1961 and used his influence to urge Secretary of the Interior Harold Ickes (in the Roosevelt administration) to recognize Touro Synagogue in addition to other historic houses of worship in the original thirteen colonies. A nonsectarian organization, now called the Touro Synagogue Foundation, was also created to help support the maintenance of the building.

Touro Synagogue has undergone several restoration projects since its designation in 1946 to improve the condition and integrity of the building for congregants and visitors alike. The Touro Synagogue Foundation has sponsored these projects and the National Park Service has consulted on proper preservation practices and methods. For example a major restoration was completed in 1963. In 2003 a federal grant of $375,000 was given to the Touro Synagogue Foundation for additional work, which was completed in 2006. Subsequently the National Trust for Historic Preservation added Touro to its list of Historic Sites.[36]

Touro Synagogue comprises two volumes, the sanctuary and the school wing. The entire building sits on a brown sandstone foundation. The walls are made of structural-supporting English red brick (presently painted a cream color), and there is an ornamental brown sandstone belt course. A steep, hipped roof supports slate shingles. The synagogue's main entrance is defined by an Ionic-columned portico (painted a sandstone color), which stands on a sandstone pad. Paneled double doors open into the sanctuary. Above the doors is a wood fan with a carved sunburst pattern. Many of the windows of the synagogue are double hung with compass heads and a twelve-over-twelve sash pattern. Beneath each window is a sandstone sill. On the front elevation of the school wing is a secondary entrance that is of the same sandstone color. It is decorated with an ornate architrave and pediment.

Touro Synagogue is special among the synagogues of the Atlantic World because it is in a pristine state of condition. However, what one sees at the site today is the c. 1780–90s appearance and not its original look from 1763. The highly visible rows of Windsor chairs and carpeting to protect the wood floors from scratching by the Windsor chairs and foot traffic were added during the twentieth century. The 1780–90s dates for the period of significance were chosen because it coincides with visits George Washington made to the synagogue. At that time the interior of the synagogue had been painted according to the color scheme that is presently visible. Originally, it is believed that the wood surfaces of the interior were stained in a similar shade to Bevis Marks in London or Esnoga in Amsterdam. Ezra Stiles recorded the following description in 1763 on the occasion of the synagogue's dedication.

> The Synagogue is about perhaps forty foot long and 30 wide, of Brick on a Foundation of Free Stone; it was begun about two years ago, and is now finished except the Porch and the Capitals of the Pillars. The Front representation of the holy of holies, or its Partition Veil, consists only of wainscoted Breast Work on the East End, in the lower part of which four long Doors cover an upright Square Closet the depth of which is about a foot long or the thickness of the Wall, and in this Apartment (vulgarly called the Ark) were deposited three copies and Rolls of Pentateuch, written on Vellum or rather tanned Calf Skin. . . . A Gallery for the Women runs around the whole Inside, except the East End, supported by Columns of Ionic order, over which are placed correspondent columns of the Corinthian order supporting the Ceiling of the Roof, the Depth of the Corinthian Pedestal is the height of the Balustrade which runs around the Gallery. The pulpit for Reading of the Law is a raised Pew with an extended front table; this placed about the center of the Synagogue or nearer the West End being a square embalustraded comparting with the length of the Indented Chancel before and at the Foot of the Ark. On the middle of the North Side and Affixed to the Wall is a raised Seat for the Parnas or Ruler, and for the Elders; the Breast and Back interlaid with Chinese Mosaic Work. A Wainscoted Seat runs around the Side of the Synagogue below and another in the Gallery. There

are no other Seats or Pews. There may be Eighty Souls of Jews or 15 miles families now in Town. The Synagogue has already cost Fifteen Hundred Pounds Sterling. There are to be five Lamps pendant from a lofty Ceiling.[37]

Unknown | St. Croix, Virgin Islands, USA

Built 1764
Years Extant 1764–65

It was recorded that a synagogue was built in the Danish colony of St. Croix in 1764 and that the following year a fire destroyed it and that it was never replaced. No images or descriptions of this synagogue could be identified.[38]

Shaar Hashamayim (II) | Gibraltar, United Kingdom

Built 1768
Years Extant 1768–81

The second Shaar Hashamayim Synagogue was built in 1768 after the first had been destroyed by a storm two years earlier. In 1781 the synagogue was destroyed during the Great Siege of 1779–83, which was an attempt by Spain to retake the peninsula during the American Revolution. Much of the British settlement was also destroyed by the siege. No images or descriptions of this synagogue could be identified.[39]

Shearith Israel | Montreal, Quebec, Canada

Built 1777–1778
Years Extant 1777–1824

Shearith Israel was founded by members of Ashkenazic origin but chose to follow the Sephardic minhag because they thought it would prove beneficial for their Jewish-mercantile relations (which it did). The synagogue was built during the American Revolution and is believed to have been a one- or one-and-a-half-story stone building, with a high red roof, and a whitewashed wall (or fence) surrounding it.[40] The congregation was also the first non-Catholic in Quebec, besides being the first Jewish.[41] The synagogue was used until 1824 when it was torn down. A second building was constructed in 1838. No images or descriptions of this synagogue could be identified.

Darkhe Yesharim | Paramaribo, Suriname

Built 1779
Years Extant 1779–1800

In 1779 the Sephardic Jews in Jodensavanne assisted the members of Darkhe Yesharim, who were of African and Jewish decent, in the construction of a synagogue in Paramaribo. At this synagogue they officiated over their own rituals without restrictions under the condition that the group remain affiliated as a satellite facility of Berakha ve Shalom and not form their own community. Darkhe Yesharim was the first and only known instance in the Atlantic World where a synagogue was built for ex-African slaves and Judeo-mulattos. The synagogue was torn down in 1800. No images or descriptions of this synagogue could be identified.[42]

Shaar Hashamayim (III), Great Synagogue of Gibraltar | Gibraltar, United Kingdom

Built 1781–1783
Years Extant 1783–present

Exterior of the Great Synagogue of Gibraltar. Drawing by Lori H. Stiefel.

The third Shaar Hashamayim Synagogue, also called the Great Synagogue of Gibraltar, is the primary synagogue in Gibraltar. It was rebuilt in 1781–83 after the destruction of the previous building during the Great Siege. However, what is seen today dates from an 1812 renovation of the building that significantly altered the design. In fact there is a keystone over the main entrance as a marker to this renovation project with Hebrew year of 5572, which corresponds to 1812. Additional alterations were made to the building over the course of the nineteenth and twentieth centuries, but these have not had a substantial affect on the integrity and historic character from 1812.

Hechal of the Great Synagogue of Gibraltar, United Kingdom. Photo from the personal collection of Barry Stiefel, picture taken by Lori H. Stiefel.

The Great Synagogue of Gibraltar is set along a narrow street and is accessed through a front courtyard. The synagogue is a two-story building with a gabled roof covered by cement tiles. Within the front pediment of the roof are a Star of David and an inscription date of 5528. This date corresponds with 1768, the year the prior synagogue building was completed, which was destroyed during the Great Siege. The front elevation is divided into three bays with a belt course visually dividing the first and second stories. The front entrance is situated within the first floor central bay and is accessed at the top of a marble front step through a wood double door. Surrounding the door is a paneled arched architrave trim with a keystone at the peak. Along the exterior wall, which continues around part of the courtyard enclosure, is an ornate tile dado with a yellow-and-blue floral pattern. The arched casement windows on this elevation are framed by an arched label mold. In the right corner of the courtyard beside the synagogue is a stairway that leads to the second floor women's balcony.

Unique to the Great Synagogue of Gibraltar's ceiling is its division into nine vaulted sections, called bays. From the center of the central row of bays are suspended the largest of many different types of silver chandeliers that illuminate the sanctuary. The largest of the chandeliers hang from chains that are connected at the ceiling with ornamental rosettes. Many of the smaller lamps date from a later period and are Moorish in style, reflecting the influence of congregants from Morocco who came from the other side of the Straits, though there were a handful that are Georgian.

The mahogany hechal on the eastern wall of the sanctuary, facing toward Jerusalem, screams of its Georgian origins through the very prominent broken pediment that frames the top. Within the broken space is placed the lukhot with a crown, representing the "Crown of the Torah." Other carved Georgian and Jewish details decorate the rest of the hechal. The hechal is on top of a duchan platform that is enclosed by an ornately carved balustrade. A Victorian-era amud was also added in the nineteenth century. In front of the hechal hang three ner tamidim. In the central-western part of the room is the tebah on top of a platform, which is enclosed by an ornately carved mahogany balustrade. At the corners of the tebah are silver candlesticks attached to the balustrade. The open central aisle of the sanctuary has been in-filled with additional benches from 1882, with the original seating along the north and south walls facing toward the center, as is typical of this synagogue plan. The seating in these areas are also of carved wood, and multiple styles are represented, testifying to the continued use of the synagogue since its 1812 renovations. The Banca is also located along the north wall. Behind the tebah is an enclosed vestibule made of carved wood and frosted glass. Above the main floor seating area is the women's balcony along the north, west, and south walls that are screened off by a paneled balustrade for the ezrat nashim.[43]

Mikveh Israel | Philadelphia, Pennsylvania, USA

Built 1782–83
Years Extant 1782–1825

Erected by John Donohue and Edward McKegan in 1782, the Mikveh Israel Synagogue was based off of New York's 1730 Shearith Israel building. The Mikveh Israel Synagogue was also the first constructed under the stars and stripes. The congregation first had difficulties making payments for the building and sought financial assistance from Jewish communities abroad as well as the local non-Jewish population. One donator was Benjamin Franklin, who gave five pounds to the congregation. By the 1820s the congregation outgrew the 1782 synagogue and built a new one in 1825 in the same location, which was in the Egyptian Revival style by William Strickland.[44]

In 1799 Hipolito Jose da Costa, a Portuguese emissary in the United States, visited the Mikveh Israel Synagogue in Philadelphia and recorded his recollection of the interior from his visit in this diary. The following is that excerpt:

> March 9, 1799. . . . Today I went to the Jews' synagogue. It was 10 o'clock and the religious service was over. The room is square with benches all around it. On one of the walls there was a kind of chest, which was open so that I could see what looked like some silver lamps inside. It was lined inside with white silk and had red curtains fringed in gold. The outside of this chest had little or no decoration. At the top there was a coat of arms of gilded and painted wood above, which was a sort of a crown. The shield was blue with gold letters in Hebrew. Further on there was a small lamp. In the middle of the room I saw a high table covered with a red cloth and beside it chairs facing the chest. The floor space occupied by the table, which was higher than the rest of the room, was surrounded by a wooden railing, as was also the area around the chest. Beneath this were two steps covered with carpet. The only man I found here seemed to be one of their priests because he went up and opened the chest looking for something and then shut it again. He invited me to come back on Saturday at 9 o'clock in the morning, or on Friday at night.[45]

In 1984 Lauren Simeone developed theoretical renderings of Mikveh Israel Synagogue; however, the level of accuracy of her project could not be determined.

Unknown | Philipsburg, St. Maarten

Built 1783
Years Extant 1783–before 1828

In 1783 the community of Jews on the Dutch half of St. Maarten built a synagogue (the other half of the island is French). Many of them were refugees from St. Eustatius. Neither the name of the synagogue and congregation nor what the building looked like is known, owing to its short existence.[46] In 1828 Marten Douwes Teenstra recorded on his travels to Philipsburg, St. Maarten that: "in former days a Synagogue existed, on the East end of the Backstreet, on the south side, is nothing more remaining than a few heaps of rubble, which stick out above the high weeds."[47]

Etz Chaim Synagogue | Gibraltar, United Kingdom

Built 1783
Years Extant 1783–present

The courtyard and vernacular front entrance to the Etz Chaim Synagogue in Gibraltar, United Kingdom. Photo from the personal collection of Barry Stiefel, picture taken by Lori H. Stiefel.

Etz Chaim Synagogue was built in 1783, shortly after the Great Siege had ended. Prior to the Great Siege it is believed that Etz Chaim started as a yeshiva in 1759. The synagogue's vernacular style and layout are possibly more typical of the clandestine, or schuilkerk-style, synagogues of the seventeenth and early eighteenth centuries built elsewhere in the Atlantic World, none of which are extant. In 1921 the building was significantly altered, and only a few historic vestiges remain.

The Etz Chaim Synagogue is a two-story building and is accessed from a passageway through a more recent building that leads to a common courtyard. This passageway entrance is modern but exhibits the dates 1759 and 5520, the year the congregation was founded. Only the front elevation of the synagogue is visible from the courtyard. The front façade has a vernacular design and is highlighted by a brown tile dado on the lower level, cream-colored stucco along the middle, and brown wood siding at the second story level. There is also a marble stairway that leads to the second story.

The sanctuary of the Etz Chaim Synagogue has been extensively modified. All that appears to date from the period of significance is a Georgian style wood cupboard on the east wall which once served as the hechal. There is now a second, more recent hechal in use. Unique to this synagogue on Gibraltar is that there is no women's balcony but a mechitzah that separates the women's section from the men.[48]

Shaare Yosher | Kingston, Jamaica

Built 1789

Years Extant 1789–1837

Completed in 1789, Shaare Yosher was the first purposely built Ashkenazic synagogue in the Americas as opposed to its counterpart, Neve Shalom in Paramaribo, Surinam, which was first built by Sephardim and then sold to the Ashkenazim. By 1837 the Ashkenazic community in Kingston had outgrown its first building and erected a second in its place. This second building was later destroyed by fire in 1882. No images or descriptions of this synagogue could be identified.[49]

Beth Elohim | Charleston, South Carolina, USA

Built 1794

Years Extant 1794–1838

Built in 1794 by Steedman and Horlbeck, the Beth Elohim Synagogue exhibits one of the more unique examples of architectural design and practice in regard to style and layout. The synagogue was a replica Wren-style church, with inspiration coming from St. Michael's Anglican Church. This was done to symbolize to the people of Charleston that the Jews were part of the community and establishment at large. The other factor that was different on the interior of the synagogue was the placement of the tebah, which was more centered in the room, giving it a slight Ashkenazic influence. This was done as a compromise between the Sephardic and Ashkenazic members of the congregations, with the Ashkenazi members wanting some say in the design of the building. For all other attributes of the interior, Beth Elohim followed the Sephardic customs defined earlier. Extant records do not indicate any substantial changes or modifications to Beth Elohim Synagogue other than the replacement of a wood fence with a wrought iron one in 1819. One historic description of the Beth Elohim Synagogue was identified, dating from 1833:

> I went to the Jews' Synagogue, it being . . . their Sabbath, to see the ceremonies of the Hebrew Church. The Synagogue outside, is very much like all our churches. Inside, there was in the centre of an area a sort of elliptical staging [Tebah] on which were mounted the Rabbi, chanting, praying and reading, all in Hebrew,—not much to

A drawing of what the exterior of Beth Elohim Synagogue of Charleston looked like, c. 1812. *Jews Synagogue in Charleston*, pencil on paper by John Rubens Smith (1775–1849), John Rubens Smith Collection, Library of Congress Prints and Photographs Division.

Interior of 1794 Beth Elohim Synagogue of Charleston. Oil on canvas by Solomon N. Carvalho, c. 1838. K. K. Beth Elohim Collection, Special Collections, College of Charleston Library.

my edification assuredly, for all that I could understand of the whole service was 'the President of the United States and his Excellency the Governor of South Carolina,' a prayer probably uttered in the same breath for each. The chants were occasionally ended by the chorus of the Jews present, whose numbers were about on hundred or more. The noise then was almost deafening for man, woman, and child screamed quite as loud as their voices would permit. The men and boys all had over their shoulders, or twined around their bodies, a short shawl—some of silk, some of worsted, and some of woolen, I believe. All the men kept their hats on, even the Rabbi. During the services a kind of cymbal, or rattle [Torah scroll which may have been decorated with a Torah Crown that was ornamented with small bells] was carried round the church by the Rabbis, and then deposited in the ark of the covenant, which was in the place where the pulpit usually is in our churches. Boys and men kept constantly going out and coming in. Many very pretty Jewesses were in the galleries. I cannot say that any of them were very attentive to the services. Probably they understood not a word of it.[50]

In 1838 Beth Elohim Synagogue was destroyed by fire, which also caused damage to parts of Charleston. In 2007 Daniel Ackerman conducted a very in-depth study of this synagogue based on surviving records. The synagogue was approximately seventy feet long and forty feet wide and was built of brick with a painted and stuccoed exterior. Defining architectural features of its Georgian style include a belt course that wrapped around the exterior of the building, rusticated quoins on the corners, a fanlight above the west entrance, compass-headed windows throughout most of the exterior walls, and a spire positioned on top of an octagonal base. The spire rose to a height of approximately seventy-five feet, which made it a very noticeable landmark on the Charleston skyline among the other prominent church spires of the city. The 1794 Beth Elohim sanctuary was mostly typical of the Atlantic World model defined by the Esnoga in Amsterdam and Bevis Marks in London. The hechal also comprised three bays divided by fluted pilasters. Crowing the piece was an ornamental lukhot with the Ten Commandments. The hechal sat on top of a platform, or duchan, which was enclosed by a balustrade and railing. At each corner of the duchan were brass candlesticks. Located in the center of the room, as a compromise with the Ashkenazic congregants, was the tebah, which stood on a platform and was enclosed by a balustrade and railing. At each corner of the tebah platform were brass candlesticks. Along the north wall of the sanctuary stood a canopied banca in which the congregation's officials sat. Seating for the rest of the congregation was provided by wood pews along the north and south walls. Above the men's first floor seating area was the women's balcony, which extended around the north, west, and south walls and was supported by Doric columns. Enclosing the women's balcony area was a geometric wainscoting along the balustrade. Illuminating the room were twenty-four compass-headed windows and brass chandeliers.[51]

Beraka ve Shalom ve Gemilut Hasadim (I) | St. Thomas, Virgin Islands, USA

Built 1796
Years Extant 1796–1804

Built in 1796 with permission from the king of Denmark, the first Beraka ve Shalom ve Gemilut Hasadim Synagogue was destroyed in 1804 by a fire that burned much of the town of Charlotte Amalie, the island's capital. It is recorded that this synagogue has been built of wood. A second synagogue was built in 1813. No images or descriptions of this synagogue could be identified.[52]

Mikveh Israel | Spanish Town, Jamaica

Built 1796
Years Extant 1796–1895

The Mikveh Israel Synagogue was built as an alternative for the Ashkenazim in Spanish Town in contrast to the Sephardic Neve Shalom Synagogue. The two congregations were completely separate and independent from one another, but from 1844 to 1860 the two Spanish Town congregations shared a rabbi. By 1860 the Ashkenazic population of Spanish Town had fallen into decline, with many relocating to Kingston or to other locations off the island entirely. The two congregations, Mikveh Israel and Neve Shalom, merged and used the Neve Shalom Synagogue building. After years of neglect and disrepair, the Mikveh Israel Synagogue was torn down in 1895, and the land was sold. No images or descriptions of this synagogue could be identified.[53]

Nefusot Yehudah, Flemish Synagogue | Gibraltar, United Kingdom

Built 1799
Years Extant 1799–present

Built in 1799, the Flemish Synagogue is unique among the synagogues of Gibraltar with its Dutch Baroque architectural style. The exterior is believed to be its original appearance, though the interior reflects the 1911–12 renovations that were constructed after a fire consumed most of the original. The new interior was inspired by the fourteenth century Samuel Ha-Levi Abulafia Synagogue in Toledo, Spain. Insufficient records survive on what the pre-1911 interior was like.

The Flemish Synagogue is named after the architectural influence of the Lowlands. However, at this time there was a stronger building tradition of synagogues in the Netherlands than in Belgium, which were then under the dominion of France. The architectural qualities of the Flemish Synagogue also bear a striking resemblance to the Snoa in Curaçao and possibly other

Exterior of the Flemish
Synagogue of Gibraltar.
Drawing by Lori H.
Stiefel.

Caribbean synagogues that are no longer extant. A Dutch gable end with
scroll detailing defines the front elevation of the two-story, yellow stucco
building. The roof is covered with Spanish tile. In the center of the pediment
is a Star of David. Gray limestone quoins decorate the corners of the building. The façade is arranged symmetrically, with bays of three windows above
and two below, and a central Roman arched doorway on the lower level. In
front of the front entrance is a gabled portico. Within the pediment of the
portico is a decorative circular molding. The arched glazed windows are decorated with terracotta hoods.[54]

Beraka ve Shalom ve Gemilut Hasadim (II) | St. Thomas, Virgin Islands, USA

Built 1812–1813
Years Extant 1813–1831

Completed in 1813 to replace the 1796 synagogue that was destroyed by fire
in 1804, the second Beraka ve Shalom ve Gemilut Hasadim Synagogue met
a similar fate. This synagogue was renovated and/or added to in 1823, before
it too was lost in a fire in 1831. A third synagogue was built in 1833, which is
used by the congregation to this day. No images or descriptions of the original
synagogue could be identified.[55]

Shearith Israel (II) | New York, New York, USA

Built 1817–1818

Years Extant 1818–1833

After eighty years of use, the 1730 Shearith Israel Synagogue was torn down and replaced by a newer and larger edifice in 1818. However, the second synagogue was used for only fifteen years, for during that time the demographics of the Mill Street neighborhood of New York changed and much of the congregation relocated further uptown. The second Shearith Israel Synagogue was thus torn down and the property sold in order to purchase a new site and build a third synagogue in 1834 on Crosby Street.

The second Shearith Israel Synagogue was a two-story building that measured thirty-five feet wide and sixty feet long, made of stone and Roman cement. Within the building were seats for 167 male congregants on the main floor and 137 in the women's balcony. In 1954 Esther Oppenheim designed a series of commemorative plates with one depicting the 1818 Mill Street Synagogue; however, it could not be determined how accurate this rendering was. A description of the synagogue's interior survives from 1828, by A. T. Goodrich:

> The Jews' Synagogue, In Mill Street, built in 1730, rebuilt in 1818, is a stone edifice. . . . The worship is here performed in the Hebrew language and in the same manner and form as in ancient times. Strangers are admitted, but females are all accommodated with seats in the gallery; the service begins on Friday evening at sunset, and is continued on Saturday morning at 10 o'clock. It is highly curious and impressive. The former Rabbi, Rev. Gersham Seixas, here officiated for 50 years regularly. The interior ornaments are elegant and costly. A lamp is kept perpetually burning before the ark. The ark is the sacred depository of the book of the law (of which a valuable manuscript copy of great antiquity belongs to the congregation) and is of a semicircular form, constructed in the most finished style of workmanship, of curled maple and satin wood, with sliding doors. The Rev. Mr. Peixotto is the present Rabbi.[56]

Artifacts originally from this building do survive and have been used in the Little Synagogue period room located in the congregation's fifth building (built 1897) on Seventieth Street and Central Park West.[57]

Mickve Israel | Savannah, Georgia, USA

Built 1820

Years Extant 1820–1829

Built in 1820 by John C. Evans, the Mickve Israel Synagogue of Savannah served its congregation for only nine years because of a fire in 1829. The synagogue was built of wood, and its architecture was most likely vernacular with Georgian and/or Federal influences. No images or descriptions of this synagogue could be identified. A second building was built in 1841.[58]

Abudarham Synagogue | Gibraltar, United Kingdom

Built 1821
Years Extant 1821–present

The front entrance to the Abudarham Synagogue in Gibraltar, United Kingdom. Photo from the personal collection of Barry Stiefel, picture taken by Lori H. Stiefel.

The Abudarham Synagogue was built in 1821 in memory of Rabbi Solomon Abudarham, who died in the yellow fever epidemic of 1804. Rabbi Abudarham had founded a yeshiva on Gibraltar in 1780, and after his death his brother Joseph Abudarham established the synagogue in his honor. The congregation may have been a continuation of this yeshiva. Records on the Abudarham Synagogue are scant, but it was altered on several occasions in the nineteenth and twentieth centuries, and restored in 2004–5. Only the front elevation of the Abudarham Synagogue is visible. The two-story building has a plain front elevation with a wood double door framed in an arched portal with stone trim. There are windows for the first and second stories, but these are concealed by closed shutters and steel grates.

Because of the 2004–5 restoration project, it is difficult to determine what fabric within the sanctuary of Abudarham Synagogue dates from the period of significance. The hechal dates from 1869 and is labeled with the corresponding Hebrew calendar date of 5629. The tebah does exhibit Georgian-style decorations; however, it is recorded as having been modified in more recent history. The wood benches along the north and south walls appear old but are also difficult to date precisely. Above the main floor is a women's balcony as well as an ornate stained glass window above the hechal.[59]

Beth Shalome | Richmond, Virginia, USA

Built 1822
Years Extant 1822–1934

Beth Shalome Synagogue as it appeared in the early twentieth century. Cook Collection, Valentine Richmond History Center.

Beth Shalome Synagogue, the last synagogue researched for this study, was built in 1822. In 1878 the synagogue was closed because of a decline in membership, and the building was sold in 1891 to the Sir Moses Montefiore congregation. Congregation Beth Shalome later merged with Beth Ahabah in 1898. In 1934 the synagogue was demolished in order to make way for redevelopment in downtown Richmond.

Based on historic photographs, we know the Beth Shalome Synagogue was a one-story brick building with a gabled roof. The front façade on the west elevation of the building was visually divided into three bays, with the central bay making up the front entrance with an entablated architrave around the entrance. Within the entrance was a wood-paneled double door. Above the entrance was a fanlight within a recessed brick frame. Flanking the main entrance were two full-height arched windows. Spanning across the top of the front elevation was a thin belt course. Inspection of the 1886 Sanborn Map revealed that there was an apse located on the rear east elevation, which most likely housed the hechal on the interior. No known surviving pictures exist of Beth Shalome's interior, but surviving written descriptions record: "The interior, decorated in white and gold, was orthodox in orientation. The pews ran lengthwise, and a reading platform was at the center of the room. The ark and pulpit were placed at one end of the sanctuary. A gallery was provided for the female members of the congregation."[60]

Glossary

Amud A pulpit or lectern from which prayers are lead.

Anusim Plural for the Hebrew word *Anus,* a Jew (or former Jew) forced to do something against his or her will. For example, the Jews that were forcibly converted in Portugal to Catholicism in 1497.

Ark Also called the *Aron Kodesh,* it is the cabinet where the Torah scrolls are stored in the sanctuary of a synagogue. The origin of the ark comes from the biblical chest that was used to transport the tablets inscribed with the Ten Commandments.

Ashkenaz Is the Hebrew word for the area in central Europe now known as Germany. It is the root for the word Ashkenazi and Ashkenazim (plural), and so on, and refers to Jews and Jewish culture that historically fell under the dominion of Christian Europe.

Auto-de-fé Literally translates from the Spanish as "act of faith" and was a public profession within Catholicism. During the Inquisition, these public professions were often associated with trials on Catholic heresy, where the punishments were often severe and included the loss of property, humiliation, and/or execution at the hands of the civil authorities. The most brutal punishment inflicted on those accused of Judaizing was being burned at the stake.

Banca A special booth set aside for the congregation's executive board in the sanctuary of the synagogue.

Beth Din A traditional Jewish court of law that is typically presided over by a tribunal of three judges.

Bimah The reader's platform situated in the middle of the sanctuary in the synagogue where the Torah scroll is read.

Chazzan Is the cantor, or precentor, that leads prayers in a synagogue.

Chevra A small Jewish communal organization that usually has little if any formal structural organization. It can be thought of as a "society."

Converso Literally translates from the Spanish as "convert," and refers to those who converted to Catholicism from Judaism in fifteenth-century Iberia or to the descendants of those who did. Conversos were also sometimes called *Nuevo Cristiano,* which means "New Christian."

Creole A person of European or African descent born in a European colony in the Americas. The word originates from the Spanish *criollo,* which has a similar meaning.

Diaspora Refers to the continued dispersal of the Jewish people that began with the conquest of the Northern Kingdom of Israel and deportation of the Ten Lost Tribes in 722 B.C.E. by the Assyrians.

Escola   Ladino word for "synagogue" and "school" (similar in concept to the Yiddish term Shul or Hebrew term Beth Midrash). Escola comes from the Latin root word *scola,* which means "school."

Esnoga   Ladino word for *synagogue.* It was usually used in reference to the second synagogue built in 1675 by Amsterdam's Talmud Torah congregation.

Ezrat Nashim   The outer courtyard in the First and Second Temples in Jerusalem that was set aside for the women. The women's area within the synagogue sanctuary is also sometimes called this.

Haham / Hahamim   The Sephardic term for "rabbi" as well as the plural version.

Halakha   Refers to the collective body of "Jewish Law" (rabbinic law).

Hascamoth   Hebrew term for a congregation's bylaws or regulations.

Haskalah   The word used to refer to a period and movement of Jewish Renaissance or Enlightenment, the most famous of which began in eighteenth-century Prussia.

Hechal   The Sephardic word for ark.

Italki   The Jews and Jewish culture associated with the Italian Peninsula.

Kahal   The Hebrew word for "congregation" or "community." Often the phrase *Kahal Ha-Kodesh* (The Holy Congregation) was placed in front of a congregation's name.

Kosher   Literally translates from the Hebrew as "fit." It is most frequently used in relation to food and its fitness within Jewish spiritual purity as described in the book of Leviticus.

Limpieza de sangre   Literally translates from the Spanish as "cleanliness of blood" and usually refers to purity of Spanish ancestry (or lack thereof).

Lukhot   An iconic representation of the Ten Commandments that is often found on top of the ark or hechal.

Mahamad   A Sephardic word used to refer to the executive board in some Jewish congregations.

Maroon   An escaped fugitive slave or descendant thereof in the Americas.

Marrano   Literally translates from the Spanish word "pig" or "swine." The word was used as a derogatory term for New Christians with Jewish ancestry. Marrano comes from the Arabic word *muharram,* which means "ritually forbidden," stemming from the prohibition of eating pork among Muslims and Jews.

Mechitzah   The divider that visually splits the men's from the women's section within the synagogue's sanctuary.

Messianism   A belief or philosophy concerned with the establishment of a Utopian world by a worldly hero. Within Judaism this belief stems from the biblical prophets that foretell a golden age brought about by the messenger of God (the Messiah) who is a descendant of King David.

Mestizo   Someone of mixed Iberian and Native American ancestry.

Mezuzah   A small box containing a piece of parchment with a specific blessing that is hung on the door and gate posts of Jewish dwellings as prescribed in Deuteronomy 6:9.

Mikvah   A Jewish ritual bath used to bring about spiritual purity. "Mikvah" should not be confused with the word *hope,* as in Mikveh Israel (Hope of Israel), which is spelled differently in Hebrew but transliterated with a very similar spelling in English.

Millenarianism Related to and influenced by messianism, the idea that human history as currently experienced will come to an end at a preordained time by a dramatic conflict between good and evil, with the forces of good led by the Messiah.

Minhag Jewish word for "custom" or "tradition."

Minyan Jewish word for a quorum of ten males over age thirteen that is necessary to perform prayer services.

Mizrach Hebrew word for "east," but also refers to the Jews and Jewish culture of North Africa and the Middle East. The direction of Mizrach is also used to indicate the direction of prayer within synagogues located west of Jerusalem.

Mulatto Someone of mixed European and African ancestry.

La Nación The Spanish-Portuguese self-identifying term used by the Sephardic Jews of the Atlantic World, which was short for the "Hebrews of the Spanish and Portuguese Nation."

Ner Tamid Literally translated from the Hebrew as "eternal light," the ner tamid is a lamp found in most synagogues that is usually placed above or in front of the ark or hechal and is kept continuously lit. The practice of the ner tamid comes from the use of the menorah in the Temple in Jerusalem.

Nusach The order of liturgy in the prayer book according to different Jewish customs, or minhag. For example, the Ashkenazic, Sephardic, and Mizrachi Jews each have their own nusach or sequential order of prayers.

Parnassim A word used to refer to the executive board in some Jewish congregations.

Rabbi The word for a religious leader within Judaism who has undergone a procedure of ordination that included supervised intensive study of Jewish texts, laws, and rituals.

Reconquista The Spanish word referring to the period and process under which the Christian kingdoms of Iberia reconquered the territories that had been ruled by the Muslims between 711 C.E. and 1492.

Reform A modern movement and practice within Judaism established simultaneously in Germany and South Carolina during the early nineteenth century, with a philosophy of not strictly following Jewish Law, or a philosophy of liberalism and modernization of Jewish practice.

Schuilkerk Dutch word for a clandestine house of worship that were (usually) established in an existing building. Varieties existed for Jews, Catholics, and dissenting Protestants across the Lowlands (Netherlands, Belgium, and Luxemburg).

Sepharad The Hebrew word for the Iberian Peninsula. It is the root for the words Sephardi and Sephardim (plural), and so on, and refers to Jews and Jewish culture that historically originated from this area of Europe and areas touched by the Sephardic Diaspora due to the Iberian expulsion edicts of the 1490s.

Shabbat The seventh day of the Jewish week and Sabbath, which is used as a day of rest within traditional Judaism.

Shamash The Hebrew word for sexton.

Shul   Yiddish word for "synagogue" and "school" (similar in concept to the Hebrew term Beth Midrash). Shul comes from the Latin root word *scola,* which means "school."

Snoa   Papiamento word for "synagogue." It is usually used in reference to the second synagogue built in 1732 by Curaçao's Mikve Israel congregation.

Surinam vs. Suriname   Within this study "Surinam" is spelled in two different ways, reflecting the addition of the "e" to the name upon the country's independence. Therefore, "Surinam" refers to the place when it was a Dutch colony and "Suriname" to when it was an independent country.

Talmud   Collection of writings constituting Jewish civil and religious law compiled during the early centuries of the common era.

Tebah   The Sephardic term for "bimah."

Torah   The Pentateuch: Genesis, Exodus, Leviticus, Numbers, and Deuteronomy. The physical Torah is traditionally a handwritten scroll on parchment.

Treif   Literally translates from the Hebrew as "unfit" and is most frequently used in relation to food and its fitness within Jewish spiritual purity as described in the book of Leviticus. It is the antonym of "kosher."

Yeshiva   A Jewish school of higher learning with an emphasis on a religious curriculum.

Notes

Introduction

1. *Converso* translates from the Spanish word "convert" and refers to those who converted to Catholicism from Judaism in fifteenth-century Iberia or to the descendants of those who did. Conversos were also sometimes called *Nuevo Cristiano,* which means "New Christian." *Marrano* comes from the Spanish word "pig" or "swine." The word was used as a derogatory term for New Christians with Jewish ancestry. Marrano comes from the Arabic word *muharram,* which means "ritually forbidden," stemming from the prohibition of eating pork among Muslims and Jews.

2. *Sepharad* is the Hebrew name for Iberia, the place of ancestral origin of Sephardic Jews.

3. Rosengarten and Stiefel, "Port Jews and Plantation Jews: Carolina-Caribbean Connections."

4. Sarna, *American Judaism: A History,* 12. For Sarna each Jewish settlement constituted a "synagogue-community," a term he uses to refer to congregants rather than to physical buildings. This one-to-one— a single congregation to a single house of worship—ratio remains, for the most part, a useful historical measure.

5. For example the official name of the Jewish congregation in Charleston, South Carolina, that dates from the eighteenth century is *Kahal Kodesh* (Holy Congregation/Community) *Beth Elohim* (House of God). Henceforth congregations will be referred to without the Kahal Kodesh prefix—for example Beth Elohim in the case of Charleston.

6. Meek, *The Synagogue,* 142–47.

7. Again Sarna's one-to-one ratio (see above) is the best overall system of measurement.

8. Within this study "Surinam" is spelled in two different ways (*Surinam* vs. *Suriname*), reflecting the addition of the "e" to the name upon the country's gaining independence in 1975.

9. See Sachar, *Farewell Espana.*

10. According to some family traditions of early Sephardic colonial families, some returnees to Judaism, such as Zipporah Nunes Machado Jacobs (1710–99), continued to use rosary beads while reciting Jewish prayers out of habit for years even after they had found refuge in the British and Dutch Empires. Bodian, *Hebrews of the Portuguese,* 155; and Marcus, *The Colonial American Jew, 1492–1776,* 2:1020.

11. Angel, *Remnant of Israel: A Portrait of America's First Jewish Congregation, Shearith Israel*, 52.

12. Studnicki-Gizbert, "La Nación among the Nations: Portuguese and Other Maritime Trading Diasporas in the Atlantic, Sixteenth to Eighteenth Centuries," 89.

13. See Bodian, *Hebrews of the Portuguese*, a publication that extensively studies this history.

14. The direction of "mizrach" is also used to indicate the direction of prayer within synagogues located west of Jerusalem by Sephardic and Ashkenazic Jewry.

15. Barnavi, ed., *A Historical Atlas of the Jewish People, From the Time of the Patriarchs to the Present*, 148–53.

16. Rupert, "Trading Globally, Speaking Locally: Curaçao's Sephardim in the Making of a Caribbean Creole," 109–17; and Marcus. *The Colonial American Jew, 1492–1776*, 3:159–60.

17. Cohen Paraira, "A Jewel in the City," 41–68; and Wiznitzer, "The Synagogue and Cemetery of the Jewish Community of Recife, Brazil (1630–1654)," 129.

18. Swierenga, *The Forerunners: Dutch Jewry in the North American Diaspora*, 23–31; and *K. K. Beth Shalome Collection*, miscellaneous papers, 1789–1898. Beth Ahabah Museum & Archives, Richmond, Virginia.

19. See Sarna, *American Judaism*.

20. Congregation Shaar Hashamaim was also known in Portuguese as Porta do Ceu, which both translate as "Gates of Heaven." Elkin, *The Jews of Latin America*, 40–44, 61–62.

21. Jick, *The Americanization of the Synagogue, 1820–1870*.

22. Ackermann, "The 1794 Synagogue of Kahal Kadosh Beth Elohim of Charleston: Reconstructed and Reconsidered," 176.

CHAPTER 1: The Origin of the Atlantic World Synagogue

1. See Levine, *The Ancient Synagogue: The First Thousand Years*, for a detailed discussion of this history.

2. "Rabbi" was the title bestowed on the sages of ancient Israel and ordained by the Sanhedrin. These sages also had authority to judge minor disputes related to Jewish law. "Rav" or "Haham" was also the title of an exceptional scholar, originating in the Babylonian academies.

3. Ladino, sometimes called *Judeo-Spanish*, is a Romance language, descended from medieval Spanish, spoken by Sephardic Jews with ancestral origins from Iberia.

4. Papiamento is a creole language derived from Spanish and Dutch, with elements of African languages, English, and Arawak.

5. Cohen, *From the Maccabees to the Mishnah*, 111.

6. Levine, *The Ancient Synagogue*, 13.

7. Levine, *The Ancient Synagogue*, 13.

8. Sarna, *American Judaism: A History*, 106, argues that Touro Synagogue (then known as Jeshuat Israel) of Newport, Rhode Island, did not originally have a lukhot above its hechal. The interior of the synagogue was modified early in its history, and it is most likely that the lukhot exhibited at Touro Synagogue presently is not from c. 1763. In the author's opinion there is insufficient evidence to prove whether or not

a lukhot was not or was part of the original installation in Touro Synagogue; however, other synagogues in the Atlantic World, such as the c. 1675 Portuguese Synagogue of Amsterdam, did, and it was documented in Emanuel de Witte's painting from the late seventeenth century.

9. The word *bimah* is Greek in origin, referring to an elevated platform.

10. See Levine, *The Ancient Synagogue.*

11. Sarna, "The Debate over Mixed Seating in the American Synagogue," 363–67.

12. This board of leaders, depending on the congregation, were given various titles: "mahamad," "parnassim," "adjunta," or "directiva."

13. Tachau, *The Architecture of the Synagogue,* 155–65.

14. Ganzfried, *Code of Jewish Law / Kitzur Shulchan Aruh, A Compilation of Jewish laws and Customs,* vol. 1; and Torah.org, *Shulchan Aruch Part I: Orach Chayim,* "Chapter 9–The Synagogue."

15. *Shulchan Aruch* (150:1–154:15).

16. Stolzman and Stolzman, *Synagogue Architecture in America, Faith, Spirit and Identity,* 29.

17. Rachel Wischnitzer claims to have identified approximately 119 synagogues built in Iberia prior to the pogroms of 1391. The earliest known synagogue in the Iberian Peninsula was built in Elche, Spain, c. 400 C.E., which established a tradition of more then one thousand continuous years of synagogue design and construction prior to the expulsions of 1492–98. Today only a very small handful of Iberian synagogues and ruins survive. The intact buildings have also had their floor plans significantly altered since 1492–98, when they were converted into churches and for other uses. Therefore it is possible that the open central aisle plan is a continuation of Sephardic synagogue design from Iberia to Amsterdam, London, and the rest of the Atlantic World, but any evidence that would support this theory has been lost over the centuries. Wischnitzer, *The Architecture of the European Synagogue,* 19, and Schapiro, "The Miniatures of the Florence Diatessaron (Laurentian ms Or. 81): Their Place in Late Medieval Art and Supposed Connection with Early Christian and Insular Art," 520.

18. Bell, *Jews in the Early Modern World,* 222–23.

19. Messinas, "Late Synagogues of Greece, Origins and Architecture: The Relationship between Greek Synagogues and Medieval Spanish Synagogues: The Bimah," 152–57.

20. Bell, *Jews in the Early Modern World,* 38–39.

21. *Tedesca,* the Italian feminine adjective for German, was also the Italkic word for "Ashkenazi." The Scuola Grande Tedesca most likely started with the central bimah-tebah plan.

22. Krinsky, *Synagogues of Europe, Architecture, History, and Meaning,* 378–86; and Comunità Israelitica di Venezia, *Jewish Art Treasures in Venice.*

23. Derived from the Greek word for geometry (*geometria*), it is a system of assigning numerical value to letters in an alphabet and is often used in association with Kabalah and its analysis of Torah and Talmud.

24. *Haham* translates into the Hebrew word "wise," whereas rabbi, from *rav,* translates into "teacher." Both are terms of endearment for Jewish sages.

25. Marcus, *The Colonial American Jew, 1492–1776*, vols. 2: and 3:542, 927, and 1333.

26. This is compared to the traditions of the local Ashkenazi rabbis, such as Rabbi Uri ben Joseph Halevi, who had different customs from their Sephardic ancestors.

27. This merged entity, the Talmud Torah, was commonly known as the Portuguese Synagogue and should not be confused with a different, far more famous building—the elegant Esnoga, completed in 1675, and referred to earlier in this text. When I use "Portuguese Synagogue" in the following discussion, I mean the 1639 structure.

28. Kaplan, "Fictions of Privacy: House Chapels and the Spatial Accommodation of Religious Dissent in Early Modern Europe."

29. Cohen Paraira, "A Jewel in the City," 41–45; Zwarts, "De eerste rabbijnen en synagogen van Amsterdam naar archivalische bronnen," 209–16 and appendices 260–64; Koen, "War en voor vie werd de synagoge van 1612 gebouwd?," 209–12; Koen "Nicolaes van Campen als huiseigenaar van de Portugees-Israelitische synagoge," *Maandblad Amstelodamum* 58 (1971).

30. van Agt, *Synagogen in Amsterdam*, 94–95.

31. Israel, *European Jewry in the Age of Mercantilism, 1550–1750*, 62–63.

32. Goldish, "The Amsterdam Portuguese Rabbinate in the Seventeenth Century: A Unique Institution Viewed from Within and Without," 9–19.

33. Altmann, "Eternality of Punishment: A Theological Controversy within the Amsterdam Rabbinate in the Thirties of the Seventeenth Century," 3.

34. Davis and Ravid, *The Jews of Early Modern Venice*, 23. Again, see early discussion of Talmud Torah and its ramifications.

35. Cyrus Adler, et al., "Pardo," *The Jewish Encyclopedia*, 524–25.

36. See Messinas, "Preserving Jewish Heritage in Greece."

37. Bodian, *Hebrews of the Portuguese Nation: Conversos and Community in Early Modern Amsterdam*, 111.

38. Davis and Ravid, *The Jews of Early Modern Venice*, 221; and Cyrus Adler, et al., "Talmud Torah," *The Jewish Encyclopedia*, 37–39.

39. Wiznitzer, "The Minute Book of Congregations Zur Israel of Recife and Magen Abraham," 217–27.

40. See Schama, *The Embarrassment of Riches: An Interpretation of Dutch Culture in the Golden Age*.

41. During the seventeenth century, there were also Protestant presses that printed in Hebrew.

42. Barnett, *Bevis Marks Records*, 7.

43. Oliel-Grausz, "A Study in Intercommunal Relations in the Sephardi Diaspora: London and Amsterdam in the Eighteenth Century," 41–58.

44. The sand was removed from Zedek ve Shalom's interior in 1999 and is no longer used for worship.

45. Kaufman, "O que se conta. . . . Quem conta. . . . Como se conta. . . . Os Judeus em Pernambuco Práticas judaicas, sinagogas."

46. Arbell, *The Jewish Nation of the Caribbean: The Spanish-Portuguese Jewish Settlements in the Caribbean and the Guianas*, 19.

47. *The Portuguese Synagogue*, 2.

48. Andriesse, <Linda@jhm.nl> personal correspondence "Zand in de synagoge / Sand in the synagogue."

49. Simonhoff, *Under Strange Skies,* 36. The author was seized with a desire for travel after World War II but does not indicate precisely when he visited each place. I am grateful to Aviva Ben-Ur of the University of Massachusetts, Amherst, for bringing this account to my attention.

50. Griffis, *The American in Holland: Sentimental Rambles in the Eleven Provinces of the Netherlands,* 65.

51. Alkmaar, *Monumentaal Alkmaar: Remonstrantse Kerk.*

52. New York Times, "De Karpershoek."

53. Fischer, *Life in New Amsterdam: Picture the Past,* 17.

54. Though officially Catholic, religious rituals at the church bear little resemblance to mainstream Catholicism, which is due to the heavy borrowing of indigenous Mayan traditions. Evans, "Coke and Conquistadors: Religious Syncretism in Latin America," 16–17.

55. Quoted in Gerard Nahon, "Les Relations entre Amsterdam et Constantinople authorities XVIIIe siecle d'apres le Copiador de Cartas de la Nation Juive d'Amsterdam," from Emmanuel and Emmanuel, *History of the Jews of the Netherlands Antilles,* 154.

56. Parry, *The Age of Reconnaissance: Discovery, Exploration, and Settlement, 1450–1650,* 74.

57. Cohen Paraira, "A Jewel in the City," 47; and Congregation Mikve Israel-Emanuel, *Our "Snoa," 5492–5742,* 24–28.

58. The second-order European synagogues (such as Plymouth or The Hague) certainly merit analysis too. These are early days still for the discipline of Atlantic World Jewish studies.

59. Durant and Durant, *The Age of Reason Begins: A History of European Civilization in the Period of Shakespeare, Bacon, Montaigne, Rembrandt, Galileo, and Descartes: 1558–1648,* 482–84.

60. Pile, *A History of Interior Design,* 189–90; and Israel, *The Dutch Republic: Its Rise, Greatness and Fall, 1477–1806,* 547, 553.

61. Exodus 20:4: "you shall not make yourself a carved image nor any likeness of that which is in the heavens above or on the earth below or in the water beneath the earth." The exact definition of engraved image is still a matter of dispute among Jewish religious traditions and authorities.

62. Louw, "Anglo-Netherlandish Architectural Interchange c. 1600–c. 1660," 1–18; and Israel, *The Dutch Republic,* 553, 872.

63. Brienen, *Visions of Savage Paradise: Albert Eckhout, Court Painter in Colonial Dutch Brazil,* 179; and da Silva and Alcides, "Collecting and Framing the Wilderness: The Garden of Johan Maurits (1604–79) in North-East Brazil," 153–76.

64. Sturgis, ed., *A Dictionary of Architecture and Building: Biographical, Historical, and Descriptive,* 195–96.

65. "Part III: The Period of Prosperity (1637–1644)," 57–77.

66. Cohen Paraira, "A Jewel in the City," 45, 49.

67. Hart, "The Glorious City: Monumentalism and Public Space in Seventeenth Century Amsterdam," 128–50.

68. Krinsky, *Synagogues of Europe, Architecture, History, and Meaning*, 389.

69. Jewish Historical Museum of Amsterdam, "New Synagogue."

70. van Oers, *Dutch Town Planning Overseas during VOC and WIC Rule (1600–1800)*, 75–90; and Hooimeijer, "The Relation between Design and Technology of Polder Cities," 80–81.

71. Hohenberg and Lees, *The Making of Urban Europe, 1000–1950*, 157; Braunfels, *Urban Design in Western Europe: Regime and Architecture, 900–1900*, 105; Norberg-Schulz, *Baroque Architecture*, 195; Dutt and Costa, *Public Planning in the Netherlands: Perspectives and Change Since the Second World War*, 65; and Antunes, *Globalisation in the Early Modern Period: The Economic Relationship between Amsterdam and Lisbon, 1640–1705*, 40.

72. See Daniel Stalpaert, *Amstelodami veteris et novissimae urbis accuratissima delineatio / geteeckent ende*. Edited by Nicolaes Visscher, 1662, located at the Universiteit van Amsterdam, Call number UB: Kaartenzl: 102.01.01. <http://dpc.uba.uva.nl/cgi/i/image/image-idx?g=all;c=carto;lasttype=boolean;view=entry;lastview=thumbnail;subview=detail;cc=carto;entryid=x-254352073;viewid=102–01–01.TIF;start=1;resnum=2%27,%20%27S_CARTO_X_254352073___102_01_01__TIF> (accessed 12 July 2010).

73. Krinsky, *Synagogues of Europe, Architecture, History, and Meaning*, 35–104.

74. Cohen Paraira, "A Jewel in the City," 56–58; and Kravtsov, "Juan Bautista Villalpando and Sacred Architecture in the Seventeenth Century," 312–39.

75. Kravtsov, "Juan Bautista Villalpando and Sacred Architecture in the Seventeenth Century," 312–39.

76. Johann Valentin Andrease introduces these concepts in *Christianopolis* by means of architectural metaphor: "that it is better to reside on the doorstep of the God's house than inside a tent of sin." Also see Reps, *Town Planning in Frontier America*, 102.

77. See Leibman, "Sephardic Sacred Space in Colonial America," 13–41.

78. Morrison, *Juan Bautista Villalpando's Ezechielem Explanationes: A Sixteenth-Century Architectural Text*, 100. An actual rendezvous between Jacob Juda Leon and Christopher Wren isn't verifiable; however, there is on record that Christiaan Huygens (1629–95), a Dutch mathematician and scientists residing in England at this time, wrote a letter to Wren introducing Leon.

79. Jews in medieval England also had "Royal Prayers" prior to the expulsion of 1290. There were also subsequent editions after Haham Leon (most notably by Chief Rabbi Hermann Adler [1839–1911] in 1895). Goldhill, *The Temple of Jerusalem*, 138.

80. Wischnitzer, *The Architecture of the European Synagogue*, 98.

81. Richardson and Gill, *London Houses from 1660 to 1820*, 37–38.

82. Temminck Groll, *De Architecture Van Suriname, 1667–1930*, 91.

83. Buddingh, "Hendrik Schielach, Builder or Bungler? The Architect of the Snoa," 115–21.

84. See Curl, *Georgian Architecture*; Roth, *American Architecture: A History*, 69–104; McAllister and McAllister, *A Field Guide to American*, 139–51; and Gura, *The Abrams Guide to Period Styles for Interiors*, 62. Indeed some architectural historians argue that for much of the eighteenth century and early nineteenth century, several architectural styles were simultaneously in fashion. Then as now architects

borrowed or mingled certain stylistic characteristics to remain popular and competi-tive in the market.

85. See Curl, *Georgian Architecture*; and Roth, *American Architecture: A History*, 69–70. Curl assigns the dates of 1714 and 1830 for when Georgian architecture was utilized, beginning with Peckwater Quadrangle at Christ Church, Oxford, by architect Henry Aldrich (26). Roth begins at c. 1700 with the completion of the Wren Building at the College of William and Mary in Williamsburg, Virginia.

86. Perrault, who built the east front of the Louvre (c. 1665), was influenced by his great contemporary Bernini, some of whose drawings he most likely surveyed. Pevsner, *An Outline of European Architecture*, 320.

87. Jones also had professional associations with Dutch architects, which led to mutually reinforcing relations in both Protestant countries. Tait, "Inigo Jones—Architectural Historian," 234–35.

88. Stimson, "Christopher Wren, F.R.S.," 360–67.

89. Pevsner, *An Outline of European Architecture*, 329.

90. Buggeln, *Temples of Grace: The Material Transformation of Connecticut's Churches, 1790–1840*, 76–79.

91. Watson, <watson_karl@yahoo.com> Fw: Your book and my article, 26 Mar. 2010 personal correspondence. Hadchity, "Of Bridges, Berths, and Hawkers," *Paintings of Bridgetown from the National Art Collection of Barbados*, the Barbados Gallery of Art and the Barbados Museum and Historical Society at the Zemicon Gallery.

92. Kadish, *Bevis Marks Synagogue, 1701–2001*, 1–5.

93. Robinson, "Robert Hooke as a Surveyor and Architect," 48–55.

94. Meek, *The Synagogue*, 146–47.

95. Lyons, Phillips, and Noah, "Historical Sketch," 194–96.

96. New-York Historical Society, *Collections of the New-York Historical Society*, 110.

97. Architecture Week, "Lord Burlington," *Great Buildings Collection*.

98. See Schless, "Peter Harrison, the Touro Synagogue, and the Wren City Church," 187–200; and Bridenbaugh, *Peter Harrison: First American Architect*.

99. Slade, "Touro Synagogue, Congregation Jeshuat Israel"; and Marcus, *The Colonial American Jew, 1492–1776*, 2:684.

100. Crain, *Historic Architecture in the Caribbean Islands*, 162.

101. See Bridenbaugh, *Peter Harrison*.

102. Morias, "Mickve Israel Congregation of Philadelphia," 15.

103. Ackermann, "The 1794 Synagogue of Kahal Kadosh Beth Elohim of Charleston: Reconstructed and Reconsidered," 159–74; and Roth, *American Architecture: A History*, 95.

104. Rubin, *Third to None: The Saga of Savannah Jewry, 1733–1983*, 64.

105. The appendix provides an "armchair survey" of forty-six known synagogues associated with the Jewish Atlantic World, including those that remain standing and that are no longer extant. A caveat: My register of forty-six known synagogues is sometimes based on the best educated guess given the surviving historical record. There were several synagogues in this study for which little material was available. Therefore the number of synagogues could be slightly lower or higher based on my interpretation of historical information or lack of information. The criterion for

their listing was that each synagogue building had to have been built for the specific purpose as a Jewish house of worship and not have been a preexisting building that was converted for the purpose.

106. See Hofstadter, *America at 1750: A Social Portrait*; and Bailyn, *The Peopling of British North America: An Introduction*.

107. The spellings of the synagogues in the index are based on what was used at the time of first identification. Many synagogues had more then one documented source that used different transliterated spellings. For example *Mikve Israel* and *Mickve Israel* are both spelled and mean the same thing in Hebrew (Hope of Israel). For the purpose of this study I have used the initial transliterated spelling at the time I first identified the synagogue and maintained its usage throughout for the sake of consistency. I apologize if this creates some confusion. The roman numerals in parentheses are an indicator to signify that a specific congregation built more than one synagogue building between 1636 and 1822. For example congregation Shearith Israel in New York built its first synagogue in 1730 (Shearith Israel [I]), which it later tore down in 1818 in order to build a second one in its place (Shearith Israel [II]).

CHAPTER 2: Jews and Conversos during the Age of Discovery

1. In the vast literature on European discovery, its ideological, technological, and economic dimensions, *loci classici* remain McNeill, *The Rise of the West: A History of the Human Community*; Braudel, *The Wheels of Commerce*; Parry, *The Age of Reconnaissance: Discovery, Exploration and Settlement, 1450–1650*; and Boorstin and Luce, *The Discoverers*. A survey with a modern bibliographical survey is Fritze, *New Worlds: The Great Voyages of Discovery, 1400–1600*. In some measure the works just cited have helped orient my thinking on European, and obviously Jewish, settlement in the Atlantic World during the Age of Discovery. This is manifestly a "perpetual subject," one that must always command the attention, and reinterpretive energy, of historians, social scientists, and scientists.

2. See Herodotus, *Histories*, book 1, 202.

3. See Obadiah 1:21.

4. Barnavi, ed., *A Historical Atlas of the Jewish People, From the Time of the Patriarchs to the Present*, 16–17.

5. Barnavi, ed., *A Historical Atlas of the Jewish People, From the Time of the Patriarchs to the Present*, 54–55.

6. McGovern, "The Archaeology of the Norse North Atlantic," 331–51.

7. See Golden, Ben-Shammai, and Róna-Tas, eds., *The World of the Khazars: New Perspectives*.

8. Roth, *Medieval Jewish Civilization: An Encyclopedia*, 558–61.

9. Sachar, *Farewell Espana: The World of the Sephardim Remembered*, 331. In this profession Judah followed his famous father Abraham, whom he may well have assisted in producing the chief work of medieval cartography, the Catalan map (1375). See also Livingstone, *Putting Science in its Place: Geographies of Scientific Knowledge*, 97.

10. See Shafer, Diffie, and Winius, *Europe and the World in the Age of Expansion*, vol. 1, *Foundations of the Portuguese Empire 1415–1580*.

11. See Livingstone, *Putting Science in its Place.*

12. Seed, "Jewish Scientists and the Origin of Modern Navigation," 73–85; Burgos and Zacuto, *Abraham Zacut, Siglo XV*; and Goldstein, "The Medieval Hebrew Tradition in Astronomy," 145–48.

13. Shafer, Diffie, and Winius, *Europe and the World in the Age of Expansion,* 1:305–8.

14. Curtin, *The Rise and Fall of the Plantation Complex: Essays in Atlantic History,* 29–46.

15. Warner, "Sugarcane: An Indigenous Papuan Cultigen," 405–11.

16. Garfield, "Public Christians, Secret Jews: Religion and Political Conflict on Sao Tome Island in the Sixteenth and Seventeenth Centuries," 645–54.

17. Schwartz, *Tropical Babylons: Sugar and the Making of the Atlantic World, 1450–1680,* 64–65.

18. See Hart, *Comparing Empires: European Colonialism from Portuguese Expansion to the Spanish-American War.* For the sugar plantation system in the Anglophone Atlantic, see Wood, *The Origins of American Slavery: Freedom and Bondage in the English Colonies;* and Dunn, *Sugar and Slaves: The Rise of the Planter Class in the English West Indies, 1624–1713.*

19. The position of the Catholic Church on slavery is an extended, complex one. It suffices to note that in the last half of the fifteenth century, the church authorized the exploitation of Africans to support the economic and colonial expansion of Iberian monarchs. But later the level of papal support diminished. The literature on African slavery and the European slave trade is enormous, with research ongoing. See Heuman and Walvin, eds., *The Slavery Reader;* and Thornton, *Africa and Africans in the Making of the Atlantic World, 1400–1800.*

20. The bulls Romanus Pontifex (1454), Ineffabilis et summi (1497), Dudum pro parte (1516), and Aequum reputamus (1534) continued to reinforce Portuguese powers of enslavement. See Sweet, "Spanish and Portuguese Influences on Racial Slavery in British North America, 1492–1619."

21. Atmore and Oliver, *Medieval Africa, 1250–1800,* 169. See also Garfield, "Public Christians, Secret Jews: Religion and Political Conflict on Sao Tome Island in the Sixteenth and Seventeenth Centuries," 645–54.

22. See Davis, *Slavery and Human Progress;* and Faber, *Jews, Slaves, and the Slave Trade: Setting the Record Straight.*

23. Suárez, *Shedding the Veil: Mapping the European Discovery of America and the World,* 8–9.

24. Rickey, "How Columbus Encountered America," 219–25.

25. Rickey, "How Columbus Encountered America," 219–25.

26. Roth, "A Note on the Astronomers of the Vecinho Family," 233–36.

27. To a surprising degree Washington Irving's fictional biography *A History of the Life and Voyages of Christopher Columbus* (London: John Murray, 1828) helped lodge the flat earth canard in Anglophone popular culture. Medieval Europeans, Irving asserted antihistorically, did not accept the earth as a sphere.

28. As Columbus frankly acknowledged, Zacuto's astronomical tables were invaluable guides in his voyages. See Humanities and Social Sciences Library, *Jews in America: Conquistadors, Knickerbockers, Pilgrims, and the Hope of Israel,* 3.

29. Zaimeche, *Granada—The Last Refuge of Muslims in Spain*, 12–13.

30. Tax farming descends from Roman practice. See Adams, *For Good and Evil: The Impact of Taxes on the Course of Civilization*.

31. Abrabanel is a fascinating, important figure. He used his wealth to help fund the final Granada campaign. Even after the Alhambra Decree, he offered large sums to the monarchs, almost certainly meant to have them reverse the decree. See Humanities and Social Sciences Library, *Jews in America: Conquistadors, Knickerbockers, Pilgrims, and the Hope of Israel*, 3; and Delevante and Alberga, *The Island of One People: An Account of the History of the Jews in Jamaica*, 7.

32. Humanities and Social Sciences Library, *Jews in America: Conquistadors, Knickerbockers, Pilgrims, and the Hope of Israel*, 3.

33. Although North African Moors conquered most of Iberia in the early decades of the eighth century, there were complex social and political tensions among various Muslim groups and their Christian neighbors over time. For a good survey, see Kennedy, *Muslim Spain and Portugal: A Political History of al-Andalus*.

34. Sachar, *Farewell Espana*, 20–22.

35. Zeitlin, "Judaism as a Religion, An Historical Study (Continued)," 115.

36. Seed, "Jewish Scientists and the Origin of Modern Navigation," 73–85.

37. See Assis, *The Jews of Spain: From Settlement to Expulsion*.

38. See Pérez, *The Spanish Inquisition: A History*; and Kamen, *The Spanish Inquisition: A Historical Revision*.

39. Columbus left for his second voyage across the Atlantic from this same port on 24 Sept. 1493.

40. The date August 2, 1492 in the Julian calendar corresponds to August 11, 1492 in the Gregorian. Additionally in the Hebrew calendar the change of one day to the next takes place at sunset, instead of 12:00 midnight in the Julian and Gregorian calendars. Therefore Av 9, 5252 began at sunset on August 1, 1492, and continued until sunset on August 2.

41. Roth, *A History of the Marranos*, 271. I have used the translation provided by Cecil Roth, which corrects Columbus's mistake of fixing the expulsion departure month as January, rather than the correct month, August. In the more precise English translation of John Thacher (1903), we find: "So that, after having banished all the Jews from all your Kingdoms and realms, in the same month of January." Columbus's deprecation of the Jewish trauma is evident in Thacher. For a similar emphasis, see Sale, *The Conquest of Paradise: Christopher Columbus and the Columbian Legacy*, 13.

42. Sachar, *Farewell Espana*, 73.

43. Seed, "Jewish Scientists and the Origin of Modern Navigation," 73–85.

44. See Couto, "The Role of Interpreters, or Linguas, in the Portuguese Empire during the 16th Century."

45. Sachar, *Farewell Espana*, 347.

46. Copy of a letter written by Amerigo Vespucci from the island of Cape Verde in the Ocean Sea to Lorenzo di Pierfrancesco de' Medici, 4 June 1501. Translated by David Jacobson. Edited and with an introduction by Luciano Formisano. *Letters from a New World: Amerigo Vespucci's Discovery of America*, 24. This letter by Vespucci was written prior to his final conclusion about the "Americas" being a separate

landmass from Asia, which is alluded in his reference to Gaspar crossing the "Indian Sea" twice, which were the Atlantic and Indian Oceans not yet conceived as two separate bodies of water.

47. See Fernández-Armesto, *Amerigo: The Man who gave his Name to America.*

48. Marcus, *The Colonial American Jew, 1492–1776,* 1:67.

49. See Liebman, "Hernando Alonso: The First Jew on the North American Continent," 291–92; and Liebman, *New World Jewry, 1493–1825: Requiem for the Forgotten,* 51. Also see Uchmany, "The Periodization of the History of the New Christians and Crypto-Jews in Spanish America," 109–47.

50. Cohen, "Some Misconceptions about the Crypto-Jews in Colonial Mexico," 277.

51. See Valencia, *The Encomenderos of New Spain, 1521–1555.*

52. See Uchmany, "The Periodization of the History of the New Christians and Crypto-Jews in Spanish America."

53. Cohen, "Some Misconceptions about the Crypto-Jews in Colonial Mexico," 277; Liebman. "Hernando Alonso," 291–96. See Uchmany, *La Vida Entre el Judaísmo y el Cristianismo en la Nueva España, 1580–1606.* In 1518 no Spaniard punished by the Inquisition could leave Spain for Crown lands abroad. "In 1552, all people of Hebraic origin were forbidden from crossing the Atlantic Ocean."

54. Liebman, "Hernando Alonso," 291–96; and Gitlitz, *Secrecy and Deceit: The Religion of the Crypto-Jews,* 54, 160, 274. See also Uchmany, *La Vida Entre el Judaísmo y el Cristianismo en la Nueva España, 1580–1606;* and White, "In the Shadows of the Inquisition: The Jews of Colonial Mexico and Their Uncertain Legacy," 2.

55. See Poole, *Pedro Moya de Contreras: Catholic Reform and Royal Power in New Spain, 1571–1591.*

56. Statistics on the numbers of Iberian Jews and New Christians prior to 1492, as well as how many who fled elsewhere or remained in Iberia is controversial. See Gitlitz, *Secrecy and Deceit,* 73–96.

57. Revisionist interpretation of the Inquisition, a complex cultural, political, and historiographic phenomenon, should be noted. Besides Kamen and Perez, an authoritative modern account placing the expulsion and Inquisition in a broader context has also been made by Lavender, "The Secret Jews of Spain, Portugal, and Italy and Their Descendants Today: Major Research Issues in a Growing Field of Academic Research," 3–16.

58. Israel, "Jews and Crypto-Jews in the Atlantic World Systems, 1500–1800," 3–17.

59. See Israel, *Diasporas within a Diaspora: Jews, Crypto-Jews, and the World of Maritime Empires (1540–1740).*

60. Precise numbers on the Iberian expulsion are hard to establish authoritatively. Kamen, *The Spanish Inquisition,* 29, estimates there were eighty thousand Spanish Jews, half of whom left Spain. Most Castilian Jews went to Portugal; Aragon's Jews to Italy. The most recent detailed work on the fate of Portuguese Jewry is Soyer's *The Persecution of the Jews and Muslims of Portugal: King Manuel I and the end of Religious Tolerance 1496–7.*

61. See Tavares, *Los Judíos en Portugal.*

62. Gampel, "The Last Jews on Iberian Soil: Navarrese Jewry, 1479–1498," 49–69.

63. Kamen, "The Mediterranean and the Expulsion of Spanish Jews in 1492," 30–55.

64. See Sumption, *The Albigensian Crusade*; and Pegg, *A Most Holy War: The Albigensian Crusade and the Battle for Christendom*.

65. See Kamen, *The Spanish Inquisition*.

66. Kamen, *The Spanish Inquisition*, 60.

67. Hessayon's review of *The Persecution of the Jews and Muslims of Portugal: King Manuel I and the End of Religious Tolerance (1496–7)*.

68. See Hessayon, review of *The Persecution of the Jews and Muslims of Portugal*.

69. See Gitlitz, *Secrecy and Deceit*, 97–135. See also Rawlings, *The Spanish Inquisition*, 47–72.

70. Gitlitz, *Secrecy and Deceit*, 38–43.

71. Kamen has influentially insisted, and his argument still carries conviction, that "Spain was not a society dominated, as often imagined, exclusively by zealots" (*The Spanish Inquisition*, 5). But neither was Spain a society driven into institutional anti-Semitism exclusively by royal whim and ecclesiastic passion. As for the case that Portuguese, as opposed to Spanish, Jews preserved a more intact sense of Jewish identity in response to the Inquisition, see Bodian, *Hebrews of the Portuguese Nation: Conversos and Community in Early Modern Amsterdam*, 11–14.

72. See Roth, *A History of the Marranos*; as well as Birnbaum, *The Long Journey of Gracia Mendes*.

73. See Uchmany, *La Vida Entre el Judaísmo y el Cristianismo en la Nueva España, 1580–1606*. See also the excellent essay by Elkin, "Imagining Idolatry: Missionaries, Indians, and Jews," 75–99.

74. An estimate for the number of crypto-Jews in the Spanish American viceroyalties (c. 1500–1600) is thirty thousand (Gitlitz, *Secrecy and Deceit*, 75). The statistics regarding demography and expulsion figures for Iberian Jewry are the subject of ongoing investigation beyond the scope of this book. But a cogent summary on estimated numbers is available in Gitlitz, 73–77. Gitlitz also examines the reliability of documentary evidence.

75. Gitlitz, *Secrecy and Deceit*, 19.

76. George Alexander Kohut, "Jewish Heretics in the Philippines in the Sixteenth and Seventeenth Century," *American Jewish Historical Society Journal* 12 (1904), 149.

77. Gitlitz, *Secrecy and Deceit*, 21–22. My treatment of Inquisitorial punishment of Judaizers leans heavily on Gitlitz.

78. See the discussions by Kamen, *The Spanish Inquisition*; and Peters, *Inquisition*. Kamen, the major modern revisionist whose research commands attention, estimates that total executions during the Inquisition came to about three thousand.

79. See Roth, *A History of the Marranos*; and Gitlitz, *Secrecy and Deceit*, 21–22.

80. Bodian, *Hebrews of the Portuguese Nation*, 13. Portuguese conversos also designated themselves as "la nacion portuguesa" or "la gente portugesa."

81. See António J. Saraiva, H. P. Salomon, and I. S. D. Sassoon, *The Marrano Factory: The Portuguese Inquisition and its New Christians, 1536–1765*.

82. Bodian, *Hebrews of the Portuguese Nation*, 7.

83. See María E. Martínez, *Genealogical Fictions: Limpieza de Sangre, Religion, and Gender in Colonial Mexico*, 1; and Bodian, *Hebrews of the Portuguese Nation*, 9. The evolution of the concept, with particular reference to Muslims, is treated by Root, "Speaking Christian: Orthodoxy and Difference in Sixteenth-Century Spain," 118–34.

84. Martínez, *Genealogical Fictions*, 200–26.

85. Friedman, "Jewish Conversion, the Spanish Pure Blood Laws and Reformation: A Revisionist View of Racial and Religious Anti-Semitism," 3–30. The repetition of decrees banning the Jews from the Spanish Americas implies that the laws were often ineffectual.

86. Weddle, "Carvajal y De La Cueva, Luis de."

87. del Hoyo, *Historia del Nuevo Reino de León, 1577–1723*, 30–41, 57–58. Also see Hordes, *To the End of the Earth: A History of the Crypto-Jews of New Mexico*.

88. Cohen, "The Letters and Last Will and Testament of Luis De Carvajal, the Younger," 451.

89. Hordes, "The Inquisition as Economic and Political Agent: The Campaign of the Mexican Holy Office against the Crypto-Jews in the Mid-Seventeenth Century," 23–38.

90. Roth, *A History of the Marranos*, 171–75; and Warshawsky, "Trans-Atlantic Crypto-Judaism and Literary Homage: Tomás Treviño de Sobremonte and the Women in his Life," 65–94.

91. Goldish, *Jewish Questions: Responsa on Sephardic Life in the Early Modern Period*, xxxvii. See also Roth, *A History of the Marranos*.

92. Sachar, *Farewell Espana*, 84–88.

93. Israel, *Conflicts of Empires: Spain, the Low Countries and the Struggle for World Supremacy, 1585–1713*, 197–203, for the activities of David Curiel in Antwerp.

94. Israel, *Conflicts of Empires*, 197.

95. Bodian, *Hebrews of the Portuguese Nation*, 38.

96. Israel, *European Jewry in the Age of Mercantilism, 1550–1750*, 108; Israel, "Jews and Crypto-Jews in the Atlantic World Systems, 1500–1800," 3–17; and Bodian, *Hebrews of the Portuguese Nation*, 38–39. Also see Elliott, *The Revolt of the Catalans: A Study in the Decline of Spain, 1598–1640*, in regards to their revolt.

97. Israel, *Conflicts of Empires: Spain, the Low Countries and the Struggle for World Supremacy, 1585–1713*, 176.

98. Israel, *European Jewry in the Age of Mercantilism, 1550–1750*, 110; Cohen, "Judaism and the History of the Church in the Inquisition Trial of António Vieira," 67–78; and Schwartz, "The Contexts of Vieira's Toleration of Jews and New Christians," 33–44.

99. See Maxwell, *Pombal: Paradox of the Enlightenment*.

100. Marcus, *The Colonial American Jew, 1492–1776*, 1:45.

101. See Graizbord, *Souls in Dispute: Converso Identities in Iberia and the Jewish Diaspora, 1580–1700*, 66–83.

102. Mentzer, "Marranos of Southern France in the Early Sixteenth Century," 303–11.

103. Israel, *European Jewry in the Age of Mercantilism, 1550–1750*, 85.

104. Krinsky, *Synagogues of Europe, Architecture, History, and Meaning*, 244. Also see Benbassa, *The Jews of France: A History from Antiquity to the Present*.

105. Benbassa, *The Jews of France: A History from Antiquity to the Present*, 50–51.

106. Job, *Les Juifs de Lunéville aux XVIIIe et XIXe Siècles: Collection Recherches en Histoire Sociale et Religieuse*, 40; and Krinsky, *Synagogues of Europe, Architecture, History, and Meaning*, 239–41. Most of the "synagogues" mentioned by Szajkowski, "Synagogues during the French Revolution of 1789–1800," 215–231, were of the clandestine type described earlier and resembled the schuilkerken of the Lowlands.

107. Kaplan, "Fictions of Privacy: House Chapels and the Spatial Accommodation of Religious Dissent in Early Modern Europe."

108. Langlais and Rome, *Jews & French Quebecers: Two Hundred Years of Shared History*, 2, 153.

109. Arbell, *The Jewish Nation of the Caribbean: The Spanish-Portuguese Jewish Settlements in the Caribbean and the Guianas*, 45–54.

110. Garrigus, "New Christians / 'New Whites,' Sephardic Jews, Free People of Color and Citizenship in French Saint Domingue, 1760–1789," 314–27.

111. Marcus, *The Colonial American Jew, 1492–1776*, 1:87–89. See also Van Ruymbeke and Sparks, *Memory and Identity: The Huguenots in France and the Atlantic Diaspora*, for an analysis of the Code Noir and the Revocation of the Edict of Nantes and its effects throughout the Atlantic World. Also see Arbell, "Jewish Settlements in the French Colonies in the Caribbean (Martinique, Guadeloupe, Haiti, Cayenne) and the 'Black Code,'" 287–313.

112. Korn, *The Early Jews of New Orleans*, 32–33.

113. Evans, *The Provincials: A Personal History of Jews in the South*, 204; and Elliott Ashkenazi. *The Business of Jews in Louisiana, 1840–1875*, 5.

114. Marcus, *The Colonial American Jew, 1492–1776*, 2:699–700; and King, *From the Ghetto to the Main: The Story of the Jews of Montreal*, 19–27.

115. See Mundill, *England's Jewish Solution: Experiment and Expulsion, 1262–1290*, 26–27.

116. See Mundill, *England's Jewish Solution: Experiment and Expulsion, 1262–1290*.

117. See Mundill, *England's Jewish Solution: Experiment and Expulsion, 1262–1290*.

118. Adler, et al., "Domus Conversorum," *The Jewish Encyclopedia*, 636–38.

119. Weiner, "A Note on Jewish Doctors in England in the Reign of Henry IV," 141–45; and Endelman, *The Jews of Britain, 1656 to 2000*, 15–18.

120. Prior, "Jewish Musicians at the Tudor Court," 253–65; and Katz, *The Jews in the History of England, 1485–1850*, 1–3.

121. Rabbi Halfan's decision in favor of Henry VIII concerned the Jewish custom of halitzah, the process by which the obligation of Levirate marriage is nullified, thus making it legal under biblical law to end the marriage. Moreover divorce was a sanctioned Jewish practice. See Katz, *The Jews in the History of England, 1485–1850*, 1–48; Adler, "Auto de fe and Jew," 698–701.

122. Hyamson, *A History of the Jews in England*, 135–36; and Feldberg, ed., "Joachim Gaunse: The Jew with Sir Walter Raleigh," 2–3.

123. Stick, *Roanoke Island: The Beginnings of English America*, 27–33. See also Wallace, "A List of Participants in the Roanoke Voyages," where the Portuguese

names Alonzo Cornieles, Enrique Lopez, Diego Menendez de Valdes, Baptista Boazio, Francisco Gomez, Anthonio de Samora Carenio, Franciscus Marquino, John de Vivia, Don John de Villa Rey, John de Viveta, Nicholas Gernandes, and Manuel Fernandez Correa appear.

124. Arbell, *The Jewish Nation of the Caribbean: The Spanish-Portuguese Jewish Settlements in the Caribbean and the Guianas*, 83, 192–93.

125. Friedman, "Boston in American Jewish History," 333–34.

126. Levinger, *A History of the Jews in the United States*, 92.

127. See Schama, *The Embarrassment of Riches: An Interpretation of Dutch Culture in the Golden Age*.

128. See Capp, *The Fifth Monarchy Men: A Study in Seventeenth-Century English Millenarianism*.

129. The historiography of the myths, movements, and theology emanating from the ten lost tribes is explored by Benite, *The Ten Lost Tribes: A World History*. For Catholic millenialist thought, see Phelan, *The Millennial Kingdom of the Franciscans in the New World*; and Kottmann, ed., *Catholic Millenarianism: From Savonarola to the Abbé Grégoire*, 2. For Jewish apocalyptic and eschatology, see Goldish and Popkin, eds., *Jewish Messianism in the Early Modern World*, 1.

130. See Lowance, *The Language of Canaan: Metaphor and Symbol in New England from the Puritans to the Transcendentalists*.

131. See Walzer, *Exodus and Revolution*.

132. See Knight, *Orthodoxies in Massachusetts: Rereading American Puritanism*; Stout, *The New England Soul: Preaching and Religious Culture in Colonial New England*; Foster, *The Long Argument: English Puritanism and the Shaping of New England Culture, 1570–1700*.

133. This is not a history that can be treated here. See Goldish and Henry Popkin, eds., *Jewish Messianism in the Early Modern World*, 1.

134. See Maimonides's discussion on the messiah in his famous work, *Mishneh Torah*, where he states "[but] in the days of the Messiah in this world things will go on as usual, except that Israel will have its own government," in Moses Maimonides, Russell, and Weinberg, *The Book of Knowledge: From the Mishneh Torah of Maimonides*, 134.

135. Levine, *Scattered Among the Peoples: The Jewish Diaspora in Twelve Portraits*, 125.

136. Quoted by Davis, "Notes on the History of the Jews in Barbados," 146, from *Mention of the Jews in the Records of Barbados*, by J. Graham Cruickshank, Esq.

137. Pestana, *The English Atlantic in An Age of Revolution, 1640–1661*, 37.

138. ben Israel and Wolf, *Menasseh ben Israel's Mission to Oliver Cromwell: Being a Reprint of the Pamphlets Published by Menasseh Ben Israel to Promote the Re-Admission of the Jews to England, 1649–1656*, xxxvi–xxxvii.

139. Delevante and Alberga, *The Island of One People: An Account of the History of the Jews of Jamaica*, 6–14; and Marcus, *The Colonial American Jew, 1492–1776*, 1:96.

140. Endelman, *The Jews of Georgian England, 1714–1830: Tradition and Change in a Liberal Society*, 16–19.

141. Wilensky, "The Royalist Position Concerning the Readmission of Jews to England," 397–409.

142. Marcus, *The Colonial American Jew, 1492–1776,* 2:500; and Wilensky, "The Royalist Position Concerning the Readmission of Jews to England," 397–409.

143. As it happens de la Penha was not a settler or colonizer, and Labrador would grow without him. Tulchinsky, *Canada's Jews: A People's Journey,* 13.

144. Gitlitz, *Secrecy and Deceit,* 509.

145. Warshawsky, "Catholic, Jewish, and Crypto Jews in the 1600s: The Geographic and Spiritual Peregrinations of Juan Pacheco de Leon in Spain, Italy, and Mexico," 121–39.

146. See Melammed, *Heretics or Daughters of Israel?: The Crypto-Jewish Women of Castile.*

147. Marcus, *The Colonial American Jew, 1492–1776,* 1:53. See also Gitlitz, *Secrecy and Deceit,* 508–13, for other examples in Iberia and Latin America.

148. Quoted by Holly Snyder, "Queens of the Household," 23, from Barnett, "Zipora Nunes's Story," 47–61.

149. A further opportunity for research on Portuguese crypto-Jewish clandestine synagogues in Brazil may exist through analysis of Dutch records on Jewish activities in the hinter regions of Pernambuco. These clandestine synagogues were carryovers from when the Dutch occupied this region of Brazil from the Portuguese. See Feitler, "Jews and New Christians in Dutch Brazil, 1630–1654," 123–52. Also see Canelo, *The Last Crypto-Jews of Portugal,* on the rediscovery of remnant crypto-Jewish communities found in Portugal during the early twentieth century.

CHAPTER 3: Brave New World

1. Bernfeld, "Financing Poor Relief in the Spanish-Portuguese Community in Amsterdam in the Seventeenth and Eighteen Centuries," 62–102.

2. See Braudel, *The Perspective of the World.* Also see Tellier, *Urban World History: An Economic and Geographical Perspective,* 308, has claimed that Antwerp, c. 1510–60, absorbed 40 percent of world trade and earned for Spain seven times the revenues of the Americas.

3. See Grell and Scribner, *Tolerance and Intolerance in the European Reformation.*

4. Kooster, "Communities of Port Jews and their Contacts in the Dutch Atlantic World," 129–45. By the 1550s, the Antwerp–south German trade was in decline, while the Baltic Sea trade was directed to Amsterdam. See Elliott, *Europe Divided, 1559–1598,* 28.

5. See Israel, *The Dutch Republic: Its Rise, Greatness and Fall, 1477–1806;* Duke, *Reformation and Revolt in the Low Countries,* Darby, ed., *The Origins and Development of the Dutch Revolt.*

6. Nahon, "The Portuguese Jewish Nation of Amsterdam as Reflected in the Memoirs of Abraham Haim Lopes, 1752," 59–78; and Belinfante, "The Sephardis, the Jews of Spain," 11–33.

7. See Nadler, *Rembrandt's Jews,* 12–25, 189. See also Kuhn, "Hugo Grotius and the Emancipation of the Jews in Holland," 173–80. Grotius claimed that Jews should

remain in Amsterdam is *Remonstrantie nopende de ordre dije in de landen van Hollandt en Westvrieslandt dijent gestelt op de Joden,* c. 1615.

8. Israel, *The Dutch Republic,* 1025.

9. Belinfante, "The Sephardis, the Jews of Spain," 11–33.

10. An example is Samuel Haas (1770–1860), who was one among the throngs of Jewish migrants who traveled to the Netherlands during this period. Born in Mardorf, Hesse, Germany, Samuel Haas traveled by foot to the Netherlands at the age of sixteen because of the bad conditions for the Jews in Hesse at the time. In 1796, Haas returned to Mardorf after conditions improved, where he settled down and had a family. Vera Hass Plotkin, "The Haas Family History" in the *History of the Katz-Stiefel Family.* Personal family papers of Barry Stiefel, 2000–2004; and Hessisches Staatsarchiv Marburg, *Jüdische Gemeinde Mardorf,* miscellaneous manuscript Jewish records of births and deaths. Also see Israel, *European Jewry in the Age of Mercantilism, 1550–1750.*

11. Israel, *The Dutch Republic: Its Rise, Greatness and Fall, 1477–1806,* 1025.

12. Bodian, "Hebrews of the Portuguese Nation: The Ambiguous Boundaries of Self-Definition," 66–80.

13. Joods Historisch Museum, *Joseph Athias.* <http://www.jhm.nl/personen.aspx?naam=Athias,%20Joseph> (29 December 2008). This material pertaining to Joseph Athias comes from the research done for Stiefel, "The Lopez Family of Newport and Charleston and a Family Heirloom," 393–405, and has been republished with the Rhode Island Jewish Historical Association's generous permission.

14. Joods Historisch Museum, *Joseph Athias.*

15. Nadler, *Rembrandt's Jews,* 140–41.

16. Picart was a deist whose foray into religious anthropology reflected the attitudes of Voltaire and Diderot. In his demythologizing eyes, Judaism was as subject to scientific criticism as Christianity. See Cohen, *Jewish Icons, Art and Society in Modern Europe,* 67. Also see Picart, *Cérémonies et coutumes religieuses de tous les peuples du monde.*

17. See Zell, *Reframing Rembrandt: Jews and the Christian Image in Seventeenth-Century Amsterdam.*

18. Nadler, *Rembrandt's Jews,* 39. See also on Rembrandt's philo-Judaism Zell, *"Eduard Kolloff and the Historiographic Romance of Rembrandt and the Jews,"* 181–97.

19. See Berger, *"Books for the Masses: The Amsterdam Yiddish Book Industry, 1650–1800,"* 24–33. Yiddish-influenced Dutch words include mokum, a nickname for "place" (from *makom*); *gabber* ("friend," from *haver*); and *stiekem* ("in secret," from *shetikah*).

20. Ruderman, *Early Modern Jewry: A New Cultural History,* 120–25.

21. Bodian, *Hebrews of the Portuguese Nation: Conversos and Community in Early Modern Amsterdam,* 126.

22. Baskind, "Bernard Picart's Etchings of Amsterdam's Jews," 40–64; and Israel, *European Jewry in the Age of Mercantilism, 1550–1750,* 155, 179.

23. Bodian, *Hebrews of the Portuguese Nation,* 25–52.

24. The three smaller congregations were Talmud Torah (Study of the Torah), Keter Torah (Crown of the Torah), and Neve Shalom (Abode of Peace). See Bell, "Ethnicity and Identity in Early Modern Hamburg," 1–16.

25. Cohen Paraira, "A Jewel in the City," 41–43.

26. Quoted in Nadler, *Rembrandt's Jews*, 25; from Perelsheim, "Great Synagogue." Also see Gans, *Memorbook: History of Dutch Jewry from the Renaissance to 1940*, 25.

27. Nadler, "Baruch Spinoza." <http://plato.stanford.edu/archives/spr2011/entries/spinoza/>. For a fuller treatment of these issues, see Nadler, *Spinoza's Heresy: Immortality and the Jewish Mind*. Also see Allison, *Benedict de Spinoza: An Introduction*; Lloyd, *Spinoza and the "Ethics,"* and Steinberg, *On Spinoza*.

28. Klooster, *The Dutch in the Americas, 1600–1800: A Narrative History with the Catalogue of an Exhibition of Rare Prints, Maps, and Illustrated Books*, 20.

29. Emmer, "The First Global War: The Dutch versus Iberia in Asia, Africa and the New World, 1590–1609," 1–14.

30. Katz and Goldberg, *The Last Jews of Cochin: Jewish Identity in Hindu India*.

31. Sarna, *American Judaism: A History*, 7–8; Israel, *The Dutch Republic: Its Rise, Greatness and Fall, 1477–1806*, 1057–62; and Katz, "The Jews of England and 1688," 217–49.

32. Stier, "South Africa's Jewish Complex," 123–42; and Green, "Further Considerations on the Sephardim of the Petite Cote," 165–83.

33. Kritzler, *Jewish Pirates of the Caribbean*, 123–28.

34. Emmer, "The History of the Dutch Slave Trade: A Bibliographical Survey," 728–47.

35. Metz, "'Those of the Hebrew Nation . . .': The Sephardic Experience in Colonial Latin America," 216–20.

36. Elkin, *The Jews of Latin America*, 16.

37. Wiznitzer, "The Minute Book of Congregation Zur Israel and Magen Abraham," 217–18.

38. Silverblatt, "New Christians and New World Fears in Seventeenth century Peru," 524–29.

39. Lasker and Lasker, "The Jewish Prayer for Rain in the Post-Talmudic Diaspora," 141–74.

40. Sarna, *American Judaism: A History*, 6–7; Sachar, *Farewell Espana: The World of the Sephardim Remembered*, 351–64.

41. Wiznitzer, "The Synagogue and Cemetery of the Jewish Community of Recife, Brazil (1630–1654)," 129; and Feitler, "Jews and New Christians in Dutch Brazil, 1630–1654," 123–52.

42. Marcus, *The Colonial American Jew, 1492–1776*, 1:75–76.

43. Wiznitzer, "Jewish Soldiers in Dutch Brazil (1630–1654)," 40–51.

44. Wiznitzer, "The Exodus from Brazil and Arrival in New Amsterdam of the Jewish Pilgrim Fathers, 1654," 80–81.

45. Arbell, *The Portuguese Jews of Jamaica*, 3.

46. Congregation Mikve Israel-Emanuel, *Our "Snoa,"* 5492–5742, 10–12.

47. See Emmanuel and Emmanuel, *History of the Jews of the Netherlands Antilles*. Also see Emmer, "The History of the Dutch Slave Trade: A Bibliographical Survey," 728–47.

48. Congregation Mikve Israel-Emanuel, *Our "Snoa,"* 5492–5742, 18–22; and Marcus, *The Colonial American Jew, 1492–1776*, 1:188.

49. Arbell, *The Jewish Nation of the Caribbean: The Spanish-Portuguese Jewish Settlements in the Caribbean and the Guianas,* 133–34.

50. Kohler, "Phases of Jewish Life in New York Before 1800," 77; and Pencak, *Jews and Gentiles in Early America, 1654–1800,* 21–29.

51. Daniels, "Colonial Jewry: Religion, Domestic and Social Relations," 375; and Sarna, *American Judaism: A History,* 9.

52. Klooster, "Networks of Colonial Entrepreneurs: The Founders of the Jewish Settlements in Dutch America, 1650s and 1660s," 33–49; and Marcus, *The Colonial American Jew, 1492–1776,* 1:147.

53. Arbell, *The Jewish Nation of the Caribbean,* 37.

54. Swierenga, *The Forerunners: Dutch Jewry in the North American Diaspora,* 33; and Rodway, *Guiana: British, Dutch, and French,* 60.

55. Cohen, *The Jewish Nation in Surinam,* 45–49.

56. Barnett, *Bevis Marks Records: Being Contributions to the History of the Spanish and Portuguese Congregation of London,* 1–3.

57. Pollins, *Economic History of the Jews in England,* 31.

58. Fischel, "The Jewish Merchant-Colony in Madras (Fort St. George) during the 17th and 18th Centuries: A Contribution to the Economic and Social History of the Jews in India (Concluded)," 175–95.

59. Pollins, *Economic History of the Jews in England,* 45–49.

60. Hyman, *The Jews of Ireland: From Earliest Times to the Year 1910,* 15.

61. Hyman, *The Jews of Ireland,* 19.

62. Israel, *European Jewry in the Age of Mercantilism, 1550–1750,* 129–31; and Childs, *The Nine Years' War and the British Army, 1688–1697: The Operations in the Low Countries,* 52.

63. Ehrlich, ed., *Encyclopedia of the Jewish Diaspora: Origins, Experiences, and Culture,* 924.

64. Samuel, *First London Synagogue of the Resettlement,* 1, 8.

65. See Kadish, et al., *Bevis Marks Synagogue, 1701–2001.*

66. Two surviving English buildings from the middle of the seventeenth century that can be used for comparison are St. Nicholas Abbey and Drax Hall (both built c. 1650s) in Barbados. Nonetheless these buildings are a product of the upper class, which was not the condition of seventeenth-century English colonial Jewry.

67. Arbell, *The Jewish Nation of the Caribbean,* 191–92, 198, 210.

68. Shilstone, *Monumental Inscriptions in the Burial Ground of the Jewish Synagogue at Bridgetown, Barbados,* vii; and Oppenheim, "The Jews in Barbados in 1739. An Attack Upon their Synagogue. Their Long Oath," 197–98, citing the *New York Gazette,* no. 725, 1–8 Oct. 1739.

69. Arbell, *The Jewish Nation of the Caribbean,* 215–16. In 1929 the congregation Nidhe Israel became defunct and was revived in the 1980s.

70. Delevante and Alberga, *The Island of One People: An Account of the History of the Jews of Jamaica,* 6–14.

71. Marcus, *The Colonial American Jew, 1492–1776,* 1:96.

72. Facsimile of correspondence between Jacob Jeosua Bueno Enriques and King Charles II. American Jewish Archives, Small Collections, document SC-3232. Dated 1661. Translation by Barry Stiefel, 18 July 2005.

73. Arbell, *The Jewish Nation of the Caribbean*, 235.

74. Cited from *Moses Cohen Naturalization*, Spanish Town Record Office, Liber 13, 1681, no. 220, as quoted by Kritzler, *Jewish Pirates of the Caribbean*, 251–52.

75. Pollins, *Economic History of the Jews in England*, 50–51.

76. See Blom, Fuks-Mansfeld, and Schöffer, *The History of the Jews in the Netherlands*, 100.

77. Sarna, *American Judaism: A History*, 6–7.

CHAPTER 4: Jewish Prosperity in the Protestant Atlantic World, 1675–1775

1. Locke, *The Fundamental Constitutions of Carolina* (1669)—*North Carolina Digital History*. <http://www.learnnc.org/lp/editions/nchist-colonial/1657> (3 January 2010).

2. Cohen, *The Jewish Nation in Surinam*, 47.

3. Arbell, *The Jewish Nation of the Caribbean: The Spanish-Portuguese Jewish Settlements in the Caribbean and the Guianas*, 92.

4. Palgrave, *Dutch Guiana*, 110.

5. Cohen, *The Jewish Nation in Surinam*, 49.

6. Much of the historical data on Jodensavanne comes from the Nationaal Archief Suriname, copy of manuscript of "Day Note Book of John Greenwood, 1757," located in the *Joden Savannah. Gezicht op de Synagoge en kerhof van de zijde van het Militar Cordonpad gezien files; and Essai historique sur la colonie de Surinam sa fondation, ses révolutions ses progrès, depuis son origine jusqu'à nos jours . . . : avec l'histoire de la nation juive portugaise & allemande y établie*, 1788. Paramaribo: n.p. Additional information was gathered from fieldwork conducted at Jodensavanne in July 2007.

7. Marcus, *The Colonial American Jew, 1492–1776*, I:153–60; and Arbell, *The Jewish Nation of the Caribbean: The Spanish-Portuguese Jewish Settlements in the Caribbean and the Guianas*, 92–95.

8. Arbell, *The Jewish Nation of the Caribbean: The Spanish-Portuguese Jewish Settlements in the Caribbean and the Guianas*, 92–93.

9. See Friedenwald, "Some Newspaper Advertisements of the Eighteenth Century," 49–51. For a general history that covers social and scientific factors, see Weinberg and Bealer, *The World of Caffeine: The Science and Culture of the World's Most Popular Drug*.

10. Ben-Ur, "Still Life: Sephardi, Ashkenazi, and West African Art and Form in Suriname's Jewish Cemeteries," 44–45; and discussed further in Ben-Ur and Frankel, *Remnant Stones: The Jewish Cemeteries and Synagogue of Suriname*.

11. Reps, *Town Planning in Frontier America*, 102; and Sennett, *Flesh and Stone: The Body and the City in Western Civilization*, 106–11. See also Higgins, *The Grid Book*.

12. This is the text used by Ben-Ur, "Still Life: Sephardi, Ashkenazi, and West African Art and Form in Suriname's Jewish Cemeteries," 44.

13. See van Oers, *Dutch Town Planning Overseas during VOC and WIC Rule (1600–1800)*.

14. Andreae's Christianopolis has a certain kinship with King Solomon's Temple as proposed in several studies written by two Spanish Jesuits, Juan Bautista Villalpando (1552–1608) and Heronimo del Prado (1547–95), and published in the 1590s

and the beginning of the next century. Their work considerably influenced seventeenth-century ecclesiastical architectural thought. See Kravtsov, "Juan Bautista Villalpando and Sacred Architecture in the Seventeenth Century," 312–39.

15. Ben-Ur and Frankel's arguments for Jodensavanne's town plan design comes from Ben-Ur, "Still Life: Sephardi, Ashkenazi, and West African Art and Form in Suriname's Jewish Cemeteries"; and Frankel, "Antecedents and Remnants of Jodensavanne: The Synagogue and Cemeteries of the First Permanent Plantation Settlement of New World Jews," 413, 419–20; Ben-Ur and Frankel, *Remnant Stones: The Jewish Cemeteries and Synagogue of Suriname*; and Archer, "Puritan Town Planning in New Haven," 140–49. The evidence for my arguments come from a site visit in July 2007; English translation by Mundigo and Crouch, reprinted in "The City Planning Ordinances of the Laws of the Indies Revisited," 247–68. Translation of ordinances 92, 102–7 by Trias; Reps, *Town Planning in Frontier America*; Held, *Johann Valentin Andreae's Christianopolis: An Ideal State of the Seventeenth Century*; and Nassy, *Historical Essay on the Colony of Surinam, 1788*.

16. Archer. "Puritan Town Planning in New Haven," 140–49.

17. See engraving of Jodensavanne by Pierre Jacques Benoit, c. 1830. William A. Rosenthall Judaica Collection, Special Collections, College of Charleston Library.

18. Ben-Ur and Frankel, *Remnant Stones: The Jewish Cemeteries of Suriname: Epitaphs*, 1–15; Arbell, *The Jewish Nation of the Caribbean: The Spanish-Portuguese Jewish Settlements in the Caribbean and the Guianas*, 82–124.

19. Cohen, *Jews in Another Environment: Surinam in the Second Half of the Eighteenth Century*, 181; and Ben-Ur and Frankel, *Remnant Stones: The Jewish Cemeteries of Suriname: Epitaphs*, 8.

20. Arbell, "Rethinking the American Jewish Experience: Rediscovering Tucacas," 35–41.

21. Rupert, "Trading Globally, Speaking Locally: Curaçao's Sephardim in the Making of a Caribbean Creole," 109–17.

22. Congregation Mikve Israel-Emanuel, *Our "Snoa,"* 5492–5742, 22–28, 58.

23. Swierenga, *The Forerunners: Dutch Jewry in the North American Diaspora*, 35.

24. Monaco, "Port Jews or a People of the Diaspora? A Critique of the Port Jew Concept," 137–66.

25. Arbell, *The Jewish Nation of the Caribbean: The Spanish-Portuguese Jewish Settlements in the Caribbean and the Guianas*, 139–40.

26. Marcus, *The Colonial American Jew, 1492–1776*, 141–42; and Hartog, "The Honen Dalim Congregation of St. Eustatius," 60–65.

27. Bernfeld, "Sephardi Women in Holland's Golden Age," 177–222; and Rottenberg, *Finding Our Fathers: A Guidebook to Jewish Genealogy*, 171.

28. Arbell, "Jewish Women in the Caribbean and the Guianas."

29. A precentor is someone who leads prayers. In Judaism the precentor is called the *chazzan*, but this is a title reserved for men in Orthodox Judaism. The Yiddish word for a female precentor is *firzogerin*. Unfortunately I was unable to identify a Sephardic term. Ben-Ur, "Still Life: Sephardi, Ashkenazi, and West African Art and Form in Suriname's Jewish Cemeteries," 64–65.

30. Ben-Naeh, *Jews in the Realm of the Sultans: Ottoman Jewish Society in the Seventeenth Century*, 224.

31. Amsterdam, The Hague, Amersfoort, Kampen, Rotterdam, Middleburg, Maarssen, Nijkerk, and Naarden are the cities and towns where organized Sephardic settlement took place in the Netherlands, identified in Israel, *The Dutch Republic: Its Rise, Greatness and Fall, 1477–1806*, 1025. This was cross-examined with the database at the Joods Historisch Museum, *Four Hundred Years of Dutch Jewry*, <http://www.jhm.nl/culture-and-history/the-netherlands>, as well as Cohen Paraira, "A Jewel in the City," 41–68. See the individual synagogues discussed throughout the narrative for the sources on the various Dutch synagogues.

32. Kisch, "The Jewish Community in Denmark: History and Present Status," 214–31.

33. Lichtenstein, "Jews in Denmark," 935.

34. Vilhjálmsson, "Iceland, the Jews, and Anti-Semitism, 1625–2004." <http://www.jcpa.org/phas/phas-vilhjalmur-f04.htm>.

35. Friedman, "Gabriel Milan, The First Jewish Governor of St. Thomas," 213.

36. Gjessing, *National Historic Landmark Nomination: St. Thomas Synagogue*; and Cohen, *Through the Sands of Time: A History of the Jewish Community of St. Thomas, U.S. Virgin Island*, 28, 35; and Arbell, *The Jewish Nation of the Caribbean*, 285. There is disagreement between Gjessing, Cohen, and Arbell as to whether or not the 1813 Beraka ve Shalom ve Gemilut Hasadim was renovated and/or added to in 1823 or if an entirely new synagogue was built. When discrepancies such as this occur, this study takes the more conservative count of synagogues. Therefore, the events surrounding the Beraka ve Shalom ve Gemilut Hasadim Synagogue in 1823 are being counted as renovation-addition until more authoritative information is found.

37. Cohen, *Through the Sands of Time*, 3.

38. Kisch, "The Jewish Community in Denmark: History and Present Status," 214–31; and Krinsky, *Synagogues of Europe, Architecture, History, and Meaning*, 403–4.

39. Marcus, *The Colonial American Jew, 1492–1776*, 2:500; and Squires, "The Significance of Religion in British Politics," 78–95.

40. Marcus, *The Jew in the American World: A Source Book*, 41–42; and Feldberg, ed., *Blessings of Freedom: Chapters in American Jewish History*, 8–9.

41. This material comes from the research done for Stiefel, "Jeshuat Israel (Touro) Synagogue's Place Within the British Empire Prior to 1776," 191–208, and has been republished with the Rhode Island Jewish Historical Association's generous permission.

42. "An Act of Denization from Queen Anne to Luis Moses Gomez Dated April 18, 1708," a special publication of the Gomez Mill House, *As A Matter of 'arti'- Fact!*, 1–2.

43. Rosengarten and Rosengarten, eds. *A Portion of the People: Three Hundred Years of Southern Jewish Life*, 76.

44. Hoyt, "Naturalization Under the American Colonies: Signs of a New Community," 248–66; Godfrey and Godfrey, *Search Out the Land: The Jews and the Growth of Equality in British Colonial America, 1740–1867*, 41–42, 54–56; and Lurbe, "John Toland and the Naturalization of the Jews," 37–48.

45. Quoted by de Bethencourt, "Notes on the Spanish and Portuguese Jews in the United States, Guiana, and the Dutch and British West Indies during the Seventeenth and Eighteenth Centuries," 7–38.

46. These counts do not include indigenous synagogue-communities outside of British Europe and the Americas. Some (not many) polities under British imperial control, such as India, had resident Jewish populations before the arrival of the English.

47. Williams, *The Making of Manchester Jewry, 1740–1875*, 5.

48. These three Dutch colonial synagogues built after 1740 were Neve Shalom (1746), Curaçao; Darkhe Yesharim (1779), Surinam; and a congregation (1783) on St. Maarten for which the name has been lost. The second Neve Shalom synagogue of Suriname, built 1833–35 (and after the period of this study), was the fourth.

49. Jacobs and Wolf, *Catalogue of Anglo-Jewish Historical Exhibition, 1887: Royal Albert Hall, and of Supplementary Exhibitions Held at the Public Record Office, British Museum, South Kensington Museum*, 73.

50. See Roth, *The Great Synagogue, London, 1690–1940*.

51. Wigoder, *The Story of the Synagogue*, 122; and Roth. "Chapter XII, The New Great Synagogue, 1790." http://www.jewishgen.org/JCR-UK/susser/roth/ch twelvehtm.

52. See Mendelsohn, *Tongue Ties: Religion, Culture and Commerce in the Making of the Anglophone Jewish Diaspora, 1840–1870*, for a more detailed discussion on this history.

53. Shawchuck and Herring, "Historic Marriage Patterns in the Sephardim of Gibraltar, 1704 to 1939," 177–200.

54. Barnett, *Bevis Marks Records: Being Contributions to the History of the Spanish and Portuguese Congregation of London*, 33.

55. Delevante and Alberga, *The Island of One People: An Account of the History of the Jews of Jamaica*, 10–14.

56. Marcus, *The Colonial American Jew, 1492–1776*, 1:123–24; Arbell, *The Jewish Nation of the Caribbean: The Spanish-Portuguese Jewish Settlements in the Caribbean and the Guianas*, 238; Delevante and Alberga, *The Island of One People: An Account of the History of the Jews of Jamaica*, 72; Holzberg, *Minorities and Power in a Black Society: The Jewish Community of Jamaica*, 9; and de Souza, *Pictorial: Featuring Some Aspects of Jamaica's Jewry and His Community Activities*, 53–55.

57. Terrell, *The Jewish Community of Early Colonial Nevis: A Historical Archaeological Study: A Historical Archaeological Study*, 41–55; and Chernow, *Alexander Hamilton*, 17–18.

58. See Morris, "Roger Williams and the Jew," 24–27.

59. Chyet, "A Synagogue in Newport," 41.

60. The Aaron Lopez papers are held at the American Jewish Historical Society at the Center for Jewish History in New York.

61. Platt, "'And Don't Forget the Guinea Voyage': The Slave Trade of Aaron Lopez of Newport," 601–18; and Snyder, *Guide to the Papers of Aaron Lopez (1731–1782)*, 1752–94, 1846, 1852, 1953. Also see Faber, *Jews, Slaves, and the Slave Trade: Setting the Record Straight*; on the extent of Aaron Lopez's and his Jewish contemporaries

involvement in the slave trade. Lopez is also recorded has having invested in whaling expeditions in the North Atlantic. These voyages most likely supplied the sperm whale oil he needed to make the spermaceti candles.

62. Marcus, *The Colonial American Jew, 1492–1776*, 2:684–85.

63. Poston, *The Buildings of Charleston: A Guide to the City's Architecture*, 473.

64. Snyder, *Guide to the Papers of Aaron Lopez (1731–1782)*, 1752–94, 1846, 1852, 1953.

65. Lyons, Phillips, and Noah, "Items Relating to the Newport Synagogue," 405–7. This material on Touro Synagogue comes from Stiefel and Goodwin, "Three New World Synagogues: Preserved Symbols of Toleration, Pride, and Continuity," 39–69; and Stiefel, "Jeshuat Israel (Touro) Synagogue's Place within the British Empire Prior to 1776," 191–208; and has been republished here with the Rhode Island Jewish Historical Association's generous permission.

66. Sarna, *American Judaism: A History*, 11.

67. Lyons, Phillips, and Noah, "Items Relating to the Newport Synagogue," 194–95.

68. Verification that the two listings of "Stanley Holmes" in 1730s New York has yet to be made. Nonetheless that it is the same person is, in the author's opinion, highly probable. John Peter Zenger's trial led to the concept of freedom of the press. Zenger was charged with printing false and seditious statements about the governor, William Crosby. James Delancey, New York's chief justice presided over the case. Delancey had been appointed by Crosby and gave specific instructions to the jury to find Zenger guilty. Despite these instructions, the jury acquitted Zenger of all charges. Andrew Hamilton, Zenger's defense lawyer, argued that because the published statements against the authorities were true, they did not constitute libel. See Rutherfurd, *John Peter Zenger: His Press, His Trial, and a Bibliography of Zenger Imprints,* for further reading.

69. Grim, *A Plan of the City and Environs of New York.*

70. Daniels, "Colonial Jewry: Religion, Domestic and Social Relations," 375–400.

71. Gelles, ed., *The Letters of Abigaill Levy Franks, 1733–1748*, xv–lii.

72. Neu, "The Jewish Businesswoman in America," 137–40; and Snyder, "Queens of the Household," 15–32.

73. Rosengarten and Rosengarten, eds., *A Portion of the People: Three Hundred Years of Southern Jewish Life*, 67.

74. Plaut, *The Jews of Windsor, 1790–1990: A Historical Chronicle*, 31–32.

75. Snyder, "'Under the Shado of Your Wings': Religiosity in the Mental World of an Eighteenth-Century Jewish Merchant," 581–622.

76. Huhner, "Jews in Connection With the Colleges of the Thirteen Original States Prior to 1800," 101–24. Franklin College is now known as Franklin and Marshall College.

77. Marcus, *The Colonial American Jew, 1492–1776*, 1:332.

78. Rezneck, "A Note on the Genealogy of an Eighteenth-Century Family of Jewish Origin: The Nunez Family of Lewes, Delaware," 20–23.

79. Pencak, *Jews and Gentiles in Early America, 1654–1800*, 45.

80. Tulchinsky, *Canada's Jews: A People's Journey*, 14.

81. Sporadically from the 1960s to the 1990s, archaeological excavations were

conducted at the old fort by Michigan State University. See Halchin, *Excavations at Fort Michilimackinac, 1983–1985: House C of the Southeast Rowhouse, The Solomon-Levy-Parant House*; Heldman, "Michigan's First Jewish Settlers: A View from the Solomon-Levy Trading House at Fort Michilimackinac, 1765–1781," 21–33; and Rubin, "Ezekiel Solomon Historical Marker Dedication," 3–7.

82. Godfrey and Godfrey, *Search Out the Land*, 88–89.

83. The oldest non-Catholic congregation established by Europeans in Canada is St. Paul's Anglican Church of Halifax, Nova Scotia, founded in 1749.

84. Marcus, *The Colonial American Jew, 1492–1776*, 1:378–80, 2:726–30; and Peterson, "The Fort of Ezekiel Solomon," 11–14.

CHAPTER 5: **Jewish Enfranchisement in the Protestant Atlantic World after 1775**

1. These guiding concepts of freedom of conscience and liberty are subject to ongoing discussion in political philosophy and the philosophy of ideas. For the English-speaking world after World War II, the point of departure is often Berlin, *Four Essays on Liberty*, later refined and developed in Berlin, Hardy, and Harris, eds., *Liberty*.

2. Isaac Harby in a letter to Secretary of States James Monroe, Charleston, 1816, is quoted in Rosengarten and Rosengarten, eds., *A Portion of the People: Three Hundred Years of Southern Jewish Life*, 75.

3. Michman, *The History of Dutch Jewry during the Emancipation Period, 1787–1815*, 1–51; and Israel, *The Dutch Republic: Its Rise, Greatness and Fall, 1477–1806*, 1057–62.

4. Michman, *The History of Dutch Jewry during the Emancipation Period, 1787–1815*, 21, 27, 191, 202, 228.

5. Michman, *The History of Dutch Jewry during the Emancipation Period, 1787–1815*, 58.

6. Michman, *The History of Dutch Jewry during the Emancipation Period, 1787–1815*, 179–80.

7. Michman, *The History of Dutch Jewry during the Emancipation Period, 1787–1815*, 21–53, 104; and Israel, *The Dutch Republic*, 1122–30.

8. Swierenga, *The Forerunners: Dutch Jewry in the North American Diaspora*, 23–31.

9. Gilmore, "Geophysics and Volcanic Islands: Resistivity and Gradiometry on St. Eustatius," 170–83.

10. Jameson, "St. Eustatius in the American Revolution," 683–708.

11. Bemis, *The Diplomacy of the American Revolution*, 113–29; and Jameson, "St. Eustatius in the American Revolution," 683–708. Also see Tuchman, *The First Salute: A View of the American Revolution*.

12. Marcus, *The Colonial American Jew, 1492–1776*, 1:141–42.

13. Cohen, *Through the Sands of Time: A History of the Jewish Community of St. Thomas, U.S. Virgin Island*, 9.

14. Jameson, "St. Eustatius in the American Revolution," 683–708; and Cohen, *Through the Sands of Time: A History of the Jewish Community of St. Thomas, U.S. Virgin Island*, 8–9.

15. Friedenwald, "Some Newspaper Advertisements of the Eighteenth Century," 51; and Sarna, *American Judaism: A History*, 33.

16. Hartog, "The Honen Dalim Congregation of St. Eustatius," 60–65.

17. Arbell, *The Jewish Nation of the Caribbean: The Spanish-Portuguese Jewish Settlements in the Caribbean and the Guianas*, 169–70.

18. Kadish, *Jewish Heritage in Gibraltar: An Architectural Guide*, 11–64. The haham was Solomon Abudarham.

19. See Kaplan, *Jewish Daily Life in Germany, 1618–1945*.

20. In fact these two were ancestors of the author who visited Rauschenburg and examined the Katz property. No document could be found pertaining to the Katz family's barn. The document verifying legal permission to erect the barn has either been lost or never existed. Translation of the text inscribed on the barn's lintel by the author.

21. Wilson, *The Southern Strategy: Britain's Conquest of South Carolina and Georgia, 1775–1780*, 270; and Cornelison and Yanak, *The Great American History Fact-Finder*, 240.

22. Marcus, *The Colonial American Jew, 1492–1776*, 1:123–24; Arbell, *The Jewish Nation of the Caribbean: The Spanish-Portuguese Jewish Settlements in the Caribbean and the Guianas*, 238; and Delevante and Alberga, *The Island of One People: An Account of the History of the Jews of Jamaica*, 72.

23. *Congregation Shearith Israel Minutes, 1778–1779*, Document SC-8355, Small Collections, American Jewish Archives.

24. Plaut, *The Jews of Windsor, 1790–1990: A Historical Chronicle*, 16.

25. Tulchinsky, *Canada's Jews: A People's Journey*, 15–16; King, *From the Ghetto to the Main: The Story of the Jews of Montreal*, 51–53; Joseph, "The Settlement of Jews in Canada," 117–20; and Godfrey and Godfrey, *Search Out the Land: The Jews and the Growth of Equality in British Colonial America, 1740–1867*, 177–85.

26. Godfrey and Godfrey, *Search Out the Land: The Jews and the Growth of Equality in British Colonial America, 1740–1867*, 186–189, 232.

27. Langlais and Rome, *Jews and French Quebecers: Two Hundred Years of Shared History*, 18.

28. Godfrey and Godfrey, *Search Out the Land: The Jews and the Growth of Equality in British Colonial America, 1740–1867*, 168.

29. Godfrey and Godfrey, *Search Out the Land: The Jews and the Growth of Equality in British Colonial America, 1740–1867*, 117.

30. Jews could not become officers in the British Army because of its requirement that an oath as a Christian had to be made. Sarna, *American Judaism: A History*, 33.

31. Kerem, "Sephardic Settlement in the British Colonies of the Americas in the 17th and 18th Centuries," 285–94.

32. *A Narrative of the Proceedings of the Jews*, 1–46. Letter writers who advocated Jewish voting rights included Philanthropos, Vetus, Candidus, Justice, A Jew and A Citizen of the World; their letters appeared in the *Kingston Chronicle*, the *Royal Gazette* (Kingston) and the *Cornwall Chronicle* (Montego Bay); quoted in Snyder, "Rules, Rights and Redemption: The Negotiation of Jewish Status in British Atlantic Port Towns, 1740–1831," 162.

33. Wiernik, *History of the Jews in America from the Period of the Discovery of the New World to the Present Day*, 60–61.

34. Hurwitz and Hurwitz, "The New World Sets an Example for the Old The Jews of Jamaica and Political Rights, 1661–1831," 37–57.

35. Barnavi, ed., *A Historical Atlas of the Jewish People, From the Time of the Patriarchs to the Present*, 140–41.

36. Benjamin Disraeli's father, Isaac Disraeli, left Bevis Marks on bad terms and had the entire family baptized. Benjamin Disraeli considered himself ethnically Jewish, but his personal religious conviction was Anglicanism—the faith he was brought up in. While today many might find this an impossible conundrum, this was something Disraeli was comfortable with, and he was an outspoken advocate for the Jews in Victorian Great Britain. Henriques, "The Jewish Emancipation Controversy in Nineteenth-Century Britain," 126–46.

37. King, *From the Ghetto to the Main: The Story of the Jews of Montreal*, 20–23.

38. Gartner, "Emancipation, Social Change and Communal Reconstruction in Anglo-Jewry, 1789–1881," 73–116.

39. Evans, *The Provincials—A Personal History of Jews in the South*, 49.

40. Faber, *The Jewish People in America: A Time for Planting, the First Migration, 1654–1820*, 63.

41. Kahal Kadosh Mikve Israel, *Address to Jewish Congregation of Surinam*.

42. Schoenberger, "The Ritual Silver Made by Myer Myers," 1–13.

43. Morris, "The Role of the Jews in the American Revolution in Historical Perspective," 49–68.

44. *Hayman Levy, Isaac Moses, Benjamin Seixas and Simon Nathan to Jonas Phillips and Bernard Gratz, New York*, 14 Mar. 1788. Misc. File. William L. Clement Library, University of Michigan.

45. Sarna, *American Judaism: A History*, 42. The prayer for the government was formally initiated as a custom in the British Empire by the Dutch haham Jacob Juda Leon, while visiting London in the mid-1670s. Goldhill, *The Temple of Jerusalem*, 138.

46. See Davis, *The History of Rodeph Shalom Congregation, Philadelphia, 1802–1926*.

47. Wischnitzer, "The Egyptian Revival in Synagogue Architecture," 61–78.

48. Sarna, *American Judaism: A History*, 11.

49. *Journal of the Senate of South Carolina*, 1794. Document SC-11217, Small Collections, American Jewish Archives.

50. Ackermann, "The 1794 Synagogue of Kahal Kadosh Beth Elohim of Charleston: Reconstructed and Reconsidered," 159–76.

51. Sarna, *American Judaism: A History*, 52.

52. Ackermann, "The 1794 Synagogue of Kahal Kadosh Beth Elohim of Charleston: Reconstructed and Reconsidered," 159–76.

53. Pencak, *Jews and Gentiles in Early America, 1654–1800*, 125–26.

54. Hagy, "Her 'Scandalous Behavior': A Jewish Divorce in Charleston, South Carolina, 1788," 185–95.

55. *Zeved Habat* is the traditional baby naming ceremony for girls among Sephardim. Though different in its composition of prayers in comparison to the Ashkenazic *Simchat Bat* ceremony it serves the equivalent purpose.

56. See Moore, "Freedom's Fruits: The Americanization of an Old-time Religion," 10–21, in which she assessed David N. Carvalho, Isaac Harby, and Abraham Moise. *The Sabbath Service and Miscellaneous Prayers Adopted by the Reformed Society of Israelites*, reprinted by Barnett A. Elzas (New York: Bloch Publishing Company, 1916). An original copy of *The Isaac Harby Prayer Book* manuscript handwritten by him from c. 1824 is at Special Collections, College of Charleston Library; however, it does not have the more proactive roles for women within it.

57. Sarna, *American Judaism: A History,* 85.

58. Linerles, "Conflict over Reforms: The Case of Congregation Beth Elohim, Charleston, South Carolina," 274–92.

59. David Lopez Jr. was a nephew of Aaron Lopez in Newport.

60. Waddell, "An Architectural History of Kahal Kadosh Beth Elohim, Charleston," 24–25. The material in this section on Beth Elohim comes from the research done for Stiefel, "The Lopez Family of Newport and Charleston and a Family Heirloom," 393–405, and is republished here with the Rhode Island Jewish Historical Association's permission.

61. Elzas, *The Jews of South Carolina: From the Earliest Times to the Present Day,* 208–19; and Sarna, "The Question of Music in American Judaism: Reflections at 350 Years," 195–203.

62. Today the congregation uses its fifth building, completed in 1897, on Central Park West at Seventieth Street.

63. Angel, *Remnant of Israel: A Portrait of America's First Jewish Congregation: Shearith Israel,* 19.

64. Sarna, *American Judaism: A History,* 56–57.

65. Mount Ararat in Turkey is the believed resting place of Noah's Ark.

66. Shalev, "'Revive, Renew, and Reestablish': Mordecai Noah's Ararat and the Limits of Biblical Imagination in the Early American Republic," 1–20.

67. Sarna, *Jacksonian Jew: The Two Worlds of Mordecai Noah,* 61–75.

68. Adler, "Moses Elias Levy and Attempts to Colonize Florida," 17–29.

69. Marcus, *The Colonial American Jew, 1492–1776,* 2:469–74, 349–67; and Pencak, *Jews and Gentiles in Early America, 1654–1800,* 141–44.

70. Pencak, *Jews and Gentiles in Early America, 1654–1800,* 162–65.

71. *K. K. Beth Shalome Collection,* miscellaneous papers, 1789–1898, Beth Ahabah Museum and Archives, Richmond, Virginia.

72. de Sola Pool and de Sola Pool, *An Old Faith in the New World: Portrait of Shearith Israel, 1654–1954,* 48, 55.

73. Rodriguez, ed., *The Louisiana Purchase: A Historical and Geographical Encyclopedia,* 313, 368–69.

74. Korn, *The Early Jews of New Orleans,* 192–208.

75. The exceptions were a splinter group from Beth Elohim in Charleston, called Shearit Israel, formed in 1841; a second Shearit Israel in Columbia, South Carolina, in 1846; and Nefusoth Yehuda of New Orleans, founded in 1847. These are the only congregations that could be accounted for in the United States to have formed during the antebellum period and follow the Sephardic minhag.

76. The members of the Reform Society of Israelites and Sephardic Beth Elohim also made amends in 1838—at least until they split again three years later.

77. Marcus, *The Colonial American Jew, 1492–1776*, 2 and 3:542, 927, and 1333. The data on congregational foundings in the United States was compiled from the finding aids and indexes of the American Jewish Historical Society Archives, Center for Jewish History; American Jewish Archives at Hebrew Union College; the Archives of the Jewish Theological Seminary; and the International Survey of Jewish Monuments.

78. On de Pinto see Bodian, "'Men of the Nation': The Shaping of Converso Identity in Early Modern Europe," 48–76. On the general problems of Voltaire's anti-Semitism, see Hertzberg, *The French Enlightenment and the Jews*, 180–83.

79. Sutcliffe, "Can a Jew Be a Philosophe? Isaac de Pinto, Voltaire, and Jewish Participation in the European Enlightenment," 31–51.

80. See *Les juifs d'Alsace doivent-ils être admis au droit de citoyens actifs? Lisez et jugez*.

81. Szajkowski, "Protestants and Jews of France in Fight for Emancipation, 1789–1791," 119–35.

82. Hyman, *The Emancipation of the Jews of Alsace: Acculturation and Tradition in the Nineteenth Century*, 15–16; and Benbassa, *The Jews of France: A History from Antiquity to the Present*, 141–47.

83. See Berlin, *Two Concepts of Liberty*.

84. Sarna, "The Impact of the American Revolution on American Jews," 149–57.

85. Zeitlin, "Judaism as a Religion, An Historical Study (Continued)," 113–16.

86. Benbassa, *The Jews of France: A History from Antiquity to the Present*, 207.

87. Benbassa, *The Jews of France: A History from Antiquity to the Present*, 208.

88. Arbell, *The Jewish Nation of the Caribbean: The Spanish-Portuguese Jewish Settlements in the Caribbean and the Guianas*, 159–60.

89. Cyrus Adler, et al., "Auto Da Fe," *The Jewish Encyclopedia*, 338–43; Elkin, *The Jews of Latin America*, 88–92; and Ezratty, *500 years in the Jewish Caribbean: The Spanish and the Portuguese Jews in the West Indies*, 89–101.

90. Cohen "Settlement of the Jews in Texas," 139–56.

91. MacLachlan, *A History of Modern Brazil: The Past Against the Future*, 16–38.

92. See Elkin, *The Jews of Latin America*; and Dias, "The Jewish Community in the Azores from 1820 to the Present," 19–34; and Igel, "Haquita as Spoken in the Brazilian Amazon," 446–56.

93. Gustavus Poznanski's dedicatory speech at the consecration of the Kahal Kadosh Beth Elohim, Charleston, March 1841, is quoted in Rosengarten and Rosengarten, eds., *A Portion of the People: Three Hundred Years of Southern Jewish Life*, 93.

CHAPTER 6: Jews and Non-Caucasians in the Atlantic World

1. See Hordes, *To the End of the Earth: A History of the Crypto-Jews of New Mexico*.

2. Perelis, "'These Indians Are Jews!' Lost Tribes, Crypto-Jews, and Jewish Self-Fashhioning in Antonio de Montezinos's Relacion of 1644," 195–211; and Popkin, "Mordecai Noah, the Abbé Grégoire and the Paris Sanhedrin," 131–48.

3. There were several David Nassys, and precise identification, apart from noting the time period itself, remains tenuous.

4. Abella, *A Coat of Many Colours: Two Centuries of Jewish Life in Canada*, 13; and Marcus, *The Colonial American Jew, 1492–1776*, 1:160.

5. Rozen, *A History of the Jewish Community in Istanbul: The Formative Years, 1453–1566*, 191–92.

6. See James W. Hagy, *This Happy Land: The Jews of Colonial and Antebellum Charleston*, 93 for 1850 census data. See also South Carolina Department of Archives and History, *Isaac Fripp of St. Helena Parish, District of Beaufort to David Lopez, Bill of Sale for a slave named Kit or Christopher, a carpenter by trade*, 30 June 1837, series S213003, vol. 005T, p. 200; and *B. R. Carroll to David Lopez, Bill of Sale for a slave named George, a carpenter*, 11 June 1839, series S213003, vol. 005W, p. 22.

7. Schorsch, *Jews and Blacks in the Early Modern World*, 226.

8. See *Minute Book of the Congregation Shearith Israel*, years 1728–30, Jacques Judah Lyons Collection, Box 1, American Jewish Historical Society, Center for Jewish History.

9. *Board of Trustee Minute Book (1838–1843)*, 146, 27 Dec. 1840 / 3 Tebet 5601, KKBE Collection, Box 1, Folder 1, Special Collections, College of Charleston.

10. See Finkelman and Miller, eds., *Macmillan Encyclopedia of World Slavery*.

11. Arbell, *The Jewish Nation of the Caribbean: The Spanish-Portuguese Jewish Settlements in the Caribbean and the Guianas*, 242.

12. Owen and Owen, eds. *History of Alabama and Dictionary of Alabama Biography*, 2:813; and Berlin, *Freedom: A Documentary History of Emancipation, 1861–1867: Selected from the Holdings of the National Archives of the United States*, 683.

13. My views on Jews in relation to slavery during the time period of this study have been shaped by two first-rate investigators: see Eli Faber, *Jews, Slaves, and the Slave Trade: Setting the Record Straight*; and Schorsch, *Jews and Blacks in the Early Modern World*.

14. Korn, "Jews and Negro Slavery in the Old South, 1789–1865, Address of the President," 155.

15. Faber, *Jews, Slaves, and the Slave Trade: Setting the Record Straight*, 1–10.

16. Korn, "Jews and Negro Slavery in the Old South, 1789–1865, Address of the President," 175–77.

17. Kiewe, "Nigerian Sculpture of a Jewish Trader," 162–68.

18. Mark and Morta, "Catholics, Jews, and Muslims in Early Seventeenth-Century Guine," 170–94.

19. See Kiewe, "Nigerian Sculpture of a Jewish Trader," 162–68.

20. Green, "Further Considerations on the Sephardim of the Petite Cote," 165–83; Schorsch, "Early Modern Sephardim and Blacks, Contact and Conflict between Two Minorities," 239–54; and Hagoort, *Beth Haim in Ouderkerk aan de Amstel: de begraafplaats van de Portugese joden in Amsterdam 1614–1945*.

21. Schorsch, "Early Modern Sephardim and Blacks, Contact and Conflict between Two Minorities," 252.

22. Ben-Ur, "A Matriarchal Matter: Slavery, Conversion, and Upward Mobility in Suriname's Jewish Community," 152–69.

23. Religious identity for a Jew descends from the mother; inheritance of a material order (property, possessions, and wealth) are normatively in the gift of the father.

24. There were already sub-Saharan African-born Jews in the seventeenth century in Ethiopia, but they had no significant involvement in the Atlantic World or links to the Jews in Amsterdam. Green, "Further Considerations on the Sephardim of the Petite Cote," 165–83.

25. See Holzberg, *Minorities and Power in a Black Society: The Jewish Community of Jamaica*.

26. Marcus, *The Colonial American Jew, 1492–1776,* 1:159.

27. Phaf-Rheinberger, "The Portuguese Jewish Nation: An Enlightenment Essay on the Colony of Suriname," 491–503.

28. Ben-Ur, "A Matriarchal Matter: Slavery, Conversion, and Upward Mobility in Suriname's Jewish Community," 152–69.

29. Arbell, *The Jewish Nation of the Caribbean: The Spanish-Portuguese Jewish Settlements in the Caribbean and the Guianas,* 106–9; and Schorsch, "Early Modern Sephardim and Blacks, Contact and Conflict between Two Minorities," 252. If the non-Jewish women of African descent voluntarily converted to Judaism, the groom's status as jahid could be restored to him.

30. Schorsch, *Jews and Blacks in the Early Modern World,* 217–53.

31. Ben-Ur, "A Matriarchal Matter: Slavery, Conversion, and Upward Mobility in Suriname's Jewish Community," 162–66.

32. Watson, *Shifting Identities: The Role of Religion, Race, and Creolization among the Sephardic Jews of Barbados, 1654 to 1900;* who quotes: "It is proper to explain that in a religious point of view we make no distinction between Mr. Brandon's son (who is a man of colour) and any other member of our community. It might truly be said of this young man that he is a Jew from inclination as he chose the religion of his father at a time of life when capable of judging for himself, for he was of age when he went to Surinam in order to be admitted within the pale of Judaism." London Metropolitan Archives, Nidhe Israel MS 397, 1820, pp. 33–34.

33. Phaf-Rheinberger, "The Portuguese Jewish Nation: An Enlightenment Essay on the Colony of Suriname," 499.

34. Ben-Ur, "Still Life: Sephardi, Ashkenazi, and West African Art and Form in Suriname's Jewish Cemeteries," 75–77. Note that few studies have been done on the Jews with sub-Saharan African ancestry from this period of history and that of the sources that could be found (Arbell, Frankel, and Ben-Ur), their information mostly overlapped.

35. Marcus, *The Colonial American Jew, 1492–1776,* 1:159–60.

36. Melnick, "Billy Simons: The Black Jew of Charleston," 3–8; and Hagy, *This Happy Land: The Jews of Colonial and Antebellum Charleston,* 101–3; and Moore, "Freedom's Fruits: The Americanization of an Old-Time Religion," 14.

Conclusion

1. See Sarna, *American Judaism: A History,* 12, though his focus is on colonial North America.

2. See Emmanuel and Emmanuel, *History of the Jews of the Netherlands Antilles;* Arbell, *The Jewish Nation of the Caribbean, the Spanish-Portuguese Jewish Settlements in the Caribbean and the Guiana;* and Cohen, *Jews in Another Environment: Surinam in the Second Half of the Eighteenth Century.*

3. This is the view of Sarna, who writes: "following publication of his book [Menasseh ben Israel's *Hope of Israel* in 1650], however, many subsequent synagogues in the New World, through the end of the eighteenth century, took on names that reflected the Dutch rabbi's millenarian belief that the colonization of Jews in the New World was both a harbinger and an instrument of messianic redemption." Sarna, "The Mystical World of Colonial American Jews," 187–88.

4. Schorsch, *Jews and Blacks in the Early Modern World*, 217–53.

5. See Bailyn, *The Peopling of British North America: An Introduction*.

6. The surviving historical record on Beth Elohim and Beth Elohim Unveh Shalom of Charleston is scant; therefore a definitive conclusion can not be made on whether the controversy in South Carolina was part of this historical trend.

7. Sarna, *American Judaism: A History*, 53.

8. Sarna's *American Judaism: A History* identifies this change as a phenomenon in American society. But an Atlanticist historiographic perspective widens the lens here: the synagogue-community fades away not only in the United States, but throughout the entire Atlantic World.

9. According to Rosenwaike, *On the Edge of Greatness: A Portrait of American Jewry in the Early National Period*, 15, the Jewish population in the United States had reached approximately four thousand in contrast to about five thousand in the Caribbean (including Surinam) in 1830. Only a very small number lived in Belém and Montreal, the only other cities with organized Jewish communities in the Americas. By the mid-1870s the Jewish population in the United States would exceed 270,000.

10. Sarna, *American Judaism: A History*, 43; and Sarna, "The Impact of the American Revolution on American Jews," 149–57.

11. See Sarna, *Jacksonian Jew: The Two Worlds of Mordecai Noah*.

12. See MacLachlan, *A History of Modern Brazil: The Past Against the Future*; MacLachlan and Beezley, *El Gran Pueblo: A History of Greater Mexico*; and Elkin, *The Jews of Latin America*.

13. See Krinsky, *Synagogues of Europe: Architecture, History, and Meaning*, 42–44.

14. Marcus, *The Colonial American Jew, 1492–1776*, 2:684.

15. Sarna, *Jacksonian Jew: The Two Worlds of Mordecai Noah*, 4, 8.

16. Picciotto, *Sketches of Anglo-Jewish History*, 300.

17. Krinsky, *Synagogues of Europe: Architecture, History, and Meaning*, 67–68, 424–26; and Kadish, *Jewish Heritage in England: An Architectural Guide*, 76–77.

18. Poston, *The Buildings of Charleston: A Guide to the City's Architecture*, 473.

19. "Zion Church," *Charleston Mercury*, 5 Apr. 1859, 1

20. See Potts, "David Lopez Cohen (1820–1893), Savannah Builder—Carpenter."

21. Poston, *The Buildings of Charleston: A Guide to the City's Architecture*, 56, 111, 409, 450, 473; and Rosen, *Confederate Charleston: An Illustrated History of the City and the People during the Civil War*, 94.

22. Breibart, et al., *Explorations in Charleston's Jewish History*, 51–54.

23. See "Consecration of the New Synagogue, Charleston, S.C," *Occident and Jewish American Advocate* 5, no. 6 (Elul 5607 / Sept. 1847). David Lopez Cohen relocated to Savannah, Georgia by 1850.

24. Rubin, *Third to None: The Saga of Savannah Jewry, 1733–1983*, 121.

25. Lerner, "The Narrating Architecture of Emancipation," 1–30; and Krinsky, *Synagogues of Europe: Architecture, History, Meaning*, 59–104.

26. Wischnitzer, *Synagogue Architecture in the United States: History and Interpretation*, 43.

27. See Holliday, *Leopold Eidlitz: Architecture and Idealism in the Gilded Age*.

28. See Snyder, "Acculturation and Particularism in the Modern City: Synagogue Building and Jewish Identity in Northern Europe"; Kadish, *The Synagogues of Britain and Ireland: An Architectural and Social History*; and Black, "The Anglicization of Orthodoxy: The Adlers, Father and Son," 295–325.

29. Kadish, *The Synagogues of Britain and Ireland: An Architectural and Social History*, 167; and Watson, "Rebuilding London: Abraham Davis and his Brothers, 1881–1924," 62–84.

30. Krinsky, *Synagogues of Europe: Architecture, History, Meaning*, 249; and Wischnitzer, *The Architecture of the European Synagogue*, 210.

31. Gans, *Memorbook: History of Dutch Jewry from the Renaissance to 1940*, 455. Coenen Snyder, *Acculturation and Particularism in the Modern City: Synagogue Building and Jewish Identity in Northern Europe*, 197-98.

32. Quoted by Lerner, "The Narrating Architecture of Emancipation," *Jewish Social Studies*, 4, from Zadoc Kahn, "Allocution prononcée à la cérémonie d'inauguration du temple israélite de Boulogne-sur-Mer le 25 août 1873," *Sermons et allocutions*. Première série (Paris, 1875), 277.

Appendix

1. See van Agt, *Synagogen in Amsterdam*.

2. Cohen Paraira, "A Jewel in the City," 42–43.

3. See Kaufman, "O que se conta. . . . Quem conta. . . . Como se conta. . . . Os Judeus em Pernambuco Práticas judaicas, sinagogas." The material in this section pertaining to Zur Israel comes from the research done for Stiefel and Goodwin, "Three New World Synagogues: Preserved Symbols of Toleration, Pride, and Continuity," 39–69.

4. Wiznitzer, "The Minute Book of Congregation Zur Israel and Magen Abraham," 217–18; and Wiznitzer, "The Synagogue and Cemetery of the Jewish Community of Recife, Brazil (1630–1654)," 129.

5. Arbell, *The Jewish Nation of the Caribbean: The Spanish-Portuguese Jewish Settlements in the Caribbean and the Guianas*, 45–54.

6. Arbell, *The Jewish Nation of the Caribbean: The Spanish-Portuguese Jewish Settlements in the Caribbean and the Guianas*, 197–98, 215.

7. Watson, *Fw: Your book and my article* personal correspondence. Hadchity, "Of Bridges, Berths, and Hawkers."

8. Miller, *Report for the Synagogue Pathway Project (Site 1 BM 4), Bridgetown, Barbados*. Also see Miller, "The Bridgetown Synagogue Pathway Archaeology Project: A Preliminary Report," 87–104.

9. Arbell, *The Jewish Nation of the Caribbean: The Spanish-Portuguese Jewish Settlements in the Caribbean and the Guianas*, 198, 207–8.

10. Nationaal Archief Suriname, *Het dorp Jodensavanne aan de Surinamerivier*.

11. Congregation Mikve Israel-Emanuel, *Our "Snoa,"* 5492–5742, 18–22; and Marcus, *The Colonial American Jew, 1492–1776*, 1:188.

12. Cohen Paraira, "A Jewel in the City," 66–67.

13. Cohen Paraira, "A Jewel in the City," 48–67.

14. Netherlands Department of Conservation, *Historic Centre of Amsterdam*; and Rosenberg, *Memory of the World Register Nomination Form*.

15. Delevante and Alberga, *The Island of One People: An Account of the History of the Jews of Jamaica*; 65–66.

16. Terrell, *The Jewish Community of Early Colonial Nevis: A Historical Archaeological Study*.

17. Nationaal Archief Suriname, *Het dorp Jodensavanne aan de Surinamerivier*; and Frankel, "Antecedents and Remnants of Jodensavanne: The Synagogue and Cemeteries of the First Permanent Plantation Settlement of New World Jews," 394–426; Groll, *De Architecture Van Suriname, 1667–1930*, 90–98; and Nassy, *Historical Essay on the Colony of Surinam, 1788*.

18. Congregation Mikve Israel-Emanuel, *Our "Snoa,"* 5492–5742, 18–22; and Marcus, *The Colonial American Jew, 1492–1776*, 1:188.

19. Kadish, et al. *Bevis Marks Synagogue, 1701–2001*.

20. Congregation Mikve Israel-Emanuel, *Our "Snoa,"* 5492–5742, 18–20.

21. "Kahal Kodesh Neveh Shalom," *Neveh Shalom Institute*. <http://www.sephardim.org/Neveh_Shalom/>.

22. Arbell, *The Jewish Nation of the Caribbean: The Spanish-Portuguese Jewish Settlements in the Caribbean and the Guianas*, 240.

23. Arbell, *The Jewish Nation of the Caribbean: The Spanish-Portuguese Jewish Settlements in the Caribbean and the Guianas*, 261–67.

24. Delevante and Alberga, *The Island of One People: An Account of the History of the Jews of Jamaica*, 66.

25. Groll, *De Architecture Van Suriname, 1667–1930*, 90–98.

26. Lyons, Phillips, and Noah, "Items Relating to the Newport Synagogue," 194–95.

27. See *Minute Book of the Congregation Shearith Israel*, years 1728–30, Jacques Judah Lyons Collection, Box 1, American Jewish Historical Society, Center for Jewish History.

28. Bangs and Bangs, *Journal of Lieutenant Isaac Bangs, April 1 to July 29, 1776*, 40–42.

29. See Congregation Mikve Israel-Emanuel, *Our "Snoa,"* 5492–5742.

30. Israel Museum, *Reconstruction and Installation of the Zedek-ve-Shalom Synagogue in the Israel Museum, Exhibition of the Jews of Suriname*; Groll, *De Architecture Van Suriname, 1667–1930*, 100–108.

31. Gilmore, *Case for Support*; Hartog, *The Jews and St. Eustatius*, 5–16.

32. Sinclair and Fyfe, *The Handbook of Jamaica, 1882*, 357, quoted in Delevante and Alberga, *The Island of One People: An Account of the History of the Jews of Jamaica*, 69–70.

33. Congregation Mikve Israel-Emanuel, *Our "Snoa,"* 5492–5742, 56–58.

34. See Kadish, *Jewish Heritage in Gibraltar: An Architectural Guide.*

35. See Stiefel and Goodwin, "Three New World Synagogues: Preserved Symbols of Toleration, Pride, and Continuity," 39–69; republished with the Rhode Island Jewish Historical Association's permission.

36. Chyet, "A Synagogue in Newport," 41; Goodwin, "The Politics of Preservation: How Touro Synagogue Became a National Historic Site," 177–207; Lewis, "History of Touro Synagogue," 305; and Touro Synagogue Foundation, "Time Line." <http://www.tourosynagogue.org/>.

37. Stiles, *Diary,* quoted in Slade, "Touro Synagogue, Congregation Jeshuat Israel."

38. Arbell, *The Jewish Nation of the Caribbean: The Spanish-Portuguese Jewish Settlements in the Caribbean and the Guianas,* 272–73.

39. See Kadish, *Jewish Heritage in Gibraltar: An Architectural Guide.*

40. Godfrey and Godfrey, *Search Out the Land: The Jews and the Growth of Equality in British Colonial America, 1740–1867,* 114; and Atherton, *Montreal, 1535–1914,* 285.

41. *Congregation Shearith Israel Minutes, 1778–1779.* Small Collections, Document SC-8355, American Jewish Archives, Cincinnati, Ohio.

42. Schorsch, *Jews and Blacks in the Early Modern World,* 217–53.

43. See Kadish, *Jewish Heritage in Gibraltar: An Architectural Guide.*

44. Pencak, *Jews and Gentiles in Early America, 1654–1800,* 208, 212, 227, 263.

45. *Excerpts from the Diary of Hipolito Jose da Costa,* quoted in Smith, "A Portuguese Naturalist in Philadelphia, 1799," 71–107.

46. Arbell, *The Jewish Nation of the Caribbean: The Spanish-Portuguese Jewish Settlements in the Caribbean and the Guianas,* 169–70.

47. Teenstra, *De Nederlandsche West-Indische eilanden in derzelver tegenwoordigen toestand* 2:252.

48. See Kadish, *Jewish Heritage in Gibraltar: An Architectural Guide.*

49. Delevante and Alberga, *The Island of One People: An Account of the History of the Jews in Jamaica,* 72.

50. "Religious Summary," 3. Reprinted from the *Portland Courier,* 30 Mar. 1833.

51. Ackermann, "The 1794 Synagogue of Kahal Kadosh Beth Elohim of Charleston: Reconstructed and Reconsidered," 159–74.

52. Cohen, *Through the Sands of Time: A History of the Jewish Community of St. Thomas, U.S. Virgin Island,* 25–28, 35.

53. Delevante and Alberga, *The Island of One People: An Account of the History of the Jews in Jamaica,* 68–69.

54. See Kadish, *Jewish Heritage in Gibraltar: An Architectural Guide.*

55. Gjessing, *National Historic Landmark Nomination: St. Thomas Synagogue;* and Cohen, *Through the Sands of Time: A History of the Jewish Community of St. Thomas, U.S. Virgin Island,* 28, 35.

56. *The Picture of New York and Stranger's Guide to the Commercial Metropolis of the United States* (New York: A. T. Goodrich, 1828), quoted in de Sola Pool, "Descriptions of the Synagogue in New York in 1776 and 1828," 189.

57. de Sola Pool and de Sola Pool, *An Old Faith in the New World: Portrait of Shearith Israel, 1654–1954*, 44–45.

58. Rubin, *Third to None: The Saga of Savannah Jewry, 1733–1983*, 64.

59. See Kadish, *Jewish Heritage in Gibraltar: An Architectural Guide*.

60. Green, Loth, and Rasmussen, *Lost Virginia, Vanished Architecture of the Old Dominion*, 142.

Bibliography

Abella, Irving. *A Coat of Many Colours: Two Centuries of Jewish Life in Canada.* Toronto: Lester and Orpen Dennys, 1990.

Ackermann, Daniel K. "The 1794 Synagogue of Kahal Kadosh Beth Elohim of Charleston: Reconstructed and Reconsidered." *American Jewish History* 93, no. 2 (June 2007), 159–74.

Adams, Charles. *For Good and Evil: The Impact of Taxes on the Course of Civilization.* London: Madison Books, 1993.

Adler, Cyrus, et al. *The Jewish Encyclopedia: A Descriptive Record of the History, Religion, Literature, and Customs of the Jewish People from the Earliest Times to the Present Day.* New York: Funk and Wagnalls, 1903–6.

Adler, E. N. "Auto de fe and Jew." *Jewish Quarterly Review* 14, no. 4 (July 1902), 698–701.

Adler, Joseph G. "Moses Elias Levy and Attempts to Colonize Florida." In *Jews of the South: Selected Essays from the Southern Jewish Historical Society.* Samuel Proctor, Louis Schmier, and Malcolm H. Stern, eds. Macon, GA: Mercer University Press, 1984, 17–29.

Agt, J. F. van. *Synagogen in Amsterdam.* Gravenhage, Netherlands: Staatsuitgeverij, 1974.

Allison, Henry E. *Benedict de Spinoza: An Introduction.* New Haven: Yale University Press, 1987.

Altmann, Alexander. "Eternality of Punishment: A Theological Controversy within the Amsterdam Rabbinate in the Thirties of the Seventeenth Century." *Proceedings of the American Academy for Jewish Research* 40 (1972), 3.

Angel, Marc D. *Remnant of Israel: A Portrait of America's First Jewish Congregation: Shearith Israel.* New York: Riverside Book Company, 2004.

Antunes, Cátia. *Globalisation in the Early Modern Period: The Economic Relationship between Amsterdam and Lisbon, 1640–1705.* Amsterdam: Aksant, 2004.

Arbell, Mordechai. *The Jewish Nation of the Caribbean: The Spanish-Portuguese Jewish Settlements in the Caribbean and the Guianas.* Jerusalem: Gefen Publishing, 2002.

———. "Jewish Settlements in the French Colonies in the Caribbean (Martinique, Guadeloupe, Haiti, Cayenne) and the 'Black Code.'" In *The Jews and the Expansion of Europe to the West, 1450 to 1800.* Paolo Bernardini and Norman Fiering, eds. New York: Berghahn Books, 2001, 287–313.

———. "Jewish Women in the Caribbean and the Guianas." In *Jewish Women: A Comprehensive Historical Encyclopedia.* Jerusalem: Shalvi Publishing, 2007, electronic resource on CD.

———. *The Portuguese Jews of Jamaica.* Kingston, Jamaica: Canoe Press, 2000.

———. "Rethinking the American Jewish Experience: Rediscovering Tucacas." *American Jewish Archives Journal* 48, no. 1 (Spring–Summer 1996), 35–41.

Archer, John. "Puritan Town Planning in New Haven." *Journal of the Society of Architectural Historians* 34, no. 2 (May 1975), 140–49.

Architecture Week. "Lord Burlington." *Great Buildings Collection.* 2010. <http://www.greatbuildings.com/architects/Lord_Burlington.html> (accessed 1 Mar. 2010).

Ashkenazi, Elliott. *The Business of Jews in Louisiana, 1840–1875.* Tuscaloosa: University of Alabama Press, 1988.

Assis, Yom Tov. *The Jews of Spain: From Settlement to Expulsion.* Jerusalem: World Zionist Organization, 1988.

Atherton, William H. *Montreal, 1535–1914.* Montreal: S. J. Clarke, 1914.

Atmore, Anthony, and Roland A. Oliver. *Medieval Africa, 1250–1800.* Cambridge, UK: Cambridge University Press, 2001.

Author Unknown. Document SC-9627. 30 Apr. 1788, Small Collections, American Jewish Archives.

Author Unknown. "Kahal Kodesh Neveh Shalom." *Neveh Shalom Institute.* 27 June 1998. <http://www.sephardim.org/Neveh_Shalom/> (accessed 15 Jan. 2008).

Author Unknown. "Part III: The Period of Prosperity (1637–1644)." *American Jewish Historical Society Journal* 33 (1934), 57–77.

Author Unknown. *The Portuguese Synagogue.* De Portuguese-Israelitsche Synagogue, n.d.

Author Unknown. "Religious Summary." *Christian Register,* 4 May 1833, 3. Reprinted from the *Portland Courier,* 30 Mar. 1833.

Bailyn, Bernard. *The Peopling of British North America: An Introduction.* New York: Knopf, 1986.

Bangs, Isaac, and Edward Bangs. *Journal of Lieutenant Isaac Bangs, April 1 to July 29, 1776.* Cambridge, UK: J. Wilson and Son, 1890.

Barnavi, Eli, ed. *A Historical Atlas of the Jewish People, From the Time of the Patriarchs to the Present.* New York: Schocken Books, 1992.

Barnett, Lionel D. *Bevis Marks Records; Being Contributions to the History of the Spanish and Portuguese Congregation of London. Part 1, The Early History of the Congregation from the Beginning until 1800.* Oxford, UK: Printed at the University Press by J. Johnson, 1940.

Barnett, Richard D. "Zipora Nunes's Story." In *A Bicentennial Festschrift for Jacob Rader Marcus.* Bertram W. Korn, ed. New York: American Jewish Historical Society and KTAV Publishing House, 1976, 47–61.

Baskind, Samantha. "Bernard Picart's Etchings of Amsterdam's Jews." *Jewish Social Studies: History, Culture, Society* new ser. 13, no. 2 (Winter 2007), 40–64.

Belinfante, Judith C. E. "The Sephardis, the Jews of Spain." In *The Esnoga: A Monument to Portuguese-Jewish Culture,* Martine Stroo and Ernest Kurpershoek, eds. Amsterdam: D'Arts, 2001: 11–33.

Bell, Dean P. "Ethnicity and Identity in Early Modern Hamburg." *Transit* 3, no. 1 (2007), 1–16.

———. *Jews in the Early Modern World.* Lanham, MD: Rowman and Littlefield, 2008.

Bemis, Samuel F. *The Diplomacy of the American Revolution.* Bloomington: Indiana University Press, 1957.

Benbassa, Esther. *The Jews of France: A History from Antiquity to the Present.* Princeton: Princeton University Press, 1999.

Benite, Zvi Ben-Dor. *The Ten Lost Tribes: A World History.* Oxford, UK: Oxford University Press, 2009.

Ben-Naeh, Yaron. *Jews in the Realm of the Sultans: Ottoman Jewish Society in the Seventeenth Century.* Tübingen, Germany: Mohr Siebeck, 2008.

Ben-Ur, Aviva. "A Matriarchal Matter: Slavery, Conversion, and Upward Mobility in Suriname's Jewish Community." In *Atlantic Diasporas: Jews, Conversos, and Crypto-Jews in the Age of Mercantilism, 1500–1800.* Richard L. Kagan and Philip D. Morgan, eds. Baltimore: Johns Hopkins University Press, 2009, 152–69.

———. "Still Life: Sephardi, Ashkenazi, and West African Art and Form in Suriname's Jewish Cemeteries." *American Jewish History* 92, no. (1 Mar. 2004), 31–79.

Ben-Ur, Aviva, and Rachel Frankel. *Remnant Stones: The Jewish Cemeteries and Synagogue of Suriname: Essays.* Cincinnati: Hebrew Union College Press, 2012.

———. *Remnant Stones: The Jewish Cemeteries of Suriname: Epitaphs.* Cincinnati: Hebrew Union College Press, 2009.

Berger, Shlomo. "Books for the Masses: The Amsterdam Yiddish Book Industry, 1650–1800." *European Judaism* 42, no. 2 (Autumn 2009), 24–33.

Berlin, Ira. *Freedom: A Documentary History of Emancipation, 1861–1867: Selected from the Holdings of the National Archives of the United States.* Cambridge, UK: Cambridge University Press, 1990.

Berlin, Isaiah. *Four Essays on Liberty.* Oxford, UK: Oxford University Press, 1969.

———. *Two Concepts of Liberty.* Oxford: Clarendon Press, 1958.

Berlin, Isaiah, Henry Hardy, and Ian Harris, eds. *Liberty.* Oxford, UK: Oxford University Press, 2002.

Bernardini, Paolo, and Norman Fiering, eds. *The Jews and the Expansion of Europe to the West, 1450 to 1800.* New York: Berghahn Books, 2001.

Bernfeld, Tirtsah L. "Financing Poor Relief in the Spanish-Portuguese Community in Amsterdam in the Seventeenth and Eighteen Centuries." In *Dutch Jewry: Its History and Secular Culture (1500–2000).* Jonathan I. Israel and R. Salverda, eds. Leiden, Netherlands: Brill, 2002), 62–102.

Bethencourt, Cardoza de. "Notes on the Spanish and Portuguese Jews in the United States, Guiana, and the Dutch and British West Indies during the Seventeenth and Eighteenth Centuries." *American Jewish Historical Society Journal* 29, no. 1–4 (1925), 7–38.

Bialik, Hayim N., and Yehoshua H. Ravnitzky. *The Book of Legends, Sefer Ha-Aggadah: Legends from the Talmud and Midrash.* Translated by William G. Braude. New York: Schoken Books, 1992.

Birnbaum, Marianna. *The Long Journey of Gracia Mendes.* Budapest: Central European University Press, 2003.

Black, Eugene C. "The Anglicization of Orthodoxy: The Adlers, Father and Son." In *Profiles in Diversity: Jews in a Changing Europe, 1750–1870.* Frances Malino and David Sorkin, eds. Detroit: Wayne State University Press, 1998, 295–325.

Blom, J. C. H., R. G. Fuks-Mansfeld, and Ivo Schöffer. *The History of the Jews in the Netherlands.* Oxford, UK: Littman Library of Jewish Civilization, 2002.

Bodian, Miriam. *Hebrews of the Portuguese Nation: Conversos and Community in Early Modern Amsterdam.* Bloomington: Indiana University Press, 1999.

———. "Hebrews of the Portuguese Nation: The Ambiguous Boundaries of Self-Definition." *Jewish Social Studies: History, Culture, Society* new ser. 15, no. 1 (Fall 2008): 66–80.

———. "'Men of the Nation': The Shaping of Converso Identity in Early Modern Europe." *Past and Present,* 143 (May 1994), 48–76.

Boorstin, Daniel J., and Clare B. Luce. *The Discoverers.* New York: Random House, 1983.

Braudel, Fernand. *The Perspective of the World.* New York: Harper and Row, 1984.

———. *The Wheels of Commerce.* New York: Harper and Row, 1982.

Braunfels, Wolfgang. *Urban Design in Western Europe: Regime and Architecture, 900–1900.* Chicago: University of Chicago Press, 1988.

Breibart, Solomon, et al. *Explorations in Charleston's Jewish History.* Charleston, SC: History Press, 2005.

Bridenbaugh, Carl. *Peter Harrison: First American Architect.* Chapel Hill: University of North Carolina Press, 1949.

Brienen, Rebecca P. *Visions of Savage Paradise: Albert Eckhout, Court Painter in Colonial Dutch Brazil.* Amsterdam: Amsterdam University Press, 2006.

Buggeln, Gretchen T. *Temples of Grace: The Material Transformation of Connecticut's Churches, 1790–1840.* Hanover, NH: Press of New England, 2003.

Burgos, F. Cantera, and A. B. S. Zacuto. *Abraham Zacut, Siglo XV.* Madrid: M. Aguilar, 1935.

Canelo, David A. *The Last Crypto-Jews of Portugal.* Portland, OR: IJS, 1990.

Capp, Bernard. *The Fifth Monarchy Men: A Study in Seventeenth-Century English Millenarianism.* London: Faber, 1972.

"Carvajal Y De La Cueva, Luis de." *Handbook of Texas Online.* 15 Feb 1999. <http:// www.tshaonline.org/handbook/online/articles/CC/fcadn.html> (accesed 31 Aug. 2010).

Carvalho, David N., Isaac Harby, and Abraham Moise. *The Sabbath Service and Miscellaneous Prayers Adopted by the Reformed Society of Israelites.* Reprinted by Barnett A. Elzas. New York: Bloch Publishing, 1916.

Cesarani, David, ed. *Port Jews: Jewish Communities in Cosmopolitan Maritime Trading Centres, 1550–1950.* London: Frank Cass, 2002.

Cesarani, David, and Gemma Romain, eds. *Jews and Port Cities, 1590–1990: Commerce, Community and Cosmopolitanism.* London: Vallentine Mitchell, 2006.

Chappel, Alonzo. *History of the World Ancient and Modern.* New York: Johnson, Fry, 1866–71.

Chernow, Ron. *Alexander Hamilton.* New York: Penguin Press, 2004.

Childs, John. *The Nine Years' War and the British Army, 1688–1697: The Operations in the Low Countries.* Manchester, UK: Manchester University Press, 1991.

Chyet, Stanley F. "A Synagogue in Newport." *American Jewish Archives* 19, no. 1 (Apr. 1967), 41.

Coenen Snyder, Saskia. "Acculturation and Particularism in the Modern City: Synagogue Building and Jewish Identity in Northern Europe." Ph.D. diss, University of Michigan, 2008.

Cohen, Judah M. *Through the Sands of Time: A History of the Jewish Community of St. Thomas, U.S. Virgin Island*. Hanover, NH: Brandeis University Press, 2004.

Cohen, Henry. "Settlement of the Jews in Texas." *Publications of the American Jewish Historical Society* 2 (1894), 139–56.

Cohen, Martin. "The Letters and Last Will and Testament of Luis De Carvajal, the Younger," *American Jewish Historical Quarterly*, 55, No. 4 (June 1966), 451–520.

———. "Some Misconceptions about the Crypto-Jews in Colonial Mexico." *Publications of the American Jewish Historical Society*, 61, No. 1–4 (Sept. 1971–June 1972), 277.

Cohen, Richard I. *Jewish Icons, Art and Society in Modern Europe*. Berkeley: University of California Press, 1998.

Cohen, Robert. *Jews in Another Environment: Surinam in the Second Half of the Eighteenth Century*. New York: E. J. Brill, 1991.

———. *The Jewish Nation in Surinam*. Amsterdam: S. Emmering, 1982.

Cohen, Shaye J. D. *From the Maccabees to the Mishnah*. Philadelphia: Westminster Press, 1987.

Cohen, Thomas. "Judaism and the History of the Church in the Inquisition Trial of António Vieira." *Luso-Brazilian Review* 40, no. 1 (Summer 2003), 67–78.

Cohen Paraira, David P. "A Jewel in the City." In *The Esnoga: A Monument to Portuguese-Jewish Culture*. Martine Stroo and Ernest Kupershoek, eds. Amsterdam: D'Arts, 2001, 41–68.

Comunità Israelitica di Venezia. *Jewish Art Treasures in Venice*. New York: International Fund for Monuments, 1973.

Congregation Mikve Israel-Emanuel. *Our "Snoa," 5492–5742*. Curaçao: Congregation Mikve Israel-Emanuel, 2001.

Congregation Shearith Israel Minutes, 1778–1779. Document SC-8355, Small Collections, American Jewish Archives.

"Consecration of the New Synagogue, Charleston, S.C." *Occident and Jewish American Advocate* 5, no. 6 (Elul 5607 / Sept. 1847).

Coomans, Henry, Michael A. Newton, and Maritza Commans-Eustatia, eds. *Building Up the Future From the Past: Studies on the Architecture and Historic Monuments in the Dutch Caribbean*. Zuphten, Netherlands: De Walburg Pers, 1990.

Cornelison, Pam, and Ted Yanak. *The Great American History Fact-Finder: The Who, What, Where, When, and Why of American History*. Boston: Houghton Mifflin, 2004.

Couto, Dejanirah. "The Role of Interpreters, or Linguas, in the Portuguese Empire during the 16th Century." *e-Journal of Portuguese History* 1, no. 2 (Winter 2003).

Crain, Edward E. *Historic Architecture in the Caribbean Islands*. Gainesville: University Press of Florida, 1994.

Curl, James S. *Georgian Architecture*. Newton Abbot, UK: David and Charles, 2002.

Curtin, Philip D. *The Rise and Fall of the Plantation Complex: Essays in Atlantic History*. Cambridge, UK: Cambridge University Press, 1990.

Daniels, Doris G. "Colonial Jewry: Religion, Domestic and Social Relations." *Publications of the American Jewish Historical Society* 66, no. 1–4 (Sept. 1976–June 1977), 375.

Darby, Graham, ed. *The Origins and Development of the Dutch Revolt*. London: Routledge, 2001.

Davis, David B. *Slavery and Human Progress*. New York: Oxford University Press, 1984.

Davis, Edward. *The History of Rodeph Shalom Congregation, Philadelphia, 1802–1926*. Philadelphia: Press of Edward Stern, 1926.

Davis, N. Darnell. "Notes on the History of the Jews in Barbados." *Publications of the American Jewish Historical Society* 18 (1909), 146.

Davis, Robert C., and Benjamin C. I. Ravid. *The Jews of Early Modern Venice*. Baltimore: Johns Hopkins University Press, 2001.

Delevante, Marilyn, and Anthony Alberga. *The Island of One People: An Account of the History of the Jews in Jamaica*. Kingston, Jamaica: Ian Randle, 2006.

Dias, Fatima D. "The Jewish Community in the Azores from 1820 to the Present." In *From Iberia to Diaspora: Studies in Sephardic History and Culture*. Yedida K. Stillman and Norman A. Stillman, eds. Boston: Brill, 1999, 19–34.

Duke, Alastair C. *Reformation and Revolt in the Low Countries*. London: Hambledon Press, 1990.

Dunn, Richard S. *Sugar and Slaves: The Rise of the Planter Class in the English West Indies, 1624–1713*. Chapel Hill: University of North Carolina Press, 1972.

Durant, Will, and Ariel Durant. *The Age of Reason Begins: A History of European Civilization in the Period of Shakespeare, Bacon, Montaigne, Rembrandt, Galileo, and Descartes: 1558–1648*. New York: Simon and Schuster, 1961.

Durkheim, Émile. *The Elementary Forms of the Religious Life*. New York: Free Press, 1965.

Dutt, Ashok K., and Frank J. Costa. *Public Planning in the Netherlands: Perspectives and Change Since the Second World War*. New York: Oxford University Press, 1985.

Ehrlich, Mark A., ed. *Encyclopedia of the Jewish Diaspora: Origins, Experiences, and Culture* Vol. 1. Santa Barbara, CA: ABC-CLIO, 2009.

Elkin, Judith L. "Imagining Idolatry: Missionaries, Indians, and Jews." *Religion and the Authority of the Past*. Tobias Siebers, ed. Ann Arbor: University of Michigan Press, 1993, 75–99.

———. *The Jews of Latin America*. New York: Holmes and Meir, 1998.

Elliott, John. *Europe Divided, 1559–1598*. New York: Harper and Row, 1969.

———. *The Revolt of the Catalans, A Study in the Decline of Spain, 1598–1640*. Cambridge, UK: Cambridge University Press, 1963.

Elzas, Barnett A. *The Jews of South Carolina: From the Earliest Times to the Present Day*. Philadelphia: J. B. Lippincott, 1905, 208–19.

Ember, Melvin, Carol R. Ember, and Ian A. Skoggard, eds. *Encyclopedia of Diasporas*. New York: Kluwer Academic Plenum, 2004.

Emmanuel, Isaac, and Suzanne Emmanuel. *History of the Jews of the Netherlands Antilles*. Cincinnati: American Jewish Archives, 1970.

Emmer, Peter C. "The First Global War: The Dutch versus Iberia in Asia, Africa and the New World, 1590–1609." *e-Journal of Portuguese History* 1, no. 1 (Summer 2003), 1–14.

———. "The History of the Dutch Slave Trade: A Bibliographical Survey." *Journal of Economic History* 32, no. 3 (Sept. 1972), 728–47.

Endelman, Todd M. *The Jews of Britain, 1656 to 2000.* Berkeley: University of California Press, 2002.

———. *The Jews of Georgian England, 1714–1830: Tradition and Change in a Liberal Society.* Philadelphia: Jewish Publication Society of America, 1979.

Enriques, Jacob Jeosua Bueno, and King Charles II, 1661. Document SC-3232, Small Collections, American Jewish Archives.

Evans, Eli N. *The Provincials: A Personal History of Jews in the South.* New York: Simon and Schuster, 1997.

Evans, Monica. "Coke and Conquistadors: Religious Syncretism in Latin America." *Just Change: Religion and Spirituality* 6 (July 2006), 16–17.

Ezratty, Harry A. *500 years in the Jewish Caribbean: The Spanish and the Portuguese Jews in the West Indies.* Baltimore: Omni Arts, 1997.

Faber, Eli. *The Jewish People in America: A Time for Planting, the First Migration, 1654–1820.* Baltimore: Johns Hopkins University Press, sponsored by the American Jewish Historical Society, 1992.

———. *Jews, Slaves, and the Slave Trade: Setting the Record Straight.* New York: New York University Press, 1998.

Feitler, Bruno. "Jews and New Christians in Dutch Brazil, 1630–1654." In *Atlantic Diasporas: Jews, Conversos, and Crypto-Jews in the Age of Mercantilism, 1500–1800.* Richard L. Kagan and Philip D. Morgan, eds. Baltimore, MD: Johns Hopkins University Press, 2009, 123–52.

Feldberg, Michael, ed. *Blessings of Freedom: Chapters in American Jewish History.* Hoboken, NJ: KTAV Publishing in association with the American Jewish Historical Society, 2002.

Fernández-Armesto, Felipe. *Amerigo: The Man Who Gave His Name to America.* New York: Random House, 2007.

Finkelman, Paul, and Joseph Calder Miller, eds. *Macmillan Encyclopedia of World Slavery.* New York: Simon & Schuster Macmillan, 1998.

Fischel, Walter J. "The Jewish Merchant-Colony in Madras (Fort St. George) during the 17th and 18th Centuries: A Contribution to the Economic and Social History of the Jews in India (Concluded)." *Journal of the Economic and Social History of the Orient* 3, no. 2 (Aug. 1960), 175–95.

Fischer, Laura. *Life in New Amsterdam: Picture the Past.* Chicago: Heinemann Library, 2003.

Formisano, Luciano. *Letters from a New World: Amerigo Vespucci's Discovery of America.* New York: Marsilio, 1992.

Foster, Stephen. *The Long Argument: English Puritanism and the Shaping of New England Culture, 1570–1700.* Chapel Hill: University of North Carolina Press, 1991.

Frankel, Rachel. "Antecedents and Remnants of Jodensavanne: The Synagogue and Cemeteries of the First Permanent Plantation Settlement of New World Jews." In *The Jews and the Expansion of Europe to the West, 1450 to 1800.* Paolo

Bernardini and Norman Fiering, eds. New York: Berghahn Books, 2001, 394–436.

Friedenwald, Herbert. "Some Newspaper Advertisements of the Eighteenth Century." *American Jewish Historical Society Journal* 6 (1898), 49–51.

Friedman, Jerome. "Jewish Conversion, the Spanish Pure Blood Laws and Reformation: A Revisionist View of Racial and Religious Anti-Semitism." *Sixteenth Century Journal* 18, no. 1 (Spring 1987), 3–30.

Friedman, Lee M. "Boston in American Jewish History." *Publications of the American Jewish Historical Society* 42, no. 1–4 (Sept. 1952–June 1953), 333–34.

———. "Gabriel Milan, The First Jewish Governor of St. Thomas." *American Jewish Historical Society Journal* 28 (1922), 213.

Fritze, Ronald H. *New Worlds: The Great Voyages of Discovery, 1400–1600.* Stroud, UK: Sutton, 2002.

Gampel, Benjamin R. "The Last Jews on Iberian Soil: Navarrese Jewry, 1479–1498." *Proceedings of the American Academy for Jewish Research* 53 (1986), 49–69.

Gans, M. H. *Memorbook: History of Dutch Jewry from the Renaissance to 1940.* Baarn, Netherlands: Bosch and Keuning, 1977.

Ganzfried, Solomon. *Code of Jewish Law/Kitzur Shulchan Aruh, A Compilation of Jewish Laws and Custom,* Vol. 1. Translated by Hyman E. Goldin. New York: Hebrew Publishing, 1961; and Torah.org, "Shulchan Aruch Part I: Orach Chayim, Chapter 9—The Synagogue." Project Genesis. 2000. <http://www.torah.org/advanced/shulchan-aruch/classes/orachchayim/chapter9.html> (accessed 20 Aug. 2007).

Garfield, Robert. "Public Christians, Secret Jews: Religion and Political Conflict on Sao Tome Island in the Sixteenth and Seventeenth Centuries." *Sixteenth Century Journal* 21, no. 4 (Winter 1990), 645–54.

Garrigus, John D. "New Christians / 'New Whites,' Sephardic Jews, Free People of Color and Citizenship in French Saint Domingue, 1760–1789." In *The Jews and the Expansion of Europe to the West, 1450 to 1800.* Paolo Bernardini and Norman Fiering, eds. New York: Berghahn Books, 2001, 314–27.

Gartner, Lloyd P. "Emancipation, Social Change and Communal Reconstruction in Anglo-Jewry, 1789–1881." *Proceedings of the American Academy for Jewish Research* 54 (1987), 73–116.

Geertz, Clifford. *The Interpretation of Cultures: Selected Essays.* New York: Basic Books, 1993.

Gelles, Edith B., ed. *The Letters of Abigaill Levy Franks, 1733–1748.* New Haven: Yale University Press, 2004.

Gemeente Alkmaar. Monumentaal Alkmaar: Remonstrantse Kerk. 2007. <http://www.alkmaar.nl/monument/monument/remokerk.htm> (accessed 31 Aug. 2007).

Gilmore, R. Grant, III, St. Eustatius Archaeologist and Director of St. Eustatius Center for Archaeological Research. "Case for Support." Unpublished manuscript. St. Eustatius Center for Archaeological Research, Oranjestad, St. Eustatius, 2007.

Gjessing, Frederik C. *National Historic Landmark Nomination: St. Thomas Synagogue.* Prepared for the U.S. Department of the Interior, National Park Service, 1997.

Glyn, Lynn B. "Israel Lyons: A Short but Starry Career. The Life of an Eighteenth-Century Jewish Botanist and Astronomer." *Notes and Records of the Royal Society of London* 56, no. 3 (Sept. 2002), 275–305.

Godfrey, Sheldon J., and Judy Godfrey. *Search Out the Land: The Jews and the Growth of Equality in British Colonial America, 1740–1867.* Montreal: McGill-Queen's University Press, 1995.

Golden, Peter B., Haggai Ben-Shammai, and András Róna-Tas, eds. *The World of the Khazars: New Perspectives.* Leiden, Netherlands: Brill, 2007.

Goldish, Matt. "The Amsterdam Portuguese Rabbinate in the Seventeenth Century: A Unique Institution Viewed from Within and Without." In *Dutch Jews as Perceived by Themselves and by Others.* Chaya Brasz and Yosef Kaplan, eds. Leiden, Netherlands: Brill, 2000, 9–19.

———. *Jewish Questions: Responsa on Sephardic Life in the Early Modern Period.* Princeton: Princeton University Press, 2008.

Goldish, Matt, and Richard Henry Popkin, eds. *Jewish Messianism in the Early Modern World.* Dordrecht, Netherlands: Kluwer Academic, 2001.

Goldstein, Bernard R. "The Medieval Hebrew Tradition in Astronomy." *Journal of the American Oriental Society* 85, no. 2 (Apr.–June 1965), 145–48.

Gomez Mill House. *As a Matter of 'arti'- Fact!* 1, no. 3 (Mar. 2004), 1–2.

Goldhill, Simon. *The Temple of Jerusalem.* Cambridge, MA: Harvard University Press, 2005.

Goodwin, George M. "The Politics of Preservation: How Touro Synagogue Became a National Historic Site." *Rhode Island Jewish Historical Notes* 13 (2000), 177–207.

Graizbord, David L. *Souls in Dispute: Converso Identities in Iberia and the Jewish Diaspora, 1580–1700.* Philadelphia: University of Pennsylvania Press, 2004.

Green, Bryan C., Calder Loth, and William M. S. Rasmussen. *Lost Virginia, Vanished Architecture of the Old Dominion.* Charlottesville, VA: Howell Press, 2001.

Green, Tobias. "Further Considerations on the Sephardim of the Petite Cote." *History in Africa* 32 (2005), 165–83.

Grell, Ole Peter, and Robert W. Scribner. *Tolerance and Intolerance in the European Reformation.* New York: Cambridge University Press, 1996.

Grell, Ole Peter, Jonathan I. Israel, and Nicholas Tyacke, eds. *From Persecution to Toleration: The Glorious Revolution and Religion in England.* Oxford, UK: Clarendon Press, 1991.

Griffis, William E. *The American in Holland: Sentimental Rambles in the Eleven Provinces of the Netherlands.* Boston: Houghton and Mifflin, 1899.

Grim, David. *A Plan of the City and Environs of New York, 1813.* New-York Historical Society Library, New York. Object LIB.NS13.M2.1.1.

Groll, C. L. Temminck. *De Architecture Van Suriname, 1667–1930.* Zutphen, Netherlands: De Walburg Pers, 1973.

Gura, Judith. *The Abrams Guide to Period Styles for Interiors.* New York: Harry N. Abrams, 2005.

Hadchity, Therese. "Of Bridges, Berths, and Hawkers." *Paintings of Bridgetown from the National Art Collection of Barbados, the Barbados Gallery of Art and the Barbados Museum and Historical Society at the Zemicon Gallery.* Barbados: Cot Caribbean Graphics, 2003.

Hagoort, Lydia. *Beth Haim in Ouderkerk aan de Amstel: debegraafplaats van de Portugese joden in Amsterdam 1614–1945*. Hilversum, Netherlands: Verloren, 2005.

Hagy, James W. "Her 'Scandalous Behavior': A Jewish Divorce in Charleston, South Carolina, 1788." *American Jewish Archives Journal* 41, no. 2 (Fall/Winter 1989), 185–95.

———. *This Happy Land: The Jews of Colonial and Antebellum Charleston*. Tuscaloosa: University of Alabama Press, 1993.

Halchin, Jill. *Excavations at Fort Michilimackinac, 1983–1985: House C of the Southeast Rowhouse, the Solomon-Levy-Parant House. Archaeological Completion Report Series*, no. 11. Mackinac Island State Park Comission, 1985.

Hart, Jonathan L. *Comparing Empires: European Colonialism from Portuguese Expansion to the Spanish-American War*. Hampshire, UK: Palgrave Macmillan, 2003.

Hart, Marjolein 't. "The Glorious City: Monumentalism and Public Space in Seventeenth Century Amsterdam." In *Urban Achievement in Early Modern Europe: Golden Ages in Antwerp, Amsterdam, and London*. Patrick K. O'Brien, ed. Cambridge, UK: Cambridge University Press, 2001, 128–50.

Hartog, Johannes. "The Honen Dalim Congregation of St. Eustatius." *American Jewish Archives* 19, no. 1 (Apr. 1967), 60–65.

———. *The Jews and St. Eustatius*. St. Maarten, Netherlands Antilles: Windward Islands Bank, 1976.

Held, Felix E. *Johann Valentin Andreae's Christianopolis: An Ideal State of the Seventeenth Century*. New York: Oxford University Press, 1916.

Heldman, Donald. "Michigan's First Jewish Settlers: A View from the Solomon-Levy Trading House at Fort Michilimackinac, 1765–1781." *Journal of New World Archaeology* 6, no. 4 (1986), 21–33.

Henriques, U. R. Q. "The Jewish Emancipation Controversy in Nineteenth-Century Britain." *Past and Present*, no. 40 (July 1968), 126–46.

Hertzberg, Arthur. *The French Enlightenment and the Jews*. New York: Columbia University Press, 1968.

Hessayon, Ariel. "Review of The Persecution of the Jews and Muslims of Portugal. King Manuel I and the End of Religious Tolerance (1496–7)" *Reviews in History*, accessed 24 Jan. 2011. http://www.history.ac.uk/reviews/review/797.

Heuman, Gad, and James Walvin, eds. *The Slavery Reader*. London: Routledge, 2004.

Higgins, Hannah. *The Grid Book*. Cambridge, MA: MIT Press, 2009.

Hofstadter, Richard. *America at 1750: A Social Portrait*. New York: Knopf, 1971.

Hohenberg, Paul M., and Lynn H. Lees. *The Making of Urban Europe, 1000–1950*. Cambridge, MA: Harvard University Press, 1985.

Holliday, Kathryn E. *Leopold Eidlitz: Architecture and Idealism in the Gilded Age*. New York: W. W. Norton, 2008.

Holzberg, Carol S. *Minorities and Power in a Black Society: The Jewish Community of Jamaica. Lanham, MD: North-South*, 1987.

Hooimeijer, F. L. "The Relation between Design and Technology of Polder Cities." In *Urbanism Laboratory for Cities and Regions: Progress of Research Issues in Urbanism*. M. Y. Berghauser-Pont, F. van der Hoeven, and Jürgen Rosemann, eds. Amsterdam: IOS, 2007, 80–81.

Hordes, Stanley M. "The Inquisition as Economic and Political Agent: The Campaign of the Mexican Holy Office against the Crypto-Jews in the Mid-Seventeenth Century." *The Americas* 39, no. 1 (July 1982), 23–38.

Hoyo, Eugenio del. *Historia del Nuevo Reino de León, 1577–1723*. Monterrey, Mexico: Publicaciones del Instituto Tecnológico y de Superiores de Monterrey, 1979.

———. *To the End of the Earth: A History of the Crypto-Jews of New Mexico*. New York: Columbia University Press, 2005.

Hoyt, Edward A. "Naturalization under the American Colonies: Signs of a New Community." *Political Science Quarterly* 67, no. 2 (June 1952), 248–66.

Huhner, Leon. "Jews in Connection with the Colleges of the Thirteen Original States Prior to 1800." *American Jewish Historical Society Journal* 19 (1910), 101–24.

Humanities and Social Sciences Library. *Jews in America: Conquistadors, Knickerbockers, Pilgrims, and the Hope of Israel*. New York: New York Public Library, 21 Sept.–13 Nov. 2004.

Hurwitz, Samuel, and Edith Hurwitz. "The New World Sets an Example for the Old: The Jews of Jamaica and Political Rights, 1661–1831." *Publications of the American Jewish Historical Society* 55, no. 1–4 (Sept. 1965–June 1966), 37–57.

Hyman, Louis. *The Jews of Ireland: From Earliest Times to the Year 1910*. Shannon: Irish University Press, 1972.

Hyman, Paula. *The Emancipation of the Jews of Alsace: Acculturation and Tradition in the Nineteenth Century*. New Haven: Yale University Press, 1991.

Hyamson, Albert M. *A History of the Jews in England*. London: Chatto and Windus, 1908.

Igel, Regina. "Haquita as Spoken in the Brazilian Amazon." In *From Iberia to Diaspora: Studies in Sephardic History and Culture*. Yedida K. Stillman and Norman A. Stillman, eds. Boston: Brill, 1999, 446–56.

Irving, Washington. *A History of the Life and Voyages of Christopher Columbus*. London: John Murray, 1828.

Israel, Jonathan I. *Conflicts of Empires: Spain, the Low Countries and the Struggle for World Supremacy, 1585–1713*. London: Hambledon Press, 1997.

———. *Diasporas within a Diaspora: Jews, Crypto-Jews, and the World of Maritime Empires (1540–1740)*. Boston: Brill, 2002.

———. *The Dutch Republic: Its Rise, Greatness and Fall, 1477–1806*. Oxford, UK: Clarendon Press, 1995.

———. *European Jewry in the Age of Mercantilism, 1550–1750*. Oxford, UK: Clarendon Press, 1985.

———. "Jews and Crypto-Jews in the Atlantic World Systems, 1500–1800." In *Atlantic Diasporas: Jews, Conversos, and Crypto-Jews in the Age of Mercantilism, 1500–1800*. Richard L. Kagan and Philip D. Morgan, eds. Baltimore: Johns Hopkins University Press, 2009), 3–17.

Israel, Manasseh ben, and Lucien Wolf. *Menasseh ben Israel's Mission to Oliver Cromwell: Being a Reprint of the Pamphlets Published by Menasseh Ben Israel to Promote the Re-Admission of the Jews to England, 1649–1656*. London, UK: Published for the Jewish Historical Society of England by Macmillan, 1901.

Jacobs, Joseph, and Lucien Wolf. *Catalogue of Anglo-Jewish Historical Exhibition, 1887: Royal Albert Hall, and of Supplementary Exhibitions Held at the Public*

Record Office, British Museum, South Kensington Museum. London: William Clowes and Sons, 1887.

Jameson, J. Franklin. "St. Eustatius in the American Revolution." *American Historical Review* 8, no. 4 (July 1903), 683–708.

Jewish Historical Museum of Amsterdam. "New Synagogue." 2010. <http://www.jhm.nl/culture-and-history/buildings/new-synagogue> (accessed 9 July 2010).

Jick, Leon A. *The Americanization of the Synagogue, 1820–1870*. Hanover, NH: University Press of New England, 1976.

Job, Françoise. *Les Juifs de Lunéville aux XVIIIe et XIXe Siècles: Collection Recherches en Histoire Sociale et Religieuse*. Nancy, France: Presses Universitaires de Nancy, 1989.

Jokilehto, Jukka. *A History of Architectural Conservation*. Oxford, UK: Butterworth-Heinemann, 2008.

Joseph, Andrew C. "The Settlement of Jews in Canada." *American Jewish Historical Society Journal* 1 (1893), 117–20.

Journal of the Senate of South Carolina. 1794. Document SC-11217, Small Collections, American Jewish Archives.

Jüdische Gemeinde Rauschenberg. Hessisches Staatsarchiv Marburg, Germany.

Kadish, Sharman. *Bevis Marks Synagogue, 1701–2001*. London: English Heritage, 2001.

———. *Jewish Heritage in Gibraltar: An Architectural Guide*. Reading, UK: Spire Books in association with Jewish Heritage UK, 2007.

———. *Jewish Heritage in England: An Architectural Guide*. Swindon, UK: English Heritage, 2006.

———. *The Synagogues of Britain and Ireland: An Architectural and Social History*. New Haven: Yale University Press, 2011.

Kahal Kadosh Mikve Israel, *Address to Jewish Congregation of Surinam*. 1790, Call P-8, Box 1, Folder 15, American Jewish Historical Society Archives, Center for Jewish History.

Kagan, Richard L., and Philip D. Morgan, eds. *Atlantic Diasporas: Jews, Conversos, and Crypto-Jews in the Age of Mercantilism, 1500–1800*. Baltimore: Johns Hopkins University Press, 2009.

Kamen, Henry. "The Mediterranean and the Expulsion of Spanish Jews in 1492." *Past and Present*, no. 119 (May 1988), 30–55.

———. *The Spanish Inquisition: A Historical Revision*. New Haven: Yale University Press, 1998.

Kaplan, Benjamin J. "Fictions of Privacy: House Chapels and the Spatial Accommodation of Religious Dissent in Early Modern Europe." *American Historical Review*, Oct. 2002. <http://www.historycooperative.org/journals/ahr/107.4/aho402001 031.html~> (accessed 16 Sept. 2007).

Kaplan, Marion A. *Jewish Daily Life in Germany, 1618–1945*. Oxford, UK: Oxford University Press, 2005.

Katz, David S. *The Jews in the History of England, 1485–1850*. Oxford, UK: Clarendon Press, 1994.

———. "The Jews of England and 1688." In *From Persecution to Toleration: The Glorious Revolution and Religion in England*. Ole P. Grell, Jonathan I. Israel, and Nicholas Tyacke, eds. Oxford, UK: Clarendon Press, 1991, 217–49.

Katz, Nathan, and Ellen S. Goldberg. *The Last Jews of Cochin: Jewish Identity in Hindu India.* Columbia: University of South Carolina Press, 1993.

Kaufman, Tania. "O que se conta . . . Quem conta . . . Como se conta . . . Os Judeus em Pernambuco Práticas judaicas, sinagogas . . ." *Arquivo Histórico Judáico de Pernambuco, Compilação.* Aleksandra Serbim, pesquisadora Arquivo Histórico Judaico de Pernambuco e e do Grupo Interdisciplinar de Estudos sobre o Judaismo, 2001.

Kennedy, Hugh. *Muslim Spain and Portugal: A Political History of al-Andalus.* London: Longman, 1996.

Kerem, Yitzchak. "Sephardic Settlement in the British Colonies of the Americas in the 17th and 18th Centuries." In *From Strangers to Citizens: The Integration of Immigrant Communities in Britain, Ireland, and Colonial America, 1550–1750.* Randolph Vigne and Charles Littleton, eds. London: Sussex Academic Press, 2001, 285–94.

Kiewe, Heinz Edgar. "Nigerian Sculpture of a Jewish Trader." *Jewish Quarterly Review,* new ser. 44, no. 2 (Oct. 1953), 162–68.

King, Joe. *From the Ghetto to the Main: The Story of the Jews of Montreal.* Montreal: Montreal Jewish Publication Society, 2003.

Kisch, Conrad. "The Jewish Community in Denmark: History and Present Status." *Judaism* 47, no. 2 (Spring 1998), 214–31.

K. K. Beth Elohim. *Board of Trustee Minute Book (1838–1843).* KKBE Collection, Box 1, Folder 1, Special Collections, College of Charleston.

K. K. Beth Shalome Collection. Miscellaneous papers, 1789–1898. Beth Ahabah Museum and Archives, Richmond, Virginia.

Klooster, Wim. "Communities of Port Jews and Their Contacts in the Dutch Atlantic World." *Jewish History* 20 (2006), 129–45.

———. *The Dutch in the Americas, 1600–1800: A Narrative History with the Catalogue of an Exhibition of Rare Prints, Maps, and Illustrated Books.* Providence: John Carter Brown Library, 1997.

———. "Networks of Colonial Entrepreneurs: The Founders of the Jewish Settlements in Dutch America, 1650s and 1660s." In *Atlantic Diasporas: Jews, Conversos, and Crypto-Jews in the Age of Mercantilism, 1500–1800.* Richard L. Kagan and Philip D. Morgan, eds. Baltimore: Johns Hopkins University Press, 2009), 33–49.

Knight, Janice. *Orthodoxies in Massachusetts: Rereading American Puritanism.* Cambridge, MA: Harvard University Press, 1994.

Koen, E. M. "War en voor vie werd de synagoge van 1612 gebouwd?" *Maandblad Amstelodamum* 57 (1970), 209–12.

Kohler, Max J. "Phases of Jewish Life in New York before 1800." *American Jewish Historical Society Journal* 2 (1894), 77.

Kohut, Alexander. "Jewish Heretics in the Philippines in the Sixteenth and Seventeenth Century." *American Jewish Historical Society Journal* 12 (1904), 149.

Korn, Bertram W., ed. *A Bicentennial Festschrift for Jacob Rader Marcus.* New York: American Jewish Historical Society and KTAV Publishing, 1976.

———. *The Early Jews of New Orleans.* Waltham, MA: American Jewish Historical Society, 1969.

————. "Jews and Negro Slavery in the Old South, 1789–1865, Address of the President." *Publications of the American Jewish Historical Society* 50, no. 1–4 (Sept. 1960–June 1961), 155.

Kottmann, Karl A., ed. *Catholic Millenarianism: From Savonarola to the Abbé Grégoire* 2. Dordrecht, Netherlands: Kluwer Academic, 2001.

Kravtsov, Sergy R. "Juan Bautista Villalpando and Sacred Architecture in the Seventeenth Century." *Journal of the Society of Architectural Historians* 64, no. 3 (Sept. 2005), 312–39.

Krinsky, Carol H. *Synagogues of Europe, Architecture, History, and Meaning*. Mineola, NY: Dover, 1985.

Kritzler, Edward. *Jewish Pirates of the Caribbean: How a Generation of Swashbuckling Jews Carved Out an Empire in the New World in Their Quest for Treasure, Religious Freedom—and Revenge*. New York: Doubleday, 2008.

Kuhn, Arthur K. "Hugo Grotius and the Emancipation of the Jews in Holland." *American Jewish Historical Society Journal* 31 (1928), 173–80.

Langlais, Jacques, and David Rome. *Jews and French Quebecers: Two Hundred Years of Shared History*. Waterloo, Ontario: Wilfrid Laurier University Press, 1991.

Lasker, Arnold A., and Daniel J. Lasker. "The Jewish Prayer for Rain in the Post-Talmudic Diaspora." *AJS Review* 9, no. 2 (Autumn 1984), 141–74.

Lavender, Abraham D. "The Secret Jews of Spain, Portugal, and Italy and Their Descendants Today: Major Research Issues in a Growing Field of Academic Research." *Journal of Spanish, Portuguese, and Italian Crypto Jews* 1 (Spring 2009), 3–16.

Leibman, Laura. "From Holy Land to New England Canaan: Rabbi Haim Carigal and Sephardic Itinerant Preaching in the Eighteenth Century." *Early American Literature* 44, no. 1 (2009), 71–93.

————. "Sephardic Sacred Space in Colonial America." *Jewish History* 25, no. 1 (2011), 13–41.

Lerner, L. Scott. "The Narrating Architecture of Emancipation." *Jewish Social Studies* new ser. 6, no. 3, (Spring/Summer 2000), 1–30.

Les juifs d'Alsace doivent-ils être admis au droit de citoyens actifs? Lisez et jugez. Strasbourg, 1790.

Leslie, John, Hugh Murray, and Robert Jameson. *Narrative of Discovery and Adventure in the Polar Seas and Regions: With illustrations of their Climate, Geology, and Natural History, and an Account of the Whale-Fishery*. New York: J. and J. Harper, 1831.

Levine, Allen. *Scattered among the Peoples: The Jewish Diaspora in Twelve Portraits*. New York: Overlook Press, 2003.

Levine, Lee I. *The Ancient Synagogue: The First Thousand Years*. New Haven: Yale University Press, 2000.

Levinger, Lee J. *A History of the Jews in the United States*. Cincinnati: Union of American Hebrew Congregations, 1952.

Levy, Hayman, Isaac Moses, Benjamin Seixas and Simon Nathan to Jonas Phillips and Bernard Gratz, New York, 14 March 1788. Misc. File. William L. Clement Library, University of Michigan.

Lewis, Theodore. "History of Touro Synagogue," *Bulletin of the Newport Historical Society* 48 (Summer 1975), 281–320.

Lichtenstein, Tatjana. "Jews in Denmark." In *Encyclopedia of Diasporas*. Melvin Ember, Carol R. Ember, and Ian A. Skoggard, eds. New York: Kluwer Academic Plenum, 2004, 935.

Lieberman, Julia R., ed. *Sephardi Family Life in the Early Modern Diaspora.* Waltham, MA: Brandeis University Press, 2011.

Liebman, Seymour B. "Hernando Alonso: The First Jew on the North American Continent." *Journal of Inter-American Studies* 5, no. 2 (Apr. 1963), 291–92.

———. *New World Jewry, 1493–1825: Requiem for the Forgotten.* New York: KTAV, 1982.

Linerles, Robert. "Conflict over Reforms: The Case of Congregation Beth Elohim, Charleston, South Carolina." In *The American Synagogue: A Sanctuary Transformed.* Jack Wertheimer, ed. Cambridge, UK: Cambridge University Press, 1987, 274–92.

Livingstone, David N. *Putting Science in its Place: Geographies of Scientific Knowledge.* Chicago: University of Chicago Press, 2003.

Lloyd, Genevieve. *Spinoza and the "Ethics."* London: Routledge, 1996.

Louw, H. J. "Anglo-Netherlandish Architectural Interchange c. 1600–c. 1660." *Architectural History* 24 (1981), 1–18.

Lowance, Mason I. *The Language of Canaan: Metaphor and Symbol in New England from the Puritans to the Transcendentalists.* Cambridge, MA: Harvard University Press, 1980.

Lurbe, Pierre. "John Toland and the Naturalization of the Jews." *Eighteenth-Century Ireland / Iris an dá chultúr* 14 (1999) 37–48.

Lyons, Jacques J., Naphtali Phillips, and M. M. Noah. "Historical Sketch." In *Publications of the American Jewish Historical Society,* no. 27, *The Lyons Collection.* Washington, DC: American Jewish Historical Society, 1913.

MacLachlan, Colin M. *A History of Modern Brazil: The Past against the Future.* Wilmington, DE: Scholarly Resources, 2003.

MacLachlan, Colin M., and William H. Beezley. *El Gran Pueblo: A History of Greater Mexico.* Upper Saddle River, NJ: Prentice Hall, 1999.

Maimonides, Moses, H. M. Russell, and J. Weinberg. *The Book of Knowledge: From the Mishneh Torah of Maimonides.* New York: KTAV, 1983.

Marcus, Jacob Rader. *The Colonial American Jew, 1492–1776.* Vols. 1–3. Detroit: Wayne State University Press, 1970.

Mark, Peter, and Jose Da Silva Morta. "Catholics, Jews, and Muslims in Early Seventeenth-Century Guine." In *Atlantic Diasporas: Jews, Conversos, and Crypto-Jews in the Age of Mercantilism, 1500–1800.* Richard L. Kagan and Philip D. Morgan, eds. Baltimore: Johns Hopkins University Press, 2009), 170–94.

Martínez, María E. *Genealogical Fictions: Limpieza de Sangre, Religion, and Gender in Colonial Mexico.* Stanford: Stanford University Press, 2008.

Maxwell, Kenneth. *Pombal: Paradox of the Enlightenment.* Cambridge, UK: Cambridge University Press, 1995.

McAllister, Lee, and Virginia McAllister. *A Field Guide to American Houses.* New York: Alfred A. Knopf, 1984.

McGovern, Thomas H. "The Archaeology of the Norse North Atlantic." *Annual Review of Anthropology* 19 (1990), 331–51.

McNeill, William H. *The Rise of the West: A History of the Human Community.* Chicago: University of Chicago Press, 1963.

Meek, H. A. *The Synagogue.* New York: Phaidon, 2003.

Mentzer, Raymond A. "Marranos of Southern France in the Early Sixteenth Century." *Jewish Quarterly Review* new ser. 72, no. 4 (Apr. 1982), 303–11.

Melammed, Renée L. *Heretics or Daughters of Israel?: The Crypto-Jewish Women of Castile.* New York: Oxford University Press, 1999.

Melnick, Ralph. "Billy Simons: The Black Jew of Charleston." *American Jewish Archives Journal* 32, no. 1 (Apr. 1980), 3–8.

Mendelsohn, Adam D. *Tongue Ties: Religion, Culture and Commerce in the Making of the Anglophone Jewish Diaspora, 1840–1870.* Ph.D. diss., Brandeis University, 2008.

Messinas, Elias V. "Late Synagogues of Greece, Origins and Architecture: The Relationship Between Greek Synagogues and Medieval Spanish Synagogues: The Bimah." In *Jewish Studies at the Turn of the Twentieth Century: Proceedings of the 6th EAJS Congress.* Judit Targarona Borrás and Angel Sáenz-Badillos, eds. Leiden, Netherlands, 1999, 152–57.

Metz, Allan. "'Those of the Hebrew Nation . . . ': The Sephardic Experience in Colonial Latin America." *American Jewish Archives Journal* 44, no. 1 (Spring/Summer 1992), 216–20.

Michman, Jozeph. *The History of Dutch Jewry during the Emancipation Period, 1787–1815: Gothic Turrets on a Corinthian Building.* Amsterdam: Amsterdam University Press, 1995.

Miller, Derek. "The Bridgetown Synagogue Pathway Archaeology Project: A Preliminary Report." *Journal of the Barbados Museum and Historical Society* 56 (Dec. 2010), 87–104.

Monaco, C. S. "Port Jews or a People of the Diaspora? A Critique of the Port Jew Concept." *Jewish Social Studies: History, Culture, Society* new ser. 15, no. 2 (Winter 2009), 137–66.

Moore, Deborah Dash. "Freedom's Fruits: The Americanization of an Old-time Religion." In *A Portion of the People: Three Hundred Years of Southern Jewish Life.* Ted Rosengarten and Dale Rosengarten, eds. Columbia: University of South Carolina Press in association with McKissick Museum, 2002), 10–21.

Morias, Sabato. "Mickve Israel Congregation of Philadelphia." *American Jewish Historical Society Journal* 1 (1893), 15.

Morris, Maxwell H. "Roger Williams and the Jew." In *American Jewish Archives Journal* 3, no. 2 (1951), 24–27.

Morris, Richard B. "The Role of the Jews in the American Revolution in Historical Perspective." In *American Jewish History: The Colonial and Early National Periods, 1654–1840.* Vol.1, Jeffrey S. Gurock, ed. New York: Routledge, 1998, 49–68.

Morrison, Tessa. *Juan Bautista Villalpando's Ezechielem Explanationes: A Sixteenth-Century Architectural Text.* Lewiston, NY: Edwin Mellen, 2009.

Mundigo, Axel, and Dora Crouch. "The City Planning Ordinances of the Laws of the Indies Revisited." *The New City* 48 (July 1977), 247–68.

Mundill, Robin R. *England's Jewish Solution: Experiment and Expulsion, 1262–1290.* Cambridge, UK: Cambridge University Press, 1998.

Nadler, Steven M. "Baruch Spinoza." In *The Stanford Encyclopedia of Philosophy.* Spring 2011 ed. Edward N. Zalta, ed. http://plato.stanford.edu/archives/spr2011/entries/spinoza/ (accessed 30 Sept. 2012.).

———. *Rembrandt's Jews.* Chicago: University of Chicago Press, 2003.

———. *Spinoza's Heresy: Immortality and the Jewish Mind.* Oxford, UK: Oxford University Press, 2001.

Nahon, Gerard. "The Portuguese Jewish Nation of Amsterdam as Reflected in the Memoirs of Abraham Haim Lopes, 1752." In *Dutch Jews as Perceived by Themselves and by Others.* Chaya Brasz and Yosef Kaplan, eds. Leiden, Netherlands: Koninklijke Brill, 2000, 59–78.

Nassy, David. *Historical Essay on the Colony of Surinam, 1788.* Cincinnati: American Jewish Archives, 1974.

Neu, Irene D. "The Jewish Businesswoman in America." *Publications of the American Jewish Historical Society* 66, no. 1–4 (Sept. 1976–June 1977), 137–40.

New-York Historical Society. *Collections of the New York Historical Society.* New York: Printed for the Society, 1886.

New York Times. "De Karpershoek." *Travel Guides: Amsterdam.* 31 Aug. 2007. <http://travel.nytimes.com/travel/guides/europe/netherlands/amsterdam/attraction-detail.html?vid=1154654658174#> (accessed 31 Aug. 2007).

Nixon, J. *European Magazine* (London), 1 Aug. 1811.

Norberg-Schulz, Christian. *Baroque Architecture.* New York: Electa, 1986.

Oers, Ron van. *Dutch Town Planning Overseas during VOC and WIC Rule (1600–1800).* Zutphen, Netherlands: Walburg Pers, 2000.

Oliel-Grausz, Evelyne. "A Study in Intercommunal Relations in the Sephardi Diaspora: London and Amsterdam in the Eighteenth Century." In *Dutch Jews as Perceived by Themselves and by Others.* Chaya Brasz and Yosef Kaplan, eds. Leiden, Netherlands: Brill, 2000, 41–58.

Oppenheim, Samuel. "The Jews in Barbados in 1739. An Attack upon Their Synagogue. Their Long Oath." *Publications of the American Jewish Historical Society,* no. 22 (1914), 197–98.

Owen, Thomas McAdory, and Marie Bankhead Owen, eds. *History of Alabama and Dictionary of Alabama Biography.* Vol. 2. Chicago: S. J. Clarke, 1921.

Palgrave, W. G. *Dutch Guiana.* London: Macmillan, 1876.

Parry, John H. *The Age of Reconnaissance: Discovery, Exploration, and Settlement, 1450–1650.* Berkeley: University of California Press, 1981.

Pegg, Mark G. *A Most Holy War: The Albigensian Crusade and the Battle for Christendom.* Oxford, UK: Oxford University Press, 2008.

Pencak, William. *Jews and Gentiles in Early America, 1654–1800.* Ann Arbor: University of Michigan Press, 2005.

Perelis, Ronnie. "'These Indians Are Jews!' Lost Tribes, Crypto-Jews, and Jewish Self-Fashioning in Antonio de Montezinos's Relacion of 1644." In *Atlantic*

Diasporas: Jews, Conversos, and Crypto-Jews in the Age of Mercantilism, 1500–1800. Richard L. Kagan and Philip D. Morgan, eds. Baltimore: Johns Hopkins University Press, 2009, 195–211.

Pérez, Joseph. *The Spanish Inquisition: A History.* New Haven: Yale University Press, 2005.

Pestana, Carla G. *The English Atlantic in An Age of Revolution, 1640–1661.* Cambridge, MA: Harvard University Press, 2004.

Peters, Edward. *Inquisition.* New York: Free Press, 1988.

Peterson, Eugene T. "The Fort of Ezekiel Solomon." *Michigan Jewish History* 3, no. 6 (June 1963), 11–14.

Pevsner, Nikolaus. *An Outline of European Architecture.* Baltimore: Pelican, 1972.

Phaf-Rheinberger, Ineke. "The Portuguese Jewish Nation: An Enlightenment Essay on the Colony of Suriname." In *A History of Literature in the Caribbean.* Vol. 2, English-and-Dutch-speaking. Albert James Arnold, Vera M. Kutzinski, and Ineke Phaf-Rheinberger, eds. Amsterdam: J. Benjamins, 2001, 491–503.

Phelan, John L. *The Millennial Kingdom of the Franciscans in the New World.* Berkeley: University of California Press, 1970.

Picart, Bernard. *Cérémonies et coutumes religieuses de tous les peuples du monde.* Amsterdam, 1723.

Picciotto, James. *Sketches of Anglo-Jewish History.* London: Trübner, 1875.

Pickard, Rob, ed. *Policy and Law in Heritage Conservation.* London: Spon, 2001.

Pile, John. *A History of Interior Design.* 2nd ed. Hoboken, NJ: John Wiley and Sons, 2005.

Platt, Virginia B. "'And Don't Forget the Guinea Voyage': The Slave Trade of Aaron Lopez of Newport." *William and Mary Quarterly* 3rd ser. 32, no. 4 (Oct. 1975), 601–18.

Plaut, Jonathan V. *The Jews of Windsor, 1790–1990: A Historical Chronicle.* Toronto: Dundurn Press, 2007.

Pollins, Harold. *Economic History of the Jews in England.* Rutherford, NJ: Fairleigh Dickinson University Press, 1982.

Poole, Stafford. *Pedro Moya de Contreras: Catholic Reform and Royal Power in New Spain, 1571–1591.* Berkeley: University of California Press, 1987.

Popkin, Richard Henry. "Mordecai Noah, the Abbé Grégoire and the Paris Sanhedrin." *Modern Judaism* 2, no. 2 (May 1982), 131–48.

Poston, Jonathan H. *The Buildings of Charleston: A Guide to the City's Architecture.* Columbia: University of South Carolina Press, 1997.

Potts, James C. "David Lopez Cohen (1820–1893), Savannah Builder—Carpenter." 1 Aug. 1977. Vertical Files of the Georgia Historical Society, Savannah.

Prior, Roger. "Jewish Musicians at the Tudor Court." *Musical Quarterly* 69, no. 2 (Spring 1983), 253–65.

Ramée, D., Nicolas-Marie-Joseph Chapuy, and Hastings. *Le moyen-âge monumental et archéologique; vues, détails et plans des monumens les plus remarquables de l'Europe, depuis le 6e jusqu'au 16e siècle.* Paris, 1843.

Rawlings, Helen. *The Spanish Inquisition.* Malden, MA: Blackwell, 2006.

Reid, Basil A., ed. *Archaeology and Geoinformatics: Case Studies from the Caribbean.* Tuscaloosa: University of Alabama Press, 2008.

Reps, William. *Town Planning in Frontier America*. Columbia: University of Missouri Press, 1980.

Rezneck, Samuel. "A Note on the Genealogy of an Eighteenth-Century Family of Jewish Origin: The Nunez Family of Lewes, Delaware." *American Jewish Archives Journal* 30, no. 1 (Apr. 1978), 20–23.

Richardson, A. E., and C. Lovett Gill. *London Houses from 1660 to 1820*. London: Batsford, 1911.

Rickey, V. Frederick. "How Columbus Encountered America." *Mathematics Magazine* 65, no. 4 (Oct. 1992), 219–25.

Robinson, H. W. "Robert Hooke as a Surveyor and Architect." *Notes and Records of the Royal Society of London* 6, no. 1 (Dec. 1948), 48–55.

Rodriguez, Junius P., ed. *The Louisiana Purchase: A Historical and Geographical Encyclopedia*. Santa Barbara, CA: ABC-CLIO, 2002.

Rodway, James. *Guiana: British, Dutch, and French*. London: T. F. Unwin, 1912.

Root, Deborah. "Speaking Christian: Orthodoxy and Difference in Sixteenth-Century Spain." *Representations*, no. 23 (Summer, 1988), 118–34.

Rosen, Robert N. *Confederate Charleston: An Illustrated History of the City and the People during the Civil War*. Columbia: University of South Carolina Press, 1994.

Rosengarten, Dale, and Barry Stiefel. "Port Jews and Plantation Jews: Carolina-Caribbean Connections." Paper presented at the Jewish Diaspora of the Caribbean International Conference, 12–14 Jan. 2010, Kingston, Jamaica.

Rosengarten, Theodore, and Dale Rosengarten, eds. *A Portion of the People: Three Hundred Years of Southern Jewish Life*. Columbia: University of South Carolina Press in association with McKissick Museum, 2002.

Rosenwaike, Ira. *On the Edge of Greatness: A Portrait of American Jewry in the Early National Period*. Cincinnati: American Jewish Archives, 1985.

Roth, Cecil. "Chapter XII, The New Great Synagogue, 1790." *Susser Archive*. 2005. <http://www.jewishgen.org/JCR-UK/susser/roth/chtwelve.htm> (accessed 5 July 2005).

———. *The Great Synagogue, London, 1690–1940*. London: E. Goldston, 1950.

———. *A History of the Marranos*. New York: Sepher-Hermon, 1992.

———. "A Note on the Astronomers of the Vecinho Family." *Jewish Quarterly Review* new ser. 27, no. 3 (Jan. 1937), 233–36.

Roth, Leland M. *American Architecture: A History*. Boulder: Westview Press, 2001.

Roth, Norman. *Medieval Jewish Civilization: An Encyclopedia*. New York: Routledge, 2003.

Rottenberg, Dan. *Finding Our Fathers: A Guidebook to Jewish Genealogy*. New York: Random House, 1977.

Rozen, Minna. *A History of the Jewish Community in Istanbul: The Formative Years, 1453–1566*. Leiden, Netherlands: Brill, 2002.

Rubin, Lawrence A. "Ezekiel Solomon Historical Marker Dedication." *Michigan Jewish History* 5, no. 1 (1964), 3–7.

Rubin, Saul J. *Third to None: The Saga of Savannah Jewry, 1733–1983*. Savannah, GA: S. J. Rubin, 1983.

Ruderman, David B. *Early Modern Jewry: A New Cultural History*. Princeton: Princeton University Press, 2010.

Rupert, Linda A. "Trading Globally, Speaking Locally: Curaçao's Sephardim in the Making of a Caribbean Creole,." In *Jews and Port Cities, 1590–1990: Commerce, Community and Cosmopolitanism*. David Cesarani and Gemma Romain, eds. London: Vallentine Mitchell, 2006, 109–17.

Rutherfurd. Livingston. *John Peter Zenger: His Press, His Trial, and a Bibliography of Zenger Imprints*. New York: Arno, 1970.

Ruymbeke, Bertrand van, and Randy J. Sparks. *Memory and Identity: The Huguenots in France and the Atlantic Diaspora*. Columbia: University of South Carolina Press, 2003.

Sachar, Howard M. *Farewell Espana: The World of the Sephardim Remembered*. New York: Vintage, 1994.

Sale, Kirkpatrick. *The Conquest of Paradise: Christopher Columbus and the Columbian Legacy*. New York: Knopf, 1990.

Samuel, Wilfred. *First London Synagogue of the Resettlement*. London: Spottiswoode, Ballantyne, 1924.

Saraiva, António J., H. P. Salomon, and I. S. D. Sassoon. *The Marrano Factory: The Portuguese Inquisition and Its New Christians, 1536–1765*. Leiden, Netherlands: Brill, 2001.

Sarna, Jonathan D. *American Judaism: A History*. New Haven: Yale University Press, 2004.

———. "The Debate over Mixed Seating in the American Synagogue." In *The American Synagogue: A Sanctuary Transformed*. Jack Wertheimer, ed. Cambridge, UK: Cambridge University Press, 1987, 363–67.

———. "The Impact of the American Revolution on American Jews." In *American Jewish History: The Colonial and Early National Periods, 1654–1840* Vol. 1. Jeffrey S. Gurock, ed. New York: Routledge, 1998, 149–57.

———. *Jacksonian Jew: The Two Worlds of Mordecai Noah*. New York: Holmes and Meier, 1981.

———. "The Mystical World of Colonial American Jews." In *Mediating Modernity: Challenges and Trends in the Jewish Encounter with the Modern World: Essays in Honor of Michael A. Meyer*. Lauren B. Strauss, Michael Brenner, and Michael A. Meyer, eds. Detroit: Wayne State University Press, 2008, 185–94.

———. "The Question of Music in American Judaism: Reflections at 350 Years." *American Jewish History* 91, no. 2 (June 2003), 195–203.

Sarna, Jonathan D., and Dvora E. Weisberg. "A Writ of Release from Levirate Marriage (Shtar Halitzah) in 1807 Charleston." *American Jewish Archives Journal* 63, no. 1 (2011), 38–55.

Schama, Simon. *The Embarrassment of Riches: An Interpretation of Dutch Culture in the Golden Age*. New York: Knopf, 1987.

Schapiro, Meyer. "The Miniatures of the Florence Diatessaron (Laurentian ms Or. 81): Their Place in Late Medieval Art and Supposed Connection with Early Christian and Insular Art." *Art Bulletin* 55, no. 4 (Dec. 1973), 520.

Schless, Nancy H. "Peter Harrison, the Touro Synagogue, and the Wren City Church." *Winterthur Portfolio* 8 (1973), 187–200.

Schoenberger, Guido. "The Ritual Silver Made by Myer Myers." *American Jewish Historical Society Journal* 43, no. 1 (Sept. 1953), 1–13.

Schorsch, Jonathan. "Early Modern Sephardim and Blacks, Contact and Conflict between Two Minorities." *Sephardic and Mizrahi Jewry: From the Golden Age of Spain to Modern Times.* Zion Zohar, ed. New York: New York University Press, 2005, 239–54.

———. *Jews and Blacks in the Early Modern World.* New York: Cambridge University Press, 2004.

Schwartz, Stuart B. "The Contexts of Vieira's Toleration of Jews and New Christians." *Luso-Brazilian Review* 40, no. 1 (Summer 2003), 33–44.

———. *Tropical Babylons: Sugar and the Making of the Atlantic World, 1450–1680.* Chapel Hill: University of North Carolina Press, 2004.

Seed, Patricia. "Jewish Scientists and the Origin of Modern Navigation." In *The Jews and the Expansion of Europe to the West, 1450 to 1800.* Paolo Bernardini and Norman Fiering, eds. New York: Berghahn Books, 2001, 73–85.

Sennett, Richard. *Flesh and Stone: The Body and the City in Western Civilization.* New York: W. W. Norton, 1994.

Shafer, Boyd C., Bailey Diffie, and George Winius. *Europe and the World in the Age of Expansion.* Vol. 1., *Foundations of the Portuguese Empire 1415–1580.* Minneapolis: University of Minnesota Press, 1977.

Shalev, Eran. "'Revive, Renew, and Reestablish': Mordecai Noah's Ararat and the Limits of Biblical Imagination in the Early American Republic." *American Jewish Archives Journal* 62, no. 1 (2010), 1–20.

Shawchuck, Lawrence A., and Doris Ann Herring. "Historic Marriage Patterns in the Sephardim of Gibraltar, 1704 to 1939." *Jewish Social Studies.* 50 (3–4), 177–200.

Shilstone, Eustace M. *Monumental Inscriptions in the Burial Ground of the Jewish Synagogue at Bridgetown, Barbados.* London: Jewish Historical Society of England, University College, 1958.

Silva, Maria Angélica da, and Melissa Mota Alcides. "Collecting and Framing the Wilderness: The Garden of Johan Maurits (1604–79) in North-East Brazil." *Garden History* 30, no. 2 (Winter 2002), 153–76.

Silverblatt, Irene. "New Christians and New World Fears in Seventeenth Century Peru." *Comparative Studies in Society and History* 42, no. 3 (July 2000), 524–29.

Simonhoff, Harry. *Under Strange Skies.* New York: Philosophical Library, 1953.

Sinclair, A. C., and Laurence R Fyfe. *The Handbook of Jamaica, 1882.* Kingston, Jamaica: Government Printing Office, 1882.

Slade, Susan R. "Touro Synagogue, Congregation Jeshuat Israel." *Historic American Building Survey, no. RI-278.* Washington, DC: National Park Service, 30 Aug. 1972.

Smith, Robert C. "A Portuguese Naturalist in Philadelphia, 1799." *Pennsylvania Magazine of History and Biography* 78 (1954), 71–107.

Smith, John Rubens. "Jews Synagogue in Charleston." John Rubens Smith Collection, Library of Congress Prints and Photographs Division.

Snyder, Holly. *Guide to the Papers of Aaron Lopez (1731–1782), 1752–94, 1846, 1852, 1953.* American Jewish Historical Society Archives at the Center for Jewish History. Collection P-11. New York, 2004.

———. "Queens of the Household." In *Women and American Judaism: Historical Perspectives, Brandeis Series in American Jewish History, Culture, and Life.* Pamela

S. Nadell and Jonathan D. Sarna, eds. Hanover, NH: University Press of New England, 2001, 15–45.

———. "Rules, Rights and Redemption: The Negotiation of Jewish Status in British Atlantic Port Towns, 1740–1831." *Jewish History* 20 (2006), 147–70.

———. "'Under the Shado of Your Wings': Religiosity in the Mental World of an Eighteenth-Century Jewish Merchant." *Early American Studies* 8, no. 3 (Fall 2010), 581–622.

Sola Pool, David de. "Descriptions of the Synagogue in New York in 1776 and 1828." *American Jewish Historical Society Journal* 40, no. 1–4 (Sept. 1950–June 1951), 189.

Sola Pool, David de, and Tamar de Sola Pool. *An Old Faith in the New World: Portrait of Shearith Israel, 1654–1954.* New York: Columbia University Press, 1955.

Souza, Ernest Henriques de. *Pictorial: Featuring Some Aspects of Jamaica's Jewry and His Community Activities.* Kingston, Jamaica: Stephensons Litho Press, 1986.

Soyer, François. *The Persecution of the Jews and Muslims of Portugal: King Manuel I and the End of Religious Tolerance 1496–7.* Leiden, Netherlands: Brill, 2007.

Squires, Josephine. "The Significance of Religion in British Politics." In *The Secular and the Sacred: Nation, Religion, and Politics.* William Safran, ed.. London: Frank Cass, 2003, 78–95.

Steinberg, Diane. *On Spinoza.* Australia: Wadsworth/Thomson Learning, 2000.

Stern, Malcom H. "The Sheftall Diaries: Vital records of Savannah Jewry 1733–1808." *American Jewish Historical Quarterly* 54 (Mar. 1965), 268.

Stick, David. *Roanoke Island: The Beginnings of English America.* Chapel Hill: University of North Carolina Press, 1983.

Stiefel, Barry. "Jeshuat Israel (Touro) Synagogue's Place within the British Empire Prior to 1776." *Rhode Island Jewish Historical Notes* 39 (2008), 191–208.

———. "The Lopez Family of Newport and Charleston and a Family Heirloom." *Rhode Island Jewish Historical Notes* 40 (2009), 393–405.

Stiefel, Barry, and George Goodwin. "Three New World Synagogues: Preserved Symbols of Toleration, Pride, and Continuity." *Rhode Island Jewish Historical Notes* 38 (2007), 39–69.

Stier, Oren B. "South Africa's Jewish Complex." *Jewish Social Studies* 10, no. 3 (2004), 123–42.

Stimson, Dorothy. "Christopher Wren, F.R.S." *Scientific Monthly* 53, no. 4 (Oct. 1941), 360–67.

Stolzman, Henry, and Daniel Stolzman. *Synagogue Architecture in America, Faith, Spirit and Identity.* Mulgrave, Australia: Images Publishing Group, 2004.

Stout, Harry. *The New England Soul: Preaching and Religious Culture in Colonial New England.* New York: Oxford University Press, 1986.

Studnicki-Gizbert, Daviken. "La Nación among the Nations: Portuguese and Other Maritime Trading Diasporas in the Atlantic, Sixteenth to Eighteenth Centuries." In *Atlantic Diasporas: Jews, Conversos, and Crypto-Jews in the Age of Mercantilism, 1500–1800.* Richard L. Kagan and Philip D. Morgan, eds.. Baltimore: Johns Hopkins University Press, 2009), 75–98.

Sturgis, Russell, ed. *A Dictionary of Architecture and Building: Biographical, Historical, and Descriptive.* New York: Macmillan, 1901.

Suárez, Thomas. *Shedding the Veil: Mapping the European Discovery of America and the World*. River Edge, NJ: World Scientific, 1992.

Sumption, Jonathan. *The Albigensian Crusade*. London: Faber, 1978.

Sutcliffe, Adam. "Can a Jew Be a Philosophe? Isaac de Pinto, Voltaire, and Jewish Participation in the European Enlightenment." *Jewish Social Studies* new ser. 6, no. 3 (Spring/Summer 2000), 31–51.

Sweet, James H. "Spanish and Portuguese Influences on Racial Slavery in British North America, 1492–1619." Paper presented at the Fifth Annual Gilder Lehrman Center International Conference, Yale University, New Haven, CT, 7–8 Nov. 2003.

Swierenga, Robert P. *The Forerunners: Dutch Jewry in the North American Diaspora*. American Jewish Civilization Series. Detroit: Wayne State University Press, 1994.

Szajkowski, Zosa. "Protestants and Jews of France in Fight for Emancipation, 1789–1791." *Proceedings of the American Academy for Jewish Research* 25 (1956), 119–35.

———. "Synagogues during the French Revolution of 1789–1800." *Jewish Social Studies* 20, no. 4 (Oct. 1958), 215–31.

Tachau, William G. *The Architecture of the Synagogue*. Philadelphia: Jewish Publication Society of America, 1926.

Tait, A. A. "Inigo Jones—Architectural Historian." *Burlington Magazine* 112, no. 805 (Apr. 1970), 234–35.

Tavares, Maria José Pimenta Ferro. *Los Judíos en Portugal*. Madrid: Editorial MAPFRE, 1992.

Teenstra, M. D. *De Nederlandsche West-Indische eilanden in derzelver tegenwoordigen toestand* Vol. 2. Amsterdam: C. G. Sulpke, 1836.

Tellier, Luc-Normand. *Urban World History: An Economic and Geographical Perspective*. Québec City: Presses de l'Université du Québec, 2009.

Terrell, Michelle M. *The Jewish Community of Early Colonial Nevis: A Historical Archaeological Study*. Gainesville: University Press of Florida, 2004.

Thornton, John K. *Africa and Africans in the Making of the Atlantic World, 1400–1800*. Cambridge, UK: Cambridge University Press, 1998.

Touro Synagogue Foundation. "Time Line." *Touro Synagogue*. 24 July 2005. <http://www.tourosynagogue.org/> (accessed 15 Sept. 2006).

Tuchman, Barbara W. *The First Salute: A View of the American Revolution*. New York: Ballantine, 1988.

Tulchinsky, Gerald J. *Canada's Jews: A People's Journey*. Toronto: University of Toronto Press, 2008.

Tyler, Norman, Ted Ligibel, and Ilene R. Tyler. *Historic Preservation: An Introduction to its History, Principles, and Practice*. New York: W. W. Norton, 2009.

Uchmany, Eva. *La Vida Entre el Judaísmo y el Cristianismo en la Nueva España, 1580–1606*. México City: Archivo General de la Nación, 1992.

———. "The Periodization of the History of the New Christians and Crypto-Jews in Spanish America." In *New Horizons in Sephardic Studies*. Yedida Stillman and George Zucker, eds. Albany: State University of New York Press, 1993, 109–47.

Valencia, Robert H. *The Encomenderos of New Spain, 1521–1555*. Austin: University of Texas Press, 1996.

Vilhjálmsson, Vilhjálmur Örn. "Iceland, the Jews, and Anti-Semitism, 1625–2004." *Jewish Political Studies Review* 16, no. 3–4 (Fall 2004). < http://www.jcpa.org/phas/phas-vilhjalmur-f04.htm> (accessed 29 Apr. 2009).

Waddell, Gene. "An Architectural History of Kahal Kadosh Beth Elohim, Charleston." *South Carolina Historical Magazine* 98, no. 1 (Jan. 1997), 6–55.

Wallace, Vickie. "A List of Participants in the Roanoke Voyages." *Fort Raleigh National Historic Site.* 6 Sept. 2007. <http://www.nps.gov/fora/forteachers/a-list-of-participants-in-the-roanoke-voyages.htm> (accessed 5 Feb. 2011).

Walzer, Michael. *Exodus and Revolution.* New York: Basic Books, 1985.

Warner, John N. "Sugarcane: An Indigenous Papuan Cultigen." *Ethnology* 1, no. 4 (Oct. 1962), 405–11.

Warshawsky, Matthew. "Catholic, Jewish, and Crypto Jews in the 1600s: The Geographic and Spiritual Peregrinations of Juan Pacheco de Leon in Spain, Italy, and Mexico." *Journal of Spanish, Portuguese, and Italian Crypto Jews* 1 (Spring 2009), 121–39.

———. "Trans-Atlantic Crypto-Judaism and Literary Homage: Tomás Treviño de Sobremonte and the Women in His Life." *Journal for the Study of Sephardic and Mizrachi Jewry* 2, no. 1 (Summer 2008), 65–94.

Watson, Isobel. "Rebuilding London: Abraham Davis and His Brothers, 1881–1924." *London Journal* 29, no. 1 (May 2004), 62–84.

Watson, Karl. "Shifting Identities: Religion, Race, and Creolization among the Sephari Jews of Barbados, 1654–1900." In *The Jews in the Caribbean.* Jane Gerber, ed. Oxford, U.K.: The Littman Library of Jewish Civilization, forthcoming.

Weinberg, Bennett A., and Bonnie K. Bealer. *The World of Caffeine: The Science and Culture of the World's Most Popular Drug.* New York: Routledge, 2001.

Weiner, A. "A Note on Jewish Doctors in England in the Reign of Henry IV." *Jewish Quarterly Review* 18, no. 1 (Oct. 1905), 141–45.

Wiernik, Peter. *History of the Jews in America from the Period of the Discovery of the New World to the Present Day.* New York: Jewish Press Publishing, 1914.

White, Libby. "In the Shadows of the Inquisition: The Jews of Colonial Mexico and Their Uncertain Legacy." *Proceedings of the 36th Annual Convention of the Association of Jewish Libraries,* 24–27 June 2001, 2.

Wigoder, Geoffrey. *The Story of the Synagogue.* San Francisco: Harper and Row, 1986.

Wilensky, M. "The Royalist Position concerning the Readmission of Jews to England." *Jewish Quarterly Review* new ser. 41, no. 4 (Apr. 1951), 397–409.

Williams, Bill. *The Making of Manchester Jewry, 1740–1875.* Manchester, UK: Manchester University Press, 1985.

Wilson, David K. *The Southern Strategy: Britain's Conquest of South Carolina and Georgia, 1775–1780.* Columbia: University of South Carolina Press, 2005.

Wischnitzer, Rachel. *The Architecture of the European Synagogue.* Philadelphia: Jewish Publication Society of America, 1964.

———. "The Egyptian Revival in Synagogue Architecture." *Publications of the American Jewish Historical Society* 41, no. 1–4 (Sept. 1951–June 1952), *AJHS Journal,* 61–78.

Wiznitzer, Arnold. "The Exodus from Brazil and Arrival in New Amsterdam of the Jewish Pilgrim Fathers, 1654." *Publications of the American Jewish Historical Society* 44, no. 1–4 (Sept. 1954–June 1955), *AJHS Journal*, 80–81.

———. "Jewish Soldiers in Dutch Brazil (1630–1654)." *Publications of the American Jewish Historical Society* 46, no. 1–4 (Sept. 1956–June 1957), *AJHS Journal*, 40–51.

———. "The Minute Book of Congregations Zur Israel of Recife and Magen Abraham." *Publications of the American Jewish Historical Society* 42, no. 1–4 (Sept. 1952–June 1953), *AJHS Journal*, 217–27.

———. "The Synagogue and Cemetery of the Jewish Community of Recife, Brazil (1630–1654)." *American Jewish History* 94 (1953), 129.

Wood, Betty. *The Origins of American Slavery: Freedom and Bondage in the English Colonies*. New York: Hill and Wang, 1997.

Zaimeche, Salah. *Granada—The Last Refuge of Muslims in Spain*. Manchester, UK: Foundation for Science, Technology, and Civilization, 2004, 12–13.

Zeitlin, Solomon. "Judaism as a Religion, An Historical Study (Continued)." *Jewish Quarterly Review* new ser. 35, no. 1 (July 1944), 115.

Zell, Michael. "Eduard Kolloff and the Historiographic Romance of Rembrandt and the Jews." *Simiolus: Netherlands Quarterly for the History of Art* 28, no. 3 (2000–2001), 181–97.

———. *Reframing Rembrandt: Jews and the Christian Image in Seventeenth-Century Amsterdam*. Berkeley: University of California Press, 2002.

"Zion Church." *Charleston Mercury,* 5 Apr. 1859, 1.

Zwarts, Jacob. *Bijdragen en Mededelingen van het Genootschap voor de Joodsche Wetenschap in Nederland*. Amsterdam: Hertzberger, 1928.

Index

Page references given in *italics* indicate illustrations or material contained in their captions.

About the Authors

BARRY L. STIEFEL is an assistant professor in the Historic Preservation and Community Planning and Urban Studies programs at the College of Charleston. He holds a Ph.D. in historic preservation from Tulane University.

DAVID RITTENBERG received his Ph.D. from Columbia University in English and Comparative Literature. He is an independent scholar and editor with interests in European history and Philosophy. Rittenberg lives in Charleston, South Carolina.